THUCYDIDES

JOWETT

THUCYDIDES

TRANSLATED INTO ENGLISH

TO WHICH IS PREFIXED

AN ESSAY ON INSCRIPTIONS AND A NOTE ON THE GEOGRAPHY OF THUCYDIDES

BY

BENJAMIN JOWETT, M.A.

LATE MASTER OF BALLIOL COLLEGE
AND REGIUS PROFESSOR OF GREEK IN THE UNIVERSITY OF OXFORD

SECOND EDITION, REVISED

VOL. I

ESSAY ON INSCRIPTIONS AND *BOOKS I–III*

WIPF & STOCK · Eugene, Oregon

[*Dedication to First Edition*, 1881.]

TO THE

RIGHT HONOURABLE VISCOUNT SHERBROOKE

ONE OF THE

BEST GREEK SCHOLARS IN ENGLAND

WHOSE

GENUINE LOVE OF ANCIENT CLASSICAL LITERATURE

(THOUGH SOMETIMES DISSEMBLED)

IS AS WELL KNOWN TO HIS FRIENDS

AS THE KINDNESS OF HIS HEART

AND THE CHARM OF HIS CONVERSATION

Wipf and Stock Publishers
199 W 8th Ave, Suite 3
Eugene, OR 97401

Thucydides Translated into English, Volume 1
To Which Is Prefixed an Essay on Inscriptions
and a Note of the Geography of Thucydides
By Jowett, Benjamin
Softcover ISBN-13: 978-1-6667-3278-8
Hardcover ISBN-13: 978-1-6667-2685-5
eBook ISBN-13: 978-1-6667-2686-2
Publication date 7/15/2021
Previously published by Oxford University Press, 1900

This edition is a scanned facsimile of the original edition published in 1900.

NOTE

The Revisors have tried, while comparing the translation carefully with the original and correcting (in accordance with the expressed wish of the late Master of Balliol) the Essay on Inscriptions by the help of recent additions to our knowledge, to make no change or insertion of which they think he would have disapproved, and to retain the general character of the work.

They desire to express their obligations, in the translation, to Mr. E. C. Marchant's edition of Books II, VI, and VII, and the late Prof. H. C. Goodhart's edition of Book VIII, and, in the Essay on Inscriptions, to Meisterhans' *Grammatik der Attischen Inschriften*, the *Corpus Inscriptionum Atticarum*, Suppl. iii., and Röhl's *Inscriptiones Graecae Antiquissimae*.

The text followed is that of Bekker, the new Oxford text by Mr. H. Stuart Jones not being available until the translation was in type.

It has been decided not to reprint the Notes, as a satisfactory revision of them would have greatly delayed the appearance of the present edition. It was, however, impossible to cancel the occasional references to the 'Notes' at the foot of the pages of the translation.

W. H. Forbes.
Evelyn Abbott.

October, 1899.

THE GREATNESS OF THUCYDIDES

'What are they all (the Roman Historians) to the great Athenian? 'I do assure you that there is no prose composition in the world, not 'even the De Corona, which I place so high as the seventh book of 'Thucydides. It is the *ne plus ultra* of human art. I was delighted 'to find in Gray's letters the other day this query to Wharton: "The 'retreat from Syracuse—Is it or is it not the finest thing you ever read 'in your life?" '—*Life of Lord Macaulay*, vol. i. p. 449.

'Most people read all the Greek that they ever read before they are 'five and twenty . . . Accordingly, almost all their ideas of Greek 'literature are ideas formed while they were still very young. A young 'man, whatever his genius may be, is no judge of such a writer as 'Thucydides. I had no high opinion of him ten years ago. I have now 'been reading him with a mind accustomed to historical researches, and 'to political affairs; and I am astonished at my own former blindness, 'and at his greatness.'—Vol. i. p. 440.

Appendix, p. 475.—'This day I finished Thucydides, after reading 'him with inexpressible interest and admiration. He is the greatest 'historian that ever lived. Feb. 27, 1835.'

'I am still of the same mind. May 30, 1836.'

'While I was reading the Annals I was reading Thucydides . . . 'What made the Annals appear cold and poor to me was the intense 'interest which Thucydides inspired. Indeed, what colouring is there 'which would not look tame when placed side by side with the mag-'nificent light, and the terrible shade, of Thucydides? Tacitus was 'a great man, but he was not up to the Sicilian expedition.'—Vol. i. p. 458.

CONTENTS

VOLUME I

PAGE

On Inscriptions of the Age of Thucydides ix

On the Geography of Thucydides cvi

Translation:

Book I 1

„ II 102

„ III 184

VOLUME II

Translation:

Book IV 2

„ V 102

„ VI 178

„ VII 262

„ VIII 335

Historical Index to Books I–VIII 421

ON INSCRIPTIONS OF THE AGE OF THUCYDIDES

SUMMARY OF CONTENTS

Nature of the study, ix; where inscriptions are found, x; process of restoring, deciphering, fixing the date, xi; Messenians of Naupactus, Alcibiades, xii; Mitylenè, xiii; ancient forms of letters and words, xiii, xiv; illustrations of Herodotus, Aristophanes, Plutarch, Pausanias, &c., xv; mention of Sophocles, xviii; inscriptions compared with MSS., xviii, xix; restoration of them assisted by uniformity of writing and contents, xix; danger of conjectural explanations, which are sometimes overthrown by later discoveries, xxi, cp. xlv, lii; inscriptions illustrate antiquities more than history, xxiv; ostracism, accounts of the 'Board of Admiralty,' and Erechtheum, xxiv, xxv; inscriptions chiefly belong to later times, use of them by the ancients, xxv; interest of them as relics of the past, xxvi; the oldest are comparatively recent, xxvii; literary interest, xxix; forgery, xxx.

Inscriptions illustrating Thucydides: The *τάξις φόρου* and quota lists, xxxii; comparison of Thucydides and the quota lists, xxxvi; doubling of the tribute in 425 (?), xliv; arrears recorded in the quota lists (?), lii; Melos and Thera, liv, lv; famine of 449 (?), lv; geographical division of the tributaries, lvi; revolt of Potidaea, &c., lvi; how was the tribute fixed? lvii.

Inventories of sacred treasure, lix; repayment of debts to Athenè and the other deities, lxiii; Kirchhoff's attempt to estimate the expenditure of Athens in 431–428 by a comparison of Thuc. ii. 13, iii. 17, 19, lxv; ordinary scale of expenditure, lxix; interest on expenditure from sacred treasure in 433-423, lxxiii; was there also a secular treasure? lxxv; Demosthenes and Nicias, lxxviii, cp. lxxxi; record of expenditure under another form, lxxviii; revolt of Samos, expedition to Corcyra and discrepancy with Thucydides, lxxix; Macedonia, Demosthenes at Argos (?), lxxx; expeditions to Melos and Sicily, lxxxi; references to the reserve fund (?) and the 400, lxxxii; exhaustion of the treasury in 410, the Propylaea, Delos, mutilation of the Hermae, Alcibiades, lxxxiv.

Decrees of the senate and people, lxxxv; Erythrae, Colophon, Chalcis, Miletus, Hestiaea, Egesta, Rhegium, Leontini, Ambracia, Methonè, Perdiccas, Argos (Thuc. v. 47), Hyperbolus, Bottiaea, Samos, Phrynichus, Daphnus, Halieis, the 'Pelasgian ground,' intercalary month, lxxxv–xcv; votive and sepulchral inscriptions, xcv; tripod dedicated after Plataea, Pisistratus son of Hippias, Dodona, tribe Erechtheis, Potidaea, other battles, xcv–xcix, cp. xvii, xxvii; fragments from the wall of Themistocles, xcix; dangerous tendency to conjecture in the study of inscriptions, c; the true value of them, ci; ostracism of Themistocles, Pythion of Megara (*addenda*), ciii.

ON INSCRIPTIONS

OF THE

AGE OF THUCYDIDES

THE study of ancient Greek inscriptions, to which so great an impulse has been given during the last sixty years by scholars, such as Boeckh, Kirchhoff, Köhler and Lolling in Germany, Lebas and Waddington in France, Mr. Charles Newton in England, as well as by Greek archaeologists such as Rangabé, throws a real but not a considerable light upon the history of Greece. Many thousands of them have been already collected; and the number may be indefinitely increased by the zeal and industry of the present generation. None hitherto found are older than the seventh century before Christ, some of the oldest being written βουστροφηδόν (i. e. returning at the end of the line like the ox in the furrow); in the sixth century and down to the Persian war they are rare; in the latter half of the fifth century they become more numerous, and there are many which have a direct connexion with the history of Thucydides; sometimes coinciding with, often supplementing his narrative; in one instance only (p. lxxix) contradicting it.

The study of inscriptions is not separable from the general study of the Ancient World. In so far as it illustrates the use of letters or words, or the growth of the dialects, or the history of prose writing, it may be included under Philology. In so far as it contributes to our knowledge of the religion, commerce, laws, political institutions, or of the private life and manners of the ancients, it may be placed under the head of Antiquities. It may also be classed with History, inasmuch as historical facts are recorded in inscriptions and the accounts of historians are confirmed or modified by them. To elevate such an accidental and multifarious kind of knowledge into a science of 'Epigraphy' is misleading. Its method, if it have any single method, is inductive, that is to say, it proceeds from the examination of facts, a general knowledge of history and of inscriptions being brought to bear on the analysis of some particular one. It has frequent recourse to hypotheses, of which many remain and will for ever remain unverified. The arrangement of inscriptions adopted by Boeckh[1] according to the countries in which they are found, or the states to which they belong, is commonly the most convenient; they may be further divided according to date, or, when the date cannot be ascertained, according to the subjects of them.

The older Attic inscriptions are generally imperfect. Of many only a few words or lines, often not more than a word or two, survive. The slabs of marble on which they are engraven are commonly broken and scattered; they are found in the beds of rivers, on the sites of temples, in the neighbourhood of the Erechtheum, on the

[1] Cp. Boeckh, Corpus Inscriptionum Graecarum, praef. p. xii ff. To this work (quoted as C. I. G.), a noble monument of learning and critical sagacity; to the admirable Corpus Inscriptionum Atticarum (vol. i and iv) of Kirchhoff, quoted in this essay as C. I. A. and Suppl., and his treatises on the Athenian treasury; to the Inscriptiones Graecae Antiquissimae of Röhl (I. G. A.); to Köhler's separate work on the Tribute Lists, as well as to the interesting essays of Mr. Charles Newton, and to the beautiful and accurate collection of ancient Greek inscriptions in the British Museum by Messrs. Newton and Hicks, the author would express his great obligations.

steps of the Parthenon, at the entrance of the Propylaea, in the Portico of Hadrian, on the banks of the Ilissus, built into the walls of a ruined church or the staircase of a monastery, here and there inserted in the pavement of a courtyard or the floor of a cottage, or forming the table of a Christian altar. Hardly any remain in their original position. From most of them there is a difficulty in extracting a continuous meaning; the result partakes of the nature of the materials. But considering the chances of destruction to which they have been exposed we may wonder that so much has been preserved, and that so many institutions and historical events receive illustration from them.

The process of deciphering Greek inscriptions may be roughly described as follows. First, the fragments must be copied and fitted into each other, allowance being made for missing portions: either they may belong to a single flat surface, or they may be the sides of a solid block. In some instances mistakes have occurred, and a further investigation or a fresh discovery has shown that pieces which at first appeared to belong to the same inscription were really parts of different ones; or, if belonging to the same, that they had been arranged in a wrong order: e.g. C. I. A. 38 and Suppl. i. 38 *a*: C. I. A. 241–254: Suppl. i. page 26. In the attempt to restore words the measure of space is one of our chief guides. When a surface was written all over, the number of letters in a particular line may be exactly known, though not a vestige of them remains. But whether the part of a marble slab or block which has been defaced or broken off contained writing or not may be uncertain. An indicator of time is the form of the letters, and this may sometimes vary in the same inscription (as in C. I. A. 40, 443). The Greek alphabet during the Peloponnesian war was in a process of transition, and the apparent variety or inconsistency in the use of some one or more letters may limit the date of an inscription to the period of the transition. Thus in

C. I. A. Suppl. i. 22 *g*, of which only three or four words are preserved,

ϽΚLΕϟΦΙ . . . .

ΜΕΣΣ . . . . ΓΡ (?)

we are able from the double form of the letter Σ (ϟ Σ) and from the syllable ΜΕΣΣ to infer with tolerable certainty that the text falls in the period of transition from one form of the letter to the other, about 460–447[1], and relates to the establishment of the Messenians at Naupactus soon after 455 B.C. (Thuc. i. 103 init.)[2]. But the period of transition may likewise introduce a new element of uncertainty in determining the date from the forms of the letters; and the matter of inscriptions may in a few instances be older than the time at which they were engraven, e.g. C. I. A. 8, 93, 283 and Suppl. ii. The country in which an inscription is found or the city to which it refers is also a criterion not to be neglected. The text itself may help to supply its own lacunae. A word, a line, several lines may be wanting, but different syllables of the imperfect word, or parts of the line, may be collected from another place in the same inscription. For example, the letters ΑΧΙ in C. I. A. 10 are the vestiges of ΞΥΜΜΑΧΙΑ, as may be easily inferred from the rest of the inscription; from the syllables ΚΟLΟΦΟ and ΟΝΙΟΝ in different parts of C. I. A. 13 the whole word ΚΟΛΟΦΩΝΙΩΝ may legitimately be extracted; in C. I. A. Suppl. i. 61 *a* (a treaty between the Selymbrians and Athenians), from ΚΙΟ . . . Σ, aided by a comparison of Xenophon, Hellenica, i. 3. 10, we can elicit without difficulty the name ΑΛΚΙΒΙΑΔΗΣ. In C. I. A. Suppl. i. 96

---

[1] Roberts, Introduction to Greek Epigraphy, pp. 106, 107.

[2] Or soon after 461 if we accept the conjecture τετάρτῳ for δεκάτῳ in Thuc. i. 103.

the word ΜΥΤΙLΕΝΑΙΟΝ and the partially effaced ΚLΓ-[ΡΟΥ]ΧΟΙΣ clearly show that the inscription relates to the events recorded in Thucydides, iii. 50. Although the first impression excited in the mind by the appearance of the half-effaced lines is one of bewilderment and unfamiliarity, out of the chaos order soon begins to arise. The experienced eye detects in the shape of the letters, in the use of Α Α for Α, of Ε for Ε, of ⊕ for Θ, of Ρ for Ρ, of Σ for Σ, of Φ for Φ, of + for Χ, and similar variations, the earlier forms of the Attic characters; and in the use of Η for the aspirate, of Ε for ΕΙ and Η, of Ο for Ω and ΟΥ, of Λ for Γ, of L for Λ, of ΧΣ for Ξ, of ΦΣ for Ψ, the old Attic alphabet, in place of which the Ionic alphabet was regularly adopted in the Archonship of Euclides, B.C. 403. There are some other particulars in which the earlier Attic usage differs from the later. In the older inscriptions, for ΕΛΠΙΣ is written ΗΕLΠΙΣ (and in many other cases the initial aspirate is inserted), for –ΕΣΘΩΝ (3 p. imp. pass.) –ΟΣΘΟΝ (e.g. 27 *a* Suppl.): there are assimilations of Ν, Κ, and Γ, as in ΕΜΠΟLΕΙ, ΤΟLLΟΓΙΣΤΟΝ, ΕΣΤΕLΕΙ, ΕΣ-ΣΑΝΙΔΙ, ΕΧΦΥLΕΣ, ΜΕΛΧΡΥΣΑ, ΕΑΜΜΕ, and also refusals to assimilate, as in ΧΣΥΝΜΑΧΟΙ, ΟLΥΝ-ΠΙΟΣ, ΣΤΡΟΝΒ[ΙΧΟΣ], (some appearing later); reduplication of Σ, as in ΑΡΙΣΣΤΑ; datives plural in ΑΣΙ, ΗΣΙ, for -ΑΙΣ, ceasing to occur in inscriptions during the 90th Olympiad, B.C. 420–417; datives in ΟΙΣΙΝ for -ΟΙΣ, up to about B.C. 444; other forms, such as ΟLΕΙΞΟΝ, the comparative of ΟΛΙΓΟΝ, which are found in inscriptions though not occurring elsewhere in Attic as known to us:—all these may be used as notes of time. We find however that some of the modern letters appear among the older ones before the archonship of Euclides[1]; it is probable that the Ionic alphabet was in literary use when it was not yet employed in public documents. There was a gradual change from slanting to upright forms; and it is interesting to trace the manner in which some refractory straggling letters, such as M and N, were coerced into regularity. In the interval between the Persian and Peloponnesian wars the archaic style disappears, and the hand of the engraver works with more clearness and precision.

Having determined the letters and from them formed a conjecture of the date of the inscription, and assisted by a knowledge of the place in which it is found, the decipherer will now proceed to gather a meaning from the words or syllables which are legible. (The reader must be reminded that in this short outline we are speaking of early imperfect inscriptions, and chiefly of those contemporary with Thucydides.) A very few scattered words are sufficient to tell the general subject: it may be a treaty of peace or alliance, the dedication of an offering, a grant of privileges to a state or an individual, an epitaph, an inventory of treasure, a boundary mark, the cost of a public edifice, a catalogue of confiscated goods, a direction for a festival or a sacrifice or the building of a temple, a prohibition, a punishment; any historical event, any incident of private life, may turn up in an inscription. We are sometimes able to trace a coincidence of names occurring in Thucydides or Xenophon which may serve as a clue. But we can seldom proceed much further. The details which we seek to extract from a fragment are necessarily incoherent, a food for guesses. A few inscriptions only preserve a clear and entire meaning, or may receive it from a comparison of contemporary history. We had better begin by moderating our expectations, if we would avoid

[1] The Ionic forms appear, often side by side with the others, with increasing frequency from 446 onwards: or in isolated cases even earlier. See Meisterhans, Grammatik der Attischen Inschriften, § 3; Roberts, Introduction to Greek Epigraphy, pp. 103-107.

disappointment. In inquiries of this kind the result is seldom very great, nor always very certain.

The task of reading ancient Greek inscriptions may be compared to the amusement of putting together a dissected puzzle, or of making out an acrostic. The ingenuity which is required in both cases is of the same kind. When all the pieces fit and all the letters fall into their places, then the solution of the puzzle has been found. And although many of the pieces have been lost and many of the words or letters are no longer legible, and fragments of different inscriptions are occasionally mixed up together, still order and consistency and exhaustiveness, in whatever degree they can be attained, are the tests of truth. Of course, as in a cipher, the possibility of arriving at a successful result depends on the definiteness of the problem and the possibility of obtaining an answer to it from a comparison of other parts of the document or of similar documents.

The broken form in which the older Greek inscriptions have been preserved to us, though impairing, is far from destroying their value. But before much use can be made of them they must be illustrated by the literary remains of antiquity. Many coincidences, slight as well as important, soon begin to appear in them which realize ancient history to us. The juxtaposition of two names, the mention of an office, of a ceremony, of a reward conferred on an individual or on a tributary state, send us to the pages of the historian, and they may often supply a test of the accuracy or knowledge of a great writer or of a scholiast. It may be truly said that the inscriptions of the fifth century before Christ, though not always agreeing with his narrative (see pp. lv, lxxix), tend upon the whole to confirm the authority of Thucydides. Again, a few letters still remain of an inscription which Herodotus records to have been engraved on the memorial (a τέθριππος χάλκεος) erected by the Athenians in honour of the victory which they gained over the Boeotians and Chalcidians soon after the expulsion of the Pisistratidae (Herod. v. 77; C. I. A. 334 and Suppl. ii)[1]. There is still to be seen the basis of some of the 'many statues' which Micythus dedicated at Olympia (Herod. vii. 171; I. G. A. 532): and 'pillars' from the ruins of the original temple of Artemis at Ephesus bear traces of the dedication Βασιλεὺς Κροῖσος ἀνέθηκε (Herod. i. 92; Hicks, Manual of Greek Historical Inscriptions, p. 5: I. G. A. 493). Such testimony is still more needed for the verification of later historians. An inscription (C. I. A. 273, cp. 22 *a* Suppl. i) corrects a name found in Diodorus, xii. 58, and also in Athenaeus, v. p. 218. By these writers the archon of the year Ol. 88. 3 (B. C. 426) is called Euthydemus, and, by the author of the argument to Aristophanes' Acharnians, Euthymenes. But, as is shown by the inscription referred to (the long inscription which records the expenditure of the sacred treasure of Athens, Ol. 86. 4—89. 2), the real name was Euthynus, a name which has been correctly preserved in the anonymous Life of Thucydides (p. 14, l. 35, Bekker), and by the Scholiast on Lucian Tim. 30. In Plutarch (Pericles xiii), we find what at first sight appears to be an unfounded and

---

[1] Ἔθνεα Βοιωτῶν καὶ Χαλκιδέων δαμάσαντες
παῖδες Ἀθηναίων ἔργμασιν ἐν πολέμου
δεσμῷ ἐν ἀχλυόεντι σιδηρέῳ ἔσβεσαν ὕβριν·
τῶν ἵππους δεκάτην Παλλάδι τάσδ' ἔθεσαν.

[Two distinct forms of the inscription existed, and fragments of both have been discovered. First were found, and edited in 1869, the letters

E NAIONEPΛM/
ΓΓΟϟΔΕΙΛ

Their appearance showed that they dated from the time of Pericles: they must therefore have been copied, or restored by memory, from the original. Of an earlier inscription, being very likely a piece of this original itself, broken up during the Persian occupation, were found, and edited in 1887, the letters

ΡΙΝ⁝ΓΑΙΑ
⁝ΤΟΝ ΗΙΓΓΟ

showing that Herodotus quotes the restored inscription, in which the two hexameters must have been transposed.]

gossiping anecdote, about a workman employed on the Propylaea, and distinguished for his skill and zeal, who had fallen from a height so that his life was despaired of. Plutarch continues: ἀθυμοῦντος δὲ τοῦ Περικλέους ἡ θεὸς ὄναρ φανεῖσα συνέταξε θεραπείαν ᾗ χρώμενος ὁ Περικλῆς ταχὺ καὶ ῥᾳδίως ἰάσατο τὸν ἄνθρωπον· ἐπὶ τούτῳ δὲ καὶ τὸ χαλκοῦν ἄγαλμα τῆς Ὑγιείας Ἀθηνᾶς ἀνέστησεν ἐν ἀκροπόλει παρὰ τὸν βωμόν, ὃς καὶ πρότερον ἦν, ὡς λέγουσιν. An inscription upon a pedestal of white marble still remaining *in situ* probably belonged to this very statue (C. I. A. 335, Ἀθηναῖοι τῇ Ἀθηναίᾳ τῇ Ὑγιείᾳ), or at least to the statue which gave rise to Plutarch's story. Pausanias, i. 29. 7, says that in the battle of Tanagra the Athenians had the assistance of troops not only from Argos (Thuc. i. 107 fin.) but from Cleonae, and that the Cleonaeans who fell were buried in the Ceramicus. Four pieces of a monumental inscription, suiting the date, and containing several Doric names, besides a trace of the word [Ταν]άγρᾳ, confirm Pausanias' statement (C. I. A. 441 and Suppl. ii).

Votive inscriptions have been discovered at Olympia which were put up by the Lacedaemonians after the revolt of the Helots in 464; by the Lacedaemonians and their allies to commemorate the victory of Tanagra; and, on the other side, by the 'Messenians and Naupactians,' together with the statue of Victory by the sculptor Paeonius, to commemorate, according to Pausanias, a victory over the Acarnanians, but, according to the account of the Messenians themselves, their great success at Sphacteria. (See I. G. A. 75, Paus. v. 24. 3: I. G. A. 26 *a*, Paus. v. 10. 4: I. G. A. 348, Paus. v. 26. 1; and cp. Hicks, Manual, pp. 81, 341.) These as well as several other inscriptions bear witness to the general trustworthiness of Pausanias, but point to several inaccuracies in detail on his part or on that of his informant. Two passages of Aristophanes may here be illustrated from inscriptions. In the Scholia on Knights, 969, Σμικύθης is asserted to have been a Thracian prince. But the occurrence of the name Σμίκυθ[ος], as the γραμματεύς of the ταμίαι τῶν ἱερῶν χρημάτων τῆς Ἀθηναίας (C. I. A. 130, Ol. 89. 1, B.C. 424–423, the year after that in which the Knights was performed), proves the futility of this statement. The name was in fact borne by more than one Athenian citizen (cp. C. I. A. 60, 432, 433, 447). The same or another scholiast is more fortunate in the illustration of Birds, 1128—

ἵππων ὑπόντων μέγεθος ὅσον ὁ δούριος,

which, he says, is a reference to a bronze figure of the Trojan horse dedicated on the Acropolis, and bearing the inscription—

Χαιρέδημος Εὐαγγέλου ἐκ Κοίλης ἀνέθηκε.

And these very words inscribed on a pedestal (C. I. A. 406) have been discovered on the Acropolis. More important contributions to history are made by the τάξις φόρου (C. I. A. 37), or estimate of the Athenian tribute, framed in 425 B.C., which has been thought by some to confirm the statements of the Orators respecting the doubling of the tribute during the Peloponnesian war (see infra, p. xlv). Still more important is the inscription (C. I. A. 433) over the Athenians of the tribe Erechtheis, who fell all in the same year (about 459 B.C.) in Cyprus, in Egypt, in Phoenicia, at Halieis, in Aegina, and at Megara: or that containing part of the treaty made by Athens with Argos (C. I. A. 46 *b*, Suppl. i) in the year 420 B.C. Both of these verify the details of Thucydides, and are worth many pages of Diodorus or Plutarch. In the tribute lists of the year 443 B.C., C. I. A. 237, we find traces of a name beloved in Greek literature—

[Σ]Ο[Φ]ΟΚL[ΕΣ] ΚΟLΟ[ΝΕΘΕΝ ΗΕLLΕΝΟΤΑΜΙΑ]Σ ΕΝ

The mutilated condition of the earlier Greek inscriptions offers a wide field for conjecture. But there are many ways in which the conjectural restoration of inscriptions is both assisted and limited; and it differs in several respects from the emendation of MSS. In the case of inscriptions we have to supply omissions rather than to correct error. The chances of error (cp. for examples C. I. A. 151, p. 72: 398, 419, 483) except in mere spelling are comparatively small. There are no recensions of the text; no glosses which have crept in from the margin, or inferences from the words of scholiasts that the reading may have been originally different. Far greater pains and time are necessarily taken in engraving than in writing; and, speaking generally, inscriptions are at first hand and there is no further risk from copying. The greater danger is from the unskilfulness or ignorance of the modern copyist, but the original is generally in existence, and the error can be corrected. Whereas MSS. have been written and rewritten many times, at each rewriting contracting some degree of inaccuracy, and changing to a certain extent their modes of spelling and forms of grammar in successive generations. Pen and ink are more pliable implements than the chisel, and the writer takes greater liberties than the engraver in the form and size of the letters. But inscriptions are monumental, and the words and letters in them have a fixed character; or, at any rate, only change with well-known changes in the alphabet. Almost invariably in inscriptions of the fifth century[1] each letter occupies the same space, and in supplying lacunae, however large, we can measure with a compass the number of letters required. Wherever the graver has been skilful the symmetry is perfect, and a straight line may be drawn horizontally, vertically, diagonally through the centre of the letters. But in some cases the miscalculation of space has led to the crowding of the latter part of the inscription: and there are other examples (cp. C. I. A. Suppl. i, 61 *a*, 71; Newton and Hicks, p. 61, 85) in which the lines are not written accurately *στοιχηδόν*. Many of the later inscriptions differ from the earlier ones as much as the fairest copperplate from the first rude attempts of an

[1] See Meisterhans, § 4.

illiterate person at writing; and may be truly called 'calligraphic' from their beauty and regularity.

But besides the greater uniformity of the writing there is also a greater similarity in the modes of expression than in literary composition. Most public inscriptions have their set beginnings and endings, their formulas of oaths, decrees, sums, dates; names of the archon, tribe, prytany, epistates. Some of them, as for example the lists of the quota (C. I. A. 226–272) paid out of the tribute of the allies to the Goddess, are arranged in years, and the imperfect members of the series may be filled up from those which exist in a more complete state. The number of such documents is considerable, and from their formal and official character they throw light upon one another. Hence it is not surprising that, while no human ingenuity, even when assisted by metre, can supply more than two or three letters in a corrupted text of the classics, and hardly so much in prose, parts of a line or of several lines in succession may be restored with comparative certainty in an ancient inscription. Even a single letter occurring in a particular place may afford a clue to the contents of a whole line if the line is repeated elsewhere. The parallel in this case is not like the parallels cited in support of emendations of the classics, from which it is often fallaciously argued that an author wrote in one place as he did in another. For inscriptions are really full of the same forms, whereas there is only a faint presumption that the same turn of expression will occur more than once in a literary composition. Similarly, two or three letters of a name which usually accompanies some other name may give the key: e. g. the letters

ΣΤΡΑΤΕΛΟΙΣ . . . . . . ΝΤΙΔΕΙΚΑΙΧΣΥΝΑΡΧΟ

indicate the words *στρατηγοῖς Νικίᾳ Νικηράτου Κυδαντίδῃ καὶ ξυνάρχουσιν*, C. I. A. 273. Many restorations which appear improbable at first sight are nevertheless true: e. g. the following, which, though seeming to depend on slender grounds, is in reality certain (C. I. A. 37; a. b. c. l. 4 ff.): ΧΕΡΟ[ΤΟΝ.........ΕΠΙ ΤΑ]Σ ΠΟΛΕΣ ΔΥΟ [ΜΕΝ ΕΠΙ ΤΑΣ ΕΠΙ ΘΡΑΙΚΕΣ] ΔΥΟ ΔΕ Ε[ΠΙ ΙΟΝΙΑΝ ΔΥΟ Δ]Ε ΕΠΙ Ν[ΕΣΟΥΣ ΔΥΟ ΔΕ ΕΠΙ ΗΕΛΛΕΣ-Π]ΟΝΤΟ[Ν. Here, out of the hint of ΗΕΛΛΕΣΠΟΝ-ΤΟΝ contained in ΟΝΤΟ, the occurrence of the word ΠΟΛΕΙΣ, the repetition of ΔΥΟ, combined with our knowledge of the division of the tributary cities into four or five groups, an important part of an inscription is recovered. So much may be made out of so little. In this, as in other cases, the power of divination is relative to the nature of the materials, which create a method for themselves. If the matter of early Greek inscriptions were varied like literary compositions, much less progress could be made in the interpretation of them. They would be curious fragments from which nothing of importance could be elicited.

It is this fragmentary character of Greek inscriptions which distinguishes the study of them from that of Assyrian or Egyptian. Before we can interpret them we have to restore them; or rather the interpretation and the restoration of them go hand in hand. It is another peculiarity in the study of them that a large literature can be brought to bear upon them; and that we do not, as in the case of most other inscriptions, derive our knowledge of them from themselves only.

Far greater than the temptation to emend is the temptation to elicit a connected meaning from them. The interpreter is apt to read into an inscription more than is really to be found in it. The record of the contemporary history is necessarily imperfect, and he exercises his ingenuity in making anything which he knows fit in with the fragmentary document which he has to decipher. If, for example, he finds in an inscription (C. I. A. 55, indicated by the occurrence of datives in αις, not -ησι, to be later than 420 B.C.) a mention of sixty ships, he immediately calls to mind the sixty ships which the Athenian assembly at first voted to the Sicilian expedition, although this vote was never carried into execution; for a larger fleet was actually sent. But is it likely that such an inoperative decree which was superseded five days afterwards (Thuc. vi. 8; cp. 25) would have been recorded in an inscription? And might not the number sixty equally well refer to the second (vii. 20) or to some other expedition? Another example of the same weakness may be found in the criticism on C. I. A. Suppl. i, 46 *a*, where the letters ꓘOPINꝊI and AΘENAI occur. It is conjectured by Kirchhoff that the inscription has reference to the visit of the Boeotian and Corinthian envoys to Athens, recorded in Thuc. v. 32. But of what value are such conjectures? Considering that some and not all the facts are narrated by the historian, and only a few legible inscriptions of the time are extant, it is *a priori* improbable that the number of coincidences should be very great. A few other instances may be given of a similar haste in drawing conclusions. In an inscription C. I. A. 54, which is again inferred from the occurrence in it of datives in αις to be later than 420 B.C., mention is made of 30 ships each having 40 hoplites on board, which are directed to collect 'the tribute in full.' These ships are identified with the 30 ships conveying 1200 Athenian hoplites which were sent to Melos in 416. But may not these numbers apply with equal probability to some other expedition in some way concerned with the tribute? The second coincidence of the 40 hoplites is of no value, as the same number of hoplites conveyed in a trireme occurs elsewhere (cp. Thuc. ii. 56 init.)[1]. Again, in a fragment of an inscription, C. I. A. 176, Boeckh (Staatsh. ii. 228) thinks that he discovers a reference to the movable plates of gold (ἐσ]θῆτα?) with which the statue of Athenè was overlaid

[1] [It should be added that the inscription speaks of 10 archers, apparently in each of the 30 ships, corresponding to the total number of 300 archers, Thucydides, v. 84. On the other hand, peltasts are mentioned in the inscription and not in Thucydides.]

(Thuc. ii. 13); but Kirchhoff, having a more accurate delineation of the text, reconstructs the inscription in an entirely different manner (ἔσ[τησαν) while retaining the reference to the statue[1].

One more warning against such divination may be added. From the fragment C. I. A. 51, when first discovered, it was inferred by Kirchhoff, (*a*) that it recorded a remission of the tribute (with the exception of the quota of one-sixtieth paid to the Goddess) made to some subject city; (*b*) that it dated from some year during the Peace of Nicias; the latter conclusion being based on the words ὅτι συνδιεπολέμησαν τομπόλεμον, an expression which was thought to imply that the war in question was concluded at the time. But six more fragments of the same inscription have since been discovered (C. I. A. Suppl. i. 51). It was then found to relate to the city of Neapolis in Thrace, and consists of two parts, the earlier dating from the archonship of Glaucippus, 410; and Kirchhoff is compelled to adopt a much more elaborate explanation of the words relating to the 'first-fruits paid to the Virgin,' which he refers not to Athenè Polias, but to the local worship of Neapolis, and supposes to have been deducted from the Athenian tribute. But this explanation is only an hypothesis. All that can be said about the recently found fragments is that they do not confirm the old theory which Kirchhoff gave up, and that they contain no resemblance to the words in which the Methonæans are excused from the payment of their tribute with the exception of the quota (C. I. A. 40). Such conjectural interpretations should be guarded with the formula, 'subject to any future discoveries.'

On the other hand, it may be objected that, if we carry our caution very far, and hesitate in attaching some fragment of an inscription to the narrative of an ancient writer, it becomes useless to us, and can be brought into no rela-

[1] New fragments of C. I. A. 298; 299 *a* (vol. iv. Suppl. iii.), show that Kirchhoff rightly referred another inscription, 298, 299, to the famous 'gold and ivory' statue.

tion with the history. And how great the temptation is to connect what we know with what we do not know may be seen in the early study of the hieroglyphics, and of the Sinaitic inscriptions. The true reply to the objection just urged is, that in any sound study of ancient Greek inscriptions we must be prepared for slender results. And the general confirmation of ancient writers afforded by those slender results is far from unimportant.

The additional facts obtained from inscriptions throw greater light upon Greek antiquities than upon Greek history. We know a good deal more than we did of the institutions and customs of the ancient Hellenes, of their family and religious life, of their games and festivals, of their public hospitalities, of their marriage and funeral ceremonies, of their military and civic divisions, of their public and private economy, of their assessments of tribute and taxation, of their societies for religious and social purposes. The constitution imposed by Athens on Erythræ (C. I. A. 9), the oaths interchanged between the Athenians and the Chalcidians of Euboea (C. I. A. Suppl. i. 27 *a*), and the inventory yearly drawn up of the treasures in the Parthenon are some of these new facts hitherto unknown to the historian. The business of life is stereotyped before our eyes. Among the débris of material on the Acropolis earlier than 480 B.C. have been found two potsherds, fragments of vases, on which two Athenian citizens,—one of them clearly a better writer than the other,—inscribed for 'ostracism,' between 487 and 484 B.C., the names of Megacles son of Hippocrates and Xanthippus son of Ariphron the father of Pericles[1]. (See Athen. Polit. c. 22: C. I. A. iv. Suppl. iii. 569, 570.) The annual accounts of the Athenian 'Board of Admiralty' are still preserved, not in books, but on tablets of Hymettian marble (C. I. A. vol. ii. part ii. p. 158 ff., 513 ff.). A report is extant of the works of the Erechtheum while in course of erection (ἐξειργασμένα καὶ ἡμίεργα), B.C. 409 (C. I. A.

[1] For a similar mention of Themistocles, see Addenda to this Essay.

321, Suppl. ii. and iii, 322; Newton and Hicks, p. 84 ff.); in a somewhat later inscription (C. I. A. 324) an estimate is given of the cost of the building, including the prices of the statues, the daily wages (in one case a drachma) of the men employed, and the quantities of the columns. And all these things, though the records of them are but fragmentary, come to us, not strained through books, but fresh from the chisel of the workman. We dig among the crumbling remains of antiquity, and out of these is gradually built up a real although very imperfect image of the past.

It must not be forgotten, however, that inscriptions begin to grow numerous and legible as Hellas declines, and that the greater part of the notices preserved in them relate to the time, not of her glory, but of her decay. The historian of Athens becomes aware that a long study such as Boeckh devoted to these ancient documents adds little to our knowledge of Greek history in the fifth century before Christ, but a great deal to that of Alexandrian and Roman times. He may add the warning that we must not antedate our knowledge, or transfer to the age of Pericles or Demosthenes institutions and forms of life which belong to succeeding centuries.

The use of inscriptions was not unknown to Herodotus (i. 51, 187; ii. 106, 136, 141; iii. 88; iv. 87, 88, 91; v. 59–61, 77; vi. 14; vii. 228; viii. 82), and Thucydides (vi. 54 fin., 59; cp. v. 18 fin., 23 fin., 47 fin., 56 med.), and became more frequent among later Greek writers. Collections were formed of them in the third and second centuries before Christ (see Boeckh, C. I. G. praef. p. viii). Thus Philochorus the historian (fl. B.C. 307–261) is recorded by Suidas to have published *ἐπιγράμματα* 'Αττικά, Attic inscriptions. Polemo, a contemporary of Aristophanes of Byzantium (about 200 B.C.), and a famous man in his day, is said to have composed, among many other works, a book upon 'inscriptions in various cities' (Athenaeus, x. p. 436 D, p. 442 E), and two other books, one 'on the votive offerings at Lacedaemon' (Athenaeus, xiii. p. 574 C), and another 'on the votive offerings in the Acropolis' (Strabo, ix. p. 396; Athenaeus, xi. p. 472 B, 486 D; xiii. 587 C). A book of Theban inscriptions is attributed to Aristodemus, a Theban historian (Schol. Apollon. Rhod. i. 906), and a work on the votive offerings of Delphi to Alcetas (Athenaeus, xiii. 591 C), and on offerings in general to Menetor (594 C); and there were other authors (fl. about 300–250 B.C.). The great collector of ancient times was Craterus the Macedonian, who published a work, Περὶ Ψηφισμάτων. From this work Boeckh supposes many of the decrees found in the Orators, especially in the Oration for the Crown, to have been extracted. The diligence of the third and second centuries before Christ, like that of our own nineteenth, had no parallel in earlier times. That the earlier historians made so little use of inscriptions is surprising to us. Again and again doubtful points of the history might have been verified or corrected, had the narrator once thought of examining the monuments of the temples. The names of the archons in Diodorus Siculus and Dionysius of Halicarnassus are probably derived from this source. But in general the examination of authorities was alien to the nature of the later Greek historians, even more than to Herodotus and Thucydides. For not only do the materials of history accumulate slowly, but the method of using them and any interest about the truth of them are even more slowly acquired. And mankind do not begin to search until the objects of their search are quite or nearly lost. The lives of hundreds and hundreds of scholars have been spent to regain, if it were possible, a small fraction of those treasures which lay open to the eyes of all Athenians and were passed by unheeded of them.

One great interest of ancient inscriptions remains to be mentioned. It is a striking thought that we have present to us some of the very words and letters on which the eye not only of the ancient historians, but of Themistocles and Pericles and Alcibiades, must have gazed. Near to the spot on which the monument bearing it was originally erected has been found the inscription by which Pisistratus the son of Hippias commemorated his archonship. On the bronze serpent which supported the tripod dedicated at Delphi, and is now preserved in the hippodrome of Constantinople, may be read to this day the names of the allied states which fought at Plataea. In the Louvre at Paris is still to be seen the tablet (already referred to) on which a record is preserved of Athenians belonging to a single tribe who fell in one year in many distant lands, a living monument of the superhuman energy which at that time inspired the Athenian people. And, although such a reflection adds nothing to our knowledge, it increases the feeling with which we regard these monuments, and quickens and enlivens the study of them. It is not that the ancients themselves thought or could have thought of them with the interest which Greek history has imparted to them, or that Themistocles and Pericles derived their greatness from the works which were the expression of it. But we, looking back, like to see with our own eyes what we have been reading and hearing about all our lives, and to be connected by a new, though a fanciful tie, with the past.

One of the most important facts to be gathered from Greek inscriptions is the very general one, that none of them are older than the seventh century before Christ. Not only is little or nothing known of the ages which preceded, but the non-existence of records and documents seems to show that there was not much to be known of them. Hellenic civilization and Hellenic art burst suddenly into life: there was no knowledge 'hoary with age' (Plato, Tim. 22 B); nor any architecture or sculpture which had existed in the same form during thousands of years; nor slow growth or change of style such as was developed in mediaeval times; at any rate there is no evidence of it[1]. Nor is there any reason to believe that

[1] [It is clear from archaeological discoveries at Mycenae and elsewhere, that what we commonly call Hellenic civilization had been preceded by an earlier form of civilization, in which it is possible to

the use of writing was common in Hellas before the Persian war. The Greek was not weighed down by records of his ancestors extending, as in Egypt, over many thousand years. The tradition of the Trojan war was the cloud which bounded his horizon; nothing which came before was known to him; nothing which followed had any real hold on his imagination. There may have been great actions performed in the Dorian settlement of the Peloponnesus or in the Messenian wars, but they made no impression on the mind of Hellas, which seemed to be absorbed and satisfied by the tale of Troy commemorating the common action of the whole people.

That in the sixth and seventh centuries B.C. the practice of writing on stone or marble was rare, and still rarer that of writing on papyri and skins, seems to be proved negatively by the silence of Homer, the scarcity of written monuments, the late rise of prose composition. But the interval between the Persian and Peloponnesian wars was prolific in inscriptions. At Athens, and probably in other centres of Greek life and religion, they must have been as numerous as the gravestones in a modern churchyard, and had as little sacredness in the eyes of posterity. And to pursue the homely simile a little further, as it is uncommon to meet with a tombstone of the seventeenth century in any parish churchyard and in any church which is not a cathedral, so in ancient times Greek inscriptions were liable to be constantly removed and were rarely preserved, except in a great temple such as the Parthenon at Athens, or the temple of Apollo at Delphi. There was not room enough for all; and the earlier and more valuable ones were buried under the accumulations of a later generation to which they yielded place. It is probably

---

trace some kind of growth. But, while we await further evidence tending to bridge over the gap between 'Mycenaean' and Hellenic civilization, the remarks in the text hold good; and no archaeological discovery is ever likely to account for the higher qualities of 'Hellenic civilization and Hellenic art.']

owing to the greater accumulation, and consequently to the greater destruction of inscriptions which took place at Athens, that fewer archaic ones are to be found there than in the islands. Many of the statues and inscriptions earlier than the Persian war which remain to us owe their preservation to the use made of them, together with other débris, as the substructure of new buildings on the artificially raised and levelled summit of the Acropolis (Prof. Gardner, New Chapters in Greek History, pp. 239, 242 ff.).

The literary or poetical value of Greek inscriptions is not great. Few, like the epitaph of Simonides on Archedicè (Thuc. vi. 59), bear the stamp of a great mind. To revert once more to our homely simile, they may be said to stand in the same relation to the works of the great lyric or dramatic poets, as the poetical or other effusions found in churches and cathedrals to the masterpieces of English literature, though preserved by Greek moderation and good taste from the absurdity and eccentricity of their modern counterparts. Two fragments in verse, and one in prose, touch us with the common feeling of humanity:

C. I. A. 463 (written *βουστροφηδόν*):—

> [Εἴτ' ἀστό]ς τις ἀνὴρ εἴτε ξένος | ἄλ(λ)οθεν ἐλθών,
> Τέτ(τ)ιχον οἰκτίρα|ς, ἄνδρ' ἀγαθόν, παρίτω,
> ἐν πολέμῳ | φθίμενον, νεαρὰν ἥβην ὀλέσαν|τα.
> ταῦτ' ἀποδυράμενοι νεῖσθε ἐπ|ὶ πρᾶγμ' ἀγαθόν.

C. I. A. 469:—

> Σῆμα Φρασικλείας· | κούρη κεκλή[σο]μαι | αἰεί,
> ἀντὶ γάμου | παρὰ θεῶν τοῦτο | λαχοῦσ' ὄνομα.

C. I. A. Suppl. ii. 491[30]:—

> ἐνθάδε Ἀρίσστυλλα κεῖται
> παῖς Ἀρίσστωνός τε καὶ Ῥοδίλλης
> σώφρων γ' ὦ θύγατερ.—Cp. also p. xciv.

Two other inscriptions have found their way into the Anthology. The first is attributed by the collector without much foundation to Anacreon.

C. I. A. 381:—

Πρὶμμὲν Καλλιτέλης ἱδρύσατ[ο· τόνδε δ' ἐκείνου
ἔ]γ[γ]ονοι ἐστήσαν[θ', οἷς χάριν ἀντιδίδου].

(Anthol. Pal. 6. 138.)

C. I. A. 403:—

[Τόνδε Πυρῆς] ἀνέθηκε Πολυμνήστου φίλο[ς υἱὸς]
εὐξάμενος δεκάτην Παλλάδι τριτογενεῖ.
Κυδωνιέτας (ιάτας or ιάτης?) Κρησίλας ἐργάσσατο.

These last words are corrupted by the MSS. of the Anthology (Anthol. Pal. 13. 13) into—

κυδωνίαι τὰς κρισίας εἰργάσατο.

The authority of Greek inscriptions is only impaired by the chance of their being more recent than the events to which they relate. When the human mind was seeking too late to recover the past, it was natural that the names of kings or magistrates should be arranged in chronological order and inscribed on monuments. But such lists are justly suspected when they extend beyond the ordinary limits of Greek history. Who will guarantee the catalogues of Olympian victors or Spartan kings whose names and dates alone are recorded, while of their actions we are ignorant? At any rate we cannot be certain of their genuineness, for they mount up to a time which is unknown to us, and we have no records by which we can test them.

A few ancient inscriptions, like that which recorded the 'treaty of Cimon' with the Great King and was suspected by Theopompus (Fragm. 167, 168) on account of the Ionic letters, may have been forgeries or perhaps restorations of older inscriptions in accordance with a later tradition. Some, like the Sigean inscription, in the opinion of Boeckh, though maintained by Kirchhoff and others to be genuine, may have been imitations of the archaic. Others again, like the Parian marble, without being forgeries may be regarded as literary works of a later age, having no more pretension to a monumental character than a MS. or printed book. Others erected by states or individuals may have been the expressions of some ancient tradition. Their character can only be determined by a familiar knowledge of the letters, words, and forms which occur in them and by their agreement with some other record of the events to which they refer. But owing to the deficiency of information, or the mutilation of the inscription itself, the diagnosis of the critic may often be at fault. The definition of forgery itself is not quite simple, for it admits of degrees; fiction may easily mingle with truth; and the deception may be more or less conscious to the inventor. In modern as well as in ancient times there have been a few instances of fraud. Cyriac of Ancona (1391—about 1450), who traversed Greece, Asia Minor, and Syria in search of MSS., inscriptions, and other antiquities, was accused by some among his contemporaries of dishonesty, though his credit has been maintained by later writers[1]. An archaeologist of the last century (Fourmont) destroyed some of his materials and invented others (Boeckh, C. I. G. p. 61 ff.). At the time the inventor escapes with impunity: there is no one to follow him in his travels through a country which can hardly be traversed with safety: the knowledge and experience do not as yet exist which can detect his forgeries. But the time comes when some internal or external evidence rises up against him; when the use of a letter or a mark, the anachronism of thought or of fact, unexpectedly betrays him. Forgery has been much more difficult in the nineteenth century than in the eighteenth, and in the later half than in the first half of the century. It should be remembered also that literary forgery easily arises out of error; like many other kinds of dishonesty, it contains an admixture of inaccuracy. The careless enthusiastic scholar makes an imperfect copy of a short fragment;

[1] Otto Jahn, Aus der Alterthumswissenschaft, Cyriacus von Ancona und Albrecht Dürer: Boeckh, C. I. G. praef. p. ix; cp. Symonds, Renaissance in Italy; Revival of Learning, pp. 156, 157.

he hastily restores it according to some preconceived idea, and he confuses in his mind or in his tablets his own restoration and the actual copy; he commits himself to some inference which he deduces from it, and the work of imposture is complete; he

> 'Makes such a sinner of his memory,

as

> To credit his own lie.'

A lively imagination, the love of creating a sensation, the habit of poring over the same words or letters during many years, may create a state of the intellect in which the distinction between truth and falsehood is lost. Theories crowd upon the discoverer thick and fast, and the facts, of which he never had a firm grasp, are easily, and perhaps unconsciously, bent or altered to suit them. But we need not pursue further the analysis of imposture. Before accepting unhesitatingly the testimony of any archaeologist to an ancient inscription, we must ask the old question, 'Where are the originals?'

The inscriptions which confirm or illustrate the narrative of Thucydides may be arranged in four classes:—

I. Those relating to finance, in which are included—

i. An estimate of the tribute to be paid by the allies, framed in 425 B.C., called *τάξις φόρου*.

ii. The quotas of the whole sum actually received which were deducted year by year from the tribute and paid over to the Goddess Athenè, being $\frac{1}{60}$th or a mina for a talent. (There were doubtless accounts of the larger sums received, but none of these have been discovered.)

iii. Inventories of gold and silver plate and of other valuables contained in the Parthenon.

iv. Accounts of sums paid out of the treasury and spent in expeditions, buildings, festivals, etc., and of debts owing or repaid to Athenè and other deities.

II. Decrees of the *βουλή* or *ἐκκλησία* (not financial) relating to persons, events, or institutions commemorated in the history. Under this head are included treaties with foreign states, agreements with allies, grants of privileges to states or individuals.

III. Dedicatory inscriptions.

IV. Sepulchral inscriptions.

The lists of quotas realize to us the greatness of the Athenian empire. Though not justifying the poetical boast of Aristophanes in the Wasps, 707, who reckons the number of Athenian tributaries at 1000, they contain the names of 257 states: if we add some other cities indicated in the *τάξις φόρου* only, the number will exceed 300. In neither are included numerous Hellenic cities on the Euxine[1] and in the interior of Lycia and Caria, which were allies, but, with a few exceptions, not tributaries; in the language of Thucydides, *σύμμαχοι* but not *ὑπήκοοι* or *φόρου ὑποτελεῖς* (vii. 57 init.). That they were present to the mind of Aristophanes when he described the Athenian empire as extending *ἀπὸ τοῦ Πόντου μέχρι Σαρδοῦς* is evident. The relation of these cities to Athens would be generally of a friendly nature. Living under her protection, but not paying tribute, they were the outer defences of her empire. The Hellenic cities of Macedonia were similarly situated, and for a similar reason were not included in the tribute lists, with the exception of three (C. I. A. 40 and 257), Methonè, Aeson, and Dicaeopolis, which about 427 B.C. had their tribute remitted, all but the quotas paid to the Goddess. They were in constant danger from the surrounding barbarians or from the Macedonian kings, and having to defend themselves could not be expected to pay for others. Since they had it in their power at any time to become a part of the Macedonian kingdom, the imposition of a heavy tax would have been too severe a test of their loyalty. (See the inscription relating to Methonè, which complained of ill-treatment from Perdiccas, C. I. A.

[1] There are traces of a few of these in the *τάξις φόρου*, see p. xlviii.

40, and, for a discussion of all these points, Köhler, Delisch-Attischer Bund, part ii. cap. 3.) There was another class of tributaries, those on the Persian border, of whom we know but little; they probably hesitated in their allegiance between the Athenians and the Persian king, and paid tribute accordingly (cp. Hdt. vi. 42; Thuc. viii. 5). There is nothing to indicate that any of the Greek cities in Cyprus and Crete ever paid tribute to Athens, or that the attempts of Athens to establish her influence in these great islands mentioned by Thucydides (i. 94, 104, 112, ii. 85) met with any success: though about and after the end of the Peloponnesian War we find Athens in friendly relations with King Evagoras of Salamis (Grote, ch. lxxvi, C. I. A. i. 64). Several states, e.g. Amphipolis, Samos, are not to be found in the quota lists, although Thucydides mentions the income derived by Athens from Amphipolis (iv. 108), and numbers Samos among the tributaries of Athens (vii. 57 init.). (See Boeckh, Staatshaush. vol. ii. p. 657 ff.)[1] By 424, when Cythera was reduced (iv. 57 fin.), the lists have become fragmentary. There is no indication that the Athenian Cleruchi paid tribute, with the exception of those in Lemnos and Imbros, colonized before the establishment of the Delian league. [Where names occur, in the quota lists, of places in which Athenian κληροῦχοι are said to have been settled, e.g. Chalcis in Euboea, the Thracian Chersonese, Naxos, Andros, the tribute was probably paid by the original inhabitants, who remained by the side of the Athenian settlers. In Lesbos, Thucydides specially mentions the fact that after the establishment of a cleruchy the Lesbians paid no tribute (iii. 50). See on the whole question Kirchhoff, Tributpflichtigkeit der Att. Kler., Abhandl. der Berl. Acad., 1878: and Beloch, Rheinisches Museum, xxxix. pp. 45, 46.]

[1] P. 411 ff. of the 3rd ed. (Fränkel) and notes. Some of the smaller cities mentioned by Boeckh probably paid with others as συντελεῖς: others never actually pay tribute in our extant lists of quotas, though they may have occurred in τάξεις.

I. i. The τάξις φόρου (C. I. A. 37 and Suppl. iii) is a vast inscription broken into about thirty fragments. Not more than a sixth part of the whole is preserved; and the position of several of the smaller fragments cannot be certainly ascertained. It is an estimate of the tribute to be paid by the allies, preceded by two decrees, out of which it is difficult to gather a connected meaning, though they evidently relate to the appointment of officers for the regulation of the tribute ('two for the Chalcidian cities, two for Ionia, two for the islands, and two for the Hellespont;' l. 5; p. xxi, supra), and contain penalties to be inflicted on the Prytanes if they fail in despatching the business before the assembly. The most interesting passages of these decrees which can be restored with any approach to certainty are the following. Line 22 ff.:—

'Let the Prytany Aegeis be required to bring these matters before the people as soon as it enters upon office, on the third day when the sacrifices are over, before anything else; and, if they be not completed on that day, let them be proceeded with on the following day before anything else; and so on until the business is finished within the term of the aforesaid Prytany: and if the Prytanes fail to bring it before the people, or do not finish the matter within their own term of office, let every one of them pay a fine of 10,000 drachmae.'

Another passage fixes the year of the inscription (l. 44 ff.): 'Thudippus proposed: That the cities for which the senate fixed the tribute, in the year of which Pleistias was the first Registrar (ἐπὶ τῆς βουλῆς ᾗ Πλειστίας πρῶτος ἐγραμμάτευε[1]), in the Archonship of Stratocles, shall all bring an ox to the great Panathenaea.' The Archonship of Stratocles falls in Ol. 88. 4, and fixes the date of the inscription, or at any rate of the decree, to this year; it probably belongs to the first half of it (the last half of B.C. 425). Once more,

[1] A γραμματεύς, or registrar to the βουλή, was appointed by lot in every Prytany. The registrar of the first Prytany is often named, as here, to mark the year.

l. 47 ff.: 'The senate fixed the tribute of the cities in the year of which Pleistias was the first Registrar, in the Archonship of Stratocles, as follows.' Then comes a long list of tributary cities, divided (as in some of the quota lists, see infra) into 4 classes: (1) the Islanders; (2) the Ionian and Carian cities; (3) the Thracian; (4) the Hellespontian cities. The list is very imperfect, and the payments imposed on the allies are still more so. The sums to be paid by the Islanders, *νησιωτικὸς φόρος*, and the names to which they are appended, are the most complete part. The names of one Ionian city and of twelve Carian (four of the Carian cities occurring nowhere else), with their tribute, are also preserved. A fragment recently discovered, fitting into part of the inscription previously known, gives us the tribute of seventeen Thracian cities, six of which, as well as two occurring on the part previously known, are found in no other list. (See C. I. A. 37. Suppl. iii.) Of the Hellespontian tribute there are a few doubtful memoranda; of Thracian and Hellespontian names there are several, and many more Ionian and Carian, but unfortunately the amount to be paid is lost; and there are some sums with no names, or only fragments of names opposite to them.

I. ii. The quota lists, like the *τάξις φόρου*, are very imperfectly preserved. They are made up of many small fragments; the number at present discovered is about 150. The first of them belongs to the year 454; the last dated to the year 421 B.C. But from 435 to 421 inclusive we have no list approaching completeness, and only three extensive fragments (428, 427 or 426, and a year between 431 and 426). The portion of them with which the series commences was originally inscribed on a single rectangular block of Pentelic marble; this ends in 440. Another, engraved on a similar block but more incomplete, extends from 439 to 432 B.C. The other extant lists are engraved on tablets. A gradual change in the form of the letters is observable in the successive years. While the more archaic nowhere appear in them, the forms ΑΑΒΝΡΣΦ still for a time remain, sometimes varying in the same inscription, sometimes recurring later than the more modern forms (Köhler, Delisch-Attischer Bund, p. 4; Roberts, Epigraphy, p. 102). An inscription which has been discovered since the time of Boeckh enables us to correct two erroneous conclusions which he drew: (1) he placed the commencement of the series in 447 B.C. instead of 454; (2) he estimated the quota paid to the Goddess as $\frac{1}{120}$ instead of $\frac{1}{60}$. The inscription which gave us the facts (C. I. A. 260) contains the words *ἦρχε δὲ Ἀθηναίοις Ἀριστίων*: and *ἐπὶ τῆς τετάρτης καὶ τρ[ιακοστῆς ἀρχῆς οἱ τρίακοντα ἀπέφηνα]ν τὴν ἀπαρχὴν τῇ θεῷ, μνᾶν ἀπὸ τοῦ ταλάν[του]*.

Of these two great monuments we may remark that they have scarcely any connexion with each other. One relates to a single year, the other extends with considerable gaps over a period of 33 years. The *τάξις φόρου* contains only the tribute to be paid by most of the Islanders, some of the Thracian cities, and a small part of the assessments made on the Ionians, Carians, and Hellespontians. The quota lists contain accounts more or less complete in different years of all these; they are in some years nearly perfect, so that we cannot suppose many cities to be accidentally wanting in them. Of those presumed to be subsequent to the *τάξις φόρου* (see p. xlv) we have only fragments of which little can be made. Nor are we certain that if both had been completely preserved to us the quota lists would have agreed precisely (*μνᾶ ἀπὸ τοῦ ταλάντου*) with the *τάξις φόρου*. For the one is a record of the sums actually received, or rather of a portion of them, the other is only an estimate of money which the Athenian magistrates meant or expected to collect. Moreover, the *τάξις φόρου* contains more than fifty names or traces of names not mentioned in the tribute lists, and these of course contain many not found in the *τάξις φόρου*.

The passages in Thucydides which relate to the tribute are five in number.

(1) i. 96. 'Thus the Athenians by the good-will of the allies, who detested Pausanias, obtained the leadership. They immediately fixed which of the cities should supply money and which of them ships for the war against the Barbarians, the avowed object being to compensate themselves and the allies for their losses by devastating the King's country. Then was first instituted at Athens the office of Hellenic treasurers (Hellenotamiae), who received the tribute, for so the contributions were termed. The amount was originally fixed at 460 talents. The island of Delos was the treasury, and the meetings of the allies were held in the temple.' This was the φόρος imposed in the time of Aristides to which allusion is made in the treaty of 421 between the Lacedaemonians and Athenians (v. 18, see infra). The time at which the transfer of the treasury from Delos to Athens was effected is not mentioned in Thucydides or in any trustworthy writer: the sole authority on which the date rests is that of Justin (iii. 6. 4), who places the event after the return of the Athenians from Ithomè, about 461. The year assumed by Köhler, 454, is a conjecture not improbable in itself, but based solely on the fact that the series of the quota lists begins in that year (p. 99 ff., 107, 108).

(2) v. 18 med. 'The inhabitants of any cities which the Lacedaemonians deliver over to the Athenians may depart whithersoever they please and take their property with them. The said cities shall be independent, but shall pay the tribute which was fixed in the time of Aristides.'

(3) i. 99 init. 'The causes which led to the defection of the allies were of different kinds, the principal being their neglect to pay the tribute or to furnish ships, and, in some cases, failure of military service. For the Athenians were exacting and oppressive, using coercive measures towards men who were neither willing nor accustomed to work hard. And for various reasons they soon began to prove less agreeable leaders than at first. They no longer

fought upon an equality with the rest of the confederates, and they had no difficulty in reducing them when they revolted. Now the allies brought all this upon themselves; for the majority of them disliked military service and absence from home, and so they agreed to contribute their share of the expense instead of ships. Whereby the Athenian navy was proportionally increased, while they themselves were always untrained and unprepared for war when they revolted.' Cp. i. 19. 'The Athenians on the other hand after a time deprived the subject cities of their ships, and made all of them pay a fixed tribute, except Chios and Lesbos.'

(4) ii. 13 med. At the commencement of the war Pericles tells the Athenians that 'the state of their finances was encouraging; they had on an average 600 talents of tribute coming in annually from their allies, to say nothing of their other revenue.'

(5) vii. 28 fin. Once more, after the fortification of Decelea we are informed, 'It was at this time that they imposed upon their allies, instead of the tribute, a duty of five per cent. on all things imported and exported by sea, thinking that this would be more productive.' (See note *in loco.*)

In these passages nothing is said (*a*) of the steps by which the tribute was raised from 460 to 600 talents; or (*b*) of the increase or diminution at different times in the number of tributaries; or (*c*) of the increase from 600 to 1200 talents mentioned in the Orators, a fact which has been doubted by Grote chiefly in consequence of the silence of Thucydides. If light can be thrown upon any of these subjects it must be obtained from inscriptions.

(*a*) and (*b*). Thucydides says that 'the amount of the tribute was originally fixed at 460 talents.' From the quota lists it appears that the amount paid by the allies was altered in the years 450 and 446 B.C., the effect of the new assessments being occasionally to raise, but far more often to lower it, while in numerous cases it remained unchanged[1]. Thasos, for example, was raised from 3 to 30 talents, while the Thracian Chersonese was lowered from 18 talents to 1 talent, paid by Agora, one of the eight small cities of the Chersonese which occur on the lists; Ephesus from 7½ to 6 talents, Lebedus from 3 to 1, Miletus from 10 to 5, Andros from 12 to 6, Colophon from 3 to 1½, Phocaea from 3 to 2; and there is a net reduction, taking the two years 450 and 446 together, of over 30 talents in all on the cities of which the names and payments have been preserved. We may conjecture that the rise in the Thasian tribute is due to the increased productiveness of the silver mines on the island or the restoration of those on the continent, or of territory there, see Thuc. i. 101. Such changes are also attributable to the rearrangement of the *συντέλειαι*, or groups of cities which contributed in common. The Sermylians (Σερβυλιῆς) in 447 pay 3 talents, but the Σερμυλιῆς καὶ συντελεῖς pay 5 talents in 445. The same cause obviously accounts in part for the extraordinary diminution of the tribute of the Thracian Chersonese, indicated above. Another cause which may have operated in this and similar cases is the occupation of certain districts by Athenian κληροῦχοι, in compensation for which the tribute paid by the original owners may have been reduced. The reduction of the tribute of Andros after 451 from 12 to 6 talents may be explained in this way. It must be remembered, however, that for the details of the establishment of κληρουχίαι we are often dependent upon late authors. Again, the average tribute between the years 446 and 440, for which years the lists are fairly complete, taken from 190 cities, amounts

[1] [In 450, about 83 cities pay the same as before.
" " 17 " are lowered.
" " 4 " are raised.
In 446, about 100 " pay the same.
" " 31 " are lowered (8 of them may have been lowered in 450).
" " 4 " are raised.
(Busolt, Philologus, 41, pp. 704–713).]

to 423 talents and 3,070 drachmae, the quota to the Goddess being 7 talents 351 drachmae, although we cannot be sure that so much was paid in any single year. It is alleged that, if we allow for defaulters, and remember that there are traces of a much larger tribute having been paid in earlier periods, this sum makes a near approach to the 460 talents fixed by Aristides.

But how are these facts to be reconciled with the other statement of Thucydides that the Athenians, 'at the beginning of the war, had on an average 600 talents coming in from their allies'? There are indications that the tribute of the cities was raised in or soon after the year 439, the net increase in the Thracian tribute being 17 talents, 2,100 drachmae [1]. Now the tribute lists are fragmentary, and the sums set against the names of the allies are only extant in a part of them. We must acknowledge therefore that most of the inferences which are drawn from them might have been different or have appeared in a different light if the whole of the great inscription had been preserved. They are all 'subject to future discoveries'; and this particular inference is drawn only from the Thracian and from some of the Carian and Ionian cities; while some cities, especially in Caria, disappear from the lists altogether, so that the increase in the payment of others may have been no more than a compensation for losses. A glance at the table of tributary states printed at the end of Kirchhoff, C. I. A. vol. i, will show how imperfect our information is; and also that in many cases the payment remained the same, and in a few was lowered instead of raised. But, while recognizing this general uncertainty, we may admit with Köhler that there appears to be a rise in the amount of the tribute shortly before the commencement of the war; this rise may explain the difference between 460 and 600 talents, especially if we suppose it to have continued during the years 435-431,

[1] Busolt, Philol. 41, p. 657.

for which our information is certainly imperfect. As however there is reason to think that not all the money paid into the Athenian treasury (see p. xxxiv above) was included in the tribute lists, we may, if the evidence of a rise in the tribute before the beginning of the war be thought too slight to explain the difference between 460 and 600 talents, resort to other hypotheses. [We may suggest with Busolt (Philol. 41, p. 703) that the annual instalments of the indemnity paid by Samos after the suppression of the Samian revolt were included by Pericles in his estimate of the *φόρος* derived from the allies: or more doubtfully with Beloch (Rhein. Mus. xxxix, p. 34 ff.) that some of the allies paid in whole or part by means of harbour duties or tolls not recorded at all on our quota lists: in fact by indirect taxation such as that which was substituted for the whole *φόρος* in 413 (Thuc. vii. 28).]

We are much more certain, however, of the general fact that the tribute was not a fixed sum, but liable to be increased or diminished on grounds at which we can only guess. It appears from the De Republica Atheniensium (wrongly ascribed to Xenophon, but dating from the period of the War preceding the Sicilian expedition), 3. 5, that new estimates were made out every fourth year: *τὸ δὲ μέγιστον εἴρηται πλὴν αἱ τάξεις τοῦ φόρου· τοῦτο δὲ γίγνεται ὡς τὰ πολλὰ δι' ἔτους πέμπτου.* As a rule they remained the same during the interval. They were originally framed in the first of the four Panathenaic years, but were afterwards transferred to the second (or from the third to the fourth year of the corresponding Olympiad), as appears probable from a comparison of the *τάξις φόρου* (425) with the quota lists (454, 450, 446) (although it must be remembered that after the first fifteen years the latter become more fragmentary). The tribute lists show a succession of slightly varying amounts, not corresponding, at any time, exactly to the sum of 460, much less to that of 600 talents. (Compare the qualifying words *ὡς ἐπὶ τὸ πολύ* in the financial statement of Pericles, ii. 13 med.) The original amount fixed by Aristides was remembered at the peace of Nicias as setting a limit to the exactions of the Athenians.

Thucydides further tells us (i. 99) that some of the allies soon began to contribute money instead of ships (*ἐτάξαντο ἀντὶ τῶν νεῶν τὸ ἱκνούμενον ἀνάλωμα φέρειν*), and we might have expected the total to be swelled by these additional contributions. But the extant quotas only begin in the year 454 B.C., and the change from ships to money may have been completed before that time. Still a difficulty remains. For the tribute imposed by Aristides, instead of falling from 460 to 423 talents, would have been proportionably increased; in other words, the defaulters in ships would have paid more money. All the allies, with the exception of the Lesbians and Chians, had been reduced to 'servitude' in the interval between the Persian and Peloponnesian wars, and they had given up supplying ships to the common cause. We should expect therefore, unless their lands were transferred to Athenian citizens, as later in the case of Lesbos (iii. 50), that the allies who had once contributed ships would have increased the tribute recorded in the quota lists. The amount would have been swelled by large sums paid by the allies, made up both of penalties reimbursing the Athenians for the expenses of the war when they rebelled (cp. i. 101 fin., *χρήματα ὅσα ἔδει ἀποδοῦναι αὐτίκα ταξάμενοι καὶ τὸ λοιπὸν φέρειν*), and of tribute exacted in lieu of the ships over and above the 460 talents. But there is no trace of any such increase. As from the first it was arranged that some were to supply money and others ships, it can hardly be supposed that the latter are included in the contributors to the 460 talents[1]. Nor is it

[1] [This explanation is certainly inconsistent with a precise interpretation of Thucydides' words in i. 96 *ἔταξαν ἅς τε ἔδει παρέχειν τῶν πόλεων χρήματα πρὸς τὸν βάρβαρον καὶ ἃς ναῦς . . . καὶ Ἑλληνοταμίαι τότε πρῶτον Ἀθηναίοις κατέστη ἀρχή, οἳ ἐδέχοντο τὸν φόρον· οὕτω γὰρ ὠνομάσθη τῶν χρημάτων ἡ φορά. ἦν δ' ὁ πρῶτος φόρος ταχθεὶς τετρακόσια τάλαντα καὶ ἑξήκοντα.* Still it is possible that Thucydides may not intend to confine the *φόρος ταχθείς* to the *χρήματα*, and that the expense of furnishing triremes (*χρήματα ἐτάξαντο ἀντὶ τῶν νεῶν τὸ ἱκνούμενον ἀνάλωμα φέρειν*,

likely that the payments of the other allies were *pro rata* diminished, for the resources of the confederacy would have been proportionably impaired; i.e. the Athenians would only have had the same amount of money and no ships or compensation for losses in war.

Other questions arise to which we can give no answers. How and when were new states admitted? Why are subject states such as Samos after 439 B.C., and certain places cited as tributaries by Stephanus Byzantinus and the lexicographers from Craterus[1] (Nymphaeum,—cp. NY in the τάξις φόρου, C. I. A. i. p. 23—Dorus, Carene, Deira, Marcaei), not included in the quota lists? Why do others, such as Melos, which we know to have been attacked in 426 by Athens without success, and Thera, which we naturally suppose to have been neutral as at the beginning of the war, occur in the τάξις φόρου? Is it possible that tribute was paid of which no quota was dedicated to the Goddess, as we remark on the other hand that in some states (Methonè, Aeson, Dicaeopolis) the quota to the Goddess continued to be paid when the tax had been remitted? Nothing either in the history or in the inscriptions throws light upon these difficulties, which, though not insuperable, can only be matters of speculation.

(*c*) No mention occurs in Thucydides of the doubling of the tribute, a measure implied in the Orators, Andocides, De Pac. (iii.) 9, Aeschines, De F. L. (ii.) 186, who speak of above 1,200 talents coming in during the peace of Nicias; and attributed to Alcibiades by the Pseudo-Andocides (in Alcib. 11).

There is nothing improbable in the fact itself. The measure could have been accomplished without risk either after the Athenian triumph at Sphacteria, when the Lacedemonian power was for a time paralyzed, or during the

---

i. 99) in the case of the cities, probably not numerous, which furnished triremes at first, may be included in the 460 talents.]

[1] Müller, F. H. G., vol. ii. pp. 617–622.

peace of Nicias. The increase in the tribute would also account for the abundance of money which Athens is recorded by Thucydides to have possessed immediately before the Syracusan expedition. And, although the authority of the Orators is in general not great, it may be argued that Andocides was contemporary with the change, and that there is no reason for questioning his testimony to a fact which must have been notorious at the time. (But are we certain that the oration De Pace is genuine?)

Many writers have spoken of this question as hitherto doubtful, but now finally determined by the evidence of the monuments. In the note on v. 18, in the first edition of this work, it was assumed, on their authority, that the *τάξις φόρου* furnished a convincing proof of a great increase of the tribute in the year to which it relates; an independent examination of the *τάξις* and a comparison of the quota lists show that the additional evidence has been greatly overstated, and that the fact still remains, as far as the testimony of inscriptions goes, unproven.

The reader may be once more reminded, (1) that the *τάξις φόρου* is an estimate of the whole tribute to be received in the single year $\frac{425}{424}$; and that it contains in anything like a complete form only the *νησιωτικὸς φόρος*, or tribute of the Islands: it also gives us the tribute of eight Carian, one Ionian, and as many as nineteen Thracian cities; and one short fragment of uncertain value, supplemented by another short fragment, relating to the Hellespontian tribute; (2) that the quota lists (though with several lacunae) extend over more than thirty years. Five small fragments (C. I. A. i. 251, 262, 263; C. I. A. Suppl. iii. 272, *d. f.*) are assigned to the same date as the *τάξις φόρου*, or to a date somewhat later, on the ground of the extensive variations which they present when compared with the earlier quota lists. A few other fragments are extant of later date, but they throw no light on the present question. (One of these, 258, is supposed to belong to the last years of the war; another, 260, supplies the date of the whole series of quota lists. See p. xxxvii.)

The facts are as follows.

The Ionian tribute, of which some record is preserved in these later fragments and in the *τάξις φόρου*, exhibits a rise from 9 talents 2,600 drachmae to 18 (or 27) talents[1] 2,100 drachmae. But (1) this calculation is made on a very inadequate basis, for only 9 out of 36 or ¼th of the payments of the Ionic cities can be compared with previous payments; and (2) the difference is more than accounted for by two cities: Clazomenae raised from 1½ to 6 or 15 talents, Miletus raised from 5 to 10 talents. On the other hand, Colophon is lowered from 1½ talents to 500 drachmae. And the one Ionian city, Elaeus in Erythraea, which appears in the *τάξις φόρου*, pays 100 drachmae as before.

A short memorandum of the Hellespontian tribute occurs in the *τάξις φόρου*[2]. It is a mere fragment, or rather we have two fragments, belonging to different inscriptions or different parts of the *τάξις* (for they overlap), of which one has been restored by conjecture from the other. They are as follows:—

---

[1] [Clazomenae appears in two of the fragments of the tribute-lists thought to be later than 425; in one it pays 6 talents (C. I. A. iv. Suppl. iii. 272 *a*), in another 15 talents (C. I. A. i. 251). The tribute of Erythrae seems also to have been raised (it paid 12 talents according to 272 *a*), but as it is impossible to be certain what it paid since 440 (7 talents) it has not been taken into account above.]

[2] [C. I. A. 259, containing a great part of the Thracian and Hellespontian tribute, is almost certainly earlier than 425: see Busolt, Philol. 41, p. 695 ff. It contains the names and payments of twenty-two Thracian and twenty-four Hellespontian cities; the Thracian tribute being slightly greater than the previous payments which we can trace; the Hellespontian tribute showing a rise of about 14 talents in the cities of which a record is preserved, chiefly due to a large and perhaps exceptional increase in the payments of three or four. As none of the Thracian cities which revolted in 432 occur among the twenty-two cities in the list, it probably belongs to one of the years 431–426, not however to 428, for which the list is extant.]

(1) C. I. A. 37. z″ (the lower portion):—

ΕΛΛΕ . ΠΟΝΤΙΟΦΟΡ
ΞΦΑΛΛ . ΟΝ
𐅅ΔΔΔΔ𐅄𐅄ΗΗΙ'
ΤΑΙΑΙΠΟΛΕΣ
ΤΑΝΤΑΝ
ΡΟΙΤΓ
ΝΕΣΟ

(2) C. I. A. 543, and Suppl. i.:—

ΚΕΦ
ΗΗ𐅄
ΑΚΤΑ

ΤΤ

Ἑλλη[σ]ποντίου φόρ[ον]
κεφάλα[ι]ον
ΗΗ𐅅ΔΔΔΔ𐅄𐅄ΗΗΗ (295 talents 5300 drachmae)

Ἀκταῖαι πόλεις
ΤΤ Ἄνταν[δρος
Ῥοίτ[ειον]
Νησο-
} Cp. Thuc. iv. 52, 75.

The restored inscription, supposing the conjectural restoration of the fragments to be admitted (and they certainly exhibit a curious coincidence)[1], would prove that the Hellespontian tribute amounted to 295 talents 5,300 drachmae. But the whole tribute calculated upon the lists of 446–440 was only about 80 talents; calculated upon the list (259) referred to on the preceding page, there is no reason to think that it amounted to more than 100 talents. The increase, therefore, would be at the rate of 3 to 1, not of 2 to 1.

[1] [But for C. I. A. 543, we might with Beloch, Rheinisches Museum, xxxix. p. 42, restore 195, not 295, talents in C. I. A. 37.]

If the total of the Hellespontian tribute, as assessed in 425 B.C., really amounted to this great sum, we may suppose the cities of the Pontus to have been included in it: of four at least of these we find traces in the *τάξις φόρου*, ΝΥ[ΜΦΑΙΟΝ], ΚΕΡ[ΑΣΟΥΣ], ΠΑΤ[ΡΑΕΥΣ], ΝΙΚ[ΩΝΙΑ] (C. I. A. 37 z'''' and z''''', and Köhler, pp. 74, 75). The magnitude of the amount and the conjectural basis on which it rests raise a suspicion: and, even if the sum was assessed, we may doubt whether anything like it was really paid.

The Thracian tribute, as assessed on a new fragment fitting on to the last two lines of C. I. A. 37. z'' quoted above (C. I. A. iv. Suppl. iii. 37), presents a striking contrast to the Island tribute. Nine small towns out of the seventeen contained in it can be compared with earlier lists [1]. Instead of paying 3 talents as before, they are rated at only 3,130 drachmae, just over half a talent. The tribute of one is doubled; of one, lowered from 500 to 100 drachmae; four remain as before. Galè, which had previously paid half a talent, Singus and Mecyberna, which had previously paid a talent each, are assessed at the nominal sum of 10 drachmae [2]. Six cities, on the other hand, occur which are not found elsewhere: of these, one is rated at two talents, and two others at a talent each.

The Carian tribute is obtained from the *τάξις φόρου*, which is compared with the quota lists of previous years, and from three fragments of the quota lists, C. I. A. 261–263. The contributions of the towns admitting com-

---

[1] Another, Potidaea, is rated at 1000 drachmae; but we cannot fairly compare this sum (imposed on the Athenian *ἔποικοι*?) with the 15 talents paid in 436, before the revolt and reduction of the town and the expulsion of the previous inhabitants.

[2] Cp. Keria in the *νησιωτικὸς φόρος*, rated at 10½ drachmae. These cities may only have been expected to pay an *ἀπαρχή* like Methonè (p. xxxiii).

parison[1] are fixed in the earlier quota lists at 15 talents 5,030 drachmae, in the fragments of quota lists supposed to be later and in the *τάξις φόρου* at 23 talents 500 drachmae.

This is the whole sum imposed upon seventeen cities, of which nine are found in the quota lists, seven in the *τάξις φόρου*, and one in both; the increase being confined entirely to the quota lists, which show a rise from 13 talents to 20 talents 2,000 drachmae, while in the *τάξις φόρου* compared with the earlier quota lists there is on the whole a very slight decrease, viz. from 2 talents 5,530 drachmae to 2 talents 5,500 drachmae. But the entire calculation rests on an insufficient basis, the names and payments legible being only 17 out of 68.

Lastly, we have the Island tribute, which is obtained from the comparison of the *τάξις φόρου* alone with the earlier quota lists. From this comparison we find that the tribute is about doubled; it increases from 51 talents 4,800 drachmae to 109 talents 5,000 drachmae[2], and several small cities or islands, appearing in no previous list, some of which probably contributed before 425 in combination with larger places, are assessed at a sum of a little over 6 talents, besides Melos, assessed at 15 talents. But here again the comparison rests on insufficient grounds, though considerably fuller than any of those which have preceded. For the names and assessments of 16 places out of 26[3] are still legible. And this is in fact the main argument: 'The *νησιωτικὸς φόρος*, of which not quite two-thirds has been preserved to us, is more than doubled; the accounts of the other tributaries, if they were preserved, would show that they had been raised in a nearly similar proportion[4].'

---

[1] Ialysus cannot fairly be taken into account, see Busolt, Rhein. Mus. 41, p. 700.

[2] Omitting both Chalcis and Eretria, the previous payment of which is not quite certain, but including Siphnos, which Busolt omits.

[3] Omitting from Kirchhoff's list Hestiaea and Aegina (now cleruchies), and Lemnos (= Hephaestia and Myrina), but adding Geraestus.

[4] [An interesting fragment of a quota list (C. I. A. iv. Suppl. iii. 272 *f.*), containing sums actually paid by eight of the Islands has been assigned

The figures which form the basis of these calculations are taken from the table of tributary cities and the amount paid by them at the end of Kirchhoff, C. I. A., vol. i, corrected from Busolt's article in Philologus 41. It is an element of uncertainty which must not be overlooked, that owing to the incomplete state of the tribute lists we can often only compare the *τάξις* of 425 or the tribute recorded in the later fragments with the tribute actually paid many years before. And there is no year for which we have both an estimate and the sum actually paid.

Let us now consider the nature of the proof, or rather want of proof, that pervades the whole argument:—

(1) None of the comparisons are made upon an adequate basis, being taken only upon about $\frac{1}{4}$th (Ionia), $\frac{1}{4}$th (Caria), $\frac{2}{3}$ (Islands): while for the Hellespont we have a questionable total without items, and for Thrace some 9 or 10 out of 30 or 40 cities, estimated not at double, but at about one-sixth of their previous payment.

(2) None of the totals exhibit an exact ratio of 2 : 1.

(3) The whole number of cities which furnish the increase is only 51. Of these 7 are precisely doubled; and 15 pay the same tribute as before.

(4) The irregularity in the increase of the tribute in the states of which the names and payments are preserved to us makes it impossible to argue with any degree of certainty from them to the states whose names and payments are unknown to us. And the comparison of the earlier quota lists shows that extensive, and to us inexplicable, changes in the amount paid were not uncommon.

The various fragments of the quota lists which have been referred to above are only dated later than 425 on

to a date later than 425, because Cythnus pays a quota on 6 talents as in the *τάξις φόρου*, instead of 3 as before, and Ceos, Paros, and Naxos pay a quota on 6, 18, and 7 talents respectively, instead of 4, $16\frac{1}{6}$, and $6\frac{2}{3}$. If this be the case, and if the fragment belongs to one of the years soon after 425, the *τάξις φόρου* was very imperfectly carried out, for in it Ceos is rated at 10, Paros at 30, and Naxos at 15 talents.]

the supposition that the Ionian and Carian, as well as the Island tribute, was greatly raised in that year [1]. Thus, apart from the uncertain and startling Hellespontian total, and from the perplexing Thracian list, the argument turns on the probability that the assessments of the other states were raised in the same proportion as those of the Islanders. It may be argued in reply to what is only a presumption that the Island tributaries were more completely under the control of the Athenians, and more likely to have had their tribute raised: a glance at a map of the Athenian empire will show that they formed the 'home circle' of it.

Thus we are driven to the conclusion that the uncertainty respecting the doubling of the tribute has not been entirely removed. It is very probable that the Athenians as they increased in power increased their demands on the allies. It is more probable than not that Andocides (granting the genuineness of the De Pace) was right when he implied that the tribute had increased from 600 to 1,200 talents, for the increase must have taken place in his own time [2]. Neither he nor any one else says that the tribute was doubled in 425; his statement would be satisfied if the Athenians were receiving 1,200 talents from their allies at any time during the peace of Nicias [3]. Nor is the argument from the silence of Thucydides against this supposition of any weight. His manner of writing is so different from that of a modern historian, that it is difficult to argue beforehand what events or measures he would have inserted in his history, and what he would have omitted. All these probabilities remain as they were before. But not much can be added to the argument from

---

[1] [May not some of them belong to the period 435–431? Cp. p. xli, and C. I. A. 251.]

[2] The Pseudo-Andocides (in Alcib., 11) cannot be right in attributing the measure, if it took place in 425, to Alcibiades, whose political influence cannot as yet have been sufficiently great.

[3] Cp. Plut. Aristides, xxiv Περικλέους δ' ἀποθανόντος ἐπιτείνοντες οἱ δημαγωγοὶ κατὰ μικρὸν εἰς χιλίων καὶ τριακοσίων ταλάντων κεφάλαιον ἀνήγαγον.

an examination of the inscriptions; except as regards the Islands they leave the question nearly as it was.

One other statement remains to be discussed. It is asserted with confidence by Köhler (p. 129) that the quota lists contain mention of arrears. This assertion rests (1) on the fact that the names of certain states occur twice or even oftener in the same lists, being those of the fifth and eighth years; and further (2), in the sixth and eighth lists some coincidences appear of defects and excesses in the payment. Abdera, for example, in the sixth year pays a quota of 1,400 drachmae to the Goddess, 100 drachmae less than the ordinary payment: in the eighth year there is no entry of a larger payment, but a small sum of 100 drachmae is recorded. It is inferred therefore that, while the regular payment is lost or effaced, the 100 drachmae represent the arrear of the sixth year. In like manner the ordinary payment of Thasos is 300 drachmae, whereas in the sixth year the treasury of the Goddess only acknowledges the receipt of 246 drachmae. But there appears in the eighth year a single payment of 54 drachmae credited to Thasos. This again is explained as an arrear, 246 drachmae and 54 drachmae = 300 drachmae. Once more, the whole payment of Dardanus in ordinary years is 100 drachmae. But Dardanus is found paying 46 drachmae in the sixth year and 54 in the eighth year. Upon these three coincidences the theory of arrears seems chiefly to rest.

We may assume that there is some explanation of the same names recurring more than once in the lists. But it does not follow that the explanation can be discovered in the extant lists with any degree of certainty. To the theory of arrears several objections may be made. (1) The alleged coincidences are only found in three instances. Thirteen other instances are cited by Köhler as of more or less weight; but in three of these the payment of the sixth year is fragmentary; in two the payment of the sixth year only, in eight the payment of the eighth year only, is preserved; so that there is no possibility of comparison.

(2) In four of the entries belonging to the eighth year we find the names recorded not twice but only once; and we conjecture from the smallness of this payment that the regular tribute must have found a place somewhere else. But of this there is no evidence. (3) In the three principal instances the arrears supposed to be paid up belong not to the previous year, but to the year before that. Are we to suppose that there was first of all a part payment and an arrear, then a full payment in the following year, and in the year after that a full payment with the arrear paid up? May we not suggest that if the quota lists had been perfect this and some other inferences which have been drawn from them would disappear? (4) There is some presumption that the arrears of the quota, if they entered into the accounts at all, would be more numerous; and (5) that they would be described under a separate heading. In the quota list of 427 or 426 a few cities appear under a heading which, as restored, runs

> [Αἴδε πό]λεις περυσ[ινοῦ]
> [φόρου τ]ὰ ὀ[φειλόμενα ἀπ]
> [έδοσαν].

Another almost equally probable explanation of the repetition may be gathered from the quota lists themselves. The names of several cities occur twice over in the years 440, 439, 437, 436, 428, the first time for a larger sum, the second time for a smaller. Against the second sum is added the word ἐπιφορᾶς, or additional tribute. For example, in the Ionian quota (440) there is an entry of a payment from the Notians, 33 drachmae 2 obols, which is immediately followed by a second entry,—'Νοτιῆς ἐπιφορᾶς 5 drachmae 3½ obols.' There are in all about fourteen cities entered in this way, some of them more than once. Cp. also in the τάξις φόρου, t-v. l. 5, ἐ[πὶ τῷ] [ἐπιφ]ορὰν [τελεῖν]. It is perhaps worth observing that these entries all belong to a period later than the supposed arrears. It may also be remarked that amongst these repeated entries occurs the following,—'Δαρδανῆς 100 drachmae, Δαρδανῆς ἐπιφορᾶς 4 drachmae 2 obols;' and that the name Δαρδανῆς also occurs among the supposed arrears in the eighth year of the lists. It is evident then that other payments besides the φόρος are included in the quota lists, and it is possible that the sums afterwards called ἐπιφοραί were inserted in the earlier lists without a distinguishing note. What was the nature of these payments we cannot precisely tell. They may have been arrears; or they may have been payments about which there was a dispute between the allies and the Athenians; possibly they were dues or fines, or rather percentages of them, paid to the Goddess. One conjecture is as good as another. But, instead of offering conjectures which are gradually assumed to be certainties, it is better simply to acknowledge that the repetition of the same names in the same year, sometimes with, sometimes without the mark ἐπιφορᾶς, is a curious fact which remains unexplained.

Some lesser points of connexion between the inscriptions relating to the tribute and the narrative of Thucydides are the following:—

(1) The name of Melos occurs among the tributaries in the τάξις φόρου (B. C. 425). But Melos was not taken by the Athenians until the year 416 B. C. There is however no necessary discrepancy between the inscription and the narrative. The τάξις φόρου, as has been already remarked, is only an estimate of money to be received, not a record of actual payments, and therefore the sum set down may not have been received. In the preceding year the Athenians had made an attack on Melos (iii. 91), but without success. It may be conjectured that they thereupon inserted the name of the island in the τάξις φόρου as a pledge to themselves of their own intention to enforce their demand: the events of 424–417 fully account for the delay. If the tribute was really paid by Melos, we must suppose Thucydides, who in his first enumeration of the allies (ii. 9 fin.) had described the Melians as not ὑπο-

τελεῖς φόρου, to have been ignorant of the fact, since in that case he would not have spoken of the Athenians as failing in their attempt to force Melos into the alliance (iii. 91 init.).

(2) A sum of three talents (i. e. a quota of 300 drachmae) is said in the list (C. I. A. 257) for the year 427 or 426 to have been paid by the islanders of Thera; and this is raised in the estimate of the τάξις φόρου, 425 B. C., to five talents. In C. I. A. 38, a decree relating to the φόρος, but of uncertain date or meaning, there occur the words [ἐξέσ]τω δὲ καὶ Σαμίοις καὶ Θηραίο[ις], showing that both were under some special regulation. Yet at the beginning of the war the Theraeans as well as the Melians are excepted from the list of the Athenian allies (πᾶσαι αἱ ἄλλαι Κυκλάδες πλὴν Μήλου καὶ Θήρας, ii. 9 fin.), and were probably, like the Melians (v. 84), neutral. Now it seems impossible that a new tribute could have been imposed before the Peloponnesian War on an island which is expressly excluded by Thucydides from the number of Athenian allies and tributaries. But it is not unlikely that at some time in the course of the war the island may have been conquered by the Athenians, or may have submitted to them, and that Thucydides may either have forgotten the fact or have not thought it worth mentioning. It is possible also that both Melos and Thera may have been original members of the Delian confederacy, and, though not included in her regular tributaries, may have made some payment to Athens.

(3) In the account of the expedition against Cyprus (Thuc. i. 112) the Athenians are said to have left Citium in consequence of the death of Cimon, and also of a famine which occurred. It is observed by Köhler (p. 130) that the year of this famine (449) coincides with the year of a defalcation in the tribute money, viz. the arrears of the sixth year just discussed. But the defalcation is itself uncertain, and it is very doubtful whether there is any trace here of a real coincidence. For the famine is in Cyprus, but the supposed defalcation is about the shores

of the Aegean extending to the Hellespont. Such an attempt to piece one fragment of knowledge with another seems to arise only out of the slenderness of our materials.

(4) Among the facts which we learn with certainty from the tribute lists is the division of the φόρος into the Ἰωνικὸς φόρος, Ἑλλησπόντιος φόρος, ἐπὶ Θρᾴκης or Θρᾴκιος φόρος, Καρικὸς φόρος, and Νησιωτικὸς φόρος. The earlier lists have no regular arrangement, or only a very rough one. E. g. at the beginning of the sixth list the Narisbareans of Caria or the adjoining countries, the Tenedians, the Gentinians of the Troad, the Stagirites, the Cerameans of Caria, the Camireans of Rhodes, the Halicarnassians, the Myrinaeans of Lemnos, and the Mecybernaeans of Chalcidicè follow each other.

After the ninth list the geographical division prevails; and in the twelfth and subsequent lists (from 443 B. C.) the cities of each division are headed by the titles Ἰωνικὸς φόρος, etc. Between 440 and 437 the Ionian and Carian tribute is united (C. I. A. 244), many Carian cities appearing for the last time in our extant lists about the same date. The names of the different states are placed under their respective heads, but no geographical or other order is observed, nor do the same names follow each other in successive lists. We seem to find traces of the division in Thucydides, ii. 9 fin.: ἄλλαι πόλεις αἱ ὑποτελεῖς οὖσαι ἐν ἔθνεσι τοσοῖσδε, Καρία ἡ ἐπὶ θαλάσσῃ, Δωριῆς Καρσὶ πρόσοικοι, Ἰωνία, Ἑλλήσποντος, τὰ ἐπὶ Θρᾴκης, νῆσοι ὅσαι ἐντὸς Πελοποννήσου καὶ Κρήτης πρὸς ἥλιον ἀνίσχοντα, πᾶσαι αἱ ἄλλαι Κυκλάδες πλὴν Μήλου καὶ Θήρας.

(5) A fragment containing a very full list of the Thracian cities was referred by Köhler to Ol. 87. 1, and was thought by him to prove that Potidaea, Olynthus, Spartolus, and other cities which revolted in that year (432) must have paid tribute just before the revolt took place. The rearrangement of the stone by Kirchhoff, who puts the list back to 436 (Ol. 86. 1), puts back also the record of the payment.

How the tribute to be paid by each city was fixed we do not know with certainty. At the end of the later lists after 437 B.C. a few cities occur under the headings *πόλεις αὐταὶ φόρον ταξάμεναι* and *πόλεις ἃς οἱ ἰδιῶται ἐνέγραψαν φόρον φέρειν*, and in a fragment which may belong to a quota list or to a *τάξις φόρου* (Köhler, p. 82, No. 7; C. I. A. 266) occur the headings—

> Πόλεις ἃς ἔτ]αξαν οἱ τάκται
>]ου γραμματεύοντος.
> Πόλεις ἃς ἡ] βουλὴ καὶ οἱ πεντακόσιο[ι]
> (?) οἱ ἡλιασταὶ ἔτ]αξαν.

Köhler, pp. 66, 136, comparing these headings with the fragment of the *τάξις φόρου* of 425, and with a report of the *ψήφισμα* of Tisamenus providing for the revision of the ancient laws after the fall of the Thirty (Andocides, De Myst. 83), and of a law preserved by Demosthenes (c. Timocr. 20 ff.), concludes that after the vote of the assembly ordering a *τάξις* to take place the amounts to be imposed upon the cities were fixed in the first instance by a board of *τάκται* (numbering 10, Köhler; 8, Kirchhoff, C. I. A. 37). The tribute as proposed by them was then discussed and passed in the senate, before which any private person (*ἰδιώτης*) might propose amendments (cp. the *ψήφισμα* of Tisamenus, *ἐξεῖναι δὲ καὶ ἰδιώτῃ τῷ βουλομένῳ εἰσιόντι εἰς τὴν βουλὴν συμβουλεύειν ὅ τι ἂν ἀγαθὸν ἔχῃ περὶ τῶν νόμων*), and there was an appeal to a court of 500 dicasts, who might grant claims for a diminution of tribute made by the cities themselves (*πόλεις αὐταί*: cp. *φόρον ὃν ἂν πείθω Ἀθηναίους*, p. lxxxvi, infra).

[Later writers (Loeschke, De Titulis aliquot Atticis, p. 16; Busolt, Philol. 41, p. 658 ff., 669 ff., partly following Boeckh) point out that the cities which fall under these two heads are all small, mostly lying in the Thracian district, and that some of them recur in more than one list, sometimes at an interval of several years. But it is unlikely that the same cities (and these small cities too) should successfully contest the Athenian assessment on different occasions. So that this circumstance points to some local reason for the special position of the *πόλεις αὐταὶ φόρον ταξάμεναι* and *πόλεις ἃς οἱ ἰδιῶται ἐνέγραψαν φόρον φέρειν*. The former may have been, for reasons at which we can only guess, allowed to fix (nominally at least) their own assessment. Similarly, the *ἰδιῶται* may have been private citizens of the states themselves; though this is even more doubtful, for what status in such a matter could private citizens of other states than Athens have had? See Fränkel on Boeckh, Staatshaushaltung, vol. ii. p. 374 (616).]

A considerable fragment of a decree respecting the tribute is contained in C. I. A. 38, but no connected meaning can be elicited from it. Certain cities seem to be spoken of as defaulters, to whom commissioners are sent to exact the tribute. The names of those who pay the tribute are to be written up on a tablet by the Hellenotamiae, and something is granted or done to 'both the Samians and the Theraeans' (cp. above, p. lv). There follows a mention of *ἐπιμεληταί*, and of a general or generals. Any attempts made by citizens of the tributary states to evade the 'decree respecting the tribute' may be prosecuted before the *ἐπιμεληταί*; the *ἐπιμεληταί* are to bring them before the dicastery, the cases being of a class which had to be tried within a month (*ἔμμηνοι*). If the accused are condemned, the dicastery is to impose a penalty. Something not very intelligible is said about the election of collectors of the tribute (*ἐκλογεῖς*). According to another fragment of the same inscription (see C. I. A. 38 *a* Suppl. i.) defaulters are to be written up. If an unjust accusation is brought, the accuser is to be fined. If no proper summons has been given, the senate is to settle the matter (*κλήσεις*, [*κ*]*λητῆρες*, cp. Aristoph. Av. 1422): these 'summoners' are also mentioned in the decree preceding the *τάξις φόρου*, C. I. A. 37 *f. g.* l. 28).

It is impossible to say whether the *ψήφισμα τὸ τοῦ φόρου*

referred to in 38 *f.* l. 10 is the τάξις φόρου of 425 or not. For the date of the inscription is uncertain, and there was a τάξις φόρου every four years.

I. iii. Another class of inscriptions illustrating Thucydides are the accounts of the treasures of Athenè. They are divided into three series: the first containing the treasures of the Pronaos, or eastern portico of the temple; the second, the treasures of the Hecatompedon, or eastern chamber; and the third, the treasures of the western chamber or Parthenon properly so called. The accounts, or, more correctly speaking, the inventories of these treasures, which were made up annually, commence in the year 434, and extend over nearly the whole of the Peloponnesian War, the account of the treasure of the Parthenon lasting, with gaps, up to 411; that of the Pronaos up to 407; that of the Hecatompedon, with gaps, to 413: there are a few later fragments of it.

Pericles, in estimating the resources of the Athenians, includes among their treasures, besides the 6,000 talents of coined money in the state treasury (ii. 13), 'uncoined gold 'and silver in the form of private and public offerings, 'sacred vessels used in processions and games, the Per'sian spoil, and other things of the like nature, worth at 'least five hundred talents more. There were also at their 'disposal, besides what they had in the Acropolis, consider'able treasures in various temples. If they were reduced 'to the last extremity, they could even take off the plates 'of gold with which the image of the Goddess was over'laid: these, as he pointed out, weighed forty talents, and 'were of refined gold, which was all removable. They 'might use the gold taken from the Goddess in self'defence, but they were bound to replace all that they had 'taken.'

These inventories are for the most part repetitions of each other. Each of them, except the last inventory of the treasures of the Pronaos (see below), is headed by a regular form of words, e.g. 'These things the stewards 'of the sacred treasure of Athenè, Eurectes of Atenè and 'his colleagues, to whom Apollodorus the son of Critias 'of Aphidnae was registrar, handed over to the stewards 'to whom Diognis the son of Isander of the Piraeus 'was registrar; having received them from the previous 'stewards to whom Euthias son of Aeschron of Anaphlys-'tus was registrar.'

'In the Pronaos.'—(C. I. A. 119.)—Then follow the actual inventories.

In the first year however of each Panathenaic period the treasures are said to be handed over to the stewards of the year by 'the officers of the four preceding years, who gave in their accounts from one Panathenaea to the next.'

During the twenty or thirty years over which the lists extend they gradually increase in length (in the language of the inscriptions, ἐπέτεια ἐπεγένετο—'these are additions of the year') until the final collapse. They are silent witnesses to the growth, decline, and fall of the first Athenian empire, the last record of the treasures of the Hecatompedon appearing in a fragment which is assigned on palaeographical and other grounds to a year subsequent to 405 B.C.[1] The inventories reappear a few years later, though the form of them is different; only a few of the articles previously mentioned are found, and many of those catalogued are described as 'out of repair.'

The treasures consisted of gold and silver plate, bowls, cups, crowns, horns, couches, tables, chairs, censers, baskets, of gilded and golden as well as of silver and plated articles, and of arms. We find among them a gilded lyre, four ivory lyres, a flute case, a 'figure of a girl upon a pillar,' a 'horse, a griffin, the face (or fore-part) of a griffin, a griffin, the head of a lion, a necklace (or wreath) of flowers, a dragon; all overlaid with gold.'

---

[1] See C. I. A. i. p. 72 b, partly corrected by C. I. A. iv. Suppl. i. p. 20, n. on p. 55.

The entire value of them, as far as can be estimated by their weight, is not great, probably not exceeding at the beginning of the war ten to twenty talents, to which must be added a moderate sum for the workmanship[1]. A sample of the character of these treasures will be given by the last inventory of the articles contained in the Πρόναος, Ol. 93. 2, 407–406 B.C. If we can trust a very conjectural restoration, which however derives some support from the exceptional character of this last inscription, they are recorded at the end of it to have been handed over to the Hellenotamiae, i.e. devoted to the purposes of the war, in the following year, Ol. 93. 3. The Athenians however do not appear to have availed themselves to any considerable extent, if at all, during the time which the lists severally cover, of the resource hinted at by Pericles.

This inventory is as follows:—

121 silver bowls . . .	weighing 2 tal.	432	drachmae.	
3 silver horns . . .	,,	528	,,	
5 silver cups . . .	,,	167	,,	
1 silver lamp . . .	,,	38	,,	
7 silver bowls . . .	,,	700	,,	
1 golden crown (in a round case)	,,	33	,,	3 obols.
2 silver bowls . . .	,,	200	,,	
4 silver bowls . . .	,,	329	,,	
1 silver Chalcidian cup .	,,	40	,,	
7 silver bowls . . .	,,	920	,,	
1 silver cup . . .	,,	40	,,	
4 silver bowls . . .	,,	420	,,	
7 silver bowls . . .	,,	643	,,	2 ,,
3 silver bowls . . .	,,	251	,,	
1 silver cup . . .	,,	66	,,	
1 silver lamp . . .	,,	22	,,	
3 silver vessels . . .	,,	294	,,	
5 silver vessels . . .	,,	413	,,	
1 silver vessel . . .	,,	112	,,	
1 silver cup . . .	,,	47	,,	

[1] It would thus appear that the articles enumerated in these records form but a small part of what may be termed the miscellaneous treasures of the Athenians, which are estimated by Thucydides at 500 talents. These, however, include uncoined gold and silver, as well as many articles of value unweighed.

1 silver vessel	weighing	60	drachmae.	
1 silver cup	,,	39	,,	
1 silver vessel	,,	153	,,	
1 silver cup	,,	30	,,	
4 silver vessels	,,	386	,,	
1 silver vessel	,,	194	,,	
4 silver vessels	,,	788	,,	
3 silver vessels	,,	718	,,	
1 silver vessel	weight wanting.			
	3 tal.	2,063	,,	5 obols.
Add for the difference between the value of gold and silver, estimated at 13 to 1,[1] in the case of the golden crown . . .		402	,,	,,
	3 ,,	2,465	,,	5 ,,

C. I. A. 194-225 are a very fragmentary series of the accounts of the 'other deities,' in which the names occur of Hephaestus, Poseidon Ἵππιος, and Poseidon of Sunium, Herè, Dionysus, the Mother of the Gods, Zeus, Artemis Ἑκάτη and Artemis Ἀγροτέρα, Apollo, and some Attic heroes (cp. C. I. A. 273). As to the amount or character of the treasure little can be made out: a 'tenth from the sale of captives,' [δ]εκάτη ἀνδραπόδων, is dedicated to Artemis Ἀγροτέρα. That the series begins before 429 is proved by words which occur in one of the inscriptions (194):—

[ἐπὶ Ἐπαμεί]
νονος ἄρχοντος, (B.C. 429)

and—

τάδε παρέδ[οσαν παραδεξάμενοι]
παρὰ τῶν π[ροτέρων ταμιῶν].

It may be worth observing (cp. Newton and Hicks, p. 47) that the words in the financial statement of Pericles τὰ ἐκ τῶν ἄλλων ἱερῶν προσετίθει χρήματα οὐκ ὀλίγα are not necessarily connected with τῶν ἄλλων θεῶν in the expression ταμίαι τῶν ἄλλων θεῶν. For Thucydides is speaking of temples 'other than those on the Acropolis,' or 'other

[1] Hdt. iii. 95. C. I. A. i. p. 160, iv. Suppl. iii. p. 146, show that the ratio (which of course varied as it does now) was higher, viz. about 14 : 1, shortly before the beginning of the Peloponnesian war.

than the Parthenon.' (Of temples on the Acropolis besides those of Athenè, Thucydides speaks in ii. 15, τὰ γὰρ ἱερὰ ἐν αὐτῇ τῇ ἀκροπόλει καὶ ἄλλων θεῶν ἐστί.) But the treasures of the other deities were certainly at a later date, and perhaps at the beginning of the war (C. I. A. 32), kept on the Acropolis and in the Parthenon.

I. iv. We will now pass to the inscriptions relating to the payment of debts to the temples and the expenditure of public money. Among them one of the most important is C. I. A 32 and Suppl. ii, a decree of the senate and people which, after mentioning the repayment of 3,000 talents to the Goddess, provides for a further repayment to 'the other deities' out of certain funds which had been already set apart for this purpose by a vote of the assembly. Part of these were in the hands of the Hellenotamiae, another part was to be obtained from a tithe of the produce of land, tolls, or spoils (?), when let out or sold (?), τὰ ἐκ τῆς δεκάτης ἐπειδὰν πραθῇ. The thirty λογισταί, or accountants, now in office are to calculate exactly the amount of the debt to the deities: these officers are to be called together at the discretion of the senate. (The τριάκοντα mentioned in the heading of the first and third quota lists are probably identical with the λογισταί, see Köhler, p. 106.) The money is to be paid back by the πρυτάνεις in the presence of the Senate, and all records of the debt are to be searched for and cancelled. The sum thus repaid is to be administered by ταμίαι. These are to be elected at the same time as the other magistrates, and in the same manner as the ταμίαι of the treasures of Athenè. They are to receive the money of the other deities from other ταμίαι, ἐπιστάται, and ἱεροποιοί of different temples who administer it at present [1], and to deposit it in the Opisthodomus of the Parthenon. They are to register the amount belonging to each deity and to all collectively, and to keep an annual

[1] I. e. after the πρυτάνεις have first paid it back to its various administrators (?).

account from one Panathenaic festival to another, like the treasurers of Athenè. Any surplus remaining after repayment is to be spent upon walls and docks.

The second part of the inscription is a decree passed somewhat later, which presupposes that the order has been given for the payment of the debt to the other deities mentioned above. Certain moneys belonging to Athenè may be used in adorning the Acropolis, and repairing (or supplying) articles employed in processions. But not more than 10,000 drachmae are to be spent on this account; and nothing at all for any other purpose without a previous vote of indemnity. The Hellenotamiae are regularly to deposit the proceeds of the *φόρος* with the *ταμίαι τῆς Ἀθηναίας*. (We cannot be quite sure whether this refers to the whole of the *φόρος*, or only to the $\frac{1}{60}$th paid to the Goddess; cp. pp. lxxvi, lxxvii.) When the sum owing to the other deities is repaid, out of the two hundred talents set apart for the purpose, it is to be kept on the left of the *ὀπισθόδομος*, and the money of Athenè on the right: *τα[μιευέσθω τὰ μὲν τῆς Ἀθη]ναίας χρήματα [ἐν τῷ] ἐπὶ δέξια τοῦ ὀπισ[θοδόμου, τὰ δὲ τῶν ἄλλων θ]εῶν ἐν τῷ ἐπ' ἀρ[ίστερ]α*[1]. Those portions of the sacred treasure which have not been weighed or counted are now to be counted in the presence of the officers of the four previous years who gave in their account from one Panathenaic festival to the next; they are to weigh such of them as are gold or silver, or silver plated with gold . . . Here the words cease to be legible.

[1] [It is a disputed question whether the Opisthodomus, in which the money under the control of the *ταμίαι* of Athene was kept, was the portico of the Parthenon west of the 'Parthenon' properly so called, or was part of a temple of Athene of which the foundation still exists between the Parthenon and the Erechtheum, destroyed in the Persian War, and, according to Dr. Dörpfeld's theory, partially rebuilt afterwards and used as a treasury. See, for arguments on both sides, Harrison and Verrall, Athens and Attica, pp. 465, 502 ff.; P. Gardner, New Chapters in Greek History, pp. 255, 256; and an elaborate criticism of Dr. Dörpfeld's theory in Frazer's Pausanias, vol. ii. pp. 553-582.]

There is no indication of a date in this inscription, except what can be gathered from the writing: *σύν* has taken the place of *ξύν*; the later and shorter form of the dative plural, and also the longer form, both occur in it (*ταμίαις* as well as *ταμίασι*), the later dative implying a year in or after Ol. 90 (420–417). It is beautifully written on two sides of a stone slab, and was once the table of an altar. Boeckh places it in the year B.C. 418.

This inscription has been made the subject of an elaborate discussion by Kirchhoff (Urkunden der Schatzmeister der 'anderen Götter,' Abhandl. der Berl. Acad. 1864, pp. 8–28, Athenischer Staatsschatz, pp. 21 ff., 43 ff., Berl. Acad. 1876), who refers it to a time before the Peloponnesian War, and draws various inferences from it. The precise year to which he assigns the inscription is the first of the Panathenaic period, Ol. 86. 3–87. 2 (434–431), or the last year of the preceding period, when the accounts of the treasure were made up, and when changes in the regulation of it would most naturally take place. He arrives at this conclusion on grounds which will be hereafter examined. To reconcile this date with the character of the writing he has recourse to the supposition that, while the substance of the document belongs to the year 434, it was not written down until after 420. Here are two improbabilities: (1) that a decree of the senate and people should not have been engraved during fifteen years; and (2) that it should have been engraved at the end of the fifteen years. Such an hypothesis would only be justified on the ground that there was no later date to which the inscription could be assigned, as in the case of C. I. A. 283; or on such palaeographical grounds as determine the date of C. I. A. 8. 93; or where, as in the case of C. I. A. 40, the interval is comparatively short and the arrangements made at the earlier date are still binding when they are recorded on the marble. But in the present case there is no necessity for any such hypothesis. The Athenians would have been quite as well able to repay a large sum to the

Goddess between B.C. 421 and 415, after a few years of peace, as before the commencement of the war. Kirchhoff, having fixed the date of the inscription on other grounds, connects the payment of the 3,000 talents with the possession of 9,700 talents by the Athenians shortly before the war (Thuc. ii. 13 med.), and with the indemnity which they exacted from the Samians after the suppression of the revolt. It is quite true that the Athenians must have been rich when they transferred so large a sum from one account to another. But they had recovered their wealth before the Syracusan expedition.

Kirchhoff argues that some words at the end of the inscription, in which provision is made for numbering and weighing some of the sacred treasures at that particular time (*νῦν*), are a decree then for the first time establishing the inventories of the sacred articles of the temple, which commence in 434 and continue in a more or less fragmentary form down to the taking of the city (C. I. A. 117–173). Thus he imagines himself to obtain an accurate determination of the date. But in reply it may be observed: (1) That the words of the inscription (32 ad fin.), *τῶν χρημάτων τῶν* [*ἱερῶ*]*ν*, seem to refer to the treasures of the Goddess and of the other deities mentioned in the words just preceding, which were kept or were henceforth to be kept in the *ὀπισθόδομος*; why should we suppose a sudden transition to the treasures of the inventories which were kept in other parts of the temple? (2) That a provision is made in the inscription for a weighing of the treasures. But several of the articles mentioned in the inventories were and continued to be unweighed. This seems to prove that the inscription has to do, not with the inventories, but with some other and more careful register of part of the sacred treasure. (3) The direction that only such of the treasures as are unweighed and uncounted are to be weighed would imply that there had been previous inventories. But, if so, the custom of having an inventory was not then established for the first time. (4) That the inscription appears to speak of a single occasion only, and not of the establishment of an annual audit. It relates to the money paid in at that time, and to the plate, which is to be numbered and weighed in the presence of the magistrates who are in the habit of accounting for it from time to time—*ἀρχαὶ αἳ ἐδίδο[σαν ἀεὶ τὸν λόγον ἐκ Παν]αθηναίων ἐς Πα[ναθήν]αια* (cp. C. I. A. 117. l. 1). Lastly, the fragmentary state of the concluding lines of the text renders it perilous to draw inferences from it, such as are drawn by Kirchhoff respecting the relation which the inscription bears to the inventories. The whole argument rests on one of those apparent coincidences which but for the slenderness of our materials would never have been observed, and when examined more closely turns out not to be a coincidence at all.

More weight is due to the argument in favour of the earlier date derived from C. I. A. 194, in which *ταμίαι τῶν ἄλλων θεῶν* are mentioned as already existing [*ἐπ' Ἀμεί*]-*νονος ἄρχοντος*, in the year 429, that is if we could be sure that they were first established by the decree contained in C. I. A. 32. But, though there appears to be a special appointment of *ταμίαι* in this inscription, the wording of it (*παρὰ δὲ τῶν νῦν ταμιῶν καὶ τῶν ἐπιστατῶν καὶ τῶν ἱεροποιῶν τῶν ἐν τοῖς ἱεροῖς οἳ νῦν διαχειρίζουσι, κ.τ.λ.*), and indeed the very fact of nearly 200 talents having been borrowed, indicate that such *ταμίαι* were already in existence. And these may be referred to in C. I. A. 194 as *ταμίαι τῶν ἄλλων θεῶν*. However this may be, the argument is hardly sufficient to counterbalance the indications given by the writing. The utmost that can be conceded is that the earlier date (Kirchhoff) is as likely as the later (Boeckh). [Beloch, Rheinisches Museum, xliii. p. 113 ff., argues strongly in favour of the later date: chiefly on the ground that a loan of 3,000 talents from the treasury of the Goddess is far more likely to have been required during the first ten years of the war than during the time between the Thirty Years' Peace and 434 B. C. With regard to the argument just referred to, from the existence of ταμίαι τῶν ἄλλων θεῶν at the date of C. I. A. 194, he observes that the enumeration of their names there, though incomplete, cannot have contained less than seven or more than five names: whereas C. I. A. 32 provides for the appointment of ταμίαι τῶν ἄλλων θεῶν by lot in the same manner as the ταμίαι τῆς Ἀθηναίας, probably implying that their number was to be ten, one from each tribe. If the later date be right, the minute statement of the sums borrowed from each of some eighteen 'other deities'—80 drachmae at an interest of half an obol from Heracles ἐν Κυνοσάργει, 2 drachmae 1½ obols from Athene ἐπὶ Παλλαδίῳ, at an interest which is lost,—represents the carrying out of the instructions given to the λογισταί in C. I. A. 32, and illustrates the difficulty of 'searching for and destroying' the records of the debt (Beloch, l. c. p. 116)[1].]

The sum of 3,000 talents repaid to the Goddess is supposed by Kirchhoff to be part of the great Athenian treasure which at some time before the Peloponnesian War had amounted to 9,700 talents (Thuc. ii. 13 med.). 'From this had to be deducted a sum of 3,700 expended on various buildings, such as the Propylaea of the Acropolis, and also on the siege of Potidaea.' Of the 6,000 talents which remained at the commencement of the war 1,000 were set apart as a reserve, and not touched until after the failure of the Syracusan expedition in 413. The remaining 5,000 might be used in the service of the state.

Now in Thucydides, iii. 19, three and a half years after the commencement of the war, towards the end of 428 B.C., the Athenians are said to have sent out twelve ships to collect tribute among their allies in Lycia and Caria; at the same time, or rather sooner, they imposed upon themselves a property tax of 200 talents. The two measures, accord-

[1] Frazer, Pausanias, vol. ii. p. 561, accepts the earlier date, 435, partly because, the Parthenon being practically completed about the time, regulations for the storage of the treasure in the ὀπισθόδομος would be necessary.

ing to Kirchhoff, Athenischer Staatsschatz, p. 26 ff., show that they were in pecuniary distress. Before they would have submitted to tax themselves they must have exhausted their whole treasure. This is the keystone of the argument: 'If there had been anything left they would never have sent out an extraordinary expedition to exact money, or have raised out of their own incomes, for the first time in the war, two hundred talents.' Hence it is inferred that during the first three years of the war the whole of their reserve fund must have been expended.

If we add to the	5,000 talents
the annual increment of the sacred treasure, calculated by Kirchhoff at 200 talents (see however infra, p. lxxxiv, note [1]) . . .	600 "
tribute for three years, at 600 talents a year	1,800 "
the whole sum spent in three years is	7,400 "
or annually	$2,466\frac{2}{3}$ "

Leaving at this point the thread of the argument, to which we will return, we may illustrate the general character of Athenian expenditure by a few easy calculations:—

(1) A fleet of 100 vessels, carrying each the ordinary crew of 200 men, or 20,000 in all, could not have been maintained in the early part of the war, when the sailors' wages were high, viz. a drachma a day, at a less cost than 100 talents a month, besides the payments to officers and marines, and the cost of the hull supplied, as well as the pay, by the state. (Thuc. iii. 17, vi. 8. 31. Cp. Thuc. viii. 45, showing that the regular rate of pay after the Sicilian expedition was half this, 3 obols per man.)

(2) The heavy-armed soldiers who served in the siege of Potidaea received each man for himself and an attendant two drachmae a day (iii. 17). They numbered in the first expedition 3,000 men, in the second 1,600, who re-

mained for only a part of the two years for which the siege lasted. Therefore under this single head an expenditure must have been incurred, while the whole 4,600 were on the spot, of more than a talent and a half a day, or at the rate of 532 talents in an ordinary year of 355 days. Thucydides expressly says that the siege cost 2,000 talents (ii. 70).

(3) The building of the Propylaea is said by Heliodorus to have cost 2,012 talents (Harpocration, s. v. p. 159).

(4) The six thousand jurymen of the court of Heliaea, if sitting at one time, would have received half a talent a day (the pay of each singly being 3 obols), or, if sitting for a month, 15 talents. Or, as Aristophanes (Wasps, 663) calculates—in 'round,' and perhaps exaggerated, numbers—the expense of 6,000 jurymen for the year, sitting 300 days,—

γίγνεται ἡμῖν ἑκατὸν δήπου καὶ πεντήκοντα τάλαντα[1].

(5) It is possible that the pay for attendance in the ἐκκλησία was introduced before the end of the war: we only know with certainty that it had been raised from 1 to 2 obols, and again, by its originator Agyrrhius, from 2 to 3 obols before the performance of Aristophanes' Ecclesiazusae in 392 (Eccl. 300, [Aristotle] Athen. Polit. 41). Even if we calculate on the basis of 5,000 as a possible maximum attendance upon ordinary occasions (cp. Thuc. viii. 72), and suppose 50 sittings in each year, viz. the four regular meetings in each of the ten prytanies, and (say) ten extraordinary meetings, the yearly cost at 1 obol a day would not have amounted to 7 talents.

(6) The total pay of 500 senators at a drachma a day, sitting 300 days in the year, would amount to 25 talents.

Such estimates give a general idea of the scale of Athenian expenditure. They may also remind us that both on the creditor and debtor side of the account should be entered many elements of revenue and expenditure which can no longer be estimated.

We may now return to the calculation of Kirchhoff. It

---

[1] Cp. Starkie, Wasps, Excursus vi.

turns, as we have already seen, upon Thucydides iii. 19, a passage in which the Athenians are described as sending ships to Caria and other places for the collection of tribute, having already raised a self-imposed tax of 200 talents among themselves. Now he infers that they would not have taken extraordinary means of raising money until their ordinary resources were exhausted. Yet surely (1) a people, like an individual, may become alarmed at its financial condition long before its capital entirely comes to an end, and, having great dangers to face, may take extraordinary measures to meet financial difficulties before the exchequer has been emptied. (2) Such expeditions were sent, not once only, but many times in the course of the war, and even before this time (Thuc. ii. 69, cp. also iv. 50, 75), to collect money from cities which were in arrears or which did not regularly pay tribute, or to exact an extraordinary tribute from those which did[1]. But (3) if so, the argument for the great expenditure of the first three years of the war falls to the ground. If there is no reason to assume that the Athenians were in extreme necessity when they sent out the squadron, neither is there any need to infer that they had spent at the rate of 2,466⅔ talents a year during the first three years of the Peloponnesian War. (4) The mere imposition of a property tax is far from proving any extreme necessity. It is a tax very likely to be imposed at all times by the growing power of a democracy on the rich, *οἵπερ καὶ*

---

[1] It cannot safely be maintained, on the strength of the doubtful passage in [Aristotle] Athen. Polit. 24 *νῆες αἱ τοὺς φόρους ἄγουσαι* (see note in Sandys), that the *ἀργυρολόγοι νῆες* collected the regular tribute: the regular tribute, as distinct from exceptional levies, appears to have been brought to Athens by the allies at the Great Dionysia: Aristoph. Ach. 504

αὐτοὶ γάρ ἐσμεν οὑπὶ Ληναίῳ τ' ἀγών,
κοὔπω ξένοι πάρεισιν· οὔτε γὰρ φόροι
ἥκουσιν οὔτ' ἐκ τῶν πόλεων οἱ ξύμμαχοι.

Schol. *εἰς δὲ τὰ Διονύσια ἐτέτακτο Ἀθήναζε κομίζειν τὰς πόλεις τοὺς φόρους ὡς Εὔπολίς φησιν ἐν Πόλεσιν.*

ταλαιπωροῦνται μάλιστα (viii. 48 init.; Aristoph. Knights, 923 ff.). (5) Kirchhoff is surely mistaken in supposing that the words of Thucydides, iii. 17, καὶ τὰ χρήματα τοῦτο μάλιστα ὑπανάλωσε μετὰ Ποτιδαίας, imply that the reserve was exhausted. They might indeed have had this meaning if any statement of such exhaustion had been previously made. But as they stand they mean no more than 'this was the great drain upon the Athenian resources.' Again (6), supposing the Athenians to have used up their capital during the first three years of the war, it is hard to see how they supported the equal if not greater strain of the seven years which followed. Can we suppose that a prudent people would have depended merely upon the limited sum which could be raised by a property tax or upon the chance sums which were brought in from time to time by the exactions of ἀργυρολόγοι νῆες? Whether the tribute was doubled in the year 425 or not, it is evident that the Athenians after a few years of peace enjoyed a plethora of wealth; cp. Thuc. vi. 26, Andoc. de Pace, (iii.) 8. 9, διὰ ταύτην τὴν εἰρήνην ἑπτακισχίλια τάλαντα νομίσματος εἰς τὴν ἀκρόπολιν ἀνηνέγκαμεν. But would they in five or six years have risen to wealth from absolute bankruptcy, which must have been their state if during five or six years of war their treasury had been empty?

Neither the notices of Thucydides nor any inscription hitherto found enable us to form a certain estimate of the total revenue or expenditure of Athens in any given year of the Peloponnesian War. We are at a loss to reconcile the words of Aristophanes, who (Wasps, 660) roughly estimates the income of Athens at 2,000 talents,—

τούτων πλήρωμα τάλαντ' ἐγγὺς δισχίλια γίγνεται ἡμῖν,—

with Xenophon's statement (Anab. vii. 1. 27) that at the beginning of the Peloponnesian War the Athenians had not less than 1,000 talents coming in yearly[1]. We cannot

[1] ['With regard to the statement of Aristoph. Wasps, 660, 422 B.C. ..., if we may venture to suppose that at that date the tribute amounted to

determine how far civil as well as military expenditure was defrayed from the treasures of the temples, or how far extraordinary expenses were defrayed out of ordinary resources: we do not know what was received from mines, public lands, law fees, harbour-dues, confiscations; how far the tribute may have risen above or fallen below 600 talents; or how much was brought in by ἀργυρολόγοι νῆες. We cannot tell to what extent the λειτουργίαι relieved the state finances of expenditure which has to be met by modern states. Neither do we know what was spent on temples and other public buildings, on theatrical performances, sacred missions and festivals, on hulls of ships, siege engines, and other munitions of war, on the maintenance of the orphans of citizens killed in battle, and other public expenses. We cannot therefore attempt to balance the accounts of the Athenian empire.

But Kirchhoff is quite right in supposing that there was a very large expenditure of capital in the first few years of the war, larger, as we gather from C. I. A. 273, than in the years which followed.

This important inscription, bearing on the preceding as well as on the following discussion, may here be conveniently introduced. It contains an account, apparently drawn up by the λογισταί, of money paid out for the public service at different times from the treasuries of Athenè Polias, Athenè Nikè, and of the other deities. The account is divided into two parts, one extending from Ol. 86. 4 to 88. 2 (433 to 427 B.C.) inclusive, the second from 88. 3 to 89. 2 (426 to 423 B.C.) inclusive. The total of the money borrowed during the first seven years from all these treasuries amounts to about 4,729 talents 2,625 drachmae 2 obols; that borrowed during the last four

---

1,200 talents' (which it may have done, in theory at least, but see p. li), 'that Aristophanes exaggerates, and lastly that the οὐ μεῖον in Xenophon is put by litotes for "fully 1,000 or more," we may reconcile the statements of the two writers.' Gilbert, Greek Constitutional Antiquities, Engl. Translation (Brooks and Nicklin), p. 358, n. 2.]

years or πεντετηρίς from the treasury of Athenè Polias—the amount borrowed from the other treasuries, though not great, is uncertain—to about 747 talents 4,178 drachmae, in all 5,477 talents 803 drachmae 2 obols. Interest is charged on the whole of this sum; calculated, during the last four years, of which alone the accounts are preserved in detail, according to Boeckh, at the 300th part of a drachma for a mina per day, or at 1⅕ per cent. for the year: a merely nominal rate, especially when we remember that 10 or 12 per cent. was considered a low rate of interest (in the third century at least), and that 18 per cent. was an ordinary rate[1].

It may be observed (1) that this inscription affords an important evidence of the existence of a sacred fund which was also public (see infra).

(2) If the 3,000 talents repaid to Athene and the 200 to be repaid to the other deities, mentioned in the last inscription (C. I. A. 32), were repaid in the year 418, as supposed by Boeckh, it is probable that they were a repayment to the temple treasures of a part of the sums here set down as borrowed. Otherwise there is no indication that the interest was ever paid or the principal returned.

(3) The inscription proves that the Athenian war expenditure was very far from being paid out of the income of the year; and that the sums borrowed were much larger, probably because there was a larger fund from which to borrow, during the first seven years than during the four subsequent years of the period to which the inscription refers. The argument of Kirchhoff supposes that the treasury was exhausted in the year 428. But the inscription tends to show, though the fragmentary state of part of it makes any inference difficult, that the treasury held out at any rate until the middle of 426. And it should be observed that the 4,729 talents form the expenditure, not

---

[1] C. I. A. 283 seems to mention a loan from the treasures of the temple at Delos at 10 per cent. ἐπιδε[κάτοις τόκοις].

only of the first five years of the war, but also of the two years which preceded it.

A question which has been discussed by Boeckh, Staatshaush. i. pp. 221, 578 ff. (199, 519 ff., ed. Fränkel), naturally arises in connexion with this inscription: in what relation did the sacred treasure stand to the secular, or rather what made the distinction between them? The φόρος would naturally at first sight appear to be secular treasure; as the quota to the Goddess and the gold and silver plate contained in the inventories are sacred treasure. The first was under the control of the Hellenotamiae, the second under that of the ταμίαι τῆς Ἀθηναίας and the ταμίαι τῶν ἄλλων θεῶν. But, besides the quota and the articles of gold and silver plate, there were large sums of money kept in the temple which had a less strictly consecrated character. These may be described as held in trust by the corporation: that is to say, they were also under the care of the ταμίαι τῆς θεοῦ, but they might be lent with the consent of the ecclesia in the service of the state, whereas no such limitation was imposed, as far as we know, on the use of the φόρος or of other moneys as long as they remained in the hands of the Hellenotamiae (see p. lxxvii). The repayment of 3,000 talents (C. I. A. 32) seems to confirm this view. For so large a sum cannot be supposed to have been the private property of the temple. Again, for the still larger sums taken from the temple treasuries the state was in the habit, as we have seen, of professing to pay a small interest. But we have no record of interest claimed on any but sacred treasure.

The following extracts from inscriptions taken from Kirchhoff, p. 36 ff., indicate a difference between the functions of the Hellenotamiae and of the ταμίαι τῆς Ἀθηναίας, and therefore between secular and sacred funds.

C. I. A. 314, 315 (430 B.C.). The payments received by the ἐπιστάται or curators of the building of the Propylaea are divided at the end into three separate accounts: of the money received, (1) παρὰ τῶμ πρ[οτέρων ἐ]πιστατ[ῶν οἷς]

Ἐπικλῆς ἐγρα[μμάτευ]ε Θορίκ[ιος]: (2) παρὰ ταμιῶν ο[ἱ τὰ τῆ]ς θεοῦ ἐτα[μίευον] οἷς Κράτης ἐγρ[αμμά]τευε Λαμπ[τρεύς]: (3) [πα]ρὰ Ἑλληνοταμ[ιῶν] οἷς Πρωτογ[ένης ἐγραμ]μάτευε Κη[φισιε]ὺς τοῦ ξυμ[μαχικοῦ φόρ]ου μνᾶ ἀπὸ τοῦ [τα]λάντου. The last words seem to indicate that the quota of the Goddess was on one occasion devoted to the building of the Propylaea. Cp. a similar division in C. I. A. 309, 310, 312.

C. I. A. 140. If the conjectural restoration of the last lines is correct, the treasures of the *πρόναος* are handed over to the Hellenotamiae for the service of the state.

C. I. A. 180–183. The Hellenotamiae are repeatedly mentioned in this inscription as having money handed over or lent to them by the *ταμίαι τῆς Ἀθηναίας*, which they applied to various military purposes (see below); and C. I. A. 188, 189 (an inscription of the end of the Peloponnesian War) contains a record of money paid to the Hellenotamiae by the *ταμίαι ἱερῶν χρημάτων τῆς Ἀθηναίας* for public purposes, *ἵπποις σῖτος, ἐς τὴν διωβελίαν*. See also C. I. A. 273.

From the evidence of these inscriptions, from the greatness of the sums taken from or paid back to the Goddess and the other deities, from the practice of reckoning interest in certain cases, it seems to be clearly proved that there was a sacred fund which was likewise capable of being used in the public service. It is probable from the different classes of officers who had the care of the public treasure that there was also a secular fund in which the *φόρος*, i.e. the $\frac{59}{60}$th (at least that which came in during the year, see below), would be included, but this is not established with equal clearness. Pericles, when he speaks of the 6,000 talents (ii. 13 med.), makes no distinction. And the amount of the sums paid into and out of the sacred fund makes it improbable that there was any other fund as large or larger which was independent of it. Whether the quota to the Goddess was included in the public sacred fund, or remained the more private property of the temple, is uncertain.

[The best explanation of the inscriptions seems to be given by the following suppositions (see Beloch, Rhein. Mus. xxxix. p. 55; Gilbert, Greek Constitutional Antiquities, Eng. Transl., pp. 332–338; and cp. Headlam, Election by Lot at Athens, pp. 132, 133).—There was no 'secular fund' at all[1], unless we give this name to the ordinary current receipts of the year, consisting principally of the $\frac{59}{60}$ths of the tribute in the hands of the Hellenotamiae. The surplus, if any, remaining over at the end of the year must, after a certain time, have been paid into the sacred treasury, for there was no other source of income from which the immense sums mentioned as sacred in C. I. A. 32, 273, can have come. The difficulty is about the application of the yearly income to current expenses. It is reasonable to suppose that part of it could be applied by the Hellenotamiae themselves to the service of the state: Beloch points out that the sums expended yearly from the treasury of Athenè Polias in 426–423 B.C. (261, 130, 133, 222 talents, C. I. A. 273) are nothing like the amounts of the tribute which must have come in and been spent in these years. If these sums or part of them were deposited with the *ταμίαι τῆς θεοῦ* at all, they could probably be drawn out again by the Hellenotamiae on the strength of a simple vote of the people (cp. the payments *ἐκ τῶν ἐπετείων, ψηφισαμένου τοῦ δήμου*, by the *ταμίαι ἱερῶν χρημάτων* to the Hellenotamiae and others in 410–9: C. I. A. 188, 189; see p. lxxxiv). After a time, any surplus remaining from these funds must have been incorporated with the sacred treasure, and could only be expended on secular objects under special restrictions; the people had to pass a previous vote of indemnity (*ψηφισαμένου τοῦ δήμου τὴν ἄδειαν*, C. I. A. 32) after 434 or 418 B.C.; and, between 433 and 423 at least, the sum was regarded as a loan bearing a small interest.]

---

[1] The 20 *ταμίαι τῶν ὁσίων* (as distinct from *ἱερῶν*) *χρημάτων* of [Aristotle] Athen. Polit. 30 may be only a part of the projected constitution of the 400; there is no trace of them in the inscriptions.

The inscription C. I. A. 273, which records the loan of the sacred treasure, has also an historical interest derived from the mention of names and events which occur in Thucydides.

Under Ol. 88. 4, 425–424 B. C., appears the name of Demosthenes, and probably that of Nicias:—

στρατηγοῖς πε[ρὶ Πε]λοπόννησον Δημοσθένει Ἀλκισθένους Αφιδ[ναίῳ] 𐅄 𐅄 𐅄 (= 30 talents).

ἑτ[έ]ρα δόσις στρατηγοῖς [Νικίᾳ Νικηράτου Κυδα]ντίδῃ 𐅅 (= 100 talents).

The first payment is made on the third day of the fourth, the second on the fifteenth day of the ninth prytany. Probably the reference is to an employment of Demosthenes in establishing and paying a garrison, including the Messenian, in Pylos, in the autumn of 425, for the date is too late for the blockade, and to the expedition of Nicias against Cythera early in the summer of 424. (Thuc. iv. 27, 53.)

Regarded from the historical point of view, C. I. A. 273 may be placed with another class of inscriptions from which the results obtained are rather historical than financial. To these we will proceed:

The money expended from the sacred treasury appears to have been reckoned in two forms. In one of these forms it was regarded as a debt to the temple, having to pay interest, of which calculation is made. In the other form the account is simply a record of sums paid to the generals or other officers to be used in the public service [1].

In the second form of the account, as might be expected,

[1] [This is only certain for the years 433–423. In C. I. A. 180–183 the treasurers of the Goddess in one special case (183, l. 6; 415 B. C.) use the word ἐδανείσα[μεν], 'we lent': not, as usual, παρέδομεν or παρέδοσαν. It must be remembered that 433–423, and the last years of the Peace of Nicias, were the only period during which the Athenians are known to have had a large surplus and a large expenditure: before 433 they had a large surplus and comparatively small expenses: after the Sicilian expedition they had a crushing expenditure and no surplus.]

no interest appears; and mention of the *ταμίαι*, not of both *ταμίαι* and *λογισταί*, occurs.

The inscriptions of the second class which relate to the narrative of Thucydides, arranged in order of time, are as follows:—

(1) The words *πρὸς Σαμίου[ς]* and the number of talents expended, 128, 368, and 908, in all 1,404, are legible on a small fragment (C. I. A. 177), which may therefore be referred with probability to the revolt of Samos (Thuc. i. 116, 117). The words *Ἀθηναίας* and *ταμιῶ[ν]* show that the sums mentioned were expended from the treasury of Athenè.

(2) Another inscription (C. I. A. 179 and Suppl. i.), clearly referring to events mentioned by Thucydides, partly agrees and partly disagrees with his narrative of them. On a fragment of marble containing 22 lines more or less complete occur the following words:—

l. 7. [*παρέδοσαν*] *στρατηγοῖς ἐς Κορκύραν τοῖς*
[*πρώτοις ἐκ*]*πλέουσι Λακεδαιμονίῳ Λακιά-*
[*δῃ, Πρωτέᾳ*] *Αἰξωνεῖ, Διοτίμῳ Εὐωνυμεῖ.*

l. 13. [*ἐπὶ Ἀψεύδους*] *ἄρχοντος καὶ ἐπὶ τῆς βουλῆς*

l. 18. [*παρέ*]*δοσαν στρατηγοῖς ἐς Κορ-*
[*κύραν τοῖς δευτέρ*]*οις ἐκπλέουσι, Γλαύκωνι*
[*ἐκ Κεραμέων, Μεταγ*]*ένει Κοιλεῖ, Δρακοντί-*
[*δῃ Βατῆθεν, ἐπὶ τῆς*] *Αἰαντίδος πρυτανείας.*

Cp. Thuc. i. 45, 51, where the Athenians send two squadrons to the aid of Corcyra, the first commanded by Lacedaemonius the son of Cimon, Diotimus the son of Strombichus, and Proteas the son of Epicles, the second by Glaucon the son of Leagrus and Andocides the son of Leogoras. The name of the Archon is lost, but the words *ἐπὶ Ἀψεύδους* (he was Archon in 433–432) exactly fill up a vacant space. In the inscription we observe that Dracon or Dracontides takes the place of Andocides the son of Leogoras as the second commander of the second expedition. There can be no doubt that Thucydides and the inscription refer to the same event, and, this being so, the authority of the marble is to be preferred to that of the book, though there is no reason for suspecting the reading.

(3) In Thucydides, ii. 23, mention is made of Carcinus, Proteas, and Socrates, who were sent with a hundred ships to devastate the coast of the Peloponnesus in the first year of the war. The three names are found in a long but fragmentary inscription (C. I. A. iv. Suppl. i. 179 *a–d.* p. 32, and Suppl. iii. p. 159 ff.). On other fragments of the same tablet, giving the expenditure of the years 431–426, are traces of money sent to troops serving against Macedonia (according to Kirchhoff this part of the inscription clearly belongs to the archonship of Euthydemus, 431–430, and so cannot refer to the expeditions of Thuc. i. 57, 61), Potidaea, Sicily (Thuc. iii. 86, 90 ?), and to '[Demo]s[th]enes of Aphi[dnae],' Thuc. iii. 91.

(4) A long but very imperfect inscription (C. I. A. 180–183, corrected in vol. iv. Suppl. ii. p. 80) records the sums paid out of the Athenian treasury in the years 418–415 (Ol. 90. 3–91. 2). The dates are fixed by the occurrence of the names of financial officers found elsewhere, and by some coincidences with the narrative of Thucydides.

In the accounts of the first year, 418–417, we find the words—

> -ους (or -ος) τοῖς μετὰ Δημοσθένους,

and again—

> -ργοῦς (or -ργος) τοῖς μετὰ Δημ [οσθένους].

The letters -ργος can hardly be a trace of anything but 'Argos,' and the date (the second prytany) is about that of the battle of Mantinea. Here we have no coincidence with Thucydides, for he only mentions the employment of Demosthenes in the following winter (v. 80). It has been suggested that Demosthenes was the unnamed commander of the 1,000 men who joined the Argive and allied forces after the battle of Mantinea (Thuc. v. 75); but of this we cannot be certain.

A little further on we probably have a trace of Nicia's abortive expedition against Perdiccas (v. 83):

[σ]τρατηγοῖς Νικίᾳ Νικηράτ[ου Κυδαντ]ίδῃ.

In the accounts of the second year, 417–416, occur the words—

[Τεισί]ᾳ Τεισιμάχου Κεφαλῆθεν, Κλεομήδει Λυκο[μήδους,]

to whom it is recorded that ten talents were paid. Cp. Thuc. v. 84, where Cleomedes the son of Lycomedes and Tisias the son of Tisimachus command the expedition against Melos.

In the accounts of the third year, 416–415, more famous names occur—

[Νικίᾳ Νι]κηράτου Κυδαντίδῃ καὶ παρεδρο . .

and—

[στρ]ατηγοῖς ἐς Σικε[λίαν Ἀ]λκιβιάδῃ Λαμάχῳ . .

and again—

στρατηγοῖς ἐς Σικελ[ίαν Ἀ[λκιβιάδῃ Λαμάχῳ . .

and again—

ΔTTTT . . . . (= 14 talents).

In the accounts of the fourth year, 415–414, occur the words, ἐπὶ τῆς Ἀντιοχίδος ὀγδόης πρυτανευούσης τρίτ[ῃ ἡμέρᾳ τῆς πρυ]τανείας Ἑλληνοταμίαις καὶ παρέδροις Ἀριστοκρ[άτ]ει Εὐωνυμεῖ καὶ ξυνάρχουσι HHH (= 300 talents) οὗτοι δ' ἔδοσαν [τῇ ἐν Σικελίᾳ στ]ρατιᾷ (Kirchhoff writes H[HH], but according to Hicks the three ciphers are quite legible); and again, Ἑλληνοταμίαις (κ.τ.λ.) ἐς τὰ[ς] ναῦς τὰς ἐς Σι[κελίαν παρέδομεν] τὰ χρή[μ]ατα TTTTXX (4 talents 2,000 drachmae).

In the summary of the accounts at the end of the year the three hundred talents reappear, together with the lesser sums expended:—

κεφάλαιον ἀνα[λώματος τ]οῦ ἐπὶ τ[ῆς] ἀρχῆς HHH𐅄TTT . . . . (353 talents).

Cp. Thuc. vi. 94 fin., καὶ ἀφικόμενοι ἐς Κατάνην καταλαμβάνουσι τούς τε ἱππέας ἥκοντας ἐκ τῶν Ἀθηνῶν πεντήκοντα καὶ διακοσίους, ἄνευ τῶν ἵππων μετὰ σκευῆς, ὡς αὐτόθεν ἵππων πορισθησομένων, καὶ ἱπποτοξότας τριάκοντα, καὶ τάλαντα ἀργυρίου τριακόσια. The prytany in which the three hundred talents are given, the eighth, corresponds exactly to the time, shortly after the beginning of spring, when, according to Thucydides, money and other supplies reached Catana for the use of the Athenian army in Sicily.

(5) A long but fragmentary inscription (C. I. A. 184–185; Newton and Hicks, xxiv), out of which it is impossible to make continuous sense, is assigned to the date Ol. 92. 1–2; 412–411. The writing and the contents are such as we should expect to find about this time; and inscriptions of the same character are extant for Ol. 90. 3–91. 2 (just quoted) and for Ol. 92. 3 and 92. 4 or 93. 2. It therefore very probably belongs to the intermediate years.

Two interesting but uncertain conjectures, if they could be accepted, would confirm this date.

Boeckh proposes to restore l. 5 (A) thus—

> [ἐκ τῶν εἰς τὰς τρι]ήρεις ὧν παρελάβομ[εν παρὰ τῶν προτέρων ταμιῶν.]

> 'From the money for the triremes which we received from the last treasurers.'

He ingeniously argues that the inscription refers to the reserve fund of 1,000 talents, which was not to be touched until Athens was threatened by an attack from the enemy's fleet. But it is not said either in ii. 24 or in viii. 15 that the 1,000 talents were especially reserved for the building of triremes. Hence the words εἰς τὰς τριήρεις do not identify this occasion with that mentioned in viii. 15, and very probably refer to some other: money must constantly have been spent 'on the triremes.' There was another provision, that 100 triremes were to be set apart annually, and only used, like the money, when the enemy menaced the Piraeus with a fleet. This latter provision it must have been impossible to observe after the Syracusan expedition. Nothing is said about it in viii. 15. And it is quite distinct from the provision respecting the 1,000 talents. The conjectural restoration, as will be seen by the letters, is of the most doubtful kind.

Again, the words ἀπὸ πρυ ταvείας] in l. 11 (A) have been thought to show that the accounts of sums paid out at the end of Ol. 92. 1 are dated 'from a (previous) prytany,' not 'in a prytany,' ἀπὸ πρυτανείας, not ἐπὶ τῆς (say Οἰνηΐδος) πρυτανείας. And here a trace has been found of the government of the 400, B.C. 411; for after the expulsion of the senate of 500 there would be no regular prytanies. But the words are too imperfect to allow any inference to be drawn from them.

[A much more certain trace of the rule of the 400 is to be found in a few words inscribed on a vacant side of the stone containing C. I. A. 179 *a–d* (Suppl. iii. p. 162, corrected by Lolling with the help of a new fragment). The rest of the inscription belongs to 432–1—426 (p. lxxx, above). The words in question record a payment of 77–78 talents at the end of Hecatombaeon, in the archonship of some one whose name ended in -χος: and instead of the usual ψηφισαμένου τοῦ δήμου we have ψηφι]σαμένης τῆς βουλῆς. The only ordinary archon during the war whose name ended in -χος was Isarchos (424–423). But the character of the writing is later than this date, and the names of the financial officers enable us to date the words in 411–10. Now the regular archon of this year was Theopompus. But in Hecatombaeon the 400 were still in power: and [Aristotle] Athen. Polit. 33 tells us that Μνασιμάχος (so the MS., probably Μνησίλοχος), one of the 400, was archon for the first two months of the year and Theopompus for the rest. There is thus no doubt about the date of the words, which must have been inscribed on a monument already partly filled up. The βουλή means of course the 400 themselves.]

(6) C. I. A. 188, 189 is an inscription of which the first part is very complete, and contains the accounts of Ol. 92. 3,

410–409, the year following that in which the history of Thucydides concludes. It illustrates the exhaustion of the Athenian finances after the Sicilian expedition and the troubles of the year 411 (cp. viii. 76, *οἵ γε μήτε ἀργύριον ἔτι εἶχον πέμπειν, ἀλλ' αὐτοὶ ἐπορίζοντο οἱ στρατιῶται*). For the heading of the inscription referring to the payments of the whole year describes them as made *ἐκ τῶν ἐπετείων*, none of them are made *ἐξ ὧν παρελάβομεν παρὰ τῶν προτέρων ταμιῶν*. So that the money belonging to the sacred treasure must have been nearly or quite exhausted by the middle of 410.

The sum expended in the year, of which the record is nearly complete, amounts to about 180 talents. On this fact Kirchhoff bases his estimate of the annual income of the sacred treasure at 200 talents [1].

There are a few other inscriptions relating to finance which stand in a more accidental relation to the narrative of Thucydides; such as the fragments of the accounts drawn up by the overseers of the Propylaea while in process of erection (C. I. A. 314, 315; cp. Thuc. iii. 17), of the accounts of the officers who had charge of the sacred islands Delos and Rhenea, belonging to the Archonship of Crates and Apseudes, 434, 433 (C. I. A. 283; cp. iii. 104), and lastly the lists of confiscated property sold by the Poletae. Some fragments of these last (C. I. A. i. 274–277 and iv. Suppl. i, ii, iii.) contain names of persons who, according to Andoc. de Myst., were punished by confiscation of their goods for the mutilation of the Hermae or the profanation of the mysteries [2].

---

[1] [But the inference is unwarranted, for only 8-9 talents are actually said in the inscription to have come from the treasury of Athene: the rest comes from other unnamed sources, and is only paid out by the 'treasurers of Athene' in the usual way as part of the public treasure (p. lxxvii). See Beloch, Rhein. Mus. xxxix. p. 59.]

[2] [One of these fragments (C. I. A. Suppl. iii. p. 178) mentions a *χαμεύνα παράκολλος* (a pallet-bed with a head-piece) worth 17 drachmae, and a *κλίν[η Μιλη]σιουργὴς [ἀ]μφ[ικν]έφα[λλος]*, a bed or sofa with cushions at both ends: along with boxes, tables, chairs, vases, &c. As

II. Decrees of the senate and people not already mentioned, and not relating to finance, but to the allies, relations with other states, &c., which illustrate the history of Thucydides, are the following:—

C. I. A. 9 is an inscription no longer existing and incorrectly copied, but of great importance[1]. It contains a decree (1) requiring the Erythraeans to contribute to the Panathenaic festival something, probably victims, worth 3 minae, under a penalty: (2) creating a *βουλή* of the democratic type consisting of 120 members, who are to be at least 30 years of age. Their oath of office and the penalties which attach to the non-enforcement of it by the existing *βουλή* are inserted in the decree. Mention occurs in the oath of [*οἱ ἐς*] *Μήδους φυγό*[*ντες*]. In another part of the decree penalties are imposed upon persons guilty of homicide, impiety, or treason.

The two fragments which follow (C. I. A. 10, 11) also relate to Erythrae, the former making mention of lawsuits, the latter of an oath to be taken by the Erythraeans. All these three relate to the times between the Persian and the Peloponnesian wars. The form of the letters is said to show that 10 belongs to a time before 450. Both 9 and 10 mention *ἐπίσκοποι*: cp. Aristoph. Birds, 1021 ff.

C. I. A. 13. Cp. 36. Both these relate to Colophon. The first is part of a decree regulating the affairs of the Colophonians, to which is attached a form of oath to be taken by them. The second is a decree conferring protection and other favours and honours on Aretus the Colophonian, for services rendered to the Athenian people and their army ([*κ*]*αὶ τοὺς στρατιώτας*), probably at the time

---

Pollux, Onomasticon, 10, 36, says, *ἐν δὲ τοῖς δημιοπράτοις πέπραται Ἀλκιβιάδου χαμεύνη παράκολλος καὶ κλίνη ἀμφικέφαλος* (for which *ἀμφικνέφαλλος* had been suggested *e conj.* before the discovery of the inscription), we probably have here a list of the confiscated furniture of Alcibiades.]

[1] For this and the following inscriptions relating to Erythrae, Colophon, Chalcis, Hestiaea, and Miletus, see Abbott, History of Greece, vol. ii., ix. 21, x. 9–11.

when Paches took Notium and restored it to the Colophonians; Thuc. iii. 34.

C. I. A. Suppl. i. 27 *a* contains two decrees of the senate and people. The first, proposed by Diognetus, prescribes the terms of an oath to be taken by the Athenian senate and dicasts to the Chalcidians, and by all the Chalcidians of full age to Athens. The Athenians promise not to expel the Chalcidians from their country, and not to disfranchise, banish, arrest, kill, or fine, any individual Chalcidian untried (ἀκ[ρ]ίτου) without the consent of the Athenian people. Compare Thuc. viii. 48 fin., on the prospects of the allies under an oligarchy, καὶ ἄκριτοι ἂν καὶ βιαιότερον ἀποθνήσκειν. They on their part promise to be faithful allies, and to pay a tribute of an amount such as the Athenians may agree to impose (ὃν ἂν πείθω Ἀθηναίους).

According to the second decree, moved by Anticles, five commissioners are sent to receive the oath. The Chalcidians are to be told that the hostages are to remain as they are for the present. Some words which follow are partly intended to guard the interests of residents in Chalcis who have received the privilege of ἀτέλεια from Athens, but are otherwise unintelligible, though quite complete. The decree is to be inscribed on a column at Athens at the expense of the Chalcidians, and in the temple of Zeus at Chalcis. Three members of the senate are to offer sacrifices on behalf of Euboea in consequence of certain oracles. An addition to the second decree, moved by Archestratus, provides that crimes involving a penalty of banishment, death, or disfranchisement, are to be sent for trial to Athens; and that the generals are to take care of Athenian interests in Euboea.

The decrees, of which the tone is conciliatory, though in fact they reduce Chalcis to a state of dependence, appear to belong to a time shortly after the reduction of Euboea by Pericles in 445, Thuc. i. 114. Anticles is the name of one of the Athenian commanders at Samos (i. 117): Archestratus, of one of the commanders at Potidaea (i. 57).

This is one of the most perfect of early Greek inscriptions, and has more the character of a regular prose composition, or of a page out of history, than any other.

Suppl. 22 *a* is a long but fragmentary inscription, probably earlier than 447, relating to the constitution of Miletus.

28 and 29 are decrees respecting the relations of Athens to the Athenian cleruchs of Hestiaea (or Oreus) in Euboea, who were settled there after the revolt, Ol. 83. 4, B. C. 445 (cp. Thucyd. i. 114 fin., vii. 57 init.). The inscription is inferred, from the writing as well as from the contents, to be older than the Peloponnesian War. It contains provisions (1) for regulating the traffic and the payment of tolls on the route between Hestiaea and Athens by way of Oropus; (2) respecting the trial of suits, either at Athens or by inhabitants of Hestiaea.

[C. I. A. Suppl. ii. 22 *k*, iii. 20 (p. 139, 140)[1], in which different parts of the archon's name Ἀρ[ιστ]ων occur, can be dated 454 B.C., and shows that the Athenians concluded in that year a treaty of some kind with the Egestaeans of Sicily:—an ἀρχὴ πολλῶν κακῶν. Diodorus, xi. 86, speaks of a war in this year between Egesta and the 'Lilybaei.' Lilybaeum was not founded until long afterwards. It has been proposed, on the strength of the letters -κυαίοις in C. I. A. ii. 22 *k*, to read [Ἁλι]κυάιοις in the inscription and (for Λιλυβαίοις) in Diodorus; Halycae being a Sicel town.

Thucydides does not mention this treaty, but it throws light upon the application of the Egestaeans to the Athenians in vi. 6, and strengthens the probability that a similar 'old treaty' existed between Athens and Leontini (see below).]

33 (cp. Suppl. i.) records a treaty with Rhegium made in Ol. 86. 4, B. C. 433. Nothing is said in Thucydides of the original making of the treaty. But compare the next:

---

[1] Wrongly copied and restored in C. I. A. i. 20: the corrections are due to Lolling.

Suppl. 33 *a* is the subscription of a treaty with Leontini also made in 433 B.C., the archonship of Apseudes, two years before the war, and apparently on the same day. Six years afterwards the Leontines and their allies, including the Rhegines, who were then engaged in a war with the Syracusans, applied for a new alliance with Athens, κατὰ παλαιὰν ξυμμαχίαν (Thuc. iii. 86 med.), being possibly that which is recorded in the inscription, but more probably a much older one.

[An inscription published by Köhler in Hermes xxvi. p. 43, cp. Arnold Behr in Hermes xxx. p. 447, seems to mention a dedication of a statue to Athene Nike, for a victory over the Ambraciots, very likely that of Thuc. iii. 107. The words as restored are

ἐπισκευὴν τοῦ ἀγ[άλ]μα
[τος τῆς Ἀθηνᾶ]ς τῆς Νίκης ἣν ἀνέ[θ]εσαν
[Ἀθηναῖοι ἀπὸ] Ἀμβρακιωτῶν καὶ τῆς ἐν
[Ὄλπαις (?) στρατ]ιᾶς.

The word Κορκυραίων also occurs, but in what connexion it is impossible to say with certainty.]

40 contains three decrees relating to the Methonaeans and Perdiccas. According to the provisions of the first decree, the Methonaeans are only to pay the quota of $\frac{1}{60}$th to the Goddess; and, if they are useful to the Athenians 'as they are now, and still better,' they are not to be subject to any general but only to a special regulation respecting arrears of tribute. To Perdiccas three ambassadors 'over fifty years of age' are sent: he is to be told that he must allow the Methonaeans the free use of the sea, and not pass through their country without permission being first obtained from them. If he and the Methonaeans consent, the ambassadors are to arrange matters between them, but if not, their differences are to be brought to Athens: if the troops at Cape Posidium report favourably on Perdiccas (ἐὰν . . . ἐπαινῶσι) the Athenians will have a good opinion of him, γνώμας ἀγαθὰς περὶ αὐτοῦ ἕξουσιν.

By tne second decree the Methonaeans receive permission to export corn up to a certain amount from Byzantium, and are not to be hindered in doing so by some officers called Wardens of the Hellespont. As in the former decree, they are only subject to special regulations about aid to be given to the Athenian state or any other service required of the allies. The differences with Perdiccas still continue. The third decree is a mere fragment.

42 is an alliance made with Perdiccas, but the fragments of the inscription have no connected meaning. The treaty refers to Arrhibaeus (Thuc. iv. 79, 83, 124), and among the names appended to it are those of Alcetas (Plato, Gorg. 471) and Philip (Thuc. i. 57), the brothers of Perdiccas, and of Archelaus the son of Perdiccas.

Suppl. iii. 42 (p. 141), apparently belonging to the last-mentioned, gives the terms of an oath to be taken by Perdiccas, and a promise not to permit the exportation of wood for oars (κωπεῖς) from Macedonia except for Athenian use.

Thucydides only mentions an agreement (ὁμολογία) made between Perdiccas and the Athenian generals in Thrace (iv. 132, 423 B.C.): but v. 6, 83, take for granted the existence of an alliance (ξυμμαχία).

In 43, to which no meaning can be given, the names of Perdiccas and perhaps Arrhibaeus also occur.

45. In the archonship of Aristion, B.C. 421, one Asteas of Alea (in Arcadia) is inscribed as proxenus and benefactor of Athens. Cp. 27 and Suppl. i, where three citizens of Thespiae are similarly described; Thuc. iv. 133, Θηβαῖοι Θεσπιέων τεῖχος περιεῖλον, ἐπικαλέσαντες Ἀττικισμόν.

46 *b* (Suppl. i). This is a fragment of a marble tablet containing the ends of twenty-six lines of the treaty between Athens, Argos, Elis and Mantinea, recorded also in Thuc. v. 47. Kirchhoff ('Hermes' xii. p. 368 ff.) notes thirty-one variations between the text of Bekker and the inscription. But of these only six occur in the inscription itself; the rest are but variations from Kirchhoff's con-

jectural restoration of the missing portions. It should be observed however that the inscription appears to have been written *στοιχηδόν*, i. e. in equal lines, so that each letter fills up the same space; hence it can in some places be restored with tolerable certainty.

The six variations between the existing part of the inscription and the text of Thucydides are as follows. In p. 346, l. 16 (Bekker) the inscription inserts *πρὸς ἀλλήλους* after Ἠλεῖοι. In ll. 25, 27, the inscription has [Μα]*ντινέας καὶ* Ἠλ[*είους*] and *Μαντινέας καὶ* for *καὶ Μαντινέας*, showing that the names of these two contracting powers were transposed; and similarly in p. 346, l. 36, and 347, l. 1, *τὴν Ἀργείων ἤ* for *ἢ τὴν Ἀργείων*. In p. 347, l. 20, it has -*νη τῇ σ*-, showing that some other word than *τὴν ἡγεμονίαν* followed *μεταπεμψαμένη* (*τῇ στρατιᾷ χρήσθω ἡγεμονεύουσα*, K.), and in l. 21 -*ις ταῖς* [*πόλεσι*], showing that some other word than *δόξῃ* (*ἁπάσαις*, K.) preceded *ταῖς*. These differences are very slight. On the other hand, it may be remarked that they occur in a fragment which amounts only to about a twelfth of the whole treaty.

Assuming for the moment the correctness of Kirchhoff's conjectures, we may compare the text of Thucydides with the whole treaty as restored by him. Of thirty-one variations (see Classen, Intr. to Thuc. Bk. viii. p. xxv ff.) thirteen are merely orthographical (*ἐάν* for *ἤν*, or *θάλατταν* for *θάλασσαν*). In three cases the order of the names 'Eleans, Mantineans, Argives,' is different[1]. In four cases the inscription inserts or repeats, probably for the sake of clearness, words which do not occur in our text. On the other hand, our text inserts *ταῖς πόλεσιν* after *δοκῇ* in p. 347, l. 7. In eight cases the variations occur in places where the restoration has little or no ground on which to rest. If we set these aside, the variations reduce themselves to two more or less probable conjectures, *ἐπὶ τὴν γῆν* for *ἐς τὴν γῆν* (p. 346, l. 36), and *ὧν ἄρχουσι* for *ὧν ἂν ἄρχωσι* (p. 347, l. 9).

---

[1] It varies in different parts of our present text.

The importance of these variations is reduced by the fact that *ὧν ἄρχουσιν* and *ἐπὶ τὴν γῆν* are apparently used as equivalents for *ὧν ἂν ἄρχωσιν* and *ἐς τὴν γῆν* in other parts of the treaty.

In three lines out of the twenty-six there is room in the missing portion of the tablet for many more letters than those found in the text of Thucydides. Here there were probably blank spaces between different articles of the treaty.

So far from the inscription tending to overthrow the text of Thucydides and (from this point of view Schöne, 'Hermes' xii. p. 476, thinks that 'its importance cannot be estimated highly enough'), no conclusion can be drawn either way from such a mere fragment. The verbal differences are very slight, and most of them may have come from Thucydides himself[1]. Nor do slight inaccuracies in the copying of a treaty afford any real ground of argument as to the text of other parts of the history.

49. The words occur Ὑπέρβολος εἶπε. If this be the demagogue Hyperbolus, ostracized about 419 B.C., the inscription would be of an earlier date.

50 is a treaty between the Athenians and Argives, not that given in v. 47, and therefore probably that referred to in v. 82 fin.

51 has important additions in Suppl. i. For a full discussion of it see supra, p. xxiii.

52, 53, and Suppl. iii. p. 142, relate to a treaty and alliance between the Athenians and Bottiaeans. Spartolus, which as we learn from Thucydides (ii. 79) was a city of the Bottiaeans, was to have been given up by the Lacedaemonians to Athens, when peace was made in 421, on condition that the place should be independent, but might be received, if willing, into the Athenian alliance (v. 18 med.). [This appears from the inscription to have been

---

[1] [Or from his informant, or from a copy of the treaty as put up at Argos, Elis, or Mantinea.]

done, though Thucydides does not mention the fact. The Bottiaeans with the Chalcidian cities had joined in the revolt of Potidaea, which was one of the original causes of the war, and Spartolus had been the scene of a grievous disaster to an Athenian army in 430 (Thuc. i. 58, ii. 79). These facts strikingly illustrate the words of the oath taken by the two parties according to the inscription, οὐ μνησικακήσω τῶν παροιχομένων ἕνεκα.]

54 is a decree about an expedition of 30 ships of war. For the question whether this is the Melian expedition (Thuc. v. 84), see supra, p. xxii.

55 also relates to an expedition, consisting of 60 ships; it is indicated by the datives in αις to be not older than Ol. 90. It has been thought to refer to the first decree for the Sicilian expedition; but see supra, pp. xxi, xxii.

56 contains a tribute of honour decreed to the Samians because they had emancipated (?) themselves, ὅτι σφᾶς αὐτοὺς [ἠλευθέρωσαν], evidently referring to the events of 412 recorded in Thucydides, viii. 21. Mention is made in the decree of deaths, exiles, and confiscations inflicted by the Samian people, and of certain offenders whom they are to send to Athens.

57 contains a decree limiting the power of the senate, probably after the overthrow of the 400. Mention occurs of 500 men, and, shortly afterwards, of 500 drachmae.

59 contains a decree in honour of Thrasybulus, Agoratus, and others, and mentioning Apoll[odorus]. It was passed in the archonship of Glaucippus (410–409), soon after the assassination of Phrynichus (Thuc. viii. 92 init.): and that the inscription has to do with the claim of Thrasybulus of *Calydon* and Apollodorus of *Megara* to be the slayers of Phrynichus appears from Lysias c. Agoratum (xiii) 76–78 (71–73), though it may not be the inscription to which he refers. Thucydides names neither the actual assassin nor his accomplice whom he calls an *Argive*. The inscription does not square with the narrative of Lysias, and cannot be said to weigh against the evidence of

Thucydides, who may have disbelieved the assertions of Thrasybulus and Apollodorus.

[An inscription recently discovered records a resolution of the senate and people, passed on the motion of Alcibiades, confirming the agreement made by the generals with 'those who settled in Daphnus,' ἐπειδὴ ἄνδρες ἐγένοντο ἀγ[αθοι]. Thuc. viii. 23, 31, refers to the settlement at Daphnus of the anti-Athenian party in Clazomenae (which city had revolted from Athens, ch. 14, and returned to its allegiance) and the refusal of the Clazomenians to retire to Daphnus at the bidding of Astyochus. The interference of the Athenian generals appears to have altered the position in Daphnus at some time between 412 and the return of Alcibiades in 407. (See, for the inscription itself, the *Athenæum*, March 5, 1898.)]

71 (Suppl. i). A defensive alliance made between the Athenians and the Halieans, indicated by the form of the letters to be not earlier than B.C. 420, and by the subject to be not later than the renewal of the war. This treaty with Halieis is not mentioned by Thucydides. But in iv. 45 we are told that the Athenians occupied a position near Methone (Methana), and ravaged the territory of Troezen, Halieis, and Epidaurus. According to iv. 118 med. an agreement was subsequently made with Troezen. And this treaty with Halieis, as well as the treaty with Epidaurus mentioned in v. 80 (unless it be the general peace of 421), may be connected with the same occurrence.

A long and almost complete inscription, C. I. A. iv. Suppl. ii, 27, *b*, lately discovered at Eleusis illustrates the sacred character of the 'Pelasgian ground' mentioned by Thucydides, ii. 17. The senate and people give directions for offering an ἀπαρχή of wheat and barley to the two goddesses of Eleusis, κατὰ τὰ πάτρια καὶ τὴν μαντείαν τὴν ἐγ Δελφῶν. The allies of Athens are required, and all the cities of Hellas are 'invited but not required' (ἐκεί[νοις] δὲ μὴ ἐπιτάττοντας κελεύοντας δὲ ἀπάρχεσθαι ἐὰν βούλωνται), to join in the offering. There is appended an amendment or additional proposal moved by Lampon, perhaps the celebrated soothsayer, part of which is as follows: *τὸν δὲ βασ[ι]λέα ὁρίσαι τὰ ἱερὰ τὰ ἐν τ[ῶ]ι Πελαργικῷ καὶ τὸ λοιπὸν μὴ ἐνίδρύεσθαι βωμοὺς ἐν τῷ Πελαργικῷ ἄνευ τῆς βουλῆς καὶ τοῦ δήμου, μηδὲ τοὺς λίθους τέμνειν ἐκ τοῦ Πελαργικοῦ, μηδὲ γῆν ἐχσάγειν μηδὲ λίθους.* The inscription was edited by M. Foucart in the Bulletin de Correspondance Hellénique, iv. p. 225. The use of Σ, not ϟ, fixes the date with probability after 454, the datives in *-ησι* before or not long after 420. As the character of the early part of the inscription seems to assign it to a time of peace, it may belong to the Peace of Nicias, or much more probably, considering the doubtful nature of that peace, to the years preceding the Peloponnesian War.

The words immediately preceding the regulation about the Pelasgicum are remarkable: *ταῦτα μὲν πε[ρ]ὶ τῆς ἀπαρχῆς τοῦ καρ[π]οῦ [τ]οῖν θεοῖν ἀναγράψαι ἐς τὼ στήλ[α]· μῆνα δὲ ἐμβάλλειν Ἑκατονβαιῶνα τὸν νέον ἄρχοντα.* It has been hitherto supposed that in the fifth century B.C., as in later times, the month intercalated was Poseideon (Dec.-Jan.). The inscription would seem to show either that any month might be intercalated, or that it was sometimes necessary to intercalate an additional month. It also raises a doubt whether the Athenians about the time of the Peloponnesian War employed a fixed cycle of years, that of Meton or any other, and did not rather intercalate a month when necessary (Droysen, in 'Hermes' for 1880, x. p. 364). The inscription affords a fresh illustration of the uncertainty of Greek chronology.

[The *a priori* difficulties urged by Adolf Schmidt (Neue Jahrbücher, 1885, i. p. 681 ff.) against this interpretation, though considerable, are not decisive. He would translate 'the new archon is to interpose the month Hecatombaeon'; i.e. grant an extension of time, consisting of that month, for the delivery of the *ἀπαρχή*. (The inscription seems to date from a time shortly before the beginning of harvest.) But it is very doubtful whether *ἐμβάλλειν μῆνα Ἑκατομβαίωνα* in this sense can be justified by expressions like *ἐμβάλλειν χρόνον*. *ἐμβάλλειν* in the sense 'intercalate' is fully justified by the word *ἐμβόλιμος*, intercalary; though, as Schmidt points out, it cannot be shown to have been the regular technical term (which was *ἐπεμβάλλειν*, *ἐπάγειν*; Hdt. ii. 4, and commonly in later writers).]

M. Foucart interprets the words as relating to the intercalation of a day or a few days in the month Hecatombaeon. But surely, as Droysen says, they must refer to the whole month.

III. Dedicatory inscriptions.

Thuc. i. 132 mentions a tripod dedicated at Delphi after the victory over the Persians, and the erasure of Pausanias' inscription; cp. Hdt. ix. 81, *δεκάτην ἐξελόντες τῷ ἐν Δελφοῖσι θεῷ, ἀπ' ἧς ὁ τρίπους ὁ χρύσεος ἀνετέθη, ὁ ἐπὶ τοῦ τρικαρήνου ὄφιος τοῦ χαλκέου ἐπεστεὼς ἄγχιστα τοῦ βωμοῦ*. A bronze column 18 feet high, believed to be identical with that which supported the tripod, still stands in the Hippodrome at Constantinople: it is in the form of three serpents twisted together. Upon it is inscribed a list of Greek states similar to that recorded by Pausanias (v. 23. 1) to have been inscribed upon the pedestal of a votive statue of Zeus at Olympia, after the victory at Plataea.

It should be observed that Thucydides speaks of the inscription as being on the tripod, while Herodotus distinguishes the tripod from the serpents on which it stood. Nevertheless the evidence (for which see Gibbon, Decline and Fall, c. xvii) seems satisfactorily to establish the identity of the monument now at Constantinople with that mentioned by Herodotus and Thucydides.

See Röhl, I. G. A., 70; Hicks, Manual of Greek Inscriptions, 11; Abbott, History of Greece, vol. ii. v. 16; Roberts, Greek Epigraphy, § 100.

Thucydides in vi. 54 quotes the inscription of Pisistratus son of Hippias on an altar in the temple of the Pythian Apollo—

Μνῆμα τόδ' ἧς ἀρχῆς Πεισίστρατου Ἱππίου υἱὸς
Θῆκεν Ἀπόλλωνος Πυθίου ἐν τεμένει.

He remarks that, though the letters were faint, it was still to be read—ἔτι καὶ νῦν δῆλά ἐστιν ἀμυδροῖς γράμμασι. '*It is equally legible to this day*, the marble on which it was inscribed having been accidentally discovered in a court-yard near the Ilissus, by M. Kumanudes, in 1877.' Newton, Essays on Art and Archaeology, p. 191. See also C. I. A. vol. iv. Suppl. i. 373 c.

The marble slab is broken into two pieces, the half-word and word -ΤΡΑΤΟΣ ΗΙΠΠΙΟ being lost by the fracture. Beneath the inscription is a leaf moulding. Thucydides tells us that in his time the letters were already 'indistinct,' ἀμυδρά. Yet there is no indistinctness in their present state, and they bear an old Athenian character, suiting the date. We may conjecture, either that they were plastered over after the fall of the Pisistratidae, and that the plaster gradually wore off: or that, at an early date, but after the age of Thucydides, they were restored without losing their antique form. [Roberts, Greek Epigraphy, § 56, suggests that the letters may originally have been coloured, and that the colour had faded by Thucydides' time.]

A curious coincidence with the words of Thucydides is presented by C. I. A. 340. A pedestal of Pentelic marble preserves the words—

ΕΠΟΙΚΟΝ | ΕΣΠΟΤΕΙΔΑΙΑΝ

Cp. Thuc. ii. 70, καὶ ὕστερον ἐποίκους ἑαυτῶν ἔπεμψαν ἐς τὴν Ποτίδαιαν καὶ κατῴκισαν.

An inscription found at Dodona (date uncertain) shows that the savage Corcyraeans were not insensible to the need of unity among themselves: they ask 'to whom of Gods or heroes they should sacrifice and pray' in order to attain it,—

Θεὸν Τ[ύ]χαν ἀγαθὰν ἐπ[ι]κοινώντᾳ τοὶ Κ[ο]ρκυρα[ῖοι τῷ Δι τῷ Νάῳ καὶ τᾷ Δ[ι]ώνᾳ τίνι κα [θεῶν ἢ] ἡρώων θύον[τ]ες καὶ εὐχ[όμενοι] ὁμονοοῖεν ἐ[π]ὶ τὠγαθόν.

(ἐπικοινώντᾳ = ἐπικοινοῦνται, 'communicate with,' or 'make inquiry of'; νάῳ = ναΐῳ)—M. Carapanos, 'Dodone,' i. p. 72; 'Hellenica,' p. 443.

IV. Sepulchral inscriptions.

The famous monument to the fallen of the tribe Erechtheis, mentioned on pp. xviii, xxvi, and referring probably to Ol. 80. 2, 459–8 B. C., certainly to the events mentioned in Thuc. i. 104, 105, runs as follows (C. I. A. 433)—

Ἐρεχθηΐδος. οἵδε ἐν τῷ πολέμῳ ἀπέθανον ἐν Κύπρῳ ἐν Αἰγ[ύπ]τῳ ἐν Φοινίκῃ ἐν Ἁλιεῦσιν ἐν Αἰγίνῃ Μεγαρο[ῖ] τοῦ αὐτοῦ ἐνιαυτοῦ—then follow 168 names.

C. I. A. 442 gives us a poem in honour of the 150 men who fell at Potidaea, Thuc. i. 63. The first two lines are given as conjecturally restored in Newton and Hicks; the rest from C. I. A.

ἀθάνατόν με θα[νοῦσι χάριν θέσαν· οἱ γὰρ ἐν ὅπλοις ?]
  σημαίνειν ἀρετ[ὴν ἵεμενοι σφετέραν ?]
καὶ προγόνω[ν] σθένος [ἐσθλὸν ἐνὶ στήθεσσιν ἔχοντες]
  νίκην εὐπόλεμον μνῆμ' ἔλαβον [σ]φ[έτερον]
αἰθὴρ μὲν ψυχὰς ὑπεδέξατο, σώ[ματα δὲ χθὼν]
  τῶνδε. Ποτειδαίας δ' ἀμφὶ πύλας ἐδ[αμεν].
ἐχθρων δ' οἱ μὲν ἔχουσι τάφου μέρος, ο[ἱ δὲ φυγόντες]
  τεῖχος πιστοτάτην ἐλπίδ' (sic) ἔθεντο [βίου]
ἄνδρας μὲν πόλις ἥδε ποθεῖ καὶ δῆ[μος Ἐρεχθέως]
  πρόσθε Ποτειδαίας οἳ θάνον ἐν πρ[ομάχοις]
παῖδες Ἀθηναίων, ψυχὰς δ' ἀντίρρο[πα θέντες]
  ἠ[λλ]άξαντ' ἀρετὴν καὶ πατ[ρίδ'] εὐκλ[έισαν].

Kirchhoff observes that the composition forms three small poems of four lines each.

Many fragments are extant containing lists of names, often arranged under tribes, which seem to belong to monuments of those who fell in battle. One of these is mentioned on p. xvii. Two others commemorate campaigns recorded in Thucydides, though there are difficulties in fixing them to any precise occasion.

[C. I. A. 432 contains over 100 names under the headings ἐν Θάσ[ῳ], ἐπὶ Σιδείῳ (no such place is known, ? Σιγείῳ), and other names of places which are lost. Some of the fallen, probably Athenian allies, are arranged under the name of their city, [Μαδ]ύτιοι, [Αἰγά]ντιοι, or [Βυζά]ντιοι. The heading ἐν Θάσῳ justifies us in referring part of the monument to the revolt of Thasos, Thuc. i. 100, 101: it will be seen that the restorations of the other headings are uncertain. It has been thought that other parts of the inscription may refer to the great disaster at Drabescus or Datum (Thuc. i. 100, Hdt. ix. 75), but neither of these names actually occurs. Köhler ('Hermes' xxiv, 1889) refers part of the monument to an expedition of Cimon against the Chersonese and the Persian garrison remaining there, mentioned only by Plutarch, Cimon xiv, between his account of the battle of the Eurymedon and the revolt of Naxos. But the authority of Plutarch as a historian is not strong enough, or the restoration of the inscription certain enough, to justify a positive conclusion.]

C. I. A. 446 contains the names of those who fell (*a*) in a battle or probably two battles which are unknown to us, (*b*) at Potidaea (three names only), (*c*) at Amphipolis, (*d*) ἐπὶ Θρᾴκης, (*e*) at Pylos, (*f*) at Sermylia (one name at each), (*g*) at Singus (one name extant). Kirchhoff (C. I. A. vol. i. p. 200) assigns the inscription to 425–424, the capture of Sphacteria and the battle of Solygea (Thuc. iv. 42 ff.), chiefly on the ground that the number of Athenians who fell in each tribe from which the loss is recorded (6 to 15 in one column, fewer still in another) represents far too small a loss for Delium or Amphipolis, but suits well with Pylos, where 'few of the Athenians fell' (Thuc. iv. 38), and Solygea. Mr. Hicks (Newton and Hicks, Greek Inscriptions in the British Museum, Part I, p. 106), following Boeckh (C. I. G. vol. i. No. 171), refers the inscription to 423, and to the expedition against Mende and Scione recorded in Thuc. iv. 129. It may be conjectured that an Athenian soldier fell in defending the bridge at Amphipolis

(iv. 103 fin.), and that some trifling engagement, which is not mentioned by Thucydides, took place at Potidaea (ch. iv. 135), Sermylia (or Sermylè), and Singus. But such hypotheses can never be brought to the test; it is therefore better to refrain from them.

The names of certain ἔγγρ[αφοι], τοξόται, and ξένοι are recorded in the inscription. Boeckh compares iv. 129 init. (ὁπλίταις δὲ χιλίοις ἑαυτῶν καὶ τοξόταις ἑξακοσίοις καὶ Θρᾳξὶ μισθωτοῖς χιλίοις καὶ ἄλλοις τῶν αὐτόθεν ξυμμάχων πελτασταῖς), and supposes the ἔγγρ[αφοι] to have been metics enrolled among the citizen hoplites (ὁπλῖται ἑαυτῶν). But, again, such combinations are hazardous, for an Athenian army would probably be composed of the same elements on many different occasions. We know of no one time at which soldiers were falling at Potidaea, at Amphipolis, and at Pylos. We are only sure that the inscription cannot be earlier than the capture of Pylos, or later than the first year of the peace, 421.

For the beautiful epitaph of Simonides on Archedicè, the daughter of Hippias, see text, vi. 59.

C. I. A. 475, [λ]οιμῷ θανούσης εἰμι σῆμα Μυρίνης, might be attributed to the time of the great plague, were not the writing (⊕ϟ) too archaic.

C. I. A. 479, 483, are fragments of sepulchral monuments found among what are supposed to be the remains of the Themistoclean walls:—

479. Σῆμα φι[λ]ου παιδὸς τόδε . . . . κατ]έθηκεν,
Στησίου, ὃν θάνατος [δακρυ]όεις καθέχει.

The inscription is broken into two pieces, and is not written metrically.

483. Ἀντιδότου. | Καλλωνίδης ἐποίει | ὁ Δεινίου.

Also iv. i. 477 *b*. Σῆμα πατὴρ Κλείβουλος ἀποφθιμένῳ Ξενοφάντῳ
θῆκε τόδ' ἀντ' ἀρετῆς ἠδὲ σαοφροσύνης.

And iv. i. 477 *h*. Ἄνθρωπε, ὅ[ς] στείχε[ι]ς καθ' ὁδὸν φρεσὶν ἄλλα μενοινῶν,
στῆθι καὶ οἴκτειρον σῆμα Θράσωνος ἰδών.

Compare Thucydides' description of the structure of the wall (i. 93 init.): 'To this day the structure shows evidence of haste. The foundations are made up of all sorts of stones, in some places unwrought, and laid just as each worker brought them; *there were many columns too, taken from sepulchres*, and many old stones already cut, inserted in the work.'

Such appears to be the amount of light thrown upon Thucydides by Greek inscriptions. The comparison of them would have been more interesting had we been able freely to accept the conjectures of archaeologists. There is always a temptation to convert the uncertain and indefinite into the definite and certain. The greater the ingenuity the greater the fascination, though often the greater the improbability. But we must remember that there are myths or romances of modern criticism as well as of early history, and in the latter half of the nineteenth century we have not so much to fear from the last as from the first. *Ἴσως τὸ μὴ μυθῶδες αὐτῶν ἀτερπέστερον φανεῖται*, but *ὠφέλιμα κρίνειν αὐτὰ ἀρκούντως ἕξει.* A few grains of fact secured to the world once for all are of more value than many brilliant theories which appear and disappear, like intellectual meteors, in successive generations.

The evil tendency of the study is that it encourages the habit of conjecture, which has already been one of the great corruptions of philology. There is a necessity for making too much out of a few letters or words, and thus appearing to obtain a result commensurate with the labour spent upon them. The slenderness of his materials leads the enquirer to snatch at chance coincidences. His honest enthusiasm will sometimes make him forget that the words or letters upon which his conclusion is based are due to conjecture. He is too apt to apply an inscription to the interpretation of a difficulty in an ancient author. Where the balance of probability is just in favour of a conclusion, it is assumed by him to be a certainty;

and the new fact which is supposed to be proved is set rolling, and draws after it other inferences still more uncertain. A possible deduction from the inscriptions, such as the doubling of the Athenian tribute in the year 425, or the transfer of the common treasury from Delos to Athens in 454 (resting only on the circumstance that in this year the quota lists begin), is repeated at second or third hand as a great historical discovery. In the absence of contemporary, we are satisfied with later, evidence; and the older history of Athens is interpreted by inscriptions of the second or third century, and inscriptions of the second or third century are explained by the older history of Athens. Where singular forms of grammar occur only once or twice, e.g. σωῶ for σώσω[1], or the omission of the article, we are not quite certain how much is to be attributed to the carelessness of the engraver. On the other hand, from the frequent repetition of it, there can be no doubt that the form of the third person plural imperative, -όσθων for -έσθων, is a real variety of inflexion. The uncertainty in the use of several letters, even in the same inscription, or the inconsistency of the writing and the subject (C. I. A. 8, 93, 283), suggests doubts as to the limits within which this undoubtedly valid argument of date may be employed. The considerable differences which occur in the interpretation and reading of the text, often incomplete, as given by various critics, are another element of uncertainty.

All these are reasons for hesitation. They show that we must not indulge in sanguine or exaggerated language, but must confine ourselves to general results. And general results, when they relate to the history of the past, are by no means to be despised. Though we cannot rewrite the history of Greece out of her stones, is it a small thing to know that inscriptions of the fifth century before Christ confirm and illustrate the great literary works of the same

[1] Cp. Meisterhans, § 143, 1.

age? They bring nearer home to us Greek political institutions, the great struggle for freedom, the writings of Herodotus, Thucydides, Xenophon. They realize to us the innumerable details of private life about which history is silent; they illustrate forcibly some of the characteristics of Athenian public life, such as the imperative nature of duty to the state, the universal responsibility and liability to audit of treasurers and other officers, the great number of citizens annually chosen by lot to take part in the administration of the city (Thuc. ii. 40 init.). They add to our previous knowledge a few facts. They make an important contribution to the history of the Greek alphabet. And the investigation of them, especially on the spot, is full of interest independently of the result. To be busy on Greek soil, under the light of the blue heaven, amid the scenes of ancient glory, in reading inscriptions, or putting together fragments of stone or marble, has a charm of another kind than that which is to be found in the language of ancient authors. Yet even to appreciate truly the value of such remains, it is to the higher study of the mind of Hellas and of her great men that we must return, finding some little pleasure by the way (like that of looking at an autograph) in deciphering the handwriting of her children amid the dust of her ruins.

ADDENDA

(*To page* xxiv)

[THERE is a second sherd bearing the name of Xanthippus, with his father's name half-written (ΑΡΡΙΦΙ), found not on the Acropolis but on the road leading to the Piraeus (C. I A. iv. Suppl. iii. 571). The writer uses two forms of P.

On a fragment of the rim of a bowl, found, in Jan. 1897, N.W. of the Areopagus, are the words

ΘΕΜΙΣΘΟΚΛΕΣ

ΦΡΕΑΡΡΙΟ[Σ]

The character of the writing does not enable us to decide whether the occasion was 483 B.C., when Aristides and not his opponent Themistocles was ostracized, or the actual ostracism of Themistocles about 471. The spelling θ for τ occurs elsewhere in Attic inscriptions. (Mittheilungen des Deutsch. Arch. Inst., Athenische Abth. 22, 1897.)

A very curious epitaph in bad hexameters (C. I. A. ii. 1675; G. F. Hill, Sources for Greek History, B. C. 478–431, iii. 206) records among other exploits of 'Pythion of Megara' that he 'saved three tribes of Athenians, bringing them from Pagae through Boeotia to Athens.' A note at the end adds Φυλαὶ αἵδ' εἰσίν· Πανδιονὶς Κεκροπὶς Ἀντιοχίς.

Köhler, 'Hermes' xxiv. (1889), sees in this an incident of the Megarian revolt of 446 (Thuc. i. 113), and is followed by Busolt, vol. iii. p. 426 ff. Seven tribes under Pericles—so they infer from the words—took part in the invasion of Euboea when it revolted, three remained behind and on the revolt of Megara threw themselves into the Megarid (Diodorus xii. 5 speaks of the Athenians sending an army against the revolted Megarians, which took much booty and won a victory), under Andocides, the grandfather of the orator, general in the Samian wars a few years later. When the Lacedaemonian army advanced into Megara on its way to Attica, the Athenian army was forced to retreat to Pagae. Pericles' willingness to negotiate with Pleistoanax is partly accounted for by the absence of nearly one-third of the Athenian army. Meanwhile Pythion, a Megarian friendly to Athens, led the Athenians over the dangerous pass by Aegosthena and Crusis on the shore of the Corinthian gulf, capturing numerous Boeotian country-people or slaves on the way; and crossing Cithaeron from the N. brought them safely back to Athens. The Athenian army was now in full force. Pleistoanax had an additional motive for retreating. Pythion was presented with the Athenian citizenship for his great services; he lived to a good old age (the inscription is mostly written in Ionic characters and bears the stamp of the end of the fifth century rather than the beginning of the fourth), and his epitaph combined with the tradition preserved in Diodorus enables us to reconstruct the history of the famous events of 446–445 B.C.

Surely this interesting story, which bids fair to become a recognized piece of Athenian history, rests on too slender a basis to be accepted. The part played in it by Andocides is taken from a line following those quoted in which Pythion is said to have 'glorified Andocides with 2000 slaves'—the number is admitted to be an exaggeration, and we cannot be sure that the line refers to the same occasion. It is fair to state that Andocides the grandfather of the orator belonged to one of the three tribes mentioned in the inscription, the Pandionis. But apart from the possibility of the inscription referring to some event of the fourth century (the counter-arguments of Köhler are not conclusive), and from the patriotic colouring of the story in Diodorus, is it likely that so romantic an exploit as this would have left no trace in literary history?

The epitaph is quite sufficiently accounted for if Pythion saved, not about a third of the Athenian army, but a few men of the garrison, forming the detachments from these tribes, who at the Megarian revolt escaped to Pegae.

The inscription, whatever its historical worth, may be given, (with its Ionicisms and metrical imperfections,) as a curious exception to the usual good taste of Greek epitaphs:

Μνῆμα [τόδ' ἐστ' ἐ]πὶ σ[ώ]ματι κείμενο[ν] ἀνδρὸς ἀρίστο·
Πυθίων εγ Μεγαρω[ν] δαΐ[ξ]ας ἑπτὰ μ[ὲ]ν ἄνδρας
Ἑπτὰ δὲ ἀπορρήσας (i. e. ἀπορρήξας) [λ]όγχας ἐνὶ σώματι ἐκείνων
Εἵλετο τὰν ἀρετὰν πατέρα εὐκλείζων ἐνὶ δέμωι.
Οὗτος ἀνὴρ ὃς ἔ[σ]ωισεν Ἀθηναίων τρε̂ς φυλὰς
Ἐκ Παγᾶν ἀγαγὼν διὰ Βοιωτῶν ἐς Ἀθήνας,
Εὐκλέϊσε Ἀνδοκίδαν δισχιλ[ί]οις ἀνδραπόδοισιν.
Οὐδένα πημάνας ἐπιχθονίων ἀνθρώπων (!)
Ἐς Ἀΐδα κατέβα πᾶσιν μακαριστὸς ἰδέσθαι.
Φυλαὶ αἵδ' εἰσίν· Πανδιονὶς Κεκροπὶς Ἀντιοχίς.]

NOTE ON THE GEOGRAPHY OF THUCYDIDES

VARIOUS difficulties have been found in the geography of Thucydides: his accounts of places are at variance sometimes (1) with facts, sometimes (2) with the statements of later writers. It may be said of his descriptions generally, as of most early descriptions, that they are graphic rather than accurate. When we try to reproduce them in the mind something is wanting. For example, we do not gather from his narrative where the Euryelus was situated by which the Athenians, and also Gylippus, ascended the heights of Epipolae (vi. 97; vii. 2, 43), or how the Syracusan defences lay after the completion of the third counter-wall (vii. 7), or, without some consideration, how the dolphins were placed for the protection of the Athenian ships in the great Syracusan harbour (vii. 38). The topography of battles is often imperfect, and sometimes leads to a difficulty in the explanation of them. The narrative of the battle of Amphipolis leads to the inference (see Arnold's Appendix) that the city was not at the top but on the slope of the hill which Cleon ascended with his army, but this can only be inferred with some uncertainty and is not definitely expressed. Perhaps without maps and plans a better delineation was impossible. The narrative of the second sea-fight in the Crisaean gulf (ii. 90 ff.) is incoherent: for we are not told what happened to that portion of the Peloponnesian fleet which was originally victorious. The manner of the attack which ended in the capture of the first Syracusan counter-wall (vi. 100) is not fully described and can only be inferred; the 'Argive hoplites' who were killed in the Syracusan out-works after the capture of the stockade must have joined the attacking party from one of the two other divisions of the army. Once more, in the calculation of distances the eye or the information of the writer was frequently at fault. For examples see below.

There has been a good deal of controversy on this subject. Even into geography the spirit of party may find a way. Some commentators have been desirous of maintaining the credit of their author, like Dr. Arnold, who was of opinion that 'when Geographers who are also Scholars visit the places of which Thucydides speaks personally, most of the difficulties in his descriptions will vanish.' That remark of course supposes that Thucydides, rightly understood, is generally or always in the right. We may imagine the writer of it to feel what he does not say: 'The most accurate and trustworthy of historians can hardly be imagined to be ignorant as a schoolboy of geography.' And certainly, in his account of Pylos and Sphacteria, Dr. Arnold is ready, in a figure, to work a miracle in order to save the reputation of Thucydides. Changes in the formation of the coast are the 'Deus ex machina' to which he has recourse.

Yet it may very likely be true that Thucydides is far behind Strabo or Pausanias or Stephanus Byzantinus in geography, though his conception of history may be quite unattainable by them. Still greater would be the disparity of his knowledge when compared with that of a modern traveller, or resident in Greece, who has perhaps surveyed and explored places which the historian himself may not have visited. For the knowledge of geography is always growing with time, while history fades into the distance. The materials of the one are increasing, while those of the other are diminishing. The credibility of an author's geography is not therefore to be judged of by the credibility of his history, because in the one far more than in the other he is dependent on the conditions of his age.

In this short note it is not intended to enter into the discussion of particular passages, but rather to urge two general principles: (1) that geographical accuracy is not to be expected from a writer of the age of Thucydides: (2) that the number of his inaccuracies show them to be attributable rather to his ignorance, than to the ignorance of later writers, or of ourselves.

To attempt to reconcile the geography of Thucydides with facts may be the same error in kind, though not in degree, as to try and adapt the drive of Telemachus between Pylos and Sparta to the present condition of the country, or to seek on the sea-shore of Ithaca for the cave by which Odysseus was deposited. As the more familiar features of a scene are likely to be reproduced in the creations of the poet, so the ancient historian will roughly guess distances. But he may often make mistakes about a region with which he was unacquainted, and he will not always be able to judge what amount of description is required in order to place before his readers a just conception of a place or of a battle. There were no surveys of countries or measurements of distances in the age of Herodotus and Thucydides (except along the course of great roads such as the Persian highways), but only the proverbially uncertain measure of a day's journey or of a day's sail (see Thuc. ii. 97, and Arnold's note). There were no correct maps, but only rude delineations such as made Herodotus laugh (iv. 36). The eye was the judge of the distance across a strait or across the entrance of a harbour. Daily experience tells us how seldom the power of judging distances is found in any one who has not been trained by long habit.

Some of the errors or misleading expressions in Thucydides which have suggested the above remarks are the following:—

ii. 86 med. The distance of Rhium in Achaia from Rhium on the opposite coast is said by Thucydides to be less than a mile (7 stadia). According to Col. Leake (Morea, ii. 148) 'the distance is little, if at all, short of a mile and a half,' and would have been considerably greater in ancient times if we assume, as in this particular instance there is reason for thinking, that the sea, owing to the deposits of rivers, has retreated about 250 yards on the south, and somewhat less on the north coast.

iv. 8 med. The southern entrance of the harbour formed by the bay of Navarino is more than three-quarters of a mile in width, and the northern is 132 yards. But according to Thucydides the northern entrance admitted the passage of only two ships, the southern of not more than eight or nine, and the Lacedaemonians had intended to block up both passages by ships placed lengthways [1].

Thucydides also underrates considerably the length of the island, which he describes (iv. 8) as 15 stadia (about 3000 yards), whereas it is really 2¾ miles (4800 yards). [Mr. Grundy (see note) points out that the distance from the place where the Athenians must have landed on the bay side of the island to its N. point is about 15 stadia.]

---

[1] [It has been suggested that Thucydides fell into the error by combining the accounts of two informants, one of whom meant by 'the harbour' the lagoon of Osmyn Aga, behind Pylos, and the other the bay of Navarino: and mistook an intended blocking of the N. entrance to the bay of Navarino at both ends (by which a passage from the bay into the lagoon, which may have existed at the time, would also have been closed to the Athenians) for a blocking of the N. and S. entrances. See Mr. G. B. Grundy's admirable monograph on Pylos and Sphacteria. If this be so, the criticism, in the Essay, on Thucydides as a geographer would only be confirmed. It is clear from iv. 8 (*τὴν δὲ νῆσον ταύτην φοβούμενοι μὴ ἐξ αὐτῆς τὸν πόλεμον σφίσι ποιῶνται, ὁπλίτας διεβίβασαν ἐς αὐτήν, καὶ παρὰ τὴν ἤπειρον ἄλλους ἔταξαν· οὕτω γὰρ τοῖς Ἀθηναίοις τήν τε νῆσον πολεμίαν ἔσεσθαι τήν τε ἤπειρον, ἀπόβασιν οὐκ ἔχουσαν· τὰ γὰρ αὐτῆς τῆς Πύλου ἔξω τοῦ ἔσπλου πρὸς τὸ πέλαγος ἀλίμενα ὄντα οὐχ ἕξειν ὅθεν ὁρμώμενοι ὠφελήσουσι τοὺς αὑτῶν*) that Thucydides believed the Lacedaemonians to have intended to block both entrances of the bay of Navarino.—And it is after all hard to believe that as a fact they did not intend to keep out the Athenian ships by occupying (if not blocking) the S. entrance.]

iv. 57 init. According to Thucydides, Thyrea was situated about 10 stadia from the sea, or about $1\frac{1}{8}$ of a mile. According to Col. Leake (Morea, ii. 492) 'it is at least three times that distance.' Other writers suggest other sites. But there are no remains which agree with the distance mentioned in Thucydides (Bursian, Geographie von Griechenland, ii. p. 70).

vi. 104 med. Gylippus sailing from Tarentum to Sicily was caught by a storm in the Terinaean gulf. But the Terinaean gulf, called also the Sinus Hipponiates, is on the west coast of Italy (Pliny, iii. 72. 5, 10). Κατὰ τὸν Τεριναῖον κόλπον cannot mean 'opposite the Terinaean gulf.'

viii. 88 init. Alcibiades is described as sailing straight from Samos to Phaselis and Caunus on his way to Aspendus, and as returning to Samos from Caunus and Phaselis (108 init.). The inverse order in both cases is the true one. Dr. Arnold supposes the words to mean 'straight to Phaselis, having first touched at Caunus'; 'from Caunus, and before that from Phaselis.' But this explanation is forced in itself, and is rendered impossible by the repetition of the wrong order in the description of the return voyage.

viii. 101 fin. Similarly, Larissa and Hamaxitus are mentioned in a wrong order (see Strabo, xiii. 1. 47, 48, pp. 604, 605).

vi. 72 init. So Naxos and Catana.

iii. 29 med. So Icarus and Myconus.

vii. 19 init. Decelea is said to be distant about 120 stadia (i. e. about fourteen miles) from Athens, and about the same or a little more from Boeotia. In reality it was much nearer Boeotia. It has been suggested that Thucydides is here thinking of the far-off corner of Boeotia at Oropus, from which an important road ran through Decelea (vii. 28 init.) to Athens. Still this would only show how different his mode of expression is from that of a modern writer.

viii. 26 med. Λέρον τὴν πρὸ Μιλήτου νῆσον. But Leros

is forty miles from Miletus. All the MSS. except the Vatican read Ἔλεον, a place which is otherwise unknown. Λέρον is probably correct, and is confirmed by the close connexion which we find existing between Leros and Miletus in the tribute lists (C. I. A. 37, 226, 251, 262, 264). The expression is natural enough for a writer who had in his mind not maps of the Aegean, but the actual voyage past Leros to Miletus.

iii. 4 fin. ὥρμουν ἐν τῇ Μαλέᾳ, πρὸς βορέαν τῆς πόλεως (compare c. 6, περιορμισάμενοι τὸ πρὸς νότον). But, according to Strabo, Malea was at the southern extremity of the island. It is possible however to take πρὸς βορέαν τῆς πόλεως not with ὥρμουν but with ἀποστέλλουσι πρέσβεις τριήρει, referring to the Mytilenaeans, above.

i. 61 med. ἀφικόμενοι ἐς Βέροιαν κἀκεῖθεν ἐπιστρέψαντες. But Beroea was several days' march out of the road from Pydna to Potidaea; nor could the Athenians possibly have reached Gigonus by slow marches three days after their departure from Beroea (κατ' ὀλίγον δὲ προϊόντες τριταῖοι ἀφίκοντο ἐς Γίγωνον). The generally received correction ἐπὶ Στρέψαν for ἐπιστρέψαντες cannot be considered certain, and does not remove the difficulty about Beroea.

We may also notice that where Thucydides evidently wants to express geographical ideas with precision, as in ii. 9 fin., νῆσοι ὅσαι ἐντὸς Πελοποννήσου καὶ Κρήτης πρὸς ἥλιον ἀνίσχοντα, πᾶσαι αἱ ἄλλαι Κυκλάδες πλὴν Μήλου καὶ Θήρας, or in the description of the island of Cythera, iv. 53 fin., πᾶσα (i. e. either ἡ νῆσος or ἡ Λακωνικὴ) γὰρ ἀνέχει πρὸς τὸ Σικελικὸν καὶ Κρητικὸν πέλαγος, he has caused a great deal of trouble to his interpreters[1]. There is a lesser degree of obscurity in the description of the country about Chimerium (i. 46 fin.), especially the words ῥεῖ δὲ καὶ Θύαμις ποταμός, ὁρίζων τὴν Θεσπρωτίδα καὶ Κεστρίνην, ὧν ἐντὸς ἡ ἄκρα ἀνέχει τὸ Χειμέριον, where ὧν refers not to τὴν Θεσπρωτίδα καὶ Κεστρίνην, but to

[1] [In ii. 9 the variations in the text give good ground for suspecting a gloss.]

ποταμῶν, gathered from the previous sentence (scil. the Acheron and the Thyamis).

It is worth while also to compare the description of the kingdom of the Odrysae in ii. 97, which, though not obscure, is cumbrous and very unlike the manner of a modern geographer.

Considering the number of these errors and vague expressions, and the probability that Thucydides from his imperfect means of knowledge would have fallen into them, is it worth while, for the sake of vindicating his credit, either to alter the text, or to assume changes in the face of nature unless there is actual proof of them in each particular case? All that we can reasonably expect of him is that he should be a little in advance of his predecessors, not that he should vie with modern accuracy, or equally with a modern historian be alive to the value of topography, or realize the fulness and minuteness of detail which are required in a describer of places or of military movements.

THUCYDIDES

BOOK I

THUCYDIDES, an Athenian, wrote the history of the war in which the Peloponnesians and the Athenians fought against one another. He began to write when they first took up arms, believing that it would be great and memorable above any previous war. For he argued that both states were then at the full height of their military power, and he saw the rest of the Hellenes either siding or intending to side with one or other of them. No movement ever stirred Hellas more deeply than this; it was shared by many of the Barbarians, and might be said even to affect the world at large. The character of the events which preceded, whether immediately or in more remote antiquity, owing to the lapse of time cannot be made out with certainty. [a] But, judging from the evidence which I am able to trust after most careful enquiry [a], I should imagine that former ages were not great either in their wars or in anything else.

Greatness of the war.

The country which is now called Hellas was not 2
regularly settled [b] in ancient times [b]. The people were

---

[a] Or, connecting ὢν with μακρότατον: 'But after carrying the enquiry to the furthest point at which any trustworthy evidence can be obtained.' [b] Or, taking οὐ πάλαι closely together: 'until recent times.'

migratory, and readily left their homes whenever they were overpowered by numbers. There was no commerce, and they could not safely hold intercourse with one another either by land or sea. The several tribes cultivated their own soil just enough to obtain a maintenance from it. But they had no accumulations of wealth, and did not plant the ground; for, being without walls, they were never sure that an invader might not come and despoil them. Living in this manner and knowing that they could anywhere obtain a bare subsistence, they were always ready to migrate; so that they had neither great cities nor any considerable resources. The richest districts were most constantly changing their inhabitants; for example, the countries which are now called Thessaly and Boeotia, the greater part of the Peloponnesus with the exception of Arcadia, and all the best parts of Hellas. For the productiveness of the land [a] increased the power of individuals; this in turn was a source of quarrels by which communities [a] were ruined, while at the same time they were more exposed to attacks from without. Certainly Attica, of which the soil was poor and thin, enjoyed a long freedom from civil strife, and therefore retained its original inhabitants. And a striking confirmation of my argument is afforded by the fact [b] that Attica through immigration increased in population more than any other region. For the leading men of Hellas [b], when driven

Weakness of ancient Hellas: readiness of the early tribes to migrate: the richer districts the more unsettled; some of the poorer, like Attica, in reality the more prosperous.

[a] Or, 'gave to some communities greater power; this was a source of quarrels, by which they' etc. [b] Or, taking ἐς τὰ ἄλλα in another sense: 'that Attica through immigration increased in population quite out of proportion to her increase in other respects;' or, supplying τὴν Ἑλλάδα and taking μετοικίας in another sense: 'And here is a striking confirmation of my argument that the constant migrations were the cause which prevented the rest of Hellas from increasing equally with Attica. The leading men of Hellas,' etc.

out of their own country by war or revolution, sought an asylum at Athens; and from the very earliest times, being admitted to rights of citizenship, so greatly increased the number of inhabitants that Attica became incapable of containing them, and was at last obliged to send out colonies to Ionia.

No unity among the early inhabitants: no common name of Hellenes or Barbarians; or common action in Hellas before the Trojan War.

The feebleness of antiquity is further proved to me by 3
the circumstance that there appears to have been no common action in Hellas before the Trojan War. And I am inclined to think that the very name was not as yet given to the whole country, and in fact did not exist at all before the time of Hellen, the son of Deucalion; the different tribes, of which the Pelasgian was the most widely spread, gave their own names to different districts. But when Hellen and his sons became powerful in Phthiotis, their aid was invoked by other cities, and those who associated with them gradually began to be called Hellenes, though a long time elapsed before the name prevailed over the whole country. Of this Homer affords the best evidence; for he, although he lived long after the Trojan War, nowhere uses this name collectively, but confines it to the followers of Achilles from Phthiotis, who were the original Hellenes; when speaking of the entire host he calls them Danaāns, or Argives, or Achaeans. Neither is there any mention of Barbarians in his poems, clearly because there were as yet no Hellenes opposed to them by a common distinctive name. Thus [a] the several Hellenic tribes (and I mean by the term Hellenes those who, while forming separate communities, had a common language, and were afterwards called by a common name)[a], owing to their weakness and isolation, were never united

[a] Or, supplying κληθέντες with both clauses: 'those who successively acquired the Hellenic name, which first spread among the several tribes speaking the same language, and afterwards became universal.'

in any great enterprise before the Trojan War. And they only made the expedition against Troy after they had gained considerable experience of the sea.

Beginnings of civilisation: Minos conquers the islands and clears the sea of pirates.

4 Minos is the first to whom tradition ascribes the possession of a navy. He made himself master of a great part of what is now termed the Hellenic sea; he conquered the Cyclades, and was the first coloniser of most of them, expelling the Carians and appointing his own sons to govern in them. Lastly, it was he who, from a natural desire to protect his growing revenues, sought, as far as he was able, to clear the sea of pirates.

5 For in ancient times both the Hellenes, and those Barbarians, whose homes were on the coast of the mainland or in islands, when they began to find their way to one another by sea had recourse to piracy. They were commanded by powerful chiefs, who took this means of increasing their wealth and providing for their poorer followers. They would fall upon the unwalled and straggling towns, or rather villages, which they plundered, and maintained themselves chiefly by the plunder of them; for, as yet, such an occupation was held to be honourable and not disgraceful. This is proved by the practice of certain tribes on the mainland who, to the present day, glory in piratical exploits, and by the witness of the ancient poets, in whose verses the question is invariably asked of newly-arrived voyagers, whether they are pirates[a]; which implies that neither those who are questioned disclaim, nor those who are interested in knowing censure the occupation. On land also neighbouring communities plundered each other; and there are many parts of Hellas in which the old practices still continue, as for example among the Ozolian Locrians, Aetolians, Acarnanians, and the adjacent regions of the continent. The fashion of wearing arms among these continental tribes is a

[a] Od. iii. 73 ff.; ix. 252; Hymn to Apoll. 452 ff.

relic of their old predatory habits. For in ancient times all Hellenes carried weapons because their homes were undefended and intercourse was unsafe; like the Barbarians they went armed in their every-day life. And the continuance of the custom in certain parts of the country indicates that it once prevailed everywhere.

Old customs which are still existing in some parts of the country: dress of Athenians and Spartans.

The Athenians were the first who laid aside arms and 6
adopted an easier and more luxurious way of life. Quite recently the old-fashioned refinement of dress still lingered among the elder men of their richer class, who wore under-garments of linen, and bound back their hair in a knot with golden clasps in the form of grasshoppers; and the same customs long survived among the elders of Ionia, having been derived from their Athenian ancestors. On the other hand, the simple dress which is now common was first worn at Sparta; and there, more than anywhere else, the life of the rich was assimilated to that of the people. The Lacedaemonians too were the first who in their athletic exercises stripped naked and rubbed themselves over with oil. But this was not the ancient custom; athletes formerly, even when they were contending at Olympia, wore girdles about their loins, a practice which lasted until quite lately, and still prevails among Barbarians, especially those of Asia, where the combatants in boxing and wrestling matches wear girdles. And many other customs which are now confined to the Barbarians might be shown to have existed formerly in Hellas.

In later times, when navigation had become general and 7
wealth was beginning to accumulate, cities were built upon the sea-shore and fortified; peninsulas too were occupied and walled-off with a view to commerce and defence against the neighbouring tribes. But the older towns both in the islands and on the continent, in order to protect themselves against the piracy which so long prevailed, were built inland; and there they remain

Fortified towns begin to be built; at first inland, afterwards on the sea-shore.

to this day. For the piratical tribes plundered, not only one another, but all those who, without being seamen, lived on the sea-coast.

8 The islanders were even more addicted to piracy than the inhabitants of the mainland. They were mostly Carian or Phoenician settlers. This is proved by the fact that when the Athenians purified Delos[a] during the Peloponnesian War and the tombs of the dead were opened, more than half of them were found to be Carians. They were known by the fashion of their arms which were buried with them, and by their mode of burial, the same which is still practised among them.

The pirates in the islands of Carian or Phoenician origin.

After Minos had established his navy, communication by sea became more general. For, he having expelled the marauders[b] when he colonised the greater part of the islands, the dwellers on the sea-coast began to grow richer and to live in a more settled manner; and some of them, finding their wealth increase beyond their expectations, surrounded their towns with walls. The love of gain made the weaker willing to serve the stronger, [c]and the command of wealth enabled the more powerful to subjugate the lesser cities[c]. This was the state of society which was beginning to prevail at the time of the Trojan War.

9 I am inclined to think that Agamemnon succeeded in collecting the expedition, not because the suitors of Helen had bound themselves by oath to Tyndareus, but because he was the most powerful king of his time. [d]Those Peloponnesians who possess the most accurate traditions say that[d] originally Pelops gained his power by the great wealth which he brought with him

Rise of the Pelopidae: the wealth and power which Agamemnon inherited from Atreus and Eurystheus enabled him to assemble the chiefs who fought at Troy.

[a] Cp. iii. 104 init. [b] Cp. i. 4. [c] Or, 'and incited the more powerful, who now had wealth at their command, to subjugate the lesser cities.' [d] Or, 'Those who possess the most accurate traditions respecting the history of Peloponnesus say that' etc.

from Asia into a poor country, whereby he was enabled, although a stranger, to give his name to the Peloponnesus; and that still greater fortune attended his descendants after the death of Eurystheus, king of Mycenae, who was slain in Attica by the Heraclidae. For Atreus the son of Pelops was the maternal uncle of Eurystheus, who, when he went on the expedition, naturally committed to his charge the kingdom of Mycenae. Now Atreus had been banished by his father on account of the murder of Chrysippus. But Eurystheus never returned; and the Mycenaeans, dreading the Heraclidae, were ready to welcome Atreus, who was considered a powerful man and had ingratiated himself with the multitude. So he succeeded to the throne of Mycenae and the other dominions of Eurystheus. Thus the house of Pelops prevailed over that of Perseus.

And it was, as I believe, because Agamemnon inherited this power and also because he was the greatest naval potentate of his time that he was able to assemble the expedition; and the other princes followed him, not from good-will, but from fear. Of the chiefs who came to Troy, he, if the witness of Homer be accepted, brought the greatest number of ships himself, besides supplying the Arcadians with them. In the 'Handing down of the Sceptre' he is described as 'The king of many islands, and of all Argos[a].' But, living on the mainland, he could not have ruled over any except the adjacent islands (which would not be 'many') unless he had possessed a considerable navy. From this expedition we must form our conjectures about the character of still earlier times.

When it is said that Mycenae was but a small place, 10
or that any other city which existed in those days is inconsiderable in our own, this argument will hardly prove that the expedition was not as great as the poets relate and as is commonly imagined. Suppose the city

---

[a] Il. ii. 108.

of Sparta to be deserted, and nothing left but the temples and the ground-plan, distant ages would be very unwilling to believe that the power of the Lacedaemonians was at all equal to their fame. And yet they own two-fifths of the Peloponnesus, and are acknowledged leaders of the whole, as well as of numerous allies in the rest of Hellas. But their city is not built continuously, and has no splendid temples or other edifices; it rather resembles a group of villages like the ancient towns of Hellas, and would therefore make a poor show. Whereas, if the same fate befell the Athenians, the ruins of Athens would strike the eye, and we should infer their power to have been twice as great as it really is. We ought not then to be unduly sceptical. The greatness of cities should be estimated by their real power and not by appearances. And we may fairly suppose the Trojan expedition to have been greater than any which preceded it, although according to Homer, if we may once more appeal to his testimony, not equal to those of our own day. He was a poet, and may therefore be expected to exaggerate; yet, even upon his showing, the expedition was comparatively small. For it numbered, as he tells us, twelve hundred ships, those of the Boeotians [a] carrying one hundred and twenty men each, those of Philoctetes [b] fifty; and by these numbers he may be presumed to indicate the largest and the smallest ships; else why in the catalogue is nothing said about the size of any others? That the crews were all fighting men as well as rowers he clearly implies when speaking of the ships of Philoctetes; for he tells us that all the oarsmen were likewise archers. And it is not to be supposed that many who were not sailors would accompany the expedition, except the kings and principal officers; for the troops had to cross the sea,

That the ancient greatness of Mycenae, or of any other city, is not to be estimated by present appearances, proved from a comparison of Athens and Sparta.

Homer's account of the number of the forces.

[a] Il. ii. 509, 510.

[b] Il. ii. 719, 720.

bringing with them the materials of war, in vessels without decks, built after the old piratical fashion. Now if we take a mean between the crews, the invading forces will appear not to have been very numerous when we remember that they were drawn from the whole of Hellas.

Considerations respecting the Trojan War.

The cause of the inferiority was not so much the want 11
of men as the want of money; the invading army was limited, by the difficulty of obtaining supplies, to such a number as might be expected to live on the country in which they were to fight. After their arrival at Troy, when they had won a battle (as they clearly did, for otherwise they could not have fortified their camp), even then they appear not to have used the whole of their force, but to have been driven by want of provisions to the cultivation of the Chersonese and to pillage. And in consequence of this dispersion of their forces, the Trojans were enabled to hold out against them during the whole ten years, being always a match for those who remained on the spot. Whereas if the besieging army had brought abundant supplies, and, instead of betaking themselves to agriculture or pillage, had carried on the war persistently with all their forces, they would easily have been masters of the field and have taken the city; since, even divided as they were, and with only a part of their army available at any one time, they held their ground. Or, again, they might have regularly invested Troy, and the place would have been captured in less time and with less trouble. Poverty was the real reason why the achievements of former ages were insignificant, and why the Trojan War, the most celebrated of them all, when brought to the test of facts, falls short of its fame and of the prevailing traditions to which the poets have given authority.

Even in the age which followed the Trojan War, Hellas 12
was still in process of ferment and settlement, and had no time for peaceful growth. The return of the Hellenes from Troy after their long absence led to many changes:

quarrels too arose in nearly every city, and those who were expelled by them went and founded other cities. Thus in the sixtieth year after the fall of Troy, the Boeotian people, having been expelled from Arnè by the Thessalians, settled in the country formerly called Cadmeis, but now Boeotia: a portion of the tribe already dwelt there, and some of these had joined in the Trojan expedition. In the eightieth year after the war, the Dorians led by the Heraclidae conquered the Peloponnesus. A considerable time elapsed before Hellas became finally settled; after a while, however, she recovered tranquillity and began to send out colonies. The Athenians colonised Ionia and most of the islands; the Peloponnesians the greater part of Italy and Sicily, and various places in Hellas. These colonies were all founded after the Trojan War.

Southward movement in Hellas after the Trojan War; Boeotians descend out of Thessalia; Dorian occupation of the Peloponnesus; Ionian and Dorian colonies.

13 As Hellas grew more powerful and the acquisition of wealth became more and more rapid, the revenues of her cities increased, and in most of them tyrannies were established; they had hitherto been ruled by hereditary kings, having fixed prerogatives. The Hellenes likewise began to build navies and to make the sea their element. The Corinthians are said to have first adopted something like the modern style of marine, and the oldest Hellenic triremes to have been constructed at Corinth. A Corinthian ship-builder, Ameinocles, appears to have built four ships for the Samians; he went to Samos
B.C. 704. Ol. 19. about three hundred years before the end of the Peloponnesian War. And the earliest naval engagement on record is that between the Corinthians and Corcyraeans
B.C. 664. Ol. 29. which occurred about forty years later. Corinth, being seated on an isthmus, was naturally from the first a centre of commerce; for the Hellenes within and without the Peloponnese in the old days, when they communicated

Rise of navies in Hellas: Corinth, Corcyra, Ionia, Samos, Phocaea.

chiefly by land, had to pass through her territory in order to reach one another. Her wealth too was a source of power, as the ancient poets testify, who speak of 'Corinth the rich[a].' When navigation grew more common, the Corinthians, having already acquired a fleet, were able to put down piracy; they offered a market both by sea and land, and with the increase of riches the power of their city increased yet more. Later, in the time of Cyrus, the B.C. 559–
first Persian king, and of Cambyses his son, the Ionians 529. Ol. 55, 2–
had a large navy; they fought with Cyrus, and were for 62, 4.
a time masters of the sea around their own coasts. Poly- B.C. 529–522.
crates, too, who was a tyrant of Samos in the reign of Ol. 62, 4–
Cambyses, had a powerful navy and subdued several of 64, 4.
the islands, among them Rhenea, which he dedicated to the Delian Apollo[b]. And the Phocaeans, when they were colonising Massalia, defeated the Carthaginians on B.C. 600.
the sea. Ol. 45.

14 *Scarcity of triremes. Smallness of the Athenian and Aeginetan fleets.*

These were the most powerful navies, and even these, which came into existence many generations after the Trojan War, appear to have consisted chiefly of fifty-oared vessels and galleys of war, as in the days of Troy; as yet triremes were not common. But a little before the Persian War and the death of Darius, B.C. 485.
who succeeded Cambyses, the Sicilian tyrants and the Ol. 73, 4.
Corcyraeans had them in considerable numbers. No other maritime powers of any consequence arose in Hellas before the expedition of Xerxes. The Aeginetans, Athenians, and a few more had small fleets, and these mostly consisted of fifty-oared vessels. [c] Even the ships which the Athenians built quite recently at the instigation of Themistocles, when they were at war with the Aeginetans

---

[a] Il. ii. 570. [b] Cp. iii. 104 init. [c] Or, 'It was quite at a recent period, when the Athenians were at war with the Aeginetans and in expectation of the Barbarian, that Themistocles persuaded them to build the ships with which they fought at Salamis; and even these were not completely decked.'

and in expectation of the Barbarian, even these ships with which they fought at Salamis were not completely decked [c].

15 So inconsiderable were the Hellenic navies in recent as well as in more ancient times. And yet those who applied their energies to the sea obtained a great accession of strength by the increase of their revenues and the extension of their dominion. For they attacked and subjugated the islands, especially when the pressure of population was felt by them. Whereas by land, no conflict of any kind which brought increase of power ever occurred; what wars they had were mere border feuds. Foreign and distant expeditions of conquest the Hellenes never undertook; for they were not as yet ranged under the command of the great states, nor did they form voluntary leagues or make expeditions on an equal footing. Their wars were only the wars of the several neighbouring tribes with one another. The conflict in which the rest of Hellas was most divided, allying itself with one side or the other, was the ancient war between the Chalcidians and Eretrians [a].

The chief power of Hellas maritime. Wars by land inconsiderable.

16 There were different impediments to the progress of the different states. The Ionians had attained great prosperity when Cyrus and the Persians, having overthrown Croesus and subdued the countries between the river Halys and the sea, made war against them and enslaved the cities on the mainland. Some time afterwards, Darius, strong in the possession of the Phoenician fleet, conquered the islands also.

Impediments to progress:

B.C. 546. Ol. 58, 3.

(1) *The rising power of the Persians.*

B.C. 493. Ol. 71, 4.

17 Nor again did the tyrants of the Hellenic cities extend their thoughts beyond their own interest, that is, the security of their persons, and the aggrandisement of themselves and their families. They were extremely cautious in the administration of their government, and nothing

(2) *The petty aims and cautious natures of the tyrants.*

---

[a] Herod. v. 99.

considerable was ever effected by them; except in wars with their neighbours, as in Sicily, where their power attained its greatest height. Thus for a long time everything conspired to prevent Hellas from uniting in any great action and to paralyse enterprise in the individual states.

They were at length overthrown by Sparta, which for four hundred years has been well governed.

At length the tyrants both at Athens and in the rest of 18
Hellas (which had been under their B.C. 510.
dominion long before Athens), at least Ol. 67, 3.
the greater number of them, and with the exception of the Sicilian the last who ever ruled, were put down by the Lacedaemonians. For although Lacedaemon, after the conquest[a] of the country by the Dorians who now inhabit it, remained long unsettled, and indeed longer than any country which we know, nevertheless she obtained good laws at an earlier period than any other, and has never been subject to tyrants; she has preserved the same form of government for rather
more than four hundred years, reckoning to the end of the B.C. 804–
Peloponnesian War. It was the excellence of her con- 404. Ol. 95.
stitution which gave her power, and thus enabled her to regulate the affairs of other states. Not long after the overthrow of the tyrants by the Lacedaemonians, the battle
of Marathon was fought between the Athenians and the B.C. 490.
Persians; ten years later, the Barbarian returned with the Ol. 72, 3. B.C. 480.
vast armament which was to enslave Hellas. In the great- Ol. 75.
ness of the impending danger, the Lacedaemonians, who were the most powerful state in Hellas, assumed the lead of the confederates, while the Athenians, as the Persian host advanced, resolved to forsake their city, broke up their homes, and, taking to their ships, became seamen. The Barbarian was repelled by a common effort; but soon the Hellenes, [b]as well those who had

The Hellenes, who had been united in resisting the Persian, soon broke up into two confederacies.

---

[a] Reading κτῆσιν, not κτίσιν.

[b] Or, 'as well those who had revolted from the King, as those who had joined with him.'

revolted from the King as those who formed the original confederacy[b], took different sides and became the allies either of the Athenians or of the Lacedaemonians; for these were now the two leading powers, the one strong by land and the other by sea. The league between them was of short duration; they speedily quarrelled and, with their respective allies, went to war. Any of the other Hellenes who had differences of their own now resorted to one or other of them. So that from the Persian to the Peloponnesian War, the Lacedaemonians and the Athenians were perpetually fighting or making peace, either with one another or with their own revolted allies; thus they attained military efficiency, and learned experience in the school of danger.

Different character of the Athenian and Spartan league.

19 The Lacedaemonians did not make tributaries of those who acknowledged their leadership, but took care that they should be governed by oligarchies in the exclusive interest of Sparta. The Athenians, on the other hand, after a time deprived the subject cities of their ships and made all of them pay a fixed tribute, except Chios and Lesbos[a]. And the single power [b]of Athens[b] at the beginning of this war was greater than that of Athens and Sparta together at their greatest, while the confederacy remained intact.

Vulgar errors.

20 Such are the results of my enquiries, [c]though the early history of Hellas is of a kind which forbids implicit reliance on every particular of the evidence[c]. Men do not discriminate, and are too ready to receive ancient traditions about their own as well as about other countries. For example, most

---

[a] Cp. i. 96, 99; iii. 39 init.; vi. 85 med.; vii. 57 init. [b] Or, 'either of Athens or Sparta.' [c] Or (1), 'Though they may not obtain entire credit, even when the proofs of them are all set down in order.' Or (2), 'Though they will not readily be believed upon a bare recital of all the proofs of them.' Or (3), 'Though it is difficult to set down all the proofs in order, so as to make the account credible.'

Athenians think that Hipparchus was actually tyrant when he was slain by Harmodius and Aristogeiton; they are not aware that Hippias was the eldest of the sons of Peisistratus, and succeeded him, and that Hipparchus and Thessalus were only his brothers [a]. At the last moment, Harmodius and Aristogeiton suddenly suspected that Hippias had been forewarned by some of their accomplices. They therefore abstained from attacking him, but, wishing to do something before they were seized, and not to risk their lives in vain, they slew Hipparchus, with whom they fell in near the temple called Leocorium as he was marshalling the Panathenaic procession. There are many other matters, not obscured by time, but contemporary, about which the other Hellenes are equally mistaken. For example, they imagine that the kings of Lacedaemon in their council have not one but two votes each [b], and that in the army of the Lacedaemonians there is a division called the Pitanate division [c]; whereas they never had anything of the sort. So little trouble do men take in the search after truth; so readily do they accept whatever comes first to hand. B.C. 514. Ol. 66, 3.

Uncertainty of early history. If estimated by facts the Peloponnesian greater than any preceding war.

Yet any one who upon the grounds which I have given arrives at some such conclusion as my own about those ancient times, would not be far wrong. He must not be misled by the exaggerated fancies of the poets, or by the tales of chroniclers who seek to please the ear rather than to speak the truth. Their accounts cannot be tested by him; and most of the facts in the lapse of ages have passed into the region of romance. At such a distance of time he must make up his mind to be satisfied with conclusions resting upon the clearest evidence which can be had. And, though men will always judge any war in which they are actually fighting to be the greatest at the time, but, after it is over, revert to their 21

[a] Cp. vi. 54 seqq. [b] Herod. vi. 57. [c] Herod. ix. 53.

admiration of some other which has preceded, still the Peloponnesian, if estimated by the actual facts, will certainly prove to have been the greatest ever known.

22 As to the speeches which were made either before or during the war, it was hard for me, and for others who reported them to me, to recollect the exact words. I have therefore put into the mouth of each speaker the sentiments proper to the occasion, expressed as I thought he would be likely to express them, while at the same time I endeavoured, as nearly as I could, to give the general purport of what was actually said. Of the events of the war I have not ventured to speak from any chance information, nor according to any notion of my own; I have described nothing but what I either saw myself, or learned from others of whom I made the most careful and particular enquiry. The task was a laborious one, because eye-witnesses of the same occurrences gave different accounts of them, as they remembered or were interested in the actions of one side or the other. And very likely the strictly historical character of my narrative may be disappointing to the ear. But if he who desires to have before his eyes a true picture of the events which have happened, and of the like events which may be expected to happen hereafter in the order of human things, shall pronounce what I have written to be useful, then I shall be satisfied. My history is an everlasting possession, not a prize composition which is heard and forgotten.

The speeches could not be exactly reported. Great pains taken to ascertain the truth about events.

23 The greatest achievement of former times was the Persian War; yet even this was speedily decided in two battles by sea and two by land. But the Peloponnesian War was a protracted struggle, and attended by calamities such as Hellas had never known within a like period of time. Never were so many cities captured and depopulated—some by Barbarians,

Length of the war, which was attended by all sorts of calamities, ordinary and extraordinary. Among the latter might be enumerated earthquakes, eclipses, droughts, and lastly, the plague.

others by Hellenes themselves fighting against one another; and several of them after their capture were repeopled by strangers. Never were exile and slaughter more frequent, whether in the war or brought about by civil strife. And traditions which had often been current before, but rarely verified by fact, were now no longer doubted. For there were earthquakes unparalleled in their extent and fury, and eclipses of the sun more numerous than are recorded to have happened in any former age; there were also in some places great droughts causing famines, and lastly the plague which did immense harm and destroyed numbers of the people. All these calamities fell upon Hellas simultaneously with the war, which began when the Athenians and Peloponnesians violated the thirty years' truce concluded by them after the recapture of Euboea[a]. Why they broke it and what were the grounds of quarrel I will first set forth, that in time to come no man may be at a loss to know what was the origin of this great war. The real though unavowed cause I believe to have been the growth of the Athenian power, which terrified the Lacedaemonians and forced them into war; but the reasons publicly alleged on either side were as follows.

The story of Epidamnus. Civil strife and war with the barbarians.

The city of Epidamnus is situated on the right hand as 24
you sail up the Ionian Gulf. The neighbouring inhabitants are the Taulantians, a barbarian tribe of the Illyrian race. The place was colonised by the Corcyraeans, but under the leadership of a Corinthian, Phalius, son of Eratocleides, who was of the lineage of Heracles; he was invited, according to ancient custom, from the mother city, and Corinthians and other Dorians joined in the colony. In process of time Epidamnus became great and populous, but there followed a long period of civil commotion, and the city is said to have been brought low in a war against the neighbouring

[a] Cp. i. 115, 146.

B.C. 435 or 434. Ol. 86, 2 or 3.

barbarians, and to have lost her ancient power. At last, shortly before the Peloponnesian War, the notables were overthrown and driven out by the people; the exiles went over to the barbarians, and, uniting with them, plundered the remaining inhabitants both by sea and land. These,

The prayer of the Epidamnians for help is rejected by their mother-city Corcyra.

finding themselves hard pressed, sent an embassy to the mother-city Corcyra, begging the Corcyraeans not to leave them to their fate, but to reconcile them to the exiles and settle the war with the barbarians. The ambassadors came, and sitting as suppliants in the temple of Herè preferred their request; but the Corcyraeans would not listen to them, and they returned without success. The Epidamnians, finding that they had no hope of assistance from Corcyra, knew not what to do, and sending to Delphi enquired of the God whether they should deliver up the city to their original founders, the Corinthians, and endeavour to obtain aid from them. The God replied that they should, and bade them place them-

They place themselves under the protection of Corinth.

selves under the leadership of the Corinthians. So the Epidamnians went to Corinth, and informing the Corinthians of the answer which the oracle had given, delivered up the city to them. They reminded them that the original leader of the colony was a citizen of Corinth; and implored the Corinthians to come and help them, and not leave them to their fate. The Corinthians took up their cause, partly in vindication of their own rights (for they considered that Epidamnus belonged to them quite as much as to the Corcyraeans), partly too because they hated the Corcyraeans, who were their own colony but slighted them. In their common festivals they would not allow them the customary privileges of founders, and at their sacrifices denied to a Corinthian the right of receiving first the lock of hair cut from the head of the victim, an honour usually granted by colonies to a representative of the mother-country. In fact they despised the Corinthians, for they were more than a match for them in military strength, and as rich as any state then existing in Hellas. They would often boast that on the sea they were very far superior to them, and would appropriate to themselves the naval renown of the Phaeacians, who were the ancient inhabitants of the island. Such feelings led them more and more to strengthen their navy, which was by no means despicable; for they had a hundred and twenty triremes when the war broke out.

The Corinthians send troops and colonists to Epidamnus. The Corcyraeans demand their dismissal; on being refused they besiege the city.

Irritated by these causes of offence, the Corinthians 26
were too happy to assist Epidamnus; accordingly they invited any one who was willing to settle there, and for the protection of the colonists despatched with them Ambracian and Leucadian troops and a force of their own. All these they sent by land as far as Apollonia, which is a colony of theirs, fearing that if they went by sea the Corcyraeans might oppose their passage. Great was the rage of the Corcyraeans when they discovered that the settlers and the troops had entered Epidamnus and that the colony had been given up to the Corinthians. They immediately set sail with five and twenty ships, followed by a second fleet, and in insulting terms bade the Epidamnians receive the exiled oligarchs, who had gone to Corcyra and implored the Corcyraeans to restore them, appealing to the tie of kindred and pointing to the sepulchres of their common ancestors[a]. They also bade them send away the troops and the new settlers. But the Epidamnians would not listen to their demands. Whereupon the Corcyraeans attacked them with forty ships. They were accompanied by the exiles whom they were to restore, and had the assistance of the native Illyrian troops. They sat down before the city, and made proclamation that any Epidamnian who chose, and the foreigners, might depart in

[a] Cp. iii. 58 med., 59 init.

safety, but that all who remained would be treated as enemies. This had no effect, and the Corcyraeans proceeded to invest the city, which is built upon an isthmus.

27 When the news reached the Corinthians that Epidamnus was besieged, they equipped an army and proclaimed that a colony was to be sent thither; all who wished might go and enjoy equal rights of citizenship; but any one who was unwilling to sail at once might remain at Corinth, and, if he made a deposit of fifty Corinthian drachmae, might still have a share in the colony[a]. Many sailed, and many deposited the money. The Corinthians also sent and requested the Megarians to assist them with a convoy in case the Corcyraeans should intercept the colonists on their voyage. The Megarians accordingly provided eight ships, and the Cephallenians of Palè four; the Epidaurians, of whom they made a similar request, five; the Hermionians one; the Troezenians two; the Leucadians ten; and the Ambraciots eight. Of the Thebans and Phliasians they begged money, and of the Eleans money, and ships without crews. On their own account they equipped thirty ships and three thousand hoplites.

The Corinthians prepare for war and proclaim a colony to Epidamnus. Megara and other friendly cities furnish ships.

28 When the Corcyraeans heard of their preparations they came to Corinth, taking with them Lacedaemonian and Sicyonian envoys, and summoned the Corinthians to withdraw the troops and the colonists, telling them that they had nothing to do with Epidamnus. If they made any claim to it, the Corcyraeans expressed themselves willing to refer the cause for arbitration to such Peloponnesian states as both parties should agree upon, and their decision was to be final; or, they were willing

The Corcyraeans propose arbitration, offering until a decision be given to withdraw their troops if the Corinthians withdraw theirs, or to allow both to remain at Epidamnus by agreement.

---

[a] The sum would amount to £2 15*s*. 4*d*., or to £1 2*s*. 6*d*., according to the two systems of reckoning discussed in the note on iii. 70, q.v.

to leave the matter in the hands of the Delphian oracle. But they deprecated war, and declared that, if war there must be, they would be compelled by the Corinthians in self-defence to discard their present friends and seek others whom they would rather not, for help they must have. The Corinthians replied that if the Corcyraeans would withdraw the ships and the barbarian troops they would consider the matter, but that it would not do for them to be litigating while Epidamnus and the colonists were in a state of siege. The Corcyraeans rejoined that they would consent to this proposal if the Corinthians on their part would withdraw their forces from Epidamnus: [a] or again, they were willing that both parties should remain [a] on the spot, and that a truce should be made until the decision was given.

The Corinthians refuse, and declare war. Sailing towards Epidamnus they are met and attacked by the Corcyraeans and completely defeated. On the same day Epidamnus surrenders.

The Corinthians turned a deaf ear to all these overtures, 29
and, when their vessels were manned and their allies had arrived, they sent a herald before them to declare war, and set sail for Epidamnus with seventy-five ships and two thousand hoplites, intending to give battle to the Corcyraeans. Their fleet was commanded by Aristeus the son of Pellichus, Callicrates the son of Callias, and Timanor the son of Timanthes; the land forces by Archetimus the son of Eurytimus, and Isarchidas the son of Isarchus. When they arrived at Actium in the territory of Anactorium, at the mouth of the Ambracian gulf, where the temple of Apollo stands, the Corcyraeans sent a herald to meet them in a small boat forbidding them to come on. Meanwhile their crews got on board; they had previously put their fleet in repair, and strengthened the old ships with cross-timbers, so as to make them serviceable. The herald brought back no message of peace

[a] Or, 'or again, they would agree to arbitration on the condition that both parties should remain' etc.

from the Corinthians. The Corcyraean ships, numbering eighty (for forty out of the hundred and twenty were engaged in the blockade of Epidamnus), were now fully manned; these sailed out against the Corinthians and, forming line, fought and won a complete victory over them, and destroyed fifteen of their ships. On the very same day the forces besieging Epidamnus succeeded in compelling the city to capitulate, the terms being that the Corinthians until their fate was determined should be imprisoned and the strangers sold.

The Corcyraeans, having command of the sea, plunder the allies of Corinth.

30 After the sea-fight the Corcyraeans raised a trophy on Leucimnè, a promontory of Corcyra, and put to death all their prisoners with the exception of the Corinthians, whom they kept in chains. The defeated Corinthians and their allies then returned home, and the Corcyraeans (who were now masters of the Ionian sea), sailing to Leucas, a Corinthian colony, devastated the country. They also burnt Cyllenè, where the Eleans had their docks, because they had supplied the Corinthians with money and ships. And, during the greater part of the summer after the battle, they retained the command of the sea and sailed about plundering the allies of the Corinthians. But, before the season was over, the Corinthians, perceiving that their allies were suffering, sent out a fleet and took up a position at Actium and near the promontory of Cheimerium in Thesprotia, that they might protect Leucas and other friendly places. The Corcyraeans with their fleet and army stationed themselves on the opposite coast at Leucimnè. Neither party attacked the other, but during the remainder of the summer they maintained their respective stations, and at the approach of winter returned home.

At length the Corinthians form a camp to protect them.

31 For the whole year after the battle and for a year after
B.C. 435, 434. Ol. 86, 2, 3. that, the Corinthians, exasperated by the war with Corcyra, were busy in building ships. They took the utmost pains

to create a great navy: rowers were collected from the Peloponnesus and from the rest of Hellas by the attraction of pay. The Corcyraeans were alarmed at the report of their preparations. They reflected that they had not enrolled themselves in the league either of the Athenians or of the Lacedaemonians, and that allies in Hellas they had none. They determined to go to Athens, join the Athenian alliance, and get what help they could from them. The Corinthians, hearing of their intentions, also sent ambassadors to Athens, fearing lest the combination of the Athenian and Corcyraean navies might prevent them from bringing the war to a satisfactory termination.

The Corinthians prepare to renew the war, and the Corcyraeans in alarm send an embassy to Athens, whither they are followed by Corinthian envoys.

Accordingly an assembly was held at which both parties B.C. 433.
came forward to plead their respective causes; and first Ol. 86, 4.
the Corcyraeans spoke as follows:—

32 'Men of Athens, those who, like ourselves, come to others who are not their allies and to whom they have never rendered any considerable service and ask help of them, are bound to show, in the first place, that the granting of their request is expedient, or at any rate not inexpedient, and, secondly, that their gratitude will be lasting. If they fulfil neither requirement they have no right to complain of a refusal. Now the Corcyraeans, when they sent us hither to ask for an alliance, were confident that they could establish to your satisfaction both these points. But, unfortunately, we have had a practice alike inconsistent with the request which we are about to make and contrary to our own interest at the present moment:—Inconsistent; for hitherto we have never, if we could avoid it, been the allies of others, and now we come and ask you to enter into an alliance with us:—Contrary to our interest; for through this practice we find ourselves isolated in our war with the Corinthians. The policy of not making alliances lest they should endanger us at another's bidding, instead of being

Speech of the Corcyraeans.

wisdom, as we once fancied, has now unmistakably proved to be weakness and folly. True, in the last naval engagement we repelled the Corinthians single-handed. But now they are on the point of attacking us with a much greater force which they have drawn together from the Peloponnesus and from all Hellas. We know that we are too weak to resist them unaided, and may expect the worst if we fall into their hands. We are therefore compelled to ask assistance of you and of all the world; and you must not be hard upon us if now, renouncing our indolent neutrality which was an error but not a crime, we dare to be inconsistent.

Our neutrality was a mistake, and has left us isolated at the mercy of the Corinthians and their allies.

33 'To you at this moment the request which we are making offers a glorious opportunity. In the first place, you will assist the oppressed and not the oppressors; secondly, you will admit us to your alliance at a time when our dearest interests are at stake, and will lay up a treasure of gratitude in our memories which will have the most abiding of all records. Lastly, we have a navy greater than any but your own. Reflect; what good fortune can be more extraordinary, what more annoying to your enemies than the voluntary accession of a power for whose alliance you would have given any amount of money and could never have been too thankful? This power now places herself at your disposal; you are to incur no danger and no expense, and she brings you a good name in the world, gratitude from those who seek your aid, and an increase of your own strength. Few have ever had all these advantages offered them at once; equally few when they come asking an alliance are able to give in the way of security and honour as much as they hope to receive.

We ask the aid of Athens, who will thus assist the oppressed, and gain our undying affection. She should not reject the offer of the Corcyraean navy.

'And if any one thinks that the war in which our services may be needed will never arrive, he is mistaken. He does not see that the Lacedaemonians, fearing the growth of your empire, are eager to take up arms, and that the Corinthians, who are your enemies, are all-powerful with them. They begin with us, but they will go on to you, that we may not stand united against them in the bond of a common enmity; they will not miss the chance of weakening us or strengthening themselves. And it is our business to strike first, we offering and you accepting our alliance, and to forestall their designs instead of waiting to counteract them.

For war is imminent.

'If they say that we are their colony and that therefore 34
you have no right to receive us, they should be made to understand that all colonies honour their mother-city when she treats them well, but are estranged from her by injustice. For colonists are not meant to be the servants but the equals of those who remain at home. And the injustice of their conduct to us is manifest: for we proposed an arbitration in the matter of Epidamnus, but they insisted on prosecuting their quarrel by arms and would not hear of a legal trial[a]. When you see how they treat us who are their own kinsmen, take warning: if they try deception, do not be misled by them; and if they make a direct request of you, refuse. For he passes through life most securely who has least reason to reproach himself with complaisance to his enemies.

True, we are a colony of the Corinthians, but that is no reason why we should be wronged by them.

'But again, you will not break the treaty with the Lace- 35
daemonians[b] by receiving us: for we are not allies either of you or of them. What says the treaty?—"Any Hellenic city which is the ally of no one may join whichever league it pleases." And how monstrous, that they should man their ships, not only from their own confederacy, but from Hellas in general, nay, even from your subjects, while they would debar us from

Reasons why the Athenians should receive the Corcyraeans into alliance. They will not break the treaty.

---

[a] Cp. i. 29 init.

[b] Cp. i. 115 init.

the alliance which naturally offers and from every other, and will denounce it as a crime if you accede to our request. With far better reason shall we complain of you if you refuse. For you will be thrusting away us who are not your enemies and are in peril; and, far from restraining the enemy and the aggressor, you will be allowing him to gather fresh forces out of your own dominions. How unjust is this! Surely if you would be impartial you should either prevent the Corinthians from hiring soldiers in your dominions, or send to us also such help as you can be induced to send; but it would be best of all if you would openly receive and assist us. Many, as we have already intimated, are the advantages which we offer. Above all, our enemies are your enemies, which is the best guarantee of fidelity in an ally; and they are not weak but well able to injure those who secede from them. Again, when the proffered alliance is that of a maritime and not of an inland power, it is a far more serious matter to refuse. You should, if possible, allow no one to have a fleet but yourselves; or, if this is impossible, whoever is strongest at sea, make him your friend.

They cannot afford to be scrupulous; Corcyra is on the way to Sicily; and is one of the three great maritime powers of Hellas.

36 'Some one may think that the course which we recommend is expedient, but he may be afraid that if he is convinced by our arguments he will break the treaty. To him we reply, that as long as he is strong he may make a present of his fears to the enemy, but that if he reject the alliance he will be weak, and then his confidence, however reassuring to himself, will be anything but terrifying to enemies who are strong. It is Athens about which he is advising, and not Corcyra: will he be providing for her best interests if, when war is imminent and almost at the door, he is so anxious about the chances of the hour that he hesitates to attach to him a state which cannot be made a friend or enemy without momentous consequences? Corcyra, besides offering many other advantages, is conveniently

situated for the coast voyage to Italy and Sicily; it stands in the way of any fleet coming from thence to the Peloponnesus, and can also protect a fleet on its way to Sicily. One word more, which is the sum of all and everything we have to say, and should convince you that you must not abandon us. Hellas has only three considerable navies:—there is ours, and there is yours, and there is the Corinthian. Now, if the Corinthians get hold of ours, and you allow the two to become one, you will have to fight against the united navies of Corcyra and the Peloponnesus. But, if you make us your allies, you will have our navy in addition to your own ranged at your side in the impending conflict.'

Thus spoke the Corcyraeans: the Corinthians replied as follows:—

'Since these Corcyraeans have chosen to speak, not 37
only of their reception into your alliance, but of our misdoings and of the unjust war which has been forced upon them by us, we too must touch on these two points before we proceed to our main argument, that you may be better prepared to appreciate our claim upon you, and may have a good reason for rejecting their petition. They pretend that they have hitherto refused to make alliances from a wise moderation, but they really adopted this policy from a mean and not from a high motive. They did not want to have an ally who might go and tell of their crimes, and who would put them to the blush whenever they called him in. Their insular position makes them judges of their own offences against others, and they can therefore afford to dispense with judges appointed under treaties; for they hardly ever visit their neighbours, but foreign ships are constantly driven to their shores by stress of weather. And all the time they screen themselves under the specious name of neutrality, making believe that they are unwilling to be the accomplices of other men's crimes. But the truth is that they wish to

The neutrality of the Corcyraeans a pretence by which they conceal their crimes.

keep their own criminal courses to themselves: where they are strong, to oppress; where they cannot be found out, to defraud; and whatever they may contrive to appropriate, never to be ashamed. If they were really upright men, as they profess to be, the greater their immunity from attack the more clearly they might have made their honesty appear by a willingness to submit differences to arbitration.

38 'But such they have not shown themselves either towards us or towards others. Although they are our colony they have always stood aloof from us, and now they are fighting against us on the plea that they were not sent out to be ill used. To which we rejoin that we did not send them out to be insulted by them, but that we might be recognised as their leaders and receive proper respect. Our other colonies at any rate honour us; no city is more beloved by her colonies than Corinth. That we are popular with the majority proves that the Corcyraeans have no reason to dislike us; [a] and, if it seems extraordinary that we should go to war with them, our defence is that the injury which they are doing us is unexampled [a]. Even if we had been misled by passion, it would have been honourable in them to make allowance for us, and dishonourable in us to use violence when they showed moderation. But they have wronged us over and over again in their insolence and pride of wealth; and now there is our colony of Epidamnus which they would not acknowledge in her distress, but, when we came to her rescue, they seized and are now holding by force.

We go to war with them because they have wronged and insulted us.

39 'They pretend that they first offered to have the matter decided by arbitration. The appeal to justice might have some meaning in the mouth of one [b] who before he had

[a] Or, 'and there is nothing extraordinary in our going to war with them, for they are doing us an unexampled injury.'

[b] Or, 'whose actions corresponded to his professions, before he entered on the struggle.'

recourse to arms acted honourably, as he now talks fairly [b], but not when it is made from a position of security and advantage. Whereas these men began by laying siege to Epidamnus, and not until they feared our vengeance did they put forward their specious offer of arbitration. And as if the wrong which they have themselves done at Epidamnus were not enough, they now come hither and ask you to be, not their allies, but their accomplices in crime, and would have you receive them when they are at enmity with us. But they ought to have come when they were out of all danger, not at a time when we are smarting under an injury and they have good reason to be afraid. You have never derived any benefit from their power, but they will now be benefited by yours, and, although innocent of their crimes, you will equally be held responsible by us. If you were to have shared the consequences with them, they ought long ago to have shared the power with you [a].

The Corcyraeans propose arbitration and request your help only when they are in danger.

'We have proved that our complaints are justified and 40
that our adversaries are tyrannical and dishonest; we will now show you that you have no right to receive them. Admitting that the treaty allows any unenrolled cities to join either league, this provision does not apply to those who have in view the injury of others, but only to him who is in need of protection,—certainly not to one who forsakes his allegiance and who will bring war instead of peace to those who receive him, or rather, if they are wise, will not receive him on such terms. And war the Corcyraeans will bring to you if you listen to them and not to us. For if you become the allies

You will break the treaty by receiving them, and will compel us to be your enemies.

---

[a] The last words of the chapter are omitted by Poppo on the authority of several of the best MSS.; they may perhaps be a gloss. If they are retained they may be translated: 'But you ought not to share all the consequences of their crimes, while in the crimes, and in them alone, you have no part.'

of the Corcyraeans you will be no longer at peace with us, but will be converted into enemies; and we must, if you take their part, in defending ourselves against them, defend ourselves against you. But you ought in common justice to stand aloof from both; or, if you must join either, you should join us and go to war with them; to Corinth you are at all events bound by treaty, but with Corcyra you never even entered into a temporary negotiation.

We did not encourage your rebellious subjects, and you should not receive ours.

B.C. 440. Ol. 85.

And do not set the precedent of receiving the rebellious subjects of others. At the revolt of Samos [a], when the other Peloponnesians were divided upon the question of giving aid to the rebels, we voted in your favour and expressly maintained "that every one should be allowed to chastise his own allies." If you mean to receive and assist evil-doers, we shall assuredly gain as many allies of yours as you will of ours; and you will establish a principle which will tell against yourselves more than against us.

41 'Such are the grounds of right which we urge; and they are sufficient according to Hellenic law. And may we venture to recall to your minds an obligation of which we claim the repayment in our present need, we and you being not enemies who seek one another's

We lent you twenty ships in the Aeginetan war.

B.C. 491. Ol. 72. 2.

hurt, nor yet friends who freely give and take? There was a time before the Persian invasion when you were in want of ships for the Aeginetan war, and we Corinthians lent you twenty: the service which we then rendered to you gave you the victory over the Aeginetans [b], as the other, which prevented the Peloponnesians from aiding the Samians, enabled you to punish Samos. Both benefits were conferred on one of those critical occasions when men in the act of attacking their enemies are utterly regardless of everything but victory, and deem him who

[a] Cp. i. 115.

[b] Cp. Herod. vi. 89.

assists them a friend though he may have previously been a foe, him who opposes them a foe, even though he may happen to be a friend; nay, they will often neglect their own interests in the excitement of the struggle.

'Think of these things; let the younger be informed 42
of them by their elders, and resolve all of you to render B.C. 433 Ol. 86, 4.
like for like. Do not say to yourselves that this is just, but that in the event of war something else is expedient; for the true path of expediency is the path of right. The war with which the Corcyraeans would frighten you into doing wrong is distant, and may never come; is it worth while to be so carried away by the prospect of it, that you bring upon yourselves the hatred of the Corinthians which is both near and certain? Would you not be wiser in seeking to mitigate the ill-feeling which your treatment of the Megarians has already inspired[a]? The later kindness done in season, though small in comparison, may cancel a greater previous offence. And do not be attracted by their offer of a great naval alliance; for to do no wrong to a neighbour is a surer source of strength than to gain a perilous advantage under the influence of a momentary illusion.

To do no wrong is better than a great naval alliance.

'We are now ourselves in the same situation in which 43
you were, when we declared at Sparta that every one so placed should be allowed to chastise his own allies; and we claim to receive the same measure at your hands. You were profited by our vote, and we ought not to be injured by yours. Pay what you owe, knowing that this is our time of need, in which a man's best friend is he who does him a service, he who opposes him, his worst enemy. Do not receive these Corcyraeans into alliance in despite of us, and do not support them in injustice. In acting thus you will act rightly, and will consult your own true interests.'

---

[a] Cp. i. 67 fin.

Such were the words of the Corinthians.

44 The Athenians heard both sides, and they held two assemblies; in the first of them they were more influenced by the words of the Corinthians, but in the second they changed their minds and inclined towards the Corcyraeans. They would not go so far as to make an alliance both offensive and defensive with them; for then, if the Corcyraeans had required them to join in an expedition against Corinth, the treaty with the Peloponnesians would have been broken. But they concluded a defensive league, by which the two states promised to aid each other if an attack were made on the territory or on the allies of either. For they knew that in any case the war with Peloponnesus was inevitable, and they had no mind to let Corcyra and her navy fall into the hands of the Corinthians. Their plan was to embroil them more and more with one another, and then, when the war came, the Corinthians and the other naval powers would be weaker. They also considered that Corcyra was conveniently situated for the coast voyage to Italy and Sicily.

The Athenians after some hesitation enter into a defensive alliance with Corcyra.

B.C. 433. Ol. 87.

Motives of the Athenians.

45 Under the influence of these feelings, they received the Corcyraeans into alliance; the Corinthians departed; and the Athenians now despatched to Corcyra ten ships commanded by Lacedaemonius the son of Cimon, Diotimus the son of Strombichus, and Proteas the son of Epicles. The commanders received orders not to engage with the Corinthians unless they sailed against Corcyra or to any place belonging to the Corcyraeans, and attempted to land there, in which case they were to resist them to the utmost. These orders were intended to prevent a breach of the treaty[a].

They send ten ships to Corcyra, giving them orders to act on the defensive.

---

[a] Cp. i. 40 init.

The Corinthians, when their preparations were completed, sailed against Corcyra with a hundred and fifty ships,—ten Elean, twelve Megarian, ten Leucadian, twenty-seven Ambraciot, one from Anactorium, and ninety of their own. The contingents of the several cities were commanded by their own generals. The Corinthian commander was Xenocleides the son of Euthycles, with four others. The fleet sailed from Leucas, and, arriving at the mainland opposite Corcyra, came to anchor at Cheimerium in the country of Thesprotia. [a] Cheimerium is only a harbour [a]; above it, at some distance from the sea, in that part of Thesprotia called Eleatis, lies the city of Ephyrè, near which the Acherusian lake finds a way out to the sea; the river Acheron, whence the name is derived, flows through Thesprotia and falls into the lake. Another river, the Thyamis, forms the boundary of Thesprotia and Cestrinè, and the promontory of Cheimerium runs out between these two rivers. Here the Corinthians anchored and formed a camp. 46

The Corinthian fleet sails against Corcyra.

B.C. 433. Ol. 86, 4.

The Corcyraeans, observing their approach, manned a hundred and ten ships. These, which were placed under the command of Meiciades, Aesimides, and Eurybatus, took up a position off one of the islands called Sybota; the ten Athenian ships accompanied them. The land forces occupied the promontory of Leucimnè, whither a thousand Zacynthians had come to the aid of Corcyra. The Corinthians on their part were supported by a large force of barbarians, which collected on the mainland; for the inhabitants of this region have always been well disposed towards them. 47

Disposition of the forces.

The Corinthians had now made their preparations, and, taking with them three days' provisions, put off by night from Cheimerium, intending to give battle: at break of day they descried the Corcyraean fleet, which had also 48

[a] Or, 'Here there is a harbour.'

put out to sea and was sailing to meet them. As soon as they saw one another, they ranged themselves in order of battle. On the right Corcyraean wing were the Athenian ships. The Corcyraeans themselves occupied the centre and the left wing, and were drawn up in three divisions, each under the command of one of the generals. On the right wing of the Corinthians were the Megarian and Ambraciot ships, in the centre the contingents of their other allies; they themselves with their swiftest vessels formed the left wing, which was opposed to the Athenians and to the right division of the Corcyraeans.

49 The standards were now raised on both sides, and the two fleets met and fought. The decks of both were crowded with heavy infantry, with archers and with javelin-men; for their naval arrangements were still of the old clumsy sort. The engagement was obstinate, but more courage than skill was displayed, and it had almost the appearance of a battle by land. When two ships once charged one another it was hardly possible to part company, for the throng of vessels was dense, and the hopes of victory lay chiefly in the heavy-armed, who maintained a steady fight upon the decks, the ships meanwhile remaining motionless. There were no attempts to break the enemy's line. Brute force and rage made up for the want of tactics. Everywhere the battle was a scene of tumult and confusion. At any point where they saw the Corcyraeans distressed, the Athenians appeared and kept the enemy in check; but the generals, who were afraid of disobeying their instructions, would not begin the attack themselves. The Corinthians suffered most on their right wing. For the Corcyraeans with twenty ships routed them, drove them in disorder to the shore, and sailed right up to their encampment; there landing, they plundered and burnt the deserted tents. So in this part of the battle the Corinthians and their allies were worsted, and the Corcyraeans

Character of the engagement.

Partial success of the Corcyraeans on the left wing and their complete defeat on the right.

prevailed. But the left wing of the Corinthians, where their own ships were stationed, had greatly the advantage, because the Corcyraeans, whose numbers were originally inferior, had now twenty vessels detached in the pursuit. When the Athenians saw the distress of the Corcyraeans, they began to assist them more openly. At first they had abstained from actual collision, but when the Corcyraeans fled outright and the Corinthians pressed them hard, then every man fell to work; all distinctions were forgotten;—the time had arrived when Corinthian and Athenian were driven to attack one another.

The Athenians share in the engagement.

The Corinthians, having put to flight their enemies, 50
never stopped to take in tow the hulls of the vessels which they had disabled, but fell upon the men; they rowed up and down and slew them, giving no quarter, and unintentionally killing their own friends; for they were not aware that their right wing had been defeated. There were so many ships on one side and on the other, and they covered so great an extent of water, that, when the engagement had once begun, it was hard among conquerors and conquered to distinguish friend from foe. For never before had two Hellenic navies so numerous met in battle.

When the Corinthians had chased the Corcyraeans to the shore, they turned their attention to their own wrecks and the bodies of their dead. Most of these were recovered by them and conveyed to Sybota, a desert harbour of Thesprotia, whither their barbarian allies had come to support them. They then formed afresh and once more made a movement towards the Corcyraeans, who, taking such vessels as had not been disabled, and any others which they had in their docks, together with the Athenian ships, put out to meet them, dreading a descent upon Corcyra. It was now late in the day and the Paean had been already sounded for the onset, when the Corinthians suddenly began to row astern. They had descried sailing towards them twenty vessels which the Athenians had sent to reinforce the former ten, fearing what had actually happened, that the Corcyraeans would be defeated, and that the original squadron would be insufficient to protect them.

Sudden appearance of twenty Athenian ships.

51 The Corinthians, who had the first view of these vessels, suspecting that they were Athenian and that there were more of them than they saw, were beginning to retreat. The Corcyraeans, owing to their position, could not see them, and they wondered why the Corinthians rowed astern. At length some of them who spied the advancing fleet exclaimed, 'Yonder are ships coming up;' and then the Corcyraeans, as it was getting dark, likewise retired, and the Corinthians turned about and sailed away. Thus the two fleets separated after a battle which lasted until nightfall. The twenty ships which came from Athens under the command of Glaucon the son of Leagrus, and Andocides the son of Leogoras, made their way through the wrecks and corpses and sailed into the Corcyraean station at Leucimnè almost as soon as they were sighted. At first in the darkness the Corcyraeans feared that they were enemies, but they soon recognised them and the Athenian vessels came to anchor.

The two fleets separate.

52 On the next day the thirty Athenian and all the Corcyraean ships which were fit for service, wanting to ascertain whether the Corinthians would fight, sailed to the harbour at Sybota where their fleet lay. The Corinthians, putting out into deep water, drew up their ships in line and so remained, but they did not intend to begin the battle. For they saw that fresh ships, which had received no damage in the action, had arrived from Athens, and their own position was one of great difficulty. They had to guard the prisoners in their vessels, and there were no means of refitting in such a desert place. They were

The Corinthians want to return home.

more disposed to consider how they should get home than to fight. For they feared that the Athenians, deeming the peace, now that blows had been exchanged, to be already broken, would intercept their return.

They therefore determined to send a few men in a boat 53
without a flag of truce to the Athenians, and so test their intentions. The men were to deliver the following message: 'You do wrong, Athenians, to begin war and violate the treaty. We were only chastising our enemies, and you come with a hostile force and place yourselves between us and them. If it is your intention to hinder us from sailing to Corcyra, or whithersoever we choose, and you are going to break the treaty, take us first and deal with us as enemies.' Whereupon all the Corcyraeans who were within hearing cried out 'Take and kill them.' But the Athenians replied: 'Men of Peloponnesus, we are not beginning war, and we are not violating the treaty; we are only aiding the Corcyraeans here, who are our allies. If you mean to sail against Corcyra or any place belonging to the Corcyraeans, we will do our utmost to prevent you, but, if you want to go anywhere else, you may.'

They hold a parley with the Athenians.

Reassured by this reply, the Corinthians prepared to 54
sail home, first setting up a trophy at the Sybota which is on the mainland. The Corcyraeans took up the wrecks and dead bodies which were carried towards them, the current and the wind which had risen during the night having scattered them in all directions. They then set up a rival trophy on the island of Sybota. Both parties claimed the victory, but on different grounds. The Corinthians had retained the advantage in the sea-fight until nightfall, and had thus secured a greater number of wrecks and dead bodies; they had taken not less than a thousand prisoners and had disabled about seventy ships. The Corcyraeans, on the other hand, had destroyed some thirty sail, and when reinforced by the Athenians had

The Corinthians return home, capturing Anactorium on the voyage.

taken up the wrecks and dead bodies which had drifted in their direction; whereas the enemy on the evening of the battle had rowed astern at sight of the Athenian ships, and after their arrival had not come out against them from Sybota. Upon these grounds both sides raised trophies
55 and claimed the victory. On their homeward voyage the Corinthians took by stratagem Anactorium, a town situated at the mouth of the Ambracian Gulf, which they and the Corcyraeans held in common; there they settled colonists of their own, and returned to Corinth. Of their Corcyraean captives eight hundred who were slaves they sold, but two hundred and fifty they detained in prison, treating them with much consideration, in the hope that, when they returned, they would win over Corcyra to the Corinthian interest [a]: it so happened that the majority of them were among the most influential men of the state. Thus the war ended to the advantage of Corcyra, and the Athenian fleet returned home. This was the first among the causes of the Peloponnesian War, the Corinthians alleging that the Athenian fleet had taken part with the Corcyraeans and had fought against them in a time of truce.

56 There soon arose another cause of quarrel between the

Quarrel with Potidaea. The Athenians command the Potidaeans to raze their walls and to give hostages.

Athenians and Peloponnesians. Potidaea, which is situated on the isthmus of Pallenè, was originally a Corinthian colony, although at this time the tribu-
B.C. 433 or 432. Ol. 86, 4; or 87, 1. tary and ally of Athens. Now the Corinthians were forming plans of vengeance, and the Athenians, who suspected their intentions, commanded the Potidaeans to raze their walls on the side of Pallenè and give hostages; also to send away and not to receive for the future the magistrates whom the Corinthians annually sent to them. For they were afraid lest the Potidaeans might be persuaded by the Corinthians and Perdiccas to revolt,

[a] Cp. iii. 70.

and might induce the rest of Chalcidicè to follow their example.

These measures of precaution were taken by the 57
Athenians immediately after the sea-fight off Corcyra. The hostility of the Corinthians was no longer doubtful, and Perdiccas, king of Macedon, the son of Alexander, hitherto the friend and ally of Athens, had now become an enemy. He had quarrelled with the Athenians because they had made an alliance with his brother Philip and with Derdas, who were leagued against him. Alarmed by their attitude, he sent envoys to Sparta and did all he could to stir up a war between Athens and the Peloponnese. He also sought the alliance of Corinth, for he had an eye to the revolt of Potidaea; and he proposed to the Chalcidians and to the Bottiaeans that they should join in the revolt, thinking, that if he had the assistance of the neighbouring peoples, the difficulties of the war would be diminished. The Athenians became aware of his designs and resolved to forestall the revolt of the cities. They were already intending to send against Perdiccas thirty ships and a thousand hoplites under the command of Archestratus the son of Lycomedes, and [a] ten others, and they told their admirals to take hostages from the Potidaeans and to demolish their wall. They were also to keep a watch over the towns in the neighbourhood and prevent any attempt at rebellion.

Perdiccas who had quarrelled with the Athenians tries to stir up war between Peloponnesus and Athens.

Meanwhile the Potidaeans sent envoys to the Athenians 58
in the hope of persuading them to take no strong measures; but at the same time other envoys of theirs accompanied a Corinthian embassy to Lacedaemon and exerted themselves to procure assistance in case of need. A long negotiation was carried on at Athens which came to no satisfactory result; the ships destined for Macedonia were

The Potidaeans send envoys to Athens and Sparta.

[a] Or *e conj.* 'four.'

also sent against Potidaea. But at Lacedaemon they were promised by the magistrates that if the Athenians attacked Potidaea they would invade Attica. So they seized the opportunity and revolted: the Chalcidians and Bottiaeans swore alliance with them and joined in the revolt. Perdiccas persuaded the Chalcidians to abandon and pull down their towns on the sea-coast, and settling at Olynthus inland, there to form one strong city. On their removal he gave them part of his own territory of Mygdonia about the lake Bolbè to cultivate while the contest lasted. So, dismantling their cities, they settled up the country and made preparation for war.

They receive promises of assistance from Sparta, and revolt.

B.C. 432. Ol. 87, 1.

59 The Athenians, when the thirty ships arrived in Chalcidicè, found that Potidaea and the other cities had already revolted. Whereupon the generals, thinking that they were not able without a stronger force to act against all the rebels as well as against Perdiccas, directed their attention to Macedonia, which was their original destination, and there carried on a regular campaign in concert with Philip and the brothers of Derdas, who had invaded the country from the interior.

The Athenians under Archestratus arrive in Chalcidicè. They first attack Macedonia.

60 Now that Potidaea had revolted and the Athenian ships were on the coast of Macedonia, the Corinthians grew anxious about the town; they felt that the danger came home to them, and despatched thither volunteers of their own and other troops whom they attracted by pay from various parts of the Peloponnese, numbering in all sixteen hundred hoplites and four hundred light-armed. Their commander was Aristeus the son of Adeimantus, who had always been a great friend of the Potidaeans; it was mainly out of regard for him that most of the Corinthian soldiers volunteered on the expedition. They arrived in Chalcidicè forty days after the revolt of Potidaea.

The Corinthians send troops to the aid of Potidaea under the command of Aristeus.

The news of the revolt in Chalcidicè quickly reached 61
Athens, and the Athenians, when they heard that Aristeus had come with reinforcements, sent against the revolted towns forty ships and two thousand of their own hoplites under the command of Callias the son of Calliades, and four others. The expedition, sailing first of all to Macedonia, found that the former thousand had just taken Thermè and were blockading Pydna; they joined in the siege themselves; but before long the Athenian army were constrained to come to an understanding and make an alliance with Perdiccas. For Potidaea, now that Aristeus had arrived, urgently demanded their presence; so they prepared to quit Macedonia. They first marched out of their way to Beroea, which they attempted to take without success. Returning to their route, they moved on by land towards Potidaea with three thousand hoplites of their own and a large force of allies; they had also six hundred Macedonian horse, who fought under Philip and Pausanias; meanwhile their ships, in number seventy, sailed along the coast. Proceeding by slow marches, they arrived on the third day at Gigonus and there encamped.

Athenian reinforcements under Callias arrive in Macedonia; the Athenians make a temporary peace with Perdiccas and move on to Potidaea.

The Potidaeans and the Peloponnesian force under 62
Aristeus had now taken up a position at the isthmus on the side towards Olynthus[a], where they awaited the coming of the Athenians; they held their market outside the walls of Potidaea. The allies had chosen Aristeus general of all the infantry, and of the cavalry Perdiccas, for he had no sooner joined than he again deserted the Athenians and was now fighting on the side of the Potidaeans, having appointed Iolaus [b]to be his lieutenant at home[b]. The plan of Aristeus was as follows:—His own army was to remain on the isthmus

Engagement at the isthmus of Pallenè.

[a] Reading πρὸς Ὀλύνθου.

[b] Or, 'to take his place with the expedition:' cp. *infra*, τὴν παρὰ Περδίκκου διακοσίαν ἵππον.

and watch for the approach of the Athenians, while the Chalcidians, their allies from beyond the isthmus, and the two hundred horse furnished by Perdiccas were stationed at Olynthus; and as soon as the Athenians attacked Aristeus himself and his army, they were to fall upon them in the rear; thus the enemy would be assailed on both sides. But Callias the Athenian general and his colleagues sent the Macedonian horse and a few of the allied troops towards Olynthus that they might check any movement in that quarter, while they themselves, quitting their position, marched against Potidaea. When they had reached the isthmus and saw the enemy preparing for battle, they did the same. The two armies soon closed. The wing led by Aristeus, which was composed of his Corinthian followers and other picked troops, routed their opponents and chased them far away; but the rest of the army, both Potidaeans and Peloponnesians, were defeated by the Athenians and fled into the city.

The army of Aristeus is partially defeated; he succeeds in making his way back to Potidaea.

63 Aristeus, when he returned from the pursuit and perceived that the other wing of his army was defeated, hesitated whether he should make for Olynthus or return to Potidaea. Both courses were hazardous; but at last he determined to contract his troops into the smallest compass and force his way at full speed into Potidaea. Harassed by the missiles of the enemy he pushed forward through the water[a] along the bank in front of the sea-wall, not without loss; but he contrived to save the greater part of his men. When the battle began, the allies of the Potidaeans in Olynthus, which is only about seven miles[b] distant, and is visible from Potidaea, seeing the signals raised, came out a little way to support their friends; and the Macedonian horse drew up in order of battle to oppose them. But victory quickly declared for

[a] Cp. Herod. viii. 129.

[b] Sixty stadia, the stadium being reckoned at two hundred and two yards.

the Athenians; and when the signals were torn down the Olynthian auxiliaries retired within the walls, and the Macedonians rejoined the Athenians: thus on neither side did the cavalry take any part in the action. The Athenians raised a trophy and granted the Potidaeans a truce for the burial of their dead. Of the Potidaeans and their allies, there fell somewhat less than three hundred; of the Athenians, a hundred and fifty, and their general Callias.

The Athenians instantly blockaded the town on the side 64
towards the isthmus, raising a wall, which they guarded; but the side towards Pallenè was left open. They were conscious that they were too weak both to guard the isthmus and, crossing over to Pallenè, there to build another wall; they feared that their forces if divided would be attacked by the Potidaeans and their allies. Afterwards, when the Athenians at home heard that on the side towards Pallenè Potidaea was not invested, they sent out sixteen hundred hoplites of their own under the command of Phormio the son of Asopius. On his arrival in Pallenè he made Aphytis his head-quarters, and brought his army by slow marches up to Potidaea, wasting the country as he went along. No one came out to meet him, and so he built a wall towards Pallenè. Potidaea was now closely invested on both sides, while the Athenian ships, lying off the city, cut off all communication from the sea.

The Athenians blockade Potidaea: at first only on the side towards the isthmus; afterwards, by the help of reinforcements under Phormio, on the side towards Pallenè.

Aristeus despaired of saving the place unless aid came 65
from Peloponnesus or he was relieved in some unforeseen manner. Being anxious to husband provisions, he proposed to the garrison that they should avail themselves of the first favourable wind and sail away, leaving behind five hundred men, of whom he offered to be one. But they would not listen to him; so, wanting to do the best he could, and to further the Peloponnesian interests beyond the walls, he sailed out undiscovered by

Aristeus leaves Potidaea and carries on the war outside the walls.

the Athenian guard-ships. He did not leave the country, but assisted the Chalcidians in carrying on the war. He succeeded in cutting off a large force of Sermylians by an ambuscade which he laid near their city; he also exerted himself to obtain aid from Peloponnesus. Phormio with his sixteen hundred hoplites, now that Potidaea was invested, ravaged Chalcidicè and Botticè, and captured several places.

66 Such were the causes of ill-feeling which at this time existed between the Athenians and Peloponnesians: the Corinthians complaining that the Athenians were blockading their colony of Potidaea, and a Corinthian and Peloponnesian garrison in it; the Athenians rejoining that a member of the Peloponnesian confederacy had excited to revolt a state which was an ally and tributary of theirs, and that they had now openly joined the Potidaeans, and were fighting on their side. The Peloponnesian war, however, had not yet broken out; the peace still continued; for thus far the Corinthians had acted alone.

Excitement of the Corinthians. Assembly at Sparta. Grievances of the Aeginetans and Megarians.

67 But now, seeing Potidaea besieged, they bestirred themselves in earnest. Corinthian troops were shut up within the walls, and they were afraid of losing the town; so without delay they invited the allies to meet at Sparta. There they inveighed against the Athenians, whom they affirmed to have broken the treaty and to be wronging the Peloponnese. The Aeginetans did not venture to send envoys openly, but secretly they acted with the Corinthians, and were among the chief instigators of the war, declaring that they had been robbed of the independence which the treaty guaranteed them. The Lacedaemonians themselves then [a]proceeded to summon any of the allies who had similar charges[a]

[a] Or, adopting the inferior reading τῶν ξυμμάχων τε καὶ εἴ τις: 'proceeded to summon any of their own allies, and any one else, who had similar charges,' etc.

to bring against the Athenians, and calling their own ordinary assembly told them to speak. Several of them came forward and stated their wrongs. The Megarians alleged, among other grounds of complaint, that they were excluded from all harbours within the Athenian dominion and from the Athenian market, contrary to the treaty. The Corinthians waited until the other allies had stirred up the Lacedaemonians; at length they came forward, and, last of all, spoke as follows:—

'The spirit of trust, Lacedaemonians, which animates 68
your own political and social life, [a]makes you distrust others who, like ourselves, have something unpleasant to say[a], and this temper of mind, though favourable to moderation, too often leaves you in ignorance of what is going on outside your own country. Time after time we have warned you of the mischief which the Athenians would do to us, but instead of taking our words to heart, you chose to suspect that we only spoke from interested motives. And this is the reason why you have brought the allies to Sparta too late, not before but after the injury has been inflicted, and when they are smarting under the sense of it. Which of them all has a better right to speak than ourselves, who have the heaviest accusations to make, outraged as we are by the Athenians, and neglected by you? If the crimes which they are committing against Hellas were being done in a corner, then you might be ignorant, and we should have to inform you of them: but now, what need of many words? Some of us, as you see, have been already enslaved; they are at this moment intriguing against others, notably against allies of ours; and long ago they had made all their preparations in the prospect of war. Else why did they seduce from her allegiance Corcyra, which they still hold in defiance of

The Corinthians complain of the delays of the Lacedaemonians,

[a] Or, 'makes you distrustful of us when we bring a charge against others.'

us, and why are they blockading Potidaea, the latter a most advantageous post for the command of the Thracian peninsula, the former a great naval power which might have assisted the Peloponnesians?

69 'And the blame of all this rests on you; for you originally allowed them to fortify their city after the Persian War[a], and afterwards to build their Long Walls[b]; and to this hour you have gone on defrauding of liberty their unfortunate subjects, and are now beginning to take it away from your own allies. For the true enslaver of a people is he who can put an end to their slavery but has no care about it; and all the more, if he be reputed the champion of liberty in Hellas.—And so we have met at last, but with what difficulty! and even now we have no definite object. By this time we ought to have been considering, not whether we are wronged, but how we are to be revenged. The aggressor is not now threatening, but advancing; he has made up his mind, while we are resolved about nothing. And we know too well how by slow degrees and with stealthy steps the Athenians encroach upon their neighbours. While they think that you are too dull to observe them, they are more careful, but, when they know that you wilfully overlook their aggressions, they will strike and not spare. Of all Hellenes, Lacedaemonians, you are the only people who never do anything: on the approach of an enemy you are content to defend yourselves against him, not by acts, but by intentions, and seek to overthrow him, not in the infancy but in the fulness of his strength. How came you to be considered safe? That reputation of yours was never justified by facts. We all know that the Persian made his way from the ends of the earth against Peloponnesus before you encountered him in a worthy manner; and now you are blind to the doings of the Athenians, who

who have enslaved Hellas by not preventing her enslavement.

---

[a] Cp. i. 90-92.

[b] Cp. i. 107.

are not at a distance as he was, but close at hand. Instead of attacking your enemy, you wait to be attacked, and take the chances of a struggle which has been deferred until his power is doubled. And you know that the Barbarian miscarried chiefly through his own errors; and that we have oftener been delivered from these very Athenians by blunders of their own, than by any aid from you. Some have already been ruined by the hopes which you inspired in them; for so entirely did they trust you that they took no precautions themselves. These things we say in no accusing or hostile spirit—let that be understood—but by way of expostulation. For men expostulate with erring friends, they bring accusation against enemies who have done them a wrong.

'And surely we have a right to find fault with our 70
neighbours, if any one ever had. There are important interests at stake to which, as far as we can see, you are insensible. And you have never considered what manner of men are these Athenians[a] with whom you will have to fight, and how utterly unlike yourselves. They are revolutionary, equally quick in the conception and in the execution of every new plan; while you are conservative—careful only to keep what you have, originating nothing, and not acting even when action is most urgent. They are bold beyond their strength; they run risks which prudence would condemn; and in the midst of misfortune they are full of hope. Whereas it is your nature, though strong, to act feebly; when your plans are most prudent, to distrust them; and when calamities come upon you, to think that you will never be delivered from them. They are impetuous, and you are dilatory; they are always abroad, and you are always at home. For they hope to gain something by leaving their homes; but you are afraid

Contrast of the Athenian and Spartan characters.

[a] For descriptions of Athenian character, cp. ii. 37 ff.; iii. 38; 42, 43; vi. 76; 87.

that any new enterprise may imperil what you have already. When conquerors, they pursue their victory to the utmost; when defeated, they fall back the least. Their bodies they devote to their country as though they belonged to other men; their true self is their mind, which is most truly their own when employed in her service. When they do not carry out an intention which they have formed, they seem to themselves to have sustained a personal bereavement; when an enterprise succeeds, they have gained a mere instalment of what is to come; but if they fail, they at once conceive new hopes and so fill up the void. With them alone to hope is to have, for they lose not a moment in the execution of an idea. This is the lifelong task, full of danger and toil, which they are always imposing upon themselves. None enjoy their good things less, because they are always seeking for more. To do their duty is their only holiday, and they deem the quiet of inaction to be as disagreeable as the most tiresome business. If a man should say of them, in a word, that they were born neither to have peace themselves nor to allow peace to other men, he would simply speak the truth.

The Lacedaemonians must lay aside their policy of inaction.

71 'In the face of such an enemy, Lacedaemonians, you persist in doing nothing. You do not see that peace is best secured by those who use their strength justly, but whose attitude shows that they have no intention of submitting to wrong. Justice with you seems to consist in giving no annoyance to others and [a] in defending yourselves only against positive injury [a]. But this policy would hardly be successful, even if your neighbours were like yourselves; and in the present case, as we pointed out just now, your ways compared with theirs are old-fashioned. And, as in the arts, so also in politics, the new must always prevail over the old. In settled times the traditions of govern-

[a] Or, 'in running no risk even in self-defence.'

ment should be observed: but when circumstances are changing and men are compelled to meet them, much originality is required. The Athenians have had a wider experience, and therefore the administration of their state unlike yours has been greatly reformed. But here let your procrastination end; send an army at once into Attica and assist your allies, especially the Potidaeans, to whom your word is pledged[a]. Do not betray friends and kindred into the hands of their worst enemies; or drive us in despair to seek the alliance of others; in taking such a course we should be doing nothing wrong either before the Gods who are the witnesses of our oaths, or before men whose eyes are upon us. For the true breakers of treaties[b] are not those who, when forsaken, turn to others, but those who forsake allies whom they have sworn to defend. We will remain your friends if you choose to bestir yourselves; for we should be guilty of an impiety if we deserted you without cause; and we shall not easily find allies equally congenial to us. Take heed then: you have inherited from your fathers the leadership of Peloponnesus; see that her greatness suffers no diminution at your hands.'

Some Athenian envoys who happen to be at Sparta desire to address the assembly.

Thus spoke the Corinthians. Now there happened to 72
be staying at Lacedaemon an Athenian embassy which had come on other business, and when the envoys heard what the Corinthians had said, they felt bound to go before the Lacedaemonian assembly, not with the view of answering the accusations brought against them by the cities, but they wanted to put the whole question before the Lacedaemonians, and make them understand that they should take time to deliberate and not be rash. They also desired to set forth the greatness of their city, reminding the elder men of what they knew, and informing the younger of what lay beyond their

[a] Cp. i. 58 med. [b] Cp. i. 123 fin.

experience. They thought that their words would sway the Lacedaemonians in the direction of peace. So they came and said that, if they might be allowed, they too would like to address the people. The Lacedaemonians invited them to come forward, and they spoke as follows:—

73 'We were not sent here to argue with your allies, but on a special mission; observing, however, that no small outcry has arisen against us, we have come forward, not to answer the accusations which they bring (for you are not judges before whom either we or they have to plead), but to prevent you from lending too ready an ear to their bad advice and so deciding wrongly about a very serious question. We propose also, in reply to the wider charges which are raised against us, to show that what we have acquired we hold rightfully and that our city is not to be despised.

They recall the memory of their services in the Persian War.

'Of the ancient deeds handed down by tradition and which no eye of any one who hears us ever saw, why should we speak? But of the Persian War, and other events which you yourselves remember, speak we must, [a]although we have brought them forward so often that the repetition of them is disagreeable to us[a]. When we faced those perils we did so for the common benefit: in the solid good you shared, and of the glory, whatever good there may be in that, we would not be wholly deprived. Our words are not designed to deprecate hostility, but to set forth in evidence the character of the city with which, unless you are very careful, you will soon be involved in war. We tell you that we, first and alone, dared to engage with the Barbarian at Marathon, and that when he came again, being too weak to defend ourselves by land, we and our whole people embarked on shipboard and shared with the other Hellenes in the victory of

---

[a] Or, 'although it may be disagreeable to you to hear what we are always bringing forward.'

Salamis. Thereby he was prevented from sailing to the Peloponnesus and ravaging city after city; for against so mighty a fleet how could you have helped one another? He himself is the best witness of our words; for when he was once defeated at sea, he felt that his power was gone and quickly retreated with the greater part of his army.

'The event proved undeniably that the fate of Hellas 74
depended on her navy. And the three chief elements of success were contributed by us; namely, the greatest number of ships, the ablest general, the most devoted patriotism. The ships in all numbered four hundred [a], and of these, our own contingent amounted to nearly two-thirds. To the influence of Themistocles our general it was chiefly due that we fought in the strait, which was confessedly our salvation; and for this service you yourselves honoured him above any stranger who ever visited you. Thirdly, we displayed the most extraordinary courage and devotion; there was no one to help us by land; for up to our frontier those who lay in the enemy's path were already slaves; so we determined to leave our city and sacrifice our homes. Even in that extremity we did not choose to desert the cause of the allies who still resisted, or by dispersing ourselves to become useless to them; but we embarked and fought, taking no offence at your failure to assist us sooner. We maintain then that we rendered you a service at least as great as you rendered us. The cities from which you came to help us were still inhabited and you might hope to return to them; your concern was for yourselves and not for us; at any rate you remained at a distance while we had anything to lose. But we went forth from a city which was no more, and fought for one of which there was small hope; and yet we saved ourselves, and bore our part in saving you. If, in order to preserve our land, like other states, we had gone over to the Persians at first, or afterwards had not ventured

---

[a] Reading with the great majority of MSS. τετρακοσίας.

to embark because our ruin was already complete, it would have been useless for you with your weak navy to fight at sea, but everything would have gone quietly just as the Persian desired.

75 'Considering, Lacedaemonians, the energy and sagacity which we then displayed, do we deserve to be so bitterly hated by the other Hellenes merely because we have an empire? That empire was not acquired by force; but you would not stay and make an end of the Barbarian, and the allies came of their own accord and asked us to be their leaders. The subsequent development of our power was originally forced upon us by circumstances; fear was our first motive; afterwards honour, and then interest stepped in. And when we had incurred the hatred of most of our allies; when some of them had already revolted and been subjugated, and you were no longer the friends to us which you once had been, but suspicious and ill-disposed, how could we without great risk relax our hold? For the cities as fast as they fell away from us would have gone over to you. And no man is to be reproached who seizes every possible advantage when the danger is so great.

Why should they be hated for having saved Hellas? Their empire was not a usurpation, but the growth of circumstances.

76 'At all events, Lacedaemonians, we may retort that you, in the exercise of your supremacy, manage the cities of Peloponnesus to suit your own views; and that if you, and not we, had persevered in the command of the allies long enough to be hated, you would have been quite as intolerable to them as we are, and would have been compelled, for the sake of your own safety, to rule with a strong hand. An empire was offered to us: can you wonder that, acting as human nature always will, we accepted it and refused to give it up again, constrained by three all-powerful motives, honour, fear, interest? We are not the first who have aspired to rule; the world has ever held that the weaker must be kept down by the stronger. And

The Lacedaemonians would have been worse than they were.

B.C. 432. Ol. 87.

we think that we are worthy of power; and there was a time when you thought so too; but now, when you mean expediency you talk about justice. Did justice ever deter any one from taking by force whatever he could? Men who indulge the natural ambition of empire deserve credit if they are in any degree more careful of justice than they need be. How moderate we are would speedily appear if others took our place; indeed our very moderation, which should be our glory, has been unjustly converted into a reproach.

'For because in our suits with our allies, regulated by 77
treaty, we do not even stand upon our rights, but have instituted the practice of deciding them at Athens and by Athenian[a] law, we are supposed to be litigious. None of our opponents observe why others, who exercise dominion elsewhere and are less moderate than we are in their dealings with their subjects, escape this reproach. Why is it? Because men who practise violence have no longer any need of law. But we are in the habit of meeting our allies on terms of equality, and, therefore, if through some legal decision of ours, or exercise of our imperial power, contrary to their own ideas of right, they suffer ever so little, they are not grateful for our moderation in leaving them so much, but are far more offended at their trifling loss than if we had from the first plundered them in the face of day, laying aside all thought of law. For then they would themselves have admitted that the weaker must give way to the stronger. Mankind resent injustice more than violence, because the one seems to be an unfair advantage taken by an equal, the other is the irresistible force of a superior. They were patient under the yoke of the Persian, who inflicted on them far more grievous wrongs; but now our dominion is odious in their eyes. And no wonder: the ruler of the day is always detested by his subjects. And

They were thought to be litigious, because they allowed their subjects a law other than the law of the stronger.

The ruler of the day is always unpopular.

[a] (?) by impartial law.

should your empire supplant ours, may not you lose the good-will which you owe to the fear of us? Lose it you certainly will, if you mean again to exhibit the temper of which you gave a specimen when, for a short time, you led the confederacy against the Persian. For the institutions under which you live are incompatible with those of foreign states; and further, when any of you goes abroad, he respects neither these nor any other Hellenic customs[a].

The Lacedaemonians should not go to war at the instigation of others, but submit to arbitration.

78 'Do not then be hasty in deciding a question which is serious; and do not, by listening to representations and complaints which concern others, bring trouble upon yourselves. Realise, while there is time, the inscrutable nature of war; and how when protracted it generally ends in becoming a mere matter of chance, over which neither of us can have any control, the event being equally unknown and equally hazardous to both. The misfortune is that in their hurry to go to war, men begin with blows, and when a reverse comes upon them, then have recourse to words. But neither you, nor we, have as yet committed this mistake; and therefore while both of us can still choose the prudent part, we tell you not to break the peace or violate your oaths. Let our differences be determined by arbitration, according to the treaty. If you refuse we call to witness the Gods, by whom your oaths were sworn, that you are the authors of the war; and we will do our best to strike in return.'

79 When the Lacedaemonians had heard the charges brought by the allies against the Athenians, and their rejoinder, they ordered everybody but themselves to withdraw, and deliberated alone. The majority were agreed that there was now a clear case against the Athenians, and that they must fight at once. But Archidamus their

[a] For the misconduct of Spartan officers abroad, cp. i. 95; 130; iii. 32; 93 fin.; viii. 84 init. Contrast Brasidas, iv. 81.

king, who was held to be both an able and a prudent man, came forward and spoke as follows:—

'At my age, Lacedaemonians, I have had experience of 80
many wars, and I see several of you who are as old as I am, and who will not, as men too often do, desire war because they have never known it, or in the belief that it is either a good or a safe thing. Any one who calmly reflects will find that the war about which you are now deliberating is likely to be a very great one. When we encounter our neighbours in the Peloponnese, their mode of fighting is like ours, and they are all within a short march. But when we have to do with men whose country is a long way off, and who are most skilful seamen and thoroughly provided with the means of war,—having wealth, private and public, ships, horses, infantry, and a population larger than is to be found in any single Hellenic territory, not to speak of the numerous allies who pay them tribute,—is this a people against whom we can lightly take up arms or plunge into a contest unprepared? To what do we trust? To our navy? There we are inferior; and to exercise and train ourselves until we are a match for them, will take time. To our money? Nay, but in that we are weaker still; we have none in a common treasury, and we are never willing to contribute out of our private means.

We are no match for the Athenians.

'Perhaps some one may be encouraged by the superior 81
equipment and numbers of our infantry, which will enable us regularly to invade and ravage their lands. But their empire extends to distant countries, and they will be able to introduce supplies by sea. Or, again, we may try to stir up revolts among their allies. But these are mostly islanders, and we shall have to employ a fleet in their defence, as well as in our own. How then shall we carry on the war? For if we can neither defeat them at

We have more hoplites, but their empire extends to distant countries, by which their navy is supported; and to ravage their land is useless.

sea, nor deprive them of the revenues by which their navy is maintained, we shall get the worst of it. And having gone so far, we shall no longer be able even to make peace with honour, especially if we are believed to have begun the quarrel. We must not for one moment flatter ourselves that if we do but ravage their country the war will be at an end. Nay, I fear that we shall bequeath it to our children; for the Athenians with their high spirit will never barter their liberty to save their land, or be terrified like novices at the sight of war.

Do not take up arms yet.

82 'Not that I would have you shut your eyes to their designs and abstain from unmasking them, or tamely suffer them to injure our allies. But do not take up arms yet. Let us first send and remonstrate with them: we need not let them know positively whether we intend to go to war or not. In the meantime our own preparations may be going forward; we may seek for allies wherever we can find them, whether in Hellas or among the Barbarians, who will supply our deficiencies in ships and money. Those who, like ourselves, are exposed to Athenian intrigue cannot be blamed if in self-defence they seek the aid not of Hellenes only, but of Barbarians. And we must develope our own resources to the utmost. If they listen to our ambassadors, well and good; but, if not, in two or three years' time we shall be in a stronger position, should we then determine to attack them. Perhaps too when they begin to see that we are getting ready, [a]and that our words are to be interpreted by our actions[a], they may be more likely to yield; for their fields will be still untouched and their goods undespoiled, and it will be in their power to save them by their decision. Think of their land simply in the light of a hostage, all the more valuable in proportion as it is better cultivated; you should spare it as long as you can, and not by reducing them to despair

[a] Or, 'and that our words too sound a note of war.'

make their resistance more obstinate. For if we allow ourselves to be stung into premature action by the reproaches of our allies, and waste their country before we are ready, we shall only involve Peloponnesus in more and more difficulty and disgrace. Charges brought by cities or persons against one another can be satisfactorily arranged; but when a great confederacy, in order to satisfy private grudges, undertakes a war of which no man can foresee the issue, it is not easy to terminate it with honour.

And let no one think that there is any want of courage 83
in cities so numerous hesitating to attack a single one. The allies of the Athenians are not less numerous; they pay them tribute too; and war is not an affair of arms, but of money which gives to arms their use, and which is needed above all things when a continental is fighting against a maritime power: let us find money first, and then we may safely allow our minds to be excited by the speeches of our allies. We, on whom the future responsibility, whether for good or evil, will chiefly fall, should calmly reflect on the consequences which may follow.

There is no cowardice in hesitation; we are fighting not against Athens, but against the great Athenian empire.

'Do not be ashamed of the slowness and procrastination 84
with which they are so fond of charging you; if you begin the war in haste, you will end it at your leisure, because you took up arms without sufficient preparation. Remember that we have always been citizens of a free and most illustrious state, and that for us the policy which they condemn may well be the truest good sense and discretion. It is a policy which has saved us from growing insolent in prosperity or giving way under adversity, like other men. We are not stimulated by the allurements of flattery into dangerous courses of which we disapprove; nor are we goaded by offensive charges into compliance with any man's wishes. Our habits of discipline

Too much haste, too little speed. Our discretion and discipline are the secret of our greatness. We must not undervalue our enemies, and we must not rely on fortune.

make us both brave and wise; brave, because the spirit of loyalty quickens the sense of honour, and the sense of honour inspires courage; wise, because we are not so highly educated that we have learned to despise the laws, and are too severely trained and of too loyal a spirit to disobey them. We have not acquired that useless over-intelligence which makes a man an excellent critic of an enemy's plans, but paralyses him in the moment of action. We think that the wits of our enemies are as good as our own, and that the element of fortune cannot be forecast in words. Let us assume that they have common prudence, and let our preparations be, not words, but deeds[a]. Our hopes ought not to rest on the probability of their making mistakes, but on our own caution and foresight. We should remember that one man is much the same as another, and that he is best who is trained in the severest school.

We can afford to wait, and should try arbitration first.

85 'These are principles which our fathers have handed down to us, and we maintain to our lasting benefit; we must not lose sight of them, and when many lives and much wealth, many cities and a great name are at stake, we must not be hasty, or make up our minds in a few short hours; we must take time. We can afford to wait, when others cannot, because we are strong. And now, send to the Athenians and remonstrate with them about Potidaea first, and also about the other wrongs of which your allies complain. They say that they are willing to have the matter tried; and against one who offers to submit to justice you must not proceed as against a criminal until his cause has been heard. In the meantime prepare for war. This decision will be the best for yourselves and the most formidable to your enemies.'

Thus spoke Archidamus. Last of all, Sthenelaidas, at that time one of the Ephors, came forward and addressed the Lacedaemonians as follows:—

---

[a] Reading παρασκευαζώμεθα.

'I do not know what the long speeches of the Athenians 86
mean. They have been loud in their own praise, but they do not pretend to say that they are dealing honestly with our allies and with the Peloponnesus. If they behaved well in the Persian War and are now behaving badly to us they ought to be punished twice over, because they were once good men and have become bad. But we are the same now as we were then, and we shall not do our duty if we allow our allies to be ill-used, and put off helping them, for they cannot put off their troubles. Others may have money and ships and horses, but we have brave allies and we must not betray them to the Athenians. If they were suffering in word only, by words and legal processes their wrongs might be redressed; but now there is not a moment to be lost, and we must help them with all our might. Let no one tell us that we should take time to think when we are suffering injustice. Nay, we reply, those who mean to do injustice should take a long time to think. Wherefore, Lacedaemonians, prepare for war as the honour of Sparta demands. Withstand the advancing power of Athens. Do not let us betray our allies, but, with the Gods on our side, let us attack the evil-doer.'

We must stand by our allies.

When Sthenelaidas had thus spoken he, being Ephor, 87
himself put the question to the Lacedaemonian assembly. Their custom is to signify their decision by cries and not by voting. But he professed himself unable to tell on which side was the louder cry, and wishing to call forth a demonstration which might encourage the warlike spirit, he said, 'Whoever of you, Lacedaemonians, thinks that the treaty has been broken and that the Athenians are in the wrong, let him rise and go yonder' (pointing to a particular spot), 'and those who think otherwise to the other side.' So the assembly rose and divided, and it was determined by a large majority that the treaty had been broken. The Lacedaemonians then recalled the allies and

The Lacedaemonians, influenced chiefly by the fear of the Athenians, resolve to go to war.

told them that in their judgment the Athenians were guilty, but that they wished to hold a general assembly of the allies and take a vote from them all; then the war, if they approved of it, might be undertaken by common consent. Having accomplished their purpose, the allies returned home; and the Athenian envoys, when their errand was
B.C. 445. Ol. 83, 4. done, returned likewise. Thirteen years of the thirty years' peace which was concluded after the recovery of Euboea had elapsed and the fourteenth year had begun when the Lacedaemonian assembly decided that the treaty had been broken.

88 In arriving at this decision and resolving to go to war, the Lacedaemonians were influenced, not so much by the speeches of their allies, as by the fear of the Athenians and of their increasing power[a]. For they saw the greater part of Hellas already subject to them.

89 How the Athenians attained the position in which they
B.C. 479. Ol. 75, 2. *The Athenians after the retreat of the Persians continue the war.* rose to greatness I will now proceed to describe. When the Persians, defeated by the Hellenes on sea and land, had retreated from Europe, and the remnant of the fleet, which had taken refuge at Mycalê, had there perished, Leotychides, the Lacedaemonian king, who had commanded the Hellenes in the battle, returned home with the allies from Peloponnesus. But the Athenians and their allies from Ionia and the Hellespont, who had now revolted from the king, persevered and besieged Sestos, at that time still in the hands of the Persians. Remaining there through the winter they took the place, which the Barbarians deserted. The allies then sailed back from the Hellespont to their respective homes. Meanwhile the Athenian people, now quit of the Barbarians, fetched their wives, their children, and the remains of their property from the places in which they had been deposited, and set to work, rebuilding the city and the walls. Of the old line of wall but

[a] Cp. i. 23 fin.

a small part was left standing. Most of the houses were in ruins, a few only remaining in which the chief men of the Persians had lodged.

The Lacedaemonians knew what would happen and sent 90
an embassy to Athens. They would rather themselves have seen neither the Athenians nor any one else protected by a wall; but their main motive was the importunity of their allies, who dreaded not only the Athenian navy, which had until lately been quite small, but also the spirit which had animated them in the Persian War. So the Lacedaemonians requested them not to restore their walls [a], but on the contrary to join with them in razing the fortifications of other towns outside the Peloponnesus which had them standing. They did not reveal their real wishes or the suspicion which they entertained of the Athenians, but argued that the Barbarian, if he again attacked them, would then have no strong place which he could make his head-quarters as he had lately made Thebes. Peloponnesus would be a sufficient retreat for all Hellas and a good base of operations. To this the Athenians, by the advice of Themistocles, replied, that they would send an embassy of their own to discuss the matter, and so got rid of the Spartan envoys. He then proposed that he should himself start at once for Sparta, and that they should give him colleagues who were not to go immediately, but were to wait until the wall reached the lowest height which could possibly be defended. The whole people, who were in the city, men, women, and children, should join in the work, and they must spare no building, private or public, which could be of use, but demolish them all. Having given these instructions and intimated that he would manage affairs at Sparta, he departed. On his arrival he did not at once present himself officially to the magistrates, but delayed and made

The Lacedaemonians at the instigation of their allies try to prevent the Athenians from rebuilding their walls.

B.C. 479–478. Ol. 75, 2, 3.

[a] Cp. i. 69 init.

excuses; and when any of them asked him 'why he did not appear before the assembly,' he said 'that he was waiting for his colleagues, who had been detained by some engagement; he was daily expecting them, and wondered that they had not appeared.'

The Lacedaemonians are outwitted by Themistocles.

91 The friendship of the Lacedaemonian magistrates for Themistocles induced them to believe him; but when everybody who came from Athens declared positively that the wall was building and had already reached a considerable height, they knew not what to think. He, aware of their suspicions, desired them not to be misled by reports, but to send to Athens men whom they could trust out of their own number who would see for themselves and bring back word. They agreed; and he at the same time privately instructed the Athenians to detain the envoys as quietly as they could, and not let them go until he and his colleagues had got safely home. For by this time Habronichus the son of Lysicles, and Aristides the son of Lysimachus, who were joined with him in the embassy, had arrived, bringing the news that the wall was of sufficient height; and he was afraid that the Lacedaemonians, when they heard the truth, might not allow them to return. So the Athenians detained the envoys, and Themistocles, coming before the Lacedaemonians, at length declared in so many words that Athens was now provided with walls and could protect her citizens; henceforward, if the Lacedaemonians or their allies wished at any time to negotiate, they must deal with the Athenians as with men who knew quite well what was for their own and the common good. When they boldly resolved to leave their city and go on board ship, they did not first ask the advice of the Lacedaemonians, and, when the two states met in council, their own judgment had been as good as that of any one. And now they had arrived at an independent opinion that it was better far, and would be more advantageous both for themselves and for the whole body of the allies, that their city

should have a wall; when any member of a confederacy had not equal military advantages, his counsel could not be of equal weight or worth. Either all the allies should pull down their walls, or they should acknowledge that the Athenians were in the right.

On hearing these words the Lacedaemonians did not 92
openly quarrel with the Athenians; for they professed that the embassy had been designed, not to interfere with them, but to offer a suggestion for the public good; besides at that time the patriotism which the Athenians had displayed in the Persian War had created a warm feeling of friendliness between the two cities. They were annoyed at the failure of their purpose, but they did not show it. And the envoys on either side returned home without any formal complaint.

But appearances are maintained, and there is no open quarrel.

In such hurried fashion did the Athenians build the 93
walls of their city. To this day the structure shows evidence of haste. The foundations are made up of all sorts of stones, in some places unwrought, and laid just as each worker brought them; there were many columns too, taken from sepulchres, and many old stones already cut, inserted in the work. The circuit of the city was extended in B.C. 478.
every direction, and the citizens, in their ardour to com- Ol. 75, 3.
plete the design, spared nothing.

Themistocles also persuaded the Athenians to finish the B.C. 482.
Piraeus, of which he had made a begin- Ol. 74, 3.
ning in his year of office as Archon. The situation of the place, which had three natural havens, was excellent; and now that the Athenians had become seamen, he thought that they had great advantage for the attainment of empire. For he first dared to say that 'they must make the sea their domain,' and he lost no time in laying the foundations of their empire. By his advice, they built the wall of such a width that two waggons carrying the stones could meet and pass on the top; this width may still be traced at the

Construction of the Piraeus, and foundation of the maritime empire of Athens.

Piraeus; inside there was no rubble or mortar, but the whole wall was made up of large stones hewn square, which were clamped on the outer face with iron and lead. The height was not more than half what he had originally intended; he had hoped by the very dimensions of the wall to paralyse the designs of an enemy, and he thought that a handful of the least efficient citizens would suffice for its defence, while the rest might man the fleet. His mind was turned in this direction, as I conceive, from observing that the King's armament had met with fewer obstacles by sea than by land. The Piraeus appeared to him to be of more real consequence than the upper city. He was fond of telling the Athenians that if ever they were hard pressed on land they should go down to the Piraeus and fight the world at sea.

Thus the Athenians built their walls and restored their city immediately after the retreat of the Persians.

94 Pausanias the son of Cleombrotus was now sent from Peloponnesus with twenty ships in command of the Hellenic forces; thirty Athenian ships and a number of the allies sailed with him. They first made an expedition against Cyprus, of which they subdued the greater part; and afterwards against Byzantium, which was in the hands of the Persians, and was taken while he was still in command.

Cyprus and Byzantium taken. Tyranny and unpopularity of Pausanias.

95 He had already begun to be oppressive[a], and the allies were offended with him, especially the Ionians and others who had been recently emancipated from the King. So they had recourse to their kinsmen the Athenians and begged them to be their leaders, and to protect them against Pausanias, if he attempted to oppress them. The Athenians took the matter up and prepared to interfere, being fully resolved to manage the confederacy in their

B.C. 477 or 476. Ol. 75, 4 or 76.

The allies transfer themselves to the Athenians.

[a] Cp. c. 130.

own way. In the meantime the Lacedaemonians summoned Pausanias to Sparta, intending to investigate certain reports which had reached them; for he was accused of numerous crimes by Hellenes returning from the Hellespont, and appeared to exercise his command more after the fashion of a tyrant than of a general. His recall occurred at the very time when the hatred which he inspired had induced the allies, with the exception of the Peloponnesians, to transfer themselves to the Athenians. On arriving at Lacedaemon he was punished for the wrongs which he had done to particular persons, but he had been also accused of conspiring with the Persians, and of this, which was the principal charge and was generally believed to be proven, he was acquitted. The government however did not continue him in his command, but sent in his place Dorcis and certain others with a small force. To these the allies refused allegiance, and Dorcis, seeing the state of affairs, returned home. Henceforth the Lacedaemonians sent out no more commanders, for they were afraid that those whom they appointed would be corrupted, as they had found to be the case with Pausanias; they had had enough of the Persian War; and they thought that the Athenians were fully able to lead, and at that time believed them to be their friends.

Thus the Athenians by the good-will of the allies, who 96
detested Pausanias, obtained the leadership. They immediately fixed which of the cities should supply money and which of them ships for the war against the Barbarians, the avowed object being to compensate themselves and the allies for their losses by devastating the King's country. Then was first instituted at Athens the office of Hellenic treasurers (Hellenotamiae), who received the tribute, for so the contributions were termed. The amount was originally fixed at 460 talents[a]. The island of Delos was the treasury, and the meetings of the allies were held in the temple.

Confederacy of Delos.

B.C. 478–477. Ol. 75, 3, 4.

[a] About £92,000.

97 At first the allies were independent and deliberated in a common assembly under the leadership of Athens. But in the interval between the Persian and the Peloponnesian Wars, by their military success and by policy in dealing with the Barbarian, with their own rebellious allies and with the Peloponnesians who came across their path from time to time, the Athenians made immense strides in power. I have gone out of my way to speak of this period because the writers who have preceded me treat either of Hellenic affairs previous to the Persian invasion or of that invasion itself; the intervening portion of history has been omitted by all of them, with the exception of Hellanicus; and he, where he has touched upon it in his Attic history, is very brief, and inaccurate in his chronology. The narrative will also serve to explain how the Athenian empire grew up.

The interval between the Persian and Peloponnesian Wars omitted in most histories.

98 First of all under the leadership of Cimon, the son of Miltiades, the Athenians besieged and took Eion upon the Strymon, then in the hands of the Persians, and sold the inhabitants into slavery. The same fate befell Scyros, an island in the Aegean inhabited by Dolopes; this they colonised themselves. They also made war on the Carystians of Euboea, who, after a time, capitulated; the other Euboeans took no part in the war. Then the Naxians revolted, and the Athenians made war against them and reduced them by blockade. This was the first of the allied cities which was enslaved contrary to Hellenic right; the turn of the others came later.

B.C. 476–466. Ol. 76–78, 3.

The Athenians subject Eion, Scyros, Carystus, Naxos.

B.C. 466. Ol. 78, 3.

99 The causes which led to the defections of the allies were of different kinds, the principal being their neglect to pay the tribute or to furnish ships, and, in some cases, failure of military service. For the Athenians were exacting and oppressive, using coercive measures towards men who were neither willing nor

Most of the allies contribute money instead of ships. As they grow weaker the Athenians become more oppressive.

accustomed to work hard. And for various reasons they soon began to prove less agreeable leaders than at first. They no longer fought upon an equality with the rest of the confederates, and they had no difficulty in reducing them when they revolted. Now the allies brought all this upon themselves; for the majority of them disliked military service and absence from home, and so they agreed to contribute their share of the expense instead of ships. Whereby the Athenian navy was proportionally increased, while they themselves were always untrained and unprepared for war when they revolted.

The Athenians conquer in a sea and land fight at the river Eurymedon. Revolt of Thasos. Attempted colonisation of Amphipolis.

A little later the Athenians and their allies fought two 100
battles, one by land and the other by sea, against the Persians, at the river Eurymedon in Pamphylia. The Athenians, under the command of Cimon the son of Miltiades, on the same day conquered in both, and took and destroyed all the Phoenician triremes numbering two hundred. After
a while the Thasians revolted; a quarrel had arisen B.C. 465.
between them and the Athenians about the Thracian Ol. 78, 4.
markets and the mine on the Thracian coast opposite, of which the Thasians received the profits. The Athenians sailed to Thasos and, gaining a victory at sea, landed upon the island. About the same time they sent ten thousand of their own people and of their allies to the Strymon, intending to colonise the place then called the Nine Ways and now Amphipolis. They gained possession of the Nine Ways, which were inhabited by the Edoni, but, advancing into the interior of Thrace, they [a]were destroyed at Drabescus in Edonia by the united Thracians[a], whose country was threatened by the new settlement.

The Thasians, now blockaded after several defeats, had 101
recourse to the Lacedaemonians and entreated them to

[a] Or, reading ξύμπαντες, as Poppo is inclined to do, 'were destroyed to a man by the Thracians.'

B.C. 464. Ol. 79. invade Attica. Unknown to the Athenians they agreed, and were on the point of setting out when the great earthquake occurred and was immediately followed by the revolt of the Helots and with them the Perioeci of Thuria and Aethaea, who seized Ithomè. These Helots were mostly the descendants of the Messenians who had been enslaved in ancient times, and hence all the insurgents were called Messenians.

Revolt of the Helots, who seize Ithomè.

B.C. 463. Ol. 79, 2. While the Lacedaemonians were thus engaged, the Thasians, who had now been blockaded for more than two years, came to terms with the Athenians; they pulled down their walls and surrendered their ships; they also agreed to pay what was required of them whether in the shape of immediate indemnity or of tribute for the future; and they gave up their claim to the mainland and to the mine.

Surrender of Thasos.

102 B.C. 463–461. Ol. 79, 2–4. The siege of Ithomè proved tedious, and the Lacedaemonians called in, among other allies, the Athenians, who sent to their aid a considerable force under Cimon. The Athenians were specially invited because they were reputed to be skilful in siege operations, and the length of the blockade proved to the Lacedaemonians their own deficiency in that sort of warfare; else why had they not taken the place by assault? This expedition of the Athenians led to the first open quarrel between them and the Lacedaemonians. For the Lacedaemonians, not succeeding in storming the place, took alarm at the bold and original spirit of the Athenians. They reflected that they were aliens in race, and fearing that, if they were allowed to remain, they might be tempted by the Helots in Ithomè to change sides, they dismissed them, while they retained the other allies. But they concealed their mistrust, and merely said that they no longer needed their services. Now the Athenians saw that their dismissal was due to some suspicion which had arisen and not to the less offensive reason which was openly avowed;

The Athenians come to the assistance of the Lacedaemonians, but being suspected by them, they are dismissed and go away in a rage.

they felt keenly that such a slight ought not to have been offered them by the Lacedaemonians; and so, on their return home, they forthwith abandoned the alliance which they had made with them against the Persians and went over to their Argive enemies. At the same time both Argos and Athens bound themselves to Thessaly by a common oath of alliance. B.C. 463–461. Ol. 79, 2–79, 4.

103 In the [a] tenth year of the siege the defenders of Ithomè were unable to hold out any longer, and capitulated to the Lacedaemonians. The terms were as follows: They were to leave Peloponnesus under a safe-conduct, and were never again to return; if any of them were taken on Peloponnesian soil, he was to be the slave of his captor. Now an ancient oracle of Delphi was current among the Lacedaemonians, bidding them let the suppliant of Ithomaean Zeus go free. So the Messenians left Ithomè with their wives and children; and the Athenians, who were now the avowed enemies of Sparta, gave them a home at Naupactus, a place which they had lately taken from the Ozolian Locrians. B.C. 455. Ol. 81, 2. [? B.C. 461. Ol. 79, 4.]

Fall of Ithomè. The Athenians settle the exiled Messenians at Naupactus.

The Athenians obtained the alliance of the Megarians, who revolted from the Lacedaemonians because the Corinthians were pressing them hard in a war arising out of a question of frontiers. Thus they gained both Megara and Pegae; and they built for the Megarians the long walls, extending from the city to the port of Nisaea, which they garrisoned themselves. This was the original and the main cause of the intense hatred which the Corinthians entertained towards the Athenians. B.C. 461–460. Ol. 79, 4–80.

Athens gains the alliance of Megara, as well as of Argos and Thessaly.

104 Meanwhile Inaros the son of Psammetichus, king of the Libyans who border on Egypt, had induced the greater part of Egypt to revolt from King Artaxerxes. He began the rebellion B.C. 460. Ol. 80.

Egyptian revolt.

[a] Or, accepting τετάρτῳ (Krüger's conj.), 'the fourth year.'

at Mareia, a city opposite the island of Pharos, and, having made himself ruler of the country, called in the Athenians. They were just then engaged in an expedition against Cyprus with two hundred ships of their own and of their allies; and, quitting the island, they went to his aid. They sailed from the sea into the Nile, and, making themselves masters of the river and of two-thirds of Memphis, proceeded to attack the remaining part called the White Castle, in which some of the Persians and Medes had taken refuge, and with them such Egyptians as had not joined in the revolt.

B.C. 460–457. Ol. 80, 1–4.

105 An Athenian fleet made a descent upon Halieis, where a battle took place against some Corinthian and Epidaurian troops; the Athenians gained the victory. Soon afterwards the Athenians fought at sea off Cecryphaleia with a Peloponnesian fleet, which they defeated. A war next broke out between the Aeginetans and the Athenians, and a great battle was fought off the coast of Aegina, in which the allies of both parties joined; the Athenians were victorious, and captured seventy of the enemy's ships; they then landed on Aegina and, under the command of Leocrates the son of Stroebus, besieged the town. Thereupon the Peloponnesians sent over to the assistance of the Aeginetans three hundred hoplites who had previously been assisting the Corinthians and Epidaurians. The Corinthians seized[a] on the heights of Geraneia, and thence made a descent with their allies into the Megarian territory, thinking that the Athenians, who had so large a force absent in Aegina and in Egypt, would be unable to assist the Megarians; or, if they did, would be obliged to raise the siege of Aegina. But the Athenians, without moving their army from Aegina, sent to Megara under the command of Myronides a force consisting of their oldest and youngest men, who had

The Athenians defeat the Aeginetans, capture seventy ships, and besiege Aegina. The Corinthians invade Megara.

[a] Omitting the stop after κατέλαβον.

remained at home. A battle was fought, which hung equally in the balance; and when the two armies separated, they both thought that they had gained the victory. The Athenians, who did however get rather the better, on the departure of the Corinthians erected a trophy. And then the Corinthians, irritated by the reproaches of the aged men in the city, after about twelve days' preparation came out again, and, claiming the victory, raised another trophy. Hereupon the Athenians sallied out of Megara, killed those who were erecting the trophy, and charged and defeated the rest of the army.

The Corinthians now retreated, but a considerable 106

They suffer great loss in their retreat.

number of them were hard pressed, and missing their way got into an enclosure belonging to a private person, which was surrounded by a great ditch and had no exit. The Athenians, perceiving their situation, closed the entrance in front with heavy-armed troops, and, placing their light troops in a circle round, stoned all who had entered the enclosure. This was a great blow to the Corinthians. The main body of their army returned home.

About this time the Athenians began to build their 107

The Athenians build their long walls. Battle of Tanagra.

B.C. 457. Ol. 80, 4.

Long Walls extending to the sea, one to the harbour of Phalerum, and the other to the Piraeus. The Phocians made an expedition against the Dorians, who inhabit Boeum, Cytinium, and Erineum, and are the mother people of the Lacedaemonians; one of these towns they took. Thereupon the Lacedaemonians under the command of Nicomedes the son of Cleombrotus, who was general in the place of the king Pleistoanax the son of Pausanias (he being at that time a minor), came to the assistance of the Dorians with fifteen hundred hoplites of their own, and, of their allies, ten thousand, and compelled the Phocians to make terms and to restore the town. They then thought of returning; but there were difficulties. Either they might go by sea across the

Crisaean Gulf, in which case the Athenian fleet would be sure to sail round and intercept them, or they might march over Mount Geraneia; but this seemed dangerous when the Athenians were holding Megara and Pegae. The pass was not easy, and was always guarded by the Athenians, who were obviously intending to stop them by that route also. So they determined to remain in Boeotia and consider how they could best get home. They had another motive:—Certain Athenians were privately making overtures to them, in the hope that they would put an end to the democracy and the building of the Long Walls. But the Athenians were aware of their embarrassment, and they also suspected their design against the democracy. So they went out to meet them with their whole force, together with a thousand Argives and contingents from the other allies; they numbered in all fourteen thousand men. Among them were some Thessalian cavalry, who came to their aid in accordance with the treaty[a], but these deserted to the Lacedaemonians during the engagement.

Battle of Oenophyta. Surrender of Aegina.

108 The battle was fought at Tanagra in Boeotia, and the Lacedaemonians and their allies, after great slaughter on both sides, gained the victory. They then marched into the Megarian territory, and, cutting down the fruit-trees, returned home by way of Geraneia and the Isthmus. But on the sixty-second day after the battle, the Athenians made another expedition into Boeotia under the command of Myronides, and there was a battle at Oenophyta, in which they defeated the Boeotians and became masters of Boeotia and Phocis. They pulled down the walls of Tanagra and took as hostages from the Opuntian Locrians a hundred of their richest citizens. They then completed their own Long Walls. Soon afterwards the Aeginetans came to terms with the Athenians, dismantling their walls, surrendering their ships, and agreeing to pay tribute for the future. The Athenians, under the command of Tolmides

B.C. 456, Ol. 81.

[a] Cp. i. 102

the son of Tolmaeus, sailed round Peloponnesus and burnt the Lacedaemonian dockyard[a]. They also took the Corinthian town of Chalcis, and, making a descent upon Sicyon, defeated a Sicyonian force. B.C. 455. Ol. 81, 2.

109 The Athenians and their allies were still in Egypt, where they carried on the war with varying fortune. At first they were masters of the country. The King sent to Lacedaemon Megabazus a Persian, who was well supplied with money, in the hope that he might persuade the Peloponnesians to invade Attica, and so draw off the Athenians from Egypt. He had no success; the money was being spent and nothing done; so, with what remained of it, he found his way back to Asia. The King then sent into Egypt Megabyzus the son of Zopyrus, a Persian, who marched overland with a large army and defeated the Egyptians and their allies. He drove the Hellenes out of Memphis, and finally shut them up in the island of Prosopitis, where he blockaded them for eighteen months. At length he drained the canal and diverted the water, thus leaving their ships high and dry and joining nearly the whole island to the mainland. He then crossed over with a land force, and took the island.

After an ineffectual attempt to obtain assistance from Lacedaemon, the Persian King at length succeeds in driving the Athenians out of Memphis.

110 Thus, after six years' fighting, the cause of the Hellenes in Egypt was lost. A few survivors of their great army found their way through Libya to Cyrenè; by far the larger number perished. Egypt again became subject to the Persians, although Amyrtaeus, the king in the fens, still held out. He escaped capture owing to the extent of the fens and the bravery of their inhabitants, who are the most warlike of all the Egyptians. Inaros, the king of Libya, the chief author of the revolt, was betrayed and impaled. Fifty additional triremes, which had been sent by the Athenians

Nearly the whole of the expedition to Egypt, including a reinforcement of fifty triremes, is destroyed.

[a] i. e. Gythium.

and their allies to relieve their other forces, in ignorance of what had happened, sailed into the Mendesian mouth of the Nile. But they were at once attacked both from the land and from the sea, and the greater part of them destroyed by the Phoenician fleet, a few ships only escaping. Thus ended the great Egyptian expedition of the Athenians and their allies.

111 About this time Orestes, the exiled son of the Thessalian king Echecratides, persuaded the Athenians to restore him. Taking with them a force of the Boeotians and Phocians, who were now their allies, they marched against Pharsalus in Thessaly. They made themselves masters of the country in the neighbourhood of their camp, but the Thessalian cavalry stopped any further advance. They could not take the place, and none of their plans prospered; so they returned unsuccessful and brought back Orestes.

Attempted restoration of Orestes, the Thessalian exile.

B.C. 454. Ol. 81, 3. A short time afterwards a thousand Athenians, under the command of Pericles the son of Xanthippus, embarking on board the fleet which they had at Pegae, now in their possession, coasted along to Sicyon, and there landing, defeated the Sicyonians who came out to meet them. With the least possible delay taking on board Achaean troops and sailing to the opposite coast, they attacked and besieged Oeniadae, a town of Acarnania; but failing to reduce it, they returned home.

The Athenians under Pericles defeat the Sicyonians.

112 B.C. 450. Ol. 82. 3. After an interval of three years a five years' truce was concluded between the Peloponnesians and Athenians. The Athenians now abstained from war in Hellas itself, but made an expedition to Cyprus with two hundred ships of their own and of their allies, under the command of Cimon. Sixty ships were detached from the armament and sailed to Egypt, at the request of Amyrtaeus the king in the fens; the remainder proceeded to blockade Citium. Here Cimon

Truce for five years. Expedition to Cyprus. More ships sent to Egypt. Death of Cimon. Battles at Salamis in Cyprus.

died, and a famine arose in the country; so the fleet B.C. 449. Ol. 82, 4.
quitted Citium. Arriving off Salamis in Cyprus they fought at sea and also on land with Phoenician and Cilician forces. Gaining a victory in both engagements, they returned home, accompanied by the ships which had gone out with them and had now come back from Egypt. After this the Lacedaemonians engaged in the so-called Sacred War and gained possession of the temple of Delphi, which they handed over to the Delphians. But no sooner had they retired than the Athenians sent an expedition and recovered the temple, which they handed over to the Phocians.

Defeat of the Athenians at Coronea. Revolution in Boeotia.

Some time afterwards the Athenians, under the com- 113 B.C. 447. Ol. 83, 2.
mand of Tolmides the son of Tolmaeus, with a thousand hoplites of their own and contingents of their allies, made an expedition against Orchomenus, Chaeronea, and certain other places in Boeotia which were in the hands of oligarchical exiles from different Boeotian towns, and so were hostile to them. They took Chaeronea, and leaving a garrison there, departed. But while they were on their march, the exiles who had occupied Orchomenus, some Locrians, some Euboean exiles and others of the same party, set upon them at Coronea and defeated them, killing many and taking many prisoners. The Athenians then agreed to evacuate the whole of Boeotia upon condition that the prisoners should be restored. And so the Boeotian exiles returned to their homes, and all the Boeotians regained their independence.

Revolt of Euboea. Slaughter of the Athenian garrison at Megara. Invasion of Attica. Retirement of the Peloponnesians, and recovery of Euboea.

Not long afterwards Euboea revolted from Athens. 114 B.C. 445. Ol. 83, 4.
Pericles had just arrived in the island with an Athenian army when the news came that Megara had likewise revolted, that the Peloponnesians were on the point of invading Attica, and that the Megarians had slaughtered the Athenian garrison, of whom a few only had escaped to

Nisaea. The Megarians had introduced a force of Corinthians, Sicyonians, and Epidaurians into the city, and by their help had effected the revolt. Pericles in haste withdrew his army from Euboea. The Peloponnesians then invaded Attica under the command of Pleistoanax son of Pausanias, the Lacedaemonian king. They advanced as far as Eleusis and Thria but no further, and after ravaging the country, returned home. Thereupon the Athenians under the command of Pericles again crossed over to Euboea and reduced the whole country; the Hestiaeans they ejected from their homes and appropriated their territory; the rest of the island they settled by agreement.

The Athenians agree to restore the places held by them in Peloponnesus. Revolt of the Samians, who are assisted by the Byzantians.

115 Soon after their return from Euboea they made a truce for thirty years with the Lacedaemonians and their allies, restoring Nisaea, Pegae, Troezen and Achaia, which were the places held by them in Peloponnesus. Six years later the Samians

B.C. 440. Ol. 85.

and Milesians went to war about the possession of Prienè, and the Milesians, who were getting worsted, came to Athens and complained loudly of the Samians. Some private citizens of Samos, who wanted to overthrow the government, supported their complaint. Whereupon the Athenians, sailing to Samos with forty ships, established a democracy, and taking as hostages fifty boys and fifty men whom they deposited at Lemnos, they returned leaving a garrison. But certain of the Samians who had quitted the island and fled to the mainland entered into an alliance with the principal oligarchs who remained in the city, and with Pissuthnes the son of Hystaspes, then governor of Sardis, and collecting troops to the number of seven hundred they crossed over by night to Samos. First of all they attacked the victorious populace and got most of them into their power; then they stole away their hostages from Lemnos, and finally revolted from Athens. The garrison of the Athenians and the officials who were in their power were delivered by them into the hands of Pissuthnes. They at once prepared to make an expedition against Miletus. The Byzantians joined in their revolt.

When the Athenians heard of the insurrection they 116
sailed for Samos with sixty ships. But of this number they sent away sixteen, some towards Caria to keep a look out for the Phoenician fleet, others to summon aid from Chios and Lesbos. With the remaining forty-four ships they fought at sea under the command of Pericles and nine others, near the island of Tragia, against seventy Samian vessels, all sailing from Miletus, of which twenty were transports; the Athenians gained the victory. After receiving a reinforcement of forty ships from Athens and of twenty-five from Chios and Lesbos they disembarked, and their infantry proving superior, invested the city with three walls; they also blockaded it by sea. At the same time Pericles took sixty ships of the blockading force and sailed hastily towards Caunus in Caria, news having arrived that a Phoenician fleet was approaching; Stesagoras and others had already gone with five ships from Samos to fetch it.

The Athenians defeat the Samians at sea.

Meanwhile the Samians made a sudden sally, and at- 117
tacking the naval station of the Athenians which was unprotected, destroyed the guard-ships and engaged and defeated the other vessels which put out to meet them. During some fourteen days they were masters of the sea about their own coasts, and carried in and out whatever they pleased. But when Pericles returned, they were B.C. 439.
again closely blockaded; and there soon arrived from Ol. 85, 2.
Athens forty additional ships under Thucydides, Hagnon, and Phormio, twenty more under Tlepolemus and Anticles, and thirty from Chios and Lesbos. The Samians made a feeble attempt at a sea-fight, but soon they were unable to resist, and after nine months were forced to surrender. The terms of capitulation were as follows:—They were to raze

Temporary success and final subjection of the Samians.

The Byzantians also submit.

their walls, give hostages, surrender their ships, and pay a full indemnity by regular instalments. The Byzantians too made terms and became subjects as before.

118 Not long afterwards occurred the affairs of Corcyra and Potidaea, which have been already narrated, and the various other circumstances which led to the Peloponnesian War. Fifty years elapsed between the retreat of Xerxes and the beginning of the war; during these years took place all those operations of the Hellenes against one another and against the Barbarian which I have been describing. The Athenians acquired a firmer hold over their empire and the city itself became a great power. The Lacedaemonians saw what was going on, but during most of the time they remained inactive and hardly attempted to interfere. They had never been of a temper prompt to take the field unless they were compelled; and they were in some degree embarrassed by wars near home. But the Athenians were growing too great to be ignored and were laying hands on their allies. They could now bear it no longer: they made up their minds that they must put out all their strength and overthrow the Athenian power by force of arms. And therefore they commenced the Peloponnesian War. They had already voted in their own assembly that the treaty had been broken and that the Athenians were guilty[a]; they now sent to Delphi and asked the God if it would be for their advantage to make war. He is reported to have answered that, if they did their best, they would be conquerors, and that he himself, invited or uninvited, would take their part.

The history is resumed from chap. 88. The Lacedaemonians, having decided to go to war, obtain the sanction of the Delphian oracle.

119 So they again summoned the allies, intending to put to them the question of war or peace. When their representatives arrived, an assembly was held; and the allies said what they had to say, most of them complaining of the

Activity of the Corinthians in pressing on the war.

[a] But cp. vii. 18 med.

Athenians and demanding that the war should proceed. B.C. 432.
The Corinthians had already gone the round of the Ol. 87.
cities and entreated them privately to vote for war; they were afraid that they would be too late to save Potidaea. At the assembly they came forward last of all and spoke as follows:—

No more fault to be found with the Lacedaemonians. The Athenians are dangerous to all alike. Men should be willing to fight, though they should be equally ready to cease from fighting.

'Fellow allies, we can no longer find fault with the 120
Lacedaemonians; they have themselves resolved upon war and have brought us hither to confirm their decision. And they have done well; for the leaders of a confederacy, while they do not neglect the interests of their own state, should look to the general weal: as they are first in honour, they should be first in the fulfilment of their duties. Now those among us who have ever had dealings with the Athenians, do not require to be warned against them; but such as live inland and not on any maritime highway should clearly understand that, if they do not protect the sea-board, they will find it more difficult to carry their produce to the sea, or to receive in return the goods which the sea gives to the land. They should not lend a careless ear to our words, for they nearly concern them; they should remember that, if they desert the cities on the sea-shore, the danger may some day reach them, and that they are consulting for their own interests quite as much as for ours. And therefore let no one hesitate to accept war in exchange for peace. Wise men refuse to move until they are wronged, but brave men as soon as they are wronged go to war, and when there is a good opportunity make peace again. They are not intoxicated by military success; but neither will they tolerate injustice from a love of peace and ease. For he whom pleasure makes a coward will quickly lose, if he continues inactive, the delights of ease which he is so unwilling to renounce; and he whose arrogance is stimulated by victory does not see how hollow is the confidence which

elates him. Many schemes which were ill-advised have succeeded through the still greater folly which possessed the enemy, and yet more, which seemed to be wisely contrived, have ended in foul disaster. The execution of an enterprise is never equal[a] to the conception of it in the confident mind of its promoter; for men are safe while they are forming plans, but, when the time of action comes, then they lose their presence of mind and fail.

We are superior to the Athenians in numbers, in military skill, in unanimity, and our fleet will soon be on a level with theirs.

121 'We, however, do not make war upon the Athenians in a spirit of vain-glory, but from a sense of wrong; there is ample justification, and when we obtain redress, we will put up the sword. For every reason we are likely to succeed. First, because we are superior in numbers and in military skill; secondly, because we all obey as one man the orders given to us. They are doubtless strong at sea, but we too will provide a navy, for which the means can be supplied partly by contributions from each state, partly out of the funds at Delphi and Olympia. A loan will be granted to us, and by the offer of higher pay we can draw away their foreign sailors. The Athenian power consists of mercenaries, and not of their own citizens; but our soldiers are not mercenaries, and therefore cannot so be bought, for we are strong in men if poor in money. Let them be beaten in a single naval engagement and they are probably conquered at once; but suppose they hold out, we shall then have more time in which to practise at sea. As soon as we have brought our skill up to the level of theirs our courage will surely give us the victory. For that is a natural gift which they cannot learn, but their superior skill is a thing acquired, [b]which we must attain by practice[b].

But we must find money.

'And the money which is required for the war, we will provide by a contribution. What! shall their allies never fail in paying the tribute which is to enslave them, and shall we refuse

[a] Reading ὅμοια.   [b] Or, 'which we must overcome by practice.'

to give freely in order to save ourselves and be avenged on our enemies, or rather to prevent the money which we refused to give from being taken from us by them and used to our destruction?

'These are some of the means by which the war may 122
be carried on; but there are others. We may induce their allies to revolt,—a sure mode of cutting off the revenues in which the strength of Athens consists; or we may plant a fort in their country; and there are many expedients which will hereafter suggest themselves. For war, least of all things, conforms to prescribed rules; it strikes out a path for itself when the moment comes. And therefore he who has his temper under control in warfare is safer far, but he who gets into a passion is, through his own fault, liable to the greater fall.

By gaining over their allies, we may cut off their resources.

'If this were merely a quarrel between one of us and our neighbours about a boundary line it would not matter; but reflect: the truth is that the Athenians are a match for us all, and much more than a match for any single city. And if we allow ourselves to be divided or are not united against them heart and soul—the whole confederacy and every nation and city in it—they will easily overpower us. It may seem a hard saying, but you may be sure that defeat means nothing but downright slavery, and the bare mention of such a possibility is a disgrace to the Peloponnese:—shall so many states suffer at the hands of one? Men will say, some that we deserve our fate, others that we are too cowardly to resist: and we shall seem a degenerate race. For our fathers were the liberators of Hellas, but we cannot secure even our own liberty; and while we make a point of overthrowing the rule of a single man in this or that city, we allow a city which is a tyrant to be set up in the midst of us. Are we not open to one of three most serious charges—folly,

If we quietly submit we shall deserve to be slaves.

cowardice, or carelessness? [a] For you certainly do not escape such imputations by wrapping yourselves in that contemptuous wisdom which has so often [a] brought men to ruin, as in the end to be pronounced contemptible folly.

123 'But why should we dwell reproachfully upon the past, except in the interest of the present? We should rather, looking to the future, devote our energies to the task which we have immediately in hand. By labour to win virtue,—that is the lesson which we [b] have learnt from our fathers, and which you ought not to unlearn, because you chance to have some trifling advantage over them in wealth and power; for men should not lose in the time of their wealth what was gained by them in their time of want. There are many reasons why you may advance with confidence. The God has spoken and has promised to take our part himself. All Hellas will fight at our side, from motives either of fear or of interest. And you will not break the treaty,—the God in bidding you go to war pronounces it to have been already broken,—but you will avenge the violation of it. For those who attack others, not those who defend themselves, are the real violators of treaties [c].

In going to war you have the God and the feeling of Hellas on your side, and you will not break the treaty.

124 'On every ground you will be right in going to war: it is our united advice; [d] and if you believe community of interests to be the surest ground of strength both to states and individuals, send speedy aid [d] to the Potidaeans, who are Dorians and now besieged by Ionians (for times have changed), and recover the

We cannot go on as we are. War is the way to peace; but peace may be the way to war.

---

[a] Or, 'For we cannot suppose that, having avoided these errors, you have wrapped yourselves in that contemptuous wisdom, which has so often' etc.

[b] Reading ἡμῖν.

[c] Cp. i. 71 fin.

[d] Reading ταὐτά: or, with all the MSS. retaining ταῦτα: 'And as it is most certain that the policy which we recommend is for our advantage both as states and individuals, send speedy aid' etc.

liberties which the rest of the allies have lost. We cannot go on as we are: for some of us are already suffering, and if it is known that we have met, but do not dare to defend ourselves, others will soon share their fate. Acknowledging then, allies, that there is no alternative, and that we are advising you for the best, vote for war; and be not afraid of the immediate danger, but fix your thoughts on the durable peace which will follow. For by war peace is assured, but to remain at peace when you should be going to war may be often very dangerous. The tyrant city which has been set up in Hellas is a standing menace to all alike; she rules over some of us already, and would fain rule over others. Let us attack and subdue her, that we may ourselves live safely for the future and deliver the Hellenes whom she has enslaved.'

Such were the words of the Corinthians.

Nearly a year is spent in preparation.

The Lacedaemonians, having heard the opinions of all 125
the allies, put the question to them all, one after the other, great and small alike, and the majority voted for war. But, although they had come to this decision, they were not ready, and could not take up arms at once; so they determined to make the necessary preparations, each for themselves, with the least possible delay. Still nearly a whole year was passed in preparation before they invaded Attica and commenced open hostilities.

The story of Cylon told in explanation of the curse of the Goddess.

During this interval they sent embassies to Athens and 126
made various complaints that their grounds for going to war might be all the stronger in case the Athenians refused to listen. The first ambassadors desired the Athenians to drive out 'the curse of the Goddess.' The B.C. 620?
curse to which they referred was as follows:—In the days Ol. 40?
of old there was an Athenian named Cylon, who had been an Olympic victor; he was powerful and of noble birth; and he had married the daughter of Theagenes, a Megarian who was at that time tyrant of Megara. In answer to an

enquiry which Cylon made at Delphi, the God told him to seize the Acropolis of Athens at the greatest festival of Zeus. Thereupon he obtained forces from Theagenes, and, persuading his friends to join him, when the time of the Olympic festival in Peloponnesus came round, he took possession of the Acropolis, intending to make himself tyrant. He thought that this was the greatest festival of Zeus, and, having been an Olympic victor, he seemed to have a special interest in it. But whether the greatest festival spoken of was in Attica or in some other part of Hellas was a question which never entered into his mind, and the oracle said nothing about it. (For the Athenians also have a greatest festival of Zeus—the festival of Zeus the Gracious, or Diasia, as it is called[a]—this is held outside the city and the whole people sacrifice at it, some, ordinary victims, others, a kind of offering peculiar to the country.) However, Cylon thought that his interpretation was right, and made the attempt at the Olympic festival. The Athenians, when they saw what had happened, came in a body from the fields and invested the Acropolis. After a time they grew tired of the siege and most of them went away, committing the guard to the nine Archons, and giving them full powers to do what they thought best in the whole matter; for in those days public affairs were chiefly administered by the nine Archons[b]. Cylon and his companions were in great distress from want of food and water. So he and his brother made their escape; the rest, being hard pressed, and some of them ready to die of hunger, sat as suppliants at the altar which is in the Acropolis. When the Athenians, to whose charge the guard had been committed, saw them dying in the temple, they bade them rise, promising to do them no harm, and then led them away and put them to death. They even slew some of them in the very presence of the awful Goddesses at whose altars, in passing by, they had sought

[a] Placing the comma before instead of after Διάσια.

[b] Cp. Herod. v. 71.

refuge. The murderers and their descendants are held to be accursed, and offenders against the Goddess. These accursed persons were banished by the Athenians; and Cleomenes, the Lacedaemonian king, again banished them from Athens in a time of civil strife by the help of the opposite faction, expelling the living and disinterring and casting forth the bones of the dead[a]. Nevertheless they afterwards returned, and to this day their race still survives in the city.

The Lacedaemonians desired the Athenians to drive 127
away this curse, as if the honour of the Gods were their first object, but in reality because they knew that the curse attached to Pericles, the son of Xanthippus, by his mother's side, and they thought that if he were banished they would find the Athenians more manageable. They did not really expect that he would be driven into exile, but they hoped to discredit him with the citizens and make them believe that his misfortune was to a certain extent the cause of the war. For he was the leader of the state and the most powerful man of his day, and his policy was utterly opposed to the Lacedaemonians. He would not suffer the Athenians to give way, but was always urging upon them the necessity of war.

This curse attached to Pericles.

The Athenians retaliated by demanding that the Lace- 128
daemonians should drive away the curse of Taenarus. They referred to the murder of certain Helots who had taken refuge in the temple of Poseidon at Taenarus; these the Lacedaemonians, having first raised by the hand, had then led away and slain. The Lacedaemonians themselves believe this act of theirs to have been the cause of the great earthquake which visited Sparta[b]. The Athenians also bade them drive out

The Athenians retaliate by desiring the Lacedaemonians to purge away other curses. The curse of the Goddess explained to be the murder of certain suppliant Helots; the curse of Athenè of the Brazen House was caused by the death of Pausanias in the precincts of her temple.

[a] Cp. Herod. v. 70, 72.

[b] Cp. i. 101, 102.

B.C. 477. Ol. 75, 4. the curse of Athenè of the Brazen House. The story is as follows:—When Pausanias the Lacedaemonian was originally summoned by the Spartans to give an account of his command at the Hellespont[a], and had been tried and acquitted, he was no longer sent out in a public capacity, but he hired a trireme of Hermionè on his own account and sailed to the Hellespont, pretending that he had gone thither to fight in the cause of the Hellenes. In reality he wanted to prosecute an intrigue with the King, by which he hoped to obtain the empire of Hellas. He had already taken the first steps after the return from

B.C. 478 or 477. Ol. 75, 3 or 4. Cyprus, when he captured Byzantium[b]. The city was at that time held by the Persians and by certain relatives and kinsmen of the King, who were taken prisoners. These he restored to the King without the knowledge of the allies, to whom he declared that they had made their escape. This act was the beginning of the whole affair, and thereby he originally placed the King under an obligation to him. His accomplice was Gongylus the Eretrian, to whose care he had entrusted Byzantium and the captives. To this same Gongylus he also gave a letter addressed to the King, of which, as was afterwards discovered, the terms were as follows:—

'Pausanias, the Spartan commander, desiring to do you a service, sends you back these captives of his spear. And I propose, if you have no objection, to marry your daughter, and to bring Sparta and the rest of Hellas under your sway. I think that I can accomplish this if you and I take counsel together. Should you approve of my proposal, send a trusty person to the sea and through him we will negotiate.' Thus far the letter.

129 Xerxes was pleased, and sent Artabazus the son of

Intrigue of Pausanias with Xerxes.

Pharnaces to the sea, commanding him to assume the government of the satrapy of Dascylium in the room of Megabates. An answer was

---

[a] Cp. i. 95.

[b] Cp. i. 94.

entrusted to him, which he was to send as quickly as possible to Pausanias at Byzantium; he was to show him at the same time the royal seal. If Pausanias gave him any order about his own affairs, he was to execute it with all diligence and fidelity. Artabazus came down to the sea, as he was desired, and transmitted the letter. The answer of the King was as follows:—

'Thus saith Xerxes, the King, to Pausanias. The benefit which thou hast done me in saving the captives who were taken at Byzantium beyond the sea is recorded in my house for ever, and thy words please me. Let neither day nor night hinder thee from fulfilling diligently the promise which thou hast made to me; spare not gold or silver, and take as large an army as thou wilt, wheresoever it may be required. I have sent to thee Artabazus, a good man; act with him for my honour and welfare, and for thine own, and be of good courage.'

B.C. 477 or 476 ff. Ol. 75, 4 or 76 ff.

Pausanias, carried away by pride, manifests his ambitious designs.

Pausanias received the letter. He had already acquired a high reputation among the Hellenes when in command at Plataea, and now he was so great that he could no longer contain himself or live like other men. Whenever he marched out of Byzantium he wore Persian apparel. On his way through Thrace he was always attended by a body-guard of Medes and Egyptians, and he had his table served after the Persian fashion. He could not conceal his ambition, but indicated by little things the greater designs which he was meditating. He made himself difficult of access, and displayed such a violent temper towards everybody that no one could come near him; and this was one of the chief reasons why the confederacy transferred themselves to the Athenians. 130

The news of his behaviour soon reached the Lacedaemonians; who had recalled him in the first instance on this ground[a]. And now, when he had sailed away in the ship 131

[a] Cp. i. 93 init.

of Hermione without leave[a], and was evidently carrying on the same practices; when he had been forced out of Byzantium and the gates had been shut against him by the Athenians; and when, instead of returning to Sparta, he settled at Colonae in Troas, and was reported to the Ephors to be negotiating with the Barbarians, and to be staying there for no good purpose, then at last they made up their minds to act. They sent a herald to him with a despatch rolled on a scytalè, commanding him to follow the officer home, and saying that, if he refused, Sparta would declare war against him. He, being desirous as far as he could to avoid suspicion and believing that he could dispose of the accusations by bribery, returned for the second time to Sparta. On his return he was at once thrown into prison by the Ephors, who have the power to imprison the king himself. But after a time he contrived to come out, and challenged any one who asserted his guilt to bring him to trial.

He is recalled a second time by the Lacedaemonians and thrown into prison, but soon comes out and offers himself for trial.

132 As yet however neither his enemies among the citizens nor the Spartan government had any trustworthy evidence such as would have justified them in inflicting punishment upon a member of the royal family holding royal office at the time. For he was the guardian as well as cousin of the king, Pleistarchus son of Leonidas, who was still a minor. But his disregard of propriety and affectation of Barbarian fashions made them strongly suspect that he was dissatisfied with his position in the state. They examined into any violation of established usage which they could find in his previous life; and they remembered among other things how in past times he had presumed on his own authority to inscribe on the tripod at Delphi, which the Hellenes

Sufficient evidence cannot be obtained. At last his confidential servant opens a letter which he was to carry to the Persian satrap, and finding an order for his own death, turns informer.

---

[a] Cp. i. 128.

dedicated as the firstfruits of their victory over the Persians, this elegiac couplet:—

> 'Pausanias, captain of the Hellenes, having destroyed the Persian host,
> Made this offering to Phoebus for a memorial.'

The Lacedaemonians had at once effaced the lines and inscribed on the tripod the names of the cities which took part in the overthrow of the Barbarian and in the dedication of the offering. But still this act of Pausanias gave offence at the time, and, now that he had again fallen under suspicion, seemed to receive a new light from his present designs. They were also informed that he was intriguing with the Helots; and this was true, for he had promised them emancipation and citizenship if they would join him in an insurrection and help to carry out his whole design. Still the magistrates would not take decided measures; they even refused to believe the distinct testimony which certain Helots brought against him; their habit having always been to be slow in taking an irrevocable decision against a Spartan without incontestable proof. At last a certain man of Argilus, who had been a favourite and was still a confidential servant of Pausanias, turned informer. He had been commissioned by him to carry to Artabazus the last letters for the King, but the thought struck him that no previous messenger had ever returned; he took alarm, and so, having counterfeited the seal of Pausanias in order to avoid discovery if he were mistaken, or if Pausanias, wanting to make some alteration, should ask him for the letter, he opened it, and among the directions given in it found written, as he had partly suspected, an order for his own death.

He showed the letter to the Ephors, who were now 133
more inclined to believe, but still they wanted to hear something from Pausanias' own mouth, and so, according to a plan preconcerted with them, the man went to Taenarus as a suppliant and there put up a hut divided by a partition. In the inner part of the hut he placed some

of the Ephors, and when Pausanias came to him and asked him why he was a suppliant, the whole truth was at once revealed to them. There was the man reproaching Pausanias with the directions which he had found in the letter, and going into minute details about the whole affair; he protested that never on any occasion had he brought him into any trouble when sent on his service in this matter to the King: why then should he share the fate of the other messengers, and be rewarded with death? And there was Pausanias, admitting the truth of his words, and telling him not to be angry at what had happened, offering to raise him by the hand that he might safely leave the temple, and bidding him start at once and not make difficulties.

His servant takes sanctuary at Taenarus, where he conceals some of the Ephors. Pausanias coming to enquire the reason reveals the whole.

134 The Ephors, who had heard every word, went away for the present, intending, now that they had certain knowledge, to take Pausanias in the city. It is said that he was on the point of being arrested in the street, when the face of one of them as they approached revealed to him their purpose, and another who was friendly warned him by a hardly perceptible nod. Whereupon he ran and fled to the temple of Athenè of the Brazen House and arrived before them, for the precinct was not far off. There, entering into a small chamber which belonged to the temple, that he might not suffer from exposure to the weather, he remained. His pursuers, failing to overtake him, afterwards unroofed the building, and watching when he was within, and preventing him from getting out, they built up the doors, and, investing the place, starved him to death. He was on the point of expiring in the chamber where he lay, when they, observing his condition, brought him out; he was still breathing, but as soon as he was brought out he died. The Spartans were going to cast his body into the Caeadas, a chasm into which they throw malefactors, but they

The Ephors attempt to arrest Pausanias. He flies to the temple of Athenè and is there shut in and starved to death.

changed their minds and buried him somewhere in the neighbourhood. The God of Delphi afterwards commanded them to transfer him to the place where he died, and he now lies in the entrance to the precinct, as the inscription on the column testifies. The oracle also told them that they had brought a curse upon themselves, and must offer two bodies for one to Athenè of the Brazen House. Whereupon they made two brazen statues, which they dedicated, intending them to be an expiation for Pausanias.

To this judgment of the God himself the Athenians 135
referred when they retorted on the Lacedaemonians, telling them to banish the curse.

Themistocles is implicated in the plot, and officers are sent to take him.

Now the evidence which proved that Pausanias was in league with Persia implicated Themistocles; and the Lacedaemonians sent ambassadors to the Athenians charging him likewise with treason, and demanding that he should receive the same punishment. The Athenians agreed, but having been ostracised he was living at the time in Argos, whence he used to visit other parts of the Peloponnese. The Lacedaemonians were very ready to join in the pursuit; so they and the Athenians sent officers, who were told to arrest him wherever they should find him.

He seeks refuge among the Corcyraeans; they are afraid of Athens and Lacedaemon, and send him away to Epirus. Coming to the house of Admetus, king of the Molossians, he sits as a suppliant at the hearth.

Themistocles received information of their purpose, and 136
fled from the Peloponnesus to the Corcyraeans, who were under an obligation to him. The Corcyraeans said that they were afraid to keep him, lest they should incur the enmity of Athens and Lacedaemon; so they conveyed him to the neighbouring continent, whither he was followed by the officers, who constantly enquired in which direction he had gone and pursued him everywhere. Owing to an accident he was compelled to stop at the house of Admetus, king of the Molossians, who was not his friend.

He chanced to be absent from home, but Themistocles presented himself as a suppliant to his wife, and was instructed by her to take their child and sit at the hearth. Admetus soon returned, and then Themistocles told him who he was, adding that if in past times he had opposed any request which Admetus had made to the Athenians, he ought not to retaliate on an exile. He was now in such extremity that a far weaker adversary than he could do him a mischief; but a noble nature should not be revenged by taking at a disadvantage one as good as himself. Themistocles further argued that he had opposed Admetus in some matter of business, and not when life was at stake; but that, if Admetus delivered him up, he would be consigning him to death. At the same time he told him who his pursuers were and what was the charge against him.

Admetus gives him protection, and when the officers arrive in pursuit, sends him to Pydna, whence he sails to Ephesus.

137 Admetus, hearing his words, raised him up, together with his own son, from the place where he sat holding the child in his arms, which was the most solemn form of supplication. Not long afterwards the Athenians and Lacedaemonians came and pressed him to give up the fugitive, but he refused; and as Themistocles wanted to go to the King, sent him on foot across the country to the sea at Pydna (which was in the kingdom of Alexander). There he found a merchant
B.C. 466. vessel sailing to Ionia, in which he embarked; it was
Ol. 78, 3. driven, however, by a storm to the station of the Athenian fleet which was blockading Naxos. He was unknown to his fellow passengers, but, fearing what might happen, he told the captain who he was and why he fled, threatening if he did not save his life to say that he had been bribed to take him on board. The only hope was that no one should be allowed to leave the ship while they had to remain off Naxos; if he complied with his request, the obligation should be abundantly repaid. The captain agreed, and after anchoring in a rough sea for a day and

a night off the Athenian station, he at length arrived at Ephesus. Themistocles rewarded him with a liberal present; for he received soon afterwards from his friends the property which they had in their keeping at Athens, and which he had deposited at Argos. He then went up the country in the company of one of the Persians who dwelt on the coast, and sent a letter to Artaxerxes the son of B.C. 465.
Xerxes, who had just succeeded to the throne. The letter Ol. 78, 4.
was in the following words:—'I, Themistocles, have come to you, I who of all

His letter to the King.

Hellenes did your house the greatest injuries so long as I was compelled to defend myself against your father; but still greater benefits when I was in safety and he in danger during his retreat. And there is a debt of gratitude due to me' (here he noted how he had forewarned Xerxes at Salamis of the resolution of the Hellenes to withdraw[a], and how through his influence, as he pretended, they had refrained from breaking down the bridges)[b]. 'Now I am here, able to do you many other services, and persecuted by the Hellenes for your sake. Let me wait a year, and then I will myself explain why I have come.'

The King is said to have been astonished at the boldness 138
of his character, and told him to wait a year as he proposed. In the interval he made himself acquainted, as far as he could, with the Persian language and the manners of the country. When

Going to the Court of Persia, he acquires the favour of the King and receives great honour, but shortly after dies.

the year was over, he arrived at the court and became a greater man there than any Hellene had ever been before. This was due partly to his previous reputation, and partly to the hope which he inspired in the King's mind that he would enslave Hellas to him; above all, his ability had been tried and

The greatness of his character. His natural acuteness and foresight: his power of persuasion, his readiness in an emergency.

not found wanting. For Themistocles was a man whose

---

[a] Cp. Herod. viii. 75.

[b] Cp. Herod. viii. 108.

natural force was unmistakeable; this was the quality for which he was distinguished above all other men; from his own native acuteness, and without any study either before or at the time, he was the ablest judge of the course to be pursued in a sudden emergency, and could best divine what was likely to happen in the remotest future. Whatever he had in hand he had the power of explaining to others, and even where he had no experience he was quite competent to form a sufficient judgment; no one could foresee with equal clearness the good or evil event which was hidden in the future. In a word, Themistocles, by natural power of mind and with the least preparation, was of all men the best able to extemporise the right thing to be done. A sickness put an end to his life, although some say that he poisoned himself because he felt that he could not accomplish what he had promised to the King. There is a monument of him in the agora of the Asiatic Magnesia, where he was governor—the King assigning to him, for bread, Magnesia, which produced a revenue of fifty talents [a] in the year; for wine, Lampsacus, which was considered to be the richest in wine of any district then known; and Myus for meat. His family say that his remains were carried home at his own request and buried in Attica, but secretly; for he had been accused of treason and had fled from his country, and he could not lawfully be interred there. Such was the end of Pausanias the Lacedaemonian, and Themistocles the Athenian, the two most famous Hellenes of their day.

139 B.C. 432. Ol. 87.

The Lacedaemonians make a final demand for the restoration of independence to the Hellenes. Speech of Pericles.

Thus the demand for the banishment of the accursed made by the Lacedaemonians on the occasion of their first embassy was met by a counter demand on the part of Athens. They came again and again, and told the Athenians that they must raise the siege of Potidaea and restore Aegina to indepen-

[a] About £10,000

dence. Above all, and in the plainest terms, they insisted B.C. 432.
that if they wanted to avert war, they must rescind the Ol. 87.
decree which excluded the Megarians from the market of Athens and the harbours in the Athenian dominions. But the Athenians would not listen to them, nor rescind the decree; alleging in reply that the Megarians had tilled the holy ground and the neutral borderland, and had received their runaway slaves. Finally, there came from Sparta an embassy, consisting of Rhamphias, Melesippus, and Hegesander, who said nothing of all this, but only, 'The Lacedaemonians desire to maintain peace; and peace there may be, if you will restore independence to the Hellenes.' Whereupon the Athenians called an assembly and held a discussion; it seemed best to them to make up their minds and to give a complete and final answer. Many came forward to speak, and much was said on both sides, some affirming that they ought to go to war, and others that this decree about the Megarians should be rescinded and not stand in the way of peace. At last Pericles the son of Xanthippus, who was the first man of his day at Athens, and the greatest orator and statesman, came forward and advised as follows:—

I still give you my old advice,—Do not yield to the Peloponnesians.

'Athenians, I say, as I always have said, that we must 140
never yield to the Peloponnesians, although I know that men are persuaded to go to war in one temper of mind, and act when the time comes in another, and that their resolutions change with the changes of fortune. But I see that I must give you the same or nearly the same advice which I gave before, and I call upon those whom my words may convince to maintain our united determination, even if we should not escape disaster; or else, if our sagacity be justified by success, to claim no share of the credit[a].

---

[a] Cp. ii. 64 init.

B.C. 432. Ol. 87. The movement of events is often as wayward and incomprehensible as the course of human thought; and this is why we ascribe to chance whatever belies our calculation.

The demands of the Lacedaemonians may seem trifling, but submission to them will only provoke fresh demands and implies the loss of our independence.

'For some time past the designs of the Lacedaemonians have been clear enough, and they are still clearer now. Our agreement says that when differences arise, the two parties shall refer them to arbitration, and in the mean time both are to retain what they have. But for arbitration they never ask; and when it is offered by us, they refuse it[a]. They want to redress their grievances by arms and not by argument; and now they come to us, using the language, no longer of expostulation, but of command. They tell us to quit Potidaea, to leave Aegina independent, and to rescind the decree respecting the Megarians. These last ambassadors go further still, and announce that we must give the Hellenes independence. I would have none of you imagine that he will be fighting for a small matter if we refuse to annul the Megarian decree, of which they make so much, telling us that its revocation would prevent the war. You should have no lingering uneasiness about this; you are not really going to war for a trifle. For in the seeming trifle is involved the trial and confirmation of your whole purpose. If you yield to them in a small matter, they will think that you are afraid, and will immediately dictate some more oppressive condition; but if you are firm, you will prove to them that they must treat you as their equals.
141 Wherefore make up your minds once for all, either to give way while you are still unharmed, or, if we are going to war, as in my judgment is best, then on no plea small or great to give way at all; we will not condescend to possess our own in fear. Any claim, the smallest as well

[a] Cp. i. 78.

as the greatest, imposed on a neighbour and an equal when there has been no legal award, can mean nothing but slavery. B.C. 432. Ol. 87.

Unless you mean to give way now, you must determine never to give way at all. Nor need you fear the result; for you have many advantages over the Peloponnesians; they are poor and till their own land, they are unaccustomed to great wars, and divided in race.

'That our resources are equal to theirs, and that we shall be as strong in the war, I will now prove to you in detail. The Peloponnesians cultivate their own lands, and they have no wealth either public or private. Nor have they any experience of long wars in countries beyond the sea; their poverty prevents them from fighting, except in person against each other, and that for a short time only. Such men cannot be often manning fleets or sending out armies. They would be at a distance from their own properties, upon which they must nevertheless draw, and they will be kept off the sea by us. Now wars are supported out of accumulated wealth, and not out of forced contributions. And men who cultivate their own lands are more ready to serve with their persons than with their property[a]; they do not despair of their lives, but they soon grow anxious lest their money should all be spent, especially if the war in which they are engaged is protracted beyond their calculation, as may well be the case. In a single pitched battle the Peloponnesians and their allies are a match for all Hellas, but they are not able to maintain a war against a power different in kind from their own[b]; they have no regular general assembly, and therefore cannot execute their plans with speed and decision. The confederacy is made up of many races; all the representatives have equal votes, and press their several interests. There follows the usual result, that nothing is ever done properly. For some are all anxiety to be revenged on an enemy, while others only want to get off with as little loss as possible. The members of such

[a] Cp. i. 121 med. [b] Cp. viii. 96 fin.

B.C. 432. Ol. 87. a confederacy are slow to meet, and when they do meet, they give little time to the consideration of any common interest, and a great deal to schemes which further the interest of their particular state. Every one fancies that his own neglect will do no harm, but that it is somebody else's business to keep a look-out for him, and this idea, cherished alike by each, is the secret ruin of all.

142 'Their greatest difficulty will be want of money, which they can only provide slowly; delay will thus occur, and war waits for no man. Further, no fortified place which they can raise against us[a] is to be feared any more than their navy. As to the first, even in time of peace it would be hard for them to build a city able to compete with Athens; and how much more so when they are in an enemy's country, and our walls will be a menace to them quite as much as theirs to us! Or, again, if they simply raise a fort in our territory, they may do mischief to some part of our lands by sallies, and the slaves may desert to them; but that will not prevent us from sailing to the Peloponnese and there raising forts against them, and defending ourselves there by the help of our navy, which is our strong arm. For we have gained more experience of fighting on land from warfare at sea than they of naval affairs from warfare on land. And they will not easily acquire the art of seamanship[b]; even you yourselves, who have been practising ever since the Persian War, are not yet perfect. How can they, who are not sailors, but tillers of the soil, do much? They will not even be permitted to practise, because a large fleet will constantly be lying in wait for them. If they were watched by a few ships only, they might run the risk, trusting to their numbers and forgetting their inexperience; but if they are kept off the sea by our superior strength, their

They cannot do you any real harm by building a rival city or fortified posts in Attica; nor can they, mere landsmen as they are, rival you at sea.

[a] Cp. i. 122 init.

[b] Cp. i. 121 med.

want of practice will make them unskilful, and their want B.C. 432.
of skill timid. Maritime skill is like skill of other kinds, Ol. 87.
not a thing to be cultivated by the way or at chance times; it is jealous of any other pursuit which distracts the mind for an instant from itself.

'Suppose, again, that they lay hands on the treasures 143
at Olympia and Delphi, and tempt our mercenary sailors with the offer of higher pay[a], there might be serious danger, if we and our metics[b] embarking alone were not still a match for them. But we are a match for them: and, best of all, our pilots are taken from our own citizens, while no sailors are to be found so good or so numerous as ours in all the rest of Hellas. None of our mercenaries will choose to fight on their side for the sake of a few days' high pay, when he will not only be an exile, but will incur greater danger, and will have less hope of victory.

Our foreign sailors will not be tempted by offers of high pay, and if they are, we can do without them.

'Such I conceive to be the prospects of the Peloponnesians. But we ourselves are free from the defects which I have noted in them; and we have great advantages. If they attack our country by land, we shall attack theirs by sea; and the devastation, even of part of Peloponnesus, will be a very different thing from that of all Attica. For they, if they want fresh territory, must take it by arms, whereas we have abundance of land both in the islands and on the continent; such is the power which the empire of the sea gives. Reflect, if we were islanders, who would be more invulnerable? Let us imagine that we are, and acting in that spirit let us give up land and houses, but keep a watch over the city and the sea. We should not under any irritation at the loss of our property give battle to the Peloponnesians, who far outnumber us. If we conquer,

We must guard the city and the sea, and not mind about our houses and lands in the country.

[a] Cp. i. 121 init. [b] Cp. iii. 16 init.

B.C. 432. Ol. 87.

we shall have to fight over again with as many more; and if we fail, besides the defeat, our confederacy, which is our strength, will be lost to us; for our allies will rise in revolt when we are no longer capable of making war upon them. Mourn not for houses and lands, but for men; men may gain these, but these will not gain men. If I thought that you would listen to me, I would say to you, "Go yourselves and destroy them, and thereby prove to the Peloponnesians that none of these things will move you."

Let our answer be: We will grant independence to our allies, if the Lacedaemonians will allow their subjects to choose their own form of government.

144 'I have many other reasons for believing that you will conquer, but you must not be extending your empire while you are at war, or run into unnecessary dangers. I am more afraid of our own mistakes than of our enemies' designs. But of all this I will speak again when the time of action comes; for the present, let us send the ambassadors away, giving them this answer: "That we will not exclude the Megarians from our markets and harbours, if the Lacedaemonians will cease to expel foreigners, whether ourselves or our allies, from Sparta; for the treaty no more forbids the one than the other. That we will concede independence to the cities, if they were independent when we made the treaty, and as soon as the Lacedaemonians allow their allied states a true independence, not for the interest of Lacedaemon, but everywhere for their own. Also that we are willing to offer arbitration according to the treaty. And that we do not want to begin a war, but intend to defend ourselves if attacked." This answer will be just, and befits the dignity of the city. We must be aware however that war will come; and the more willing we are to accept the situation, the less ready will our enemies be to lay hands upon us. Remember that where dangers are greatest, there the greatest honours are to be won by men and states. Our

We do not want war, but offer arbitration. Still peace is hopeless; and we must prepare for war in a spirit worthy of our fathers.

fathers, when they withstood the Persian, had no such power as we have; what little they had they forsook: not by good fortune but by wisdom, and not by power but by courage, they drove the Barbarian away and raised us to our present height of greatness. We must be worthy of them, and resist our enemies to the utmost, that we may hand down our empire unimpaired to posterity.' B.C. 432. Ol. 87.

145 Such were the words of Pericles. The Athenians, approving, voted as he told them, and on his motion answered the Lacedaemonians in detail as he had suggested, and on the whole question to the effect 'that they would do nothing upon compulsion, but were ready to settle their differences by arbitration upon fair terms according to the treaty.' So the ambassadors went home and came no more.

The Athenians adopt Pericles' advice.

146 These were the causes of offence alleged on either side before the war began. The quarrel arose immediately out of the affair of Epidamnus and Corcyra. But, although the contest was imminent, the contending parties still kept up intercourse and visited each other, without a herald, but not with entire confidence. For the situation was really an abrogation of the treaty, and might at any time lead to war.

War, though not formally proclaimed, is imminent.

BOOK II

1 AND now the war between the Athenians and Peloponnesians and the allies of both actually began. Henceforward the struggle was uninterrupted, and they communicated with one another only by heralds. The narrative is arranged according to summers and winters and follows the order of events.

B.C. 431. Ol. 87, 2.

Outbreak of the war.

2 For fourteen years the thirty years' peace which was concluded after the recovery of Euboea remained unbroken. But in the fifteenth year, when Chrysis the high-priestess of Argos was in the forty-eighth year of her priesthood, Aenesias being Ephor at Sparta, and at Athens Pythodorus having two months of his archonship to run[a], in the sixth month after the engagement at Potidaea and at the beginning of spring, about the first watch of the night an armed force of somewhat more than three hundred Thebans entered Plataea, a city of Boeotia, which was an ally of Athens, under the command of two Boeotarchs, Pythangelus the son of Phyleides, and Diemporus the son of Onetorides. They were invited by Naucleides, a Plataean, and his partisans, who opened the gates to them. These men wanted to kill certain citizens of the opposite faction and to make over the city to the Thebans, in the hope of getting the power into their own hands. The intrigue had been conducted by Eurymachus the son of Leontiades,

The Thebans enter Plataea by night.

[a] For the difficulties attending the chronology see note on the passage.

one of the chief citizens of Thebes. There was an old quarrel between the two cities, and the Thebans, seeing that war was inevitable, were anxious to surprise the place while the peace lasted and before hostilities had actually broken out. No watch had been set; and so they were enabled to enter the city unperceived. They grounded their arms in the Agora, but instead of going to work at once and making their way into the houses of their enemies, as those who invited them suggested, they resolved to issue a conciliatory proclamation and try to make friends with the citizens. The herald announced that if any one wished to become their ally and return to the ancient constitution of Boeotia, he should join their ranks. In this way they thought that the inhabitants would easily be induced to come over to them.

B.C. 431. Ol. 87, 2.

The Plataeans, when they found that the city had been 3
surprised and taken and that the Thebans were within their walls, were panic-stricken. In the darkness they were unable to see them and greatly over-estimated their numbers. So they came to terms, and accepting the proposals which were made to them, remained quiet, the more readily since the Thebans offered violence to no one. But in the course of the negotiations they somehow discovered that their enemies were not so numerous as they had supposed, and concluded that they could easily attack and master them. They determined to make the attempt, for the commons at Plataea were strongly attached to the Athenian alliance. They began to collect inside the houses, breaking through the party-walls that they might not be seen going along the streets; they likewise raised barricades of waggons (without the beasts which drew them), and took other measures suitable to the emergency. When they had done all which could be done under the circumstances, they sallied forth from their houses, choosing the time of night just before daybreak,

The Plataeans, terrified by the sudden attack, come to terms. But afterwards, discovering the weakness of the enemy, they gather and fall upon the Thebans.

B.C. 431. Ol. 87, 2.

lest, if they put off the attack until dawn, the enemy might be more confident and more a match for them. While darkness lasted they would be timid, and at a disadvantage, not knowing the streets so well as themselves. So they fell upon them at once hand to hand.

The Thebans, after some resistance, turn and fly. Being ignorant of the way, many are slain in the streets; a few escape; the remainder surrender.

4 When the Thebans found that they had been deceived they closed their ranks and resisted their assailants on every side. Two or three times they drove them back. But when at last the Plataeans charged them, and the women and slaves on the housetops screamed and yelled and pelted them with stones and tiles, the confusion, which was aggravated by the rain which had been falling heavily during the night, became too much for them, and they turned and fled in terror through the city. Hardly any of them knew the way out, and the streets were dark as well as muddy, for the affair happened at the end of the month when there was no moon; whereas their pursuers knew well enough how to prevent their escape; and thus many of them perished. The gates by which they entered were the only ones open, and these a Plataean fastened with the spike of a javelin, which he thrust into the bar instead of the pin. So this exit too was closed and they were chased up and down the city. Some of them mounted upon the wall and cast themselves down into the open. Most of these were killed. Others got out by a deserted gate, cutting through the bar unperceived with an axe which a woman gave them; but only a few, for they were soon found out. Others lost themselves in different parts of the city, and were put to death. But the greater number kept together and took refuge in a large building abutting upon the wall, of which the doors on the near side chanced to be open, they thinking them to be the gates of the city, and expecting to find a way through them into the country. The Plataeans, seeing that they were in a trap, began to consider whether they should not set the building on fire,

B.C. 431. Ol. 87, 2.

and burn them where they were. At last they and the other Thebans who were still alive, and were wandering about the city, agreed to surrender themselves and their arms unconditionally. Thus fared the Thebans in Plataea.

Reinforcements come from Thebes. The Plataeans, suspecting that the Thebans intend to seize their citizens outside the walls, send a herald, promising with an oath (according to the Theban account) to restore the prisoners if the Thebans retired. The prisoners are put to death.

The main body of the Theban army, which should have 5
come during the night to the support of the party entering the city in case of a reverse, having on their march heard of the disaster, were now hastening to the rescue. Plataea is about eight miles distant from Thebes, and the heavy rain which had fallen in the night delayed their arrival; for the river Asopus had swollen, and was not easily fordable. Marching in the rain, and with difficulty crossing the river, they came up too late, some of their friends being already slain and others captives. When the Thebans became aware of the state of affairs, they resolved to lay hands on what was outside the walls; for there were men and property left in the fields, as would naturally happen when a sudden blow was struck in time of peace. They meant to keep any one whom they caught as a hostage and exchange him for one of their own men, if any of them were still alive. But before they had executed their plan, the Plataeans, suspecting their intentions, and fearing for their friends outside, sent a herald to the Thebans protesting against the crime of which they had been guilty in trying to seize their city during peace, and warning them not to touch anything which was outside the walls. If they persisted they threatened in return to kill the prisoners; but if they retired, they would give them up. This is the Theban account, and they add that the Plataeans took an oath. The Plataeans do not admit that they ever promised to restore the captives at once, but only if they could agree after negotiations; and they deny that they took an oath. However this may have been, the

B.C. 431. Ol. 87, 2. Thebans withdrew, leaving the Platáean territory unhurt; but the Plataeans had no sooner got in their property from the country than they put the prisoners to death. Those who were taken were a hundred and eighty in number, and Eurymachus, with whom the betrayers of the city had negotiated, was one of them.

The Athenians, knowing only of the attempt on the city, bid the Plataeans spare their prisoners. Learning the truth, they garrison Plataea and remove the women and children.

6 When they had killed their prisoners, they sent a messenger to Athens and gave back the dead to the Thebans under a flag of truce; they then took the necessary measures for the security of the city. The news had already reached Athens, and the Athenians had instantly seized any Boeotians who were in Attica, and sent a herald to Plataea bidding them do no violence to the Theban prisoners, but wait for instructions from Athens. The news of their death had not arrived. For the first messenger had gone out when the Thebans entered, and the second when they were just defeated and captured; but of what followed the Athenians knew nothing; they sent the message in ignorance, and the herald, when he arrived, found the prisoners dead. The Athenians next despatched an army to Plataea, and brought in supplies. Then leaving a small force in the place they conveyed away the least serviceable of the citizens, together with the women and children.

Both sides now prepare for the struggle.

7 The affair of Plataea was a glaring violation of the thirty years' truce, and the Athenians now made preparations for war. The Lacedaemonians and their allies made similar preparations. Both they and the Athenians meditated sending embassies to the King[a], and to the other Barbarian potentates[b] from whom either party might hope to obtain aid; they likewise sought the alliance of independent cities outside their own dominion. The Lacedaemonians ordered their friends in

---

[a] Cp. ii. 67 init.; iv. 50.

[b] Cp. ii. 29, 67.

Italy and Sicily to build others in number proportioned to the size of their cities, in addition to the ships which they had on the spot; for they intended to raise the Peloponnesian navy to a total of five hundred. The cities were also required to furnish a fixed sum of money; they were not to receive more than one ship of the Athenians at a time, but were to take no further measures until these preparations had been completed. The Athenians reviewed their confederacy, and sent ambassadors to the places immediately adjacent to Peloponnesus—Corcyra, Cephallenia, Acarnania, and Zacynthus. They perceived that if they could only rely upon the friendship of these states[a], they might completely encircle Peloponnesus with war.

B.C. 431. Ol. 87, 2.

Excitement and enthusiasm in Hellas.

On neither side were there any mean thoughts; they 8
were both full of enthusiasm: and no wonder, for all men are energetic when they are making a beginning. At that time the youth of Peloponnesus and the youth of Athens were numerous; they had never seen war, and were therefore very willing to take up arms. All Hellas was excited by the coming conflict between her two chief cities. Many were the prophecies circulated and many the oracles chanted by diviners, not only in the cities about to engage in the struggle, but throughout Hellas. Quite recently the island of Delos had been shaken by an earthquake for the first time within the memory of the Hellenes; this was interpreted and generally believed to be a sign of coming events. And everything of the sort which occurred was curiously noted.

Universal hatred and fear of the Athenians.

The feeling of mankind was strongly on the side of 9
the Lacedaemonians; for they professed to be the liberators of Hellas. Cities and individuals were eager to assist them to the utmost, both by word and deed; and where a man could not hope

---

[a] Taking βεβαίως with εἰ σφίσι φίλια ταῦτα εἴη.

B.C. 431. Ol. 87, 2.

to be present, there it seemed to him that all things were at a stand. For the general indignation against the Athenians was intense; some were longing to be delivered from them, others fearful of falling under their sway.

List of the allies on either side.

Such was the temper which animated the Hellenes, and such were the preparations made by the two powers for the war. Their respective allies were as follows:—The Lacedaemonian confederacy included all the Peloponnesians with the exception of the Argives and the Achaeans—they were both neutral; only the Achaeans of Pellene took part with the Lacedaemonians at first; afterwards all the Achaeans joined them [a]. Beyond the borders of the Peloponnese, the Megarians, Phocians, Locrians, Boeotians, Ambraciots, Leucadians, and Anactorians were their allies. Of these the Corinthians, Megarians, Sicyonians, Pellenians, Eleans, Ambraciots, and Leucadians provided a navy, the Boeotians, Phocians, and Locrians furnished cavalry, the other states only infantry. The allies of the Athenians were Chios, Lesbos, Plataea, the Messenians of Naupactus, the greater part of Acarnania, Corcyra, Zacynthus, and cities in many other countries which were their tributaries. There was the maritime region of Caria, the adjacent Dorian peoples, Ionia, the Hellespont, the Thracian coast, the islands that lie to the east within the line of Peloponnesus and Crete, including all the Cyclades with the exception of Melos and Thera. Chios, Lesbos, and Corcyra furnished a navy; the rest, land forces and money. Thus much concerning the two confederacies, and the character of their respective forces.

The Lacedaemonians summon their allies to meet at the Isthmus.

10 Immediately after the affair at Plataea the Lacedaemonians sent round word to their Peloponnesian and other allies, bidding them equip troops and provide all things necessary for a foreign expedition, with the object

[a] Cp. v. 82 init.

of invading Attica. The various states made their preparations as fast as they could, and at the appointed time, with contingents numbering two-thirds of the forces of each, met at the Isthmus. When the whole army was assembled, Archidamus, the king of the Lacedaemonians, and the leader of the expedition, called together the generals of the different states and their chief officers and most distinguished men, and spoke as follows:— B.C. 431. Ol. 87, 2.

Speech of Archidamus.

11 'Men of Peloponnesus, and you, allies, many are the expeditions which our fathers made both within and without the Peloponnese, and the veterans among ourselves are experienced in war; and yet we never went forth with a greater army than this. But then we should remember that, whatever may be our numbers or our valour, we are going against a most powerful city. And we are bound to show ourselves worthy of our fathers, and not wanting to our own reputation. For all Hellas is stirred by our enterprise, and her eyes are fixed upon us: she is friendly and would have us succeed because she hates the Athenians. Now although some among you, surveying this great host, may think that there is very little risk of the enemy meeting us in the field, we ought not on that account to advance heedlessly; but the general and the soldier of every state should be always expecting that his own division of the army will be the one first in danger. War is carried on in the dark; attacks are generally sudden and furious, and often the smaller army, animated by a proper fear, has been more than a match for a larger force which, disdaining their opponent, were taken unprepared by him. When invading an enemy's country, men should always be confident in spirit, but they should fear too, and take measures of precaution; and thus they will be at once most valorous in attack and impregnable in defence.

We have had great experience in war, and our army was never finer. But we must beware of haste, and not hold our enemy too cheap.

B.C. 431. Ol. 87, 2.

'And the city which we are attacking is not so utterly powerless against an invader, but is in the best possible state of preparation, and for this reason our enemies may be quite expected to meet us in the field. Even if they have no such intention beforehand, yet as soon as they see us in Attica, wasting and destroying their property, they will certainly change their mind. For all men are angry when they not only suffer but see, and some strange form of calamity strikes full upon the eye; the less they reflect the more ready they are to fight; above all men the Athenians, who claim imperial power, and are more disposed to invade and waste their neighbour's land than to look on while their own is being wasted. Remembering how great this city is which you are attacking, and what a fame you will bring on your ancestors and yourselves for good or evil according to the result, follow whithersoever you are led; maintain discipline and caution above all things, and be on the alert to obey the word of command. It is both the noblest and the safest thing for a great army to be visibly animated by one spirit.'

For they are thoroughly prepared, and the least likely of all men to sit idly by while we waste their lands.

12 Having thus spoken, Archidamus dismissed the assembly. His first step was to send Melesippus, the son of Diacritus, a Spartan, to Athens in the hope that the Athenians might after all give way, when they saw their enemies actually on the march. But they would not admit him to the assembly, nor even into the city. For Pericles had already carried a motion to the effect that they would have nothing to do with herald or embassy while the Lacedaemonians were in the field. So Melesippus was sent away without a hearing and told that he must cross the frontier before sunset; if the Lacedaemonians wanted to hold any parley with the Athenians, they must go home first. He was attended by an escort in order to prevent his communi-

Archidamus sends Melesippus to Athens, but he is refused admission to the city, and immediately sent across the frontier.

cating with any one. When he arrived at the Athenian frontier, and was about to leave them, he uttered these words: 'This day will be to the Hellenes the beginning of great sorrows.' On the return of the herald to the camp Archidamus learned that the Athenians were not as yet at all in the mood to yield; so at last he moved forward his army and prepared to enter Attica. The Boeotians who had sent their contingent of two-thirds, including their cavalry, to the Peloponnesian army, marched to Plataea with the remainder of their forces and wasted the country. B.C. 431. Ol. 87, 2.

While the Peloponnesians were gathering at the Isthmus, 13
and were still on their way, but before they entered Attica, Pericles the son of Xanthippus, who was one of the ten Athenian generals, knowing that the invasion was inevitable, and suspecting that Archidamus in wasting the country might very likely spare his lands, either out of courtesy and because he happened to be his friend, or by the order of the Lacedaemonian authorities (who had already attempted to raise a prejudice against him[a] when they demanded the expulsion of the polluted family, and might take this further means of injuring him in the eyes of the Athenians), openly declared in the assembly that Archidamus was his friend, but was not so to the injury of the state, and that supposing the enemy did not destroy his lands and buildings like the rest, he would make a present of them to the public; and he desired that the Athenians would have no suspicion of him on that account. As to the general situation, he repeated his previous advice; they must prepare for war and bring their property from the country into the city; they must defend their walls but not go out to battle; they should also equip for service the fleet in which lay their strength. Their allies

Pericles, suspecting that Archidamus will spare his lands, either from friendship, or to prejudice him with the Athenians, promises to give them to the public if they are uninjured by the enemy.

[a] Cp. i. 126 init. and 127.

B.C. 431. Ol. 87, 2.

should be kept well in hand, for their power depended on the revenues which they derived from them; military successes were generally gained by a wise policy and command of money. The state of their finances was encouraging; they had on an average six hundred talents[a] of tribute coming in annually from their allies, to say nothing of their other revenue; and there were still remaining in the Acropolis six thousand talents of coined silver. (The whole amount had once been as much as nine thousand seven hundred talents[b], but from this had to be deducted a sum of three thousand seven hundred expended on various buildings, such as the Propylaea of the Acropolis, and also on the siege of Potidaea.) Moreover there was uncoined gold and silver in the form of private and public offerings, sacred vessels used in processions and games, the Persian spoil and other things of the like nature, worth at least five hundred talents[c] more. There were also at their disposal, besides what they had in the Acropolis, considerable treasures in various temples. If they were reduced to the last extremity they could even take off the plates of gold with which the image of the goddess was overlaid; these, as he pointed out, weighed forty talents, and were of refined gold, which was all removeable. They might use this treasure in self-defence, but they were bound to replace all that they had taken. By this estimate of their wealth he strove to encourage them. He added that they had thirteen thousand hoplites, besides the sixteen thousand who occupied the fortresses or who manned the walls of the city. For this was the number engaged on garrison duty at the beginning of the war[d], whenever the enemy invaded Attica; they were made up of the elder and younger men, and of such metics as bore

He reminds the Athenians of their enormous wealth and military and naval resources, telling them that victory is certain if they act with prudence.

[a] About £120,000. [b] About £1,940,000. [c] About £100,000.

[d] Cp. what is said of the citizens on garrison duty, vii. 28 init.

heavy arms. The Phaleric wall extended four miles from Phalerum to the city walls: the portion of the city wall which was guarded was somewhat less than five miles; that between the Long Wall and the Phaleric requiring no guard. The Long Walls running down to the Piraeus were rather more than four and a half miles in length; the outer only was guarded. The whole circuit of the Piraeus and of Munychia was not quite seven miles, of which half required a guard. The Athenian cavalry, so Pericles pointed out, numbered twelve hundred, including mounted archers; the foot-archers, sixteen hundred; of triremes fit for service the city had three hundred.—The forces of various kinds which Athens possessed at the commencement of the war, when the first Peloponnesian invasion was impending, cannot be estimated at less.—To these Pericles added other arguments, such as he was fond of using, which were intended to prove to the Athenians that victory was certain.

The citizens, following his advice, gather into the city;

The citizens were persuaded, and brought into the city 14
their children and wives, their household goods, and even the wood-work of their houses, which they took down. Their flocks and beasts of burden they conveyed to Euboea and the adjacent islands.

but reluctantly, for they had ever loved a country life. In old times they lived in separate communes, until Theseus united them into the one city of Athens.

The removal of the inhabitants was painful; for the Athenians had always been accustomed to reside in the
country. Such a life had been characteristic of them, 15
more than of any other Hellenic people, from very early times. In the days of Cecrops and the first kings, down to the reign of Theseus, Attica was divided into communes, having their own town halls and magistrates. Except in case of alarm the whole people did not assemble in council under the king, but administered their own affairs, and advised together in their several townships. Some of them at times even

went to war with him, as the Eleusinians under Eumolpus with Erectheus. But when Theseus came to the throne, he, being a powerful as well as a wise ruler, among other improvements in the administration of the country, dissolved the councils and separate governments, and united all the inhabitants of Attica in the present city, establishing one council and town hall. They continued to live on their own lands, but he compelled them to resort to Athens as their metropolis, and henceforward they[a] were all inscribed in the roll of her citizens[a]. A great city thus arose which was handed down by Theseus to his descendants, and from his day to this the Athenians have regularly celebrated the national festival of the Synoecia, or 'union of the communes' in honour of the Goddess Athenè.

Small extent of the ancient city.

Before his time, what is now the Acropolis and the ground lying under it to the south was the city. Many reasons may be urged in proof of this statement:—The temples of Athenè and of other divinities are situated in the Acropolis itself, and those which are not lie chiefly thereabouts; the temples of Olympian Zeus, for example, and of the Pythian Apollo, and the temple of Earth and of Dionysus in the Marshes, in honour of whom the more ancient Dionysia are celebrated on the twelfth day of the month Anthesterion[b], a festival which also continues to be observed by the Ionian descendants of the Athenians. In the same quarter are other ancient temples, and not far off is the fountain now called Enneacrounos, or the Nine Conduits, from the form given to it by the tyrants, but originally, before the springs were covered in, Callirrhoè, or the Fair Stream. The water of this fountain was used by the ancient Athenians on great occasions, it being near the original city; and at marriage rites and other ceremonies the custom is still retained. To this day the Acropolis or

---

[a] Or, 'all paid taxes to Athens.'

[b] February–March.

Citadel is called by the Athenians *Polis,* or City, because that neighbourhood was first inhabited.

Thus for a long time the ancient Athenians enjoyed 16
a country life in self-governing communities; and although they were now united in a single city, they and their descendants, down to the time of this war, from old habit generally resided with their households in the country where they had been born. For this reason, and also because they had recently restored their country-houses and estates after the Persian War, they had a disinclination to move. They were depressed at the thought of forsaking their homes and the temples which had come down to them from their fathers and were the abiding memorials of their early constitution. They were going to change their manner of life, and in leaving their villages were in fact each of them going into exile.

The new-comers, having no homes of their own, occupy the temples and waste spaces in the city.

When they came to Athens, only a few of them had 17
houses or could find homes among friends or kindred. The majority took up their abode in the vacant spaces of the city, and in the temples and shrines of heroes, with the exception of those on the Acropolis, the Eleusinium, and any other precinct which could be securely closed. The Pelasgian ground, as it was called, which lay at the foot of the citadel, was under a curse forbidding its occupation. There was also a half-line of a Pythian oracle to the same effect:—

'Better the Pelasgian ground left waste.'

Yet even this was filled under the sudden pressure of necessity. And to my mind the oracle came true in a sense exactly contrary to the popular expectation; for the unlawful occupation to which men were driven was not the cause of the calamities which befell the city, but the war was the cause of the occupation; and the oracle without mentioning the war foresaw that the place would be inhabited some day for no good. Many also established themselves in the turrets of the walls, or in any other place which they could find; for the city could not contain them when they first came in. But afterwards they divided among them the Long Walls and the greater part of the Piraeus. At the same time the Athenians applied themselves vigorously to the war, summoning their allies, and preparing an expedition of a hundred ships against the Peloponnese.

18 While they were thus engaged, the Peloponnesian army was advancing: it arrived first of all at Oenoè, a fortress on the confines of Attica and Boeotia, which was garrisoned by the Athenians whenever war broke out, and was the point at which the Peloponnesians intended to enter the enemy's country. There they encamped and prepared to assault the walls by means of engines and siege works. But these and other measures took up time and detained them in the neighbourhood. Archidamus was severely blamed for the delay; he was also thought not to have been energetic enough in levying war, and to have done the Athenians good service by discouraging vigorous action. After the muster of the forces he had been accused of delay at the isthmus, and of loitering on the march. But his reputation was most affected by his halt at Oenoè. For the Athenians employed the interval in getting away their property; and the Peloponnesians fancied that, if they had advanced quickly and he had not lingered, they could have seized everything before it was conveyed within the walls. Such were the feelings entertained towards Archidamus by his troops during the halt. He is said to have held back in the belief that the Athenians, while their lands were still unravaged[a], would yield, and that the thought of allowing them to be devastated would be too much for them.

The Peloponnesians advance to Oenoè, which they attempt in vain to capture.

19 But when they had assaulted Oenoè, and after leaving no means untried were unable to take it, and no herald

[a] Cp. i. 82 med.

Leaving Oenoë, they enter Attica and march to Acharnae,

came from the Athenians, at last they marched on, and about the eightieth day after the entry of the Thebans into Plataea, in the middle of the summer [a], when the corn was in full ear, invaded Attica, under the command of Archidamus the son of Zeuxidamus the Lacedaemonian king. They encamped and ravaged, first of all, Eleusis and the plain of Thria, where they put to flight some Athenian horse near the streams called Rheiti; they then advanced, keeping Mount Aegaleos on the right hand, through the district of Kropeia until they reached Acharnae, which is the largest of the Athenian townships or demes, as they are called; and at Acharnae they encamped, and remained there a considerable time ravaging the country.

where they linger, in the hope that the Athenians will come out to fight.

In this first invasion Archidamus is said to have lingered 20
about Acharnae with his army ready for battle, instead of descending into the plain [b], in the hope that the Athenians, who were now flourishing in youth and numbers and provided for war as they had never been before, would perhaps meet them in the field rather than allow their lands to be ravaged. When therefore they did not appear at Eleusis or in the plain of Thria, he tried once more whether by encamping in the neighbourhood of Acharnae he could induce them to come out. The situation appeared to be convenient, and the Acharnians, being a considerable section of the city and furnishing three thousand hoplites, were likely to be impatient at the destruction of their property, and would communicate to the whole people a desire to fight. Or if the Athenians did not come out to meet him during this invasion, he could henceforward ravage the plain with more confidence, and march right up to the walls of the city. The Acharnians, having lost their own possessions, would be less willing to hazard their lives on behalf of their neighbours,

[a] i.e. of the Attic summer, including spring, see note.

[b] i.e. the plain round Athens.

and so there would be a division in the Athenian counsels. Such was the motive of Archidamus in remaining at Acharnae.

21 The Athenians, so long as the Lacedaemonians were in the neighbourhood of Eleusis and the plain of Thria, entertained a hope that they would come no further. They remembered how, fourteen years before [a], the Lacedaemonian king, Pleistoanax the son of Pausanias, invaded Attica with a Peloponnesian army, and how after advancing as far as Eleusis and Thria he came no further, but retreated. And indeed this retreat was the cause of his exile; for he was thought to have been bribed. But when they saw the army in the neighbourhood of Acharnae, and barely seven miles from the city, they felt the presence of the invader to be intolerable. The devastation of their country before their eyes, which the younger men had never seen at all, nor the elder except in the Persian invasion, naturally appeared to them a horrible thing, and the whole people, the young men especially, were anxious to go forth and put a stop to it. Knots were formed in the streets, and there were loud disputes, some eager to go out, a minority resisting. Soothsayers were repeating oracles of the most different kinds, which all found in some one or other enthusiastic listeners. The Acharnians, who in their own estimation were no small part of the Athenian state, seeing their land ravaged, strongly insisted that they should go out and fight. The excitement in the city was universal; the people were furious with Pericles, and, forgetting all his previous warnings, they abused him for not leading them to battle, as their general should, and laid all their miseries to his charge.

Rage and excitement of the Athenians. Unpopularity of Pericles.

22 But he, seeing that they were overcome by the irritation of the moment and inclined to evil counsels, and confident that he was right in refusing to go out, would not

---

[a] Cp. i. 114 fin.

summon an assembly or meeting of any kind, lest, coming together more in anger than in prudence, they might take some false step. He maintained a strict watch over the city, and sought to calm the irritation as far as he could. Meanwhile he sent out horsemen from time to time to prevent flying parties finding their way into the fields near the city and doing mischief. A skirmish took place at Phrygia between one of the divisions of the Athenian horse assisted by their Thessalian allies on the one hand, and the Boeotian cavalry on the other, in which the Athenians and Thessalians were at least a match for their opponents, until, the Boeotian infantry coming up to support the horse, they were compelled to fly. The Athenians and Thessalians lost a few men, but recovered their bodies on the same day without asking for a truce. On the morrow the Peloponnesians raised a trophy. The forces which the Thessalians brought to the aid of the Athenians, according to the terms of their old alliance[a], consisted of Larissaeans, Pharsalians, Cranonians, Pyrasians, Gyrtonians, and Pheraeans. The leaders of the Larissaeans were Polymedes and Aristonous, one from each of the two leading factions of their city; the Pharsalians were commanded by Meno. The forces of the other cities had likewise generals of their own.

He refuses to comply with their wishes.

Skirmish at Phrygia, in which the Athenians are worsted.

When the Peloponnesians found that the Athenians did 23
not come out to meet them, they moved their army from Acharnae, and ravaged some of the townships which lie between Mount Parnes and Mount Brilessus. While they were still in the country, the Athenians sent the fleet of a hundred ships which they had been equipping on an expedition round the Peloponnese. These ships carried on board a thousand hoplites and four hundred archers; they were under the

The Athenians send one hundred ships to cruise round Peloponnesus. The enemy retire from Attica.

---

[a] Cp. i. 102 fin., 107 fin.; iv. 78 med.

command of Carcinus the son of Xenotimus, Proteas the son of Epicles, and Socrates the son of Antigenes. After the departure of the fleet the Peloponnesians remained in Attica as long as their provisions lasted, and then, taking a new route, retired through Boeotia. In passing by Oropus they wasted the country called Peiraïkè[a], inhabited by the Oropians, who are subjects of the Athenians. On their return to Peloponnesus the troops dispersed to their several cities.

24 When they had retreated, the Athenians posted guards to keep watch both by land and sea, a precaution which they maintained throughout the war. They then passed a decree reserving of the treasure in the Acropolis a thousand talents[b]: this sum was set apart and was not to be expended unless the enemy attacked the city with a fleet and they had to defend it. In any other case, he who brought forward or put to the vote a proposal to touch the money was to be punished with death. They also resolved to set apart yearly a hundred triremes, the finest of the year, and to appoint trierarchs for them; these they were only to use at the same time with the money, and in the same emergency.

The Athenians set aside a thousand talents and a hundred triremes in case of an attack by sea.

25 The Athenian forces, which had lately been dispatched to Peloponnesus in the hundred vessels, and were assisted by the Corcyraeans with fifty ships and by some of the allies from the same region, did considerable damage on the Peloponnesian coast. They also disembarked and attacked Methonè, a fortress in Laconia, which was weak and had no regular garrison. Now Brasidas the son of Tellis, a Spartan, happened to be in those parts in command of a force, and, seeing the danger, he came to the aid of the inhabitants

Proceedings of the Athenian fleet.

[a] Reading with the MSS. τὴν γῆν τὴν Πειραϊκήν. Cp. iii. 91 med., ἐς Ὠρωπὸν τῆς πέραν γῆς, i.e. the coast opposite Euboea.

[b] About £200,000.

with a hundred hoplites. He dashed through the scattered parties of Athenian troops, whose attention was occupied with the fortress, and threw himself into Methonè, suffering a slight loss; he thus saved the place. The exploit was publicly acknowledged at Sparta, Brasidas being the first Spartan who obtained this distinction in the war. The Athenians, proceeding on their voyage, ravaged the territory of Pheia in Elis for two days, and defeated three hundred chosen men from the vale of Elis, as well as some Elean perioeci from the neighbourhood of Pheia who came to the rescue. But a violent storm arose, and there was no harbour in which the fleet could find shelter; so the greater part of the army re-embarked and sailed round the promontory called Ichthys towards the harbour of Pheia. Meanwhile the Messenians and others who were unable to get on board marched by land and captured Pheia. The fleet soon sailed into the harbour and took them up; they then evacuated Pheia and put to sea. By this time the main army of the Eleans had arrived; whereupon the Athenians proceeded on their way to other places, which they ravaged.

About the same time the Athenians sent thirty ships to 26
cruise off Locris, having an eye also to the safety of Euboea. Cleopompus the son of Cleinias was their commander. He made descents on the Locrian coast and ravaged various places. He also captured Thronium, taking hostages of the inhabitants, and at Alopè defeated the Locrians who came to defend the place.

Thirty ships are sent to Locris.

In the same summer the Athenians expelled the 27
Aeginetans and their families from Aegina, alleging that they had been the main cause of the war. The island lies close to Peloponnesus, and they thought it safer to send thither settlers of their own, an intention which they shortly afterwards carried out. The Lacedaemonians gave the Aeginetan exiles the

The Athenians expel the Aeginetans from their country. Some of the exiles are settled by the Lacedaemonians in Thyrea.

town of Thyrea to occupy and the adjoining country to cultivate, partly in order to annoy the Athenians, partly out of gratitude to the Aeginetans, who had done them good service at the time of the earthquake and the revolt of the Helots. The Thyrean territory is a strip of land coming down to the sea on the borders of Argolis and Laconia. There some of them found a home; others dispersed over Hellas.

Eclipse of the sun.

28 During the same summer, at the beginning of the lunar month (apparently the only time when such an event is possible), and in the afternoon, there was an eclipse of the sun, which took the form of a crescent, and then became full again; during the eclipse a few stars were visible.

The Athenians make Nymphodorus their proxenus, hoping that he will gain over Sitalces, king of Thrace.

29 In the same summer, Nymphodorus the son of Pythes, a native of Abdera and a man of great influence with Sitalces who had married his sister, was made by the Athenians their proxenus at that place and invited by them to Athens. He had formerly been considered their enemy, but now they hoped that he would gain over to their alliance Sitalces, who was the son of Teres and king of Thrace.

Sitalces was the son of Teres, the founder of the Odrysian empire. This Teres has no connexion with the Tereus of mythology.

This Teres, the father of Sitalces, was the first founder of the great Odrysian empire, which he extended over a large part of Thrace, although many of the Thracian tribes are still independent. He has no connexion with Tereus who took to wife from Athens Procnè, the daughter of Pandion; they do not even belong to the same Thrace. For Tereus dwelt in Daulia, a part of the region which is now called Phocis but in those days was inhabited by Thracians, and in that country Itys suffered at the hands of the women Procnè and Philomela. Many of the poets when they make mention of the nightingale (Philomela) apply to the bird the epithet Daulian. Further, Pandion would surely have formed a marriage connexion for his daughter among his neighbours with a view to mutual protection, and not at a distance of so many days' journey, among the Odrysian Thracians. And the Teres of whom I am speaking, and who was the first powerful king of the Odrysae, has not even the same name [a].

Sitalces becomes an ally of Athens, and his son is made an Athenian citizen: Perdiccas is also reconciled.

Now Sitalces, whom the Athenians made their ally, was the son of this Teres; they wanted him to assist them in the conquest of Chalcidicè and of Perdiccas. So Nymphodorus came to Athens, negotiated the alliance with Sitalces, and got his son Sadocus enrolled an Athenian citizen. He also undertook to terminate the war in Chalcidicè, promising that he would persuade Sitalces to send the Athenians an army of Thracian horsemen and targeteers. He further reconciled Perdiccas with the Athenians, and persuaded them to restore Thermè to him [b]. Whereupon Perdiccas joined the Athenian army under Phormio [c], and with him fought against the Chalcidians. Thus Sitalces the son of Teres king of Thrace, and Perdiccas son of Alexander king of Macedonia, entered into the Athenian alliance.

The Athenians capture Sollium and Astacus, and gain over Cephallenia.

The Athenians, in the hundred ships which were still 30
cruising about Peloponnesus, took Sollium, a town belonging to the Corinthians, which they handed over to the Palaereans of Acarnania, giving to them alone of the Acarnanians the right of occupying the city and country. They also stormed the town of Astacus, and driving out Evarchus who was tyrant there, added it to the Athenian confederacy. They next sailed to the island of Cephallenia, which they gained over without fighting. The island lies over against Acarnania and Leucas, and contains four cities inhabited by the Paleans,

---

[a] i. e. is called Teres, not Tereus.

[b] Cp. i. 61 init.

[c] Cp. i. 64 med.

Cranians, Samaeans, and Pronnaeans. Soon afterwards the fleet proceeded on its voyage homewards.

31 About the end of the summer the entire Athenian force, including the metics, invaded the territory of Megara, under the command of Pericles the son of Xanthippus. The Athenian fleet had reached Aegina on its way home, and when the commanders heard that the whole armed force of the city was in Megara, they sailed thither and joined them. This was the largest army which the Athenians ever had in one place; for the city was still in her full strength, and had not as yet suffered from the plague. The Athenians themselves numbered not less than ten thousand hoplites, exclusive of the remaining three thousand who were engaged at Potidaea. A force of metic hoplites amounting to at least three thousand took part in the invasion, and also a large number of light-armed troops. After ravaging the greater part of the country they retired. They repeated the invasion, sometimes with cavalry, sometimes with the whole Athenian army, every year during the war until Nisaea was taken[a].

The Athenians under the command of Pericles march into the Megarid and ravage the country.

32 At the end of this summer the island of Atalantè, which lies off the coast of the Opuntian Locrians and had hitherto been uninhabited, was fortified and made a guard-station by the Athenians. They wanted to prevent pirates sailing from Opus and other places in Locris and plundering Euboea. Such were the events which occurred during the remainder of the summer after the Peloponnesians had retired from Attica.

The Athenians fortify the island of Atalantè.

33 During the following winter, Evarchus the Acarnanian, desiring to be restored to Astacus, persuaded the Corinthians to sail with forty ships and fifteen hundred hoplites and reinstate him, he

The Corinthians restore the tyrant Evarchus to Astacus. On their return they attack Cephallenia, but are defeated.

[a] Cp. iv. 66 init., 69 fin.

himself hiring some mercenaries. Of this expedition Euphamidas the son of Aristonymus, Timoxenus the son of Timocrates, and Eumachus the son of Chrysis, were the commanders. They sailed to Astacus, and restored Evarchus; they then tried to gain over certain other towns on the coast of Acarnania; but, failing in their attempt, they proceeded homewards. Touching at Cephallenia on their voyage, they made a descent on the country of the Cranians, but being entrapped by means of a pretended agreement, and then unexpectedly attacked, they lost a part of their forces; at length, not without a severe struggle, they put to sea again and returned home.

The Athenians celebrate the funeral of their citizens who had died in the war.

During the same winter, in accordance with an old 34
national custom, the funeral of those who first fell in this war was celebrated by the Athenians at the public charge. The ceremony is as follows: Three days before the celebration they erect a tent in which the bones of the dead are laid out, and every one brings to his own dead any offering which he pleases. At the time of the funeral the bones are placed in chests of cypress wood, which are conveyed on hearses; there is one chest for each tribe. They also carry a single empty litter decked with a pall for all whose bodies are missing, and cannot be recovered after the battle. The procession is accompanied by any one who chooses, whether citizen or stranger, and the female relatives of the deceased are present at the place of interment and make lamentation. The public sepulchre is situated in the most beautiful spot outside the walls; there they always bury those who fall in war; only after the battle of Marathon the dead, in recognition of their pre-eminent valour, were interred on the field. When the remains have been laid in the earth, some man of known ability and high reputation, chosen by the city, delivers a suitable oration over them; after which the people depart. Such is the manner of interment; and

the ceremony was repeated from time to time throughout the war. Over those who were the first buried Pericles was chosen to speak. At the fitting moment he advanced from the sepulchre to a lofty stage, which had been erected in order that he might be heard as far as possible by the multitude, and spoke as follows:—

(FUNERAL SPEECH.)

The law which enjoins this oration has been often praised. But I should prefer to praise the brave by deeds only, not to imperil their reputation on the skill of an orator. Still, our ancestors approved the practice, and I must obey.

35 'Most of those who have spoken here before me have commended the lawgiver who added this oration to our other funeral customs; it seemed to them a worthy thing that such an honour should be given at their burial to the dead who have fallen on the field of battle. But I should have preferred that, when men's deeds have been brave, they should be honoured in deed only, and with such an honour as this public funeral, which you are now witnessing. Then the reputation of many would not have been imperilled on the eloquence or want of eloquence of one, and their virtues believed or not as he spoke well or ill. For it is difficult to say neither too little nor too much; and even moderation is apt not to give the impression of truthfulness. The friend of the dead who knows the facts is likely to think that the words of the speaker fall short of his knowledge and of his wishes; another who is not so well informed, when he hears of anything which surpasses his own powers, will be envious and will suspect exaggeration. Mankind are tolerant of the praises of others so long as each hearer thinks that he can do as well or nearly as well himself, but, when the speaker rises above him, jealousy is aroused and he begins to be incredulous. However, since our ancestors have set the seal of their approval upon the practice, I must obey, and to the utmost of my power shall endeavour to satisfy the wishes and beliefs of all who hear me.

'I will speak first of our ancestors, for it is right and 36
seemly that now, when we are lamenting the dead, a tribute should be paid to their memory. There has never been a time when they did not inhabit this land, which by their valour they have handed down from generation to generation, and we have received from them a free state. But if they were worthy of praise, still more were our fathers, who added to their inheritance, and after many a struggle transmitted to us their sons this great empire. And we ourselves assembled here to-day, who are still most of us in the vigour of life, have carried the work of improvement further, and have richly endowed our city with all things, so that she is sufficient for herself both in peace and war. Of the military exploits by which our various possessions were acquired, or of the energy with which we or our fathers drove back the tide of war, Hellenic or Barbarian, I will not speak; for the tale would be long and is familiar to you. But before I praise the dead, I should like to point out by what principles of action we rose[a] to power, and under what institutions and through what manner of life our empire became great. For I conceive that such thoughts are not unsuited to the occasion, and that this numerous assembly of citizens and strangers may profitably listen to them.

I will first commemorate our predecessors, who gave us freedom and empire. And before praising the dead, I will describe how Athens has won her greatness.

'Our form of government does not enter into rivalry 37
with the institutions of others. We do not copy our neighbours, but are an example to them. It is true that we are called a democracy, for the administration is in the hands of the many and not of the few. But while the law secures equal justice to all alike in their private disputes, the claim of excellence is also recognised; and when a

Our government is a democracy, but we honour men of merit, whether rich or poor. Our public life is free from exclusiveness, our private from suspicion; yet we revere alike the injunctions of law and custom.

[a] Reading ἤλθομεν.

citizen is in any way distinguished, he is preferred to the public service, not as a matter of privilege, but as the reward of merit. Neither is poverty a bar, but a man may benefit his country whatever be the obscurity of his condition. There is no exclusiveness in our public life, and in our private intercourse we are not suspicious of one another, nor angry with our neighbour if he does what he likes; we do not put on sour looks at him which, though harmless, are not pleasant. While we are thus unconstrained in our private intercourse, a spirit of reverence pervades our public acts; we are prevented from doing wrong by respect for the authorities and for the laws, having an especial regard to those which are ordained for the protection of the injured as well as to those unwritten laws which bring upon the transgressor of them the reprobation of the general sentiment.

We find relaxation in our amusements, and in our homes; and the whole world contributes to our enjoyment.

38 'And we have not forgotten to provide for our weary spirits many relaxations from toil; we have regular games and sacrifices throughout the year; our homes are beautiful and elegant; and the delight which we daily feel in all these things helps to banish melancholy. Because of the greatness of our city the fruits of the whole earth flow in upon us; so that we enjoy the goods of other countries as freely as of our own.

In war we singly are a match for the Peloponnesians united; though we have no secrets and undergo no laborious training.

39 'Then, again, our military training is in many respects superior to that of our adversaries. Our city is thrown open to the world, and we never expel a foreigner or prevent him from seeing or learning anything of which the secret if revealed to an enemy might profit him. We rely not upon management or trickery, but upon our own hearts and hands. And in the matter of education, whereas they from early youth are always undergoing laborious exercises which are to make them brave, we live at ease, and yet are equally

ready to face [a]the perils which they face[a]. And here is the proof. The Lacedaemonians come into Attica not by themselves, but with their whole confederacy following; we go alone into a neighbour's country; and although our opponents are fighting for their homes and we on a foreign soil, we have seldom any difficulty in overcoming them. Our enemies have never yet felt our united strength; the care of a navy divides our attention, and on land we are obliged to send our own citizens everywhere. But they, if they meet and defeat a part of our army, are as proud as if they had routed us all, and when defeated they pretend to have been vanquished by us all.

We are not enervated by culture, or vulgarised by wealth. We are all interested in public affairs, believing that nothing is lost by free discussion. Our goodness to others springs not from interest, but from the generous confidence of freedom.

'If then we prefer to meet danger with a light heart but without laborious training, and with a courage which is gained by habit and not enforced by law, are we not greatly the gainers? Since we do not anticipate the pain, although, when the hour comes, we can be as brave as those who never allow themselves to rest; and thus too our city is equally admirable in peace and in war. For we 40
are lovers of the beautiful, yet simple in our tastes, and we cultivate the mind without loss of manliness. Wealth we employ, not for talk and ostentation, but when there is a real use for it. To avow poverty with us is no disgrace; the true disgrace is in doing nothing to avoid it. An Athenian citizen does not neglect the state because he takes care of his own household; and even those of us who are engaged in business have a very fair idea of politics. We alone regard a man who takes no interest in public affairs, not as a harmless, but as a useless character; and if few of us are originators, we are all sound judges of a policy. The great impediment to action

[a] Or, 'perils such as our strength can bear;' or 'perils which are enough to daunt us.'

is, in our opinion, not discussion, but the want of that knowledge which is gained by discussion preparatory to action. For we have a peculiar power of thinking before we act and of acting too, whereas other men are courageous from ignorance but hesitate upon reflection. And they are surely to be esteemed the bravest spirits who, having the clearest sense both of the pains and pleasures of life, do not on that account shrink from danger. In doing good, again, we are unlike others; we make our friends by conferring, not by receiving favours. Now he who confers a favour is the firmer friend, because he would fain by kindness keep alive the memory of an obligation; but the recipient is colder in his feelings, because he knows that in requiting another's generosity he will not be winning gratitude but only paying a debt. We alone do good to our neighbours not upon a calculation of interest, but in the confidence of freedom and in a frank

41 *In fine, Athens is the school of Hellas. She alone in the hour of trial rises above her reputation. Her citizens need no poet to sing their praises: for every land bears witness to their valour.*

and fearless spirit. To sum up: I say that Athens is the school of Hellas, and that the individual Athenian in his own person seems to have the power of adapting himself to the most varied forms of action with the utmost versatility and grace. This is no passing and idle word, but truth and fact; and the assertion is verified by the position to which these qualities have raised the state. For in the hour of trial Athens alone among her contemporaries is superior to the report of her. No enemy who comes against her is indignant at the reverses which he sustains at the hands of such a city; no subject complains that his masters are unworthy of him. And we shall assuredly not be without witnesses; there are mighty monuments of our power which will make us the wonder of this and of succeeding ages; we shall not need the praises of Homer or of any other panegyrist whose poetry may please for the moment [a],

[a] Cp. i. 10 med., and 21.

although his representation of the facts will not bear the light of day. For we have compelled every land and every sea to open a path for our valour, and have everywhere planted eternal memorials of our friendship and of our enmity. Such is the city for whose sake these men nobly fought and died; they could not bear the thought that she might be taken from them; and every one of us who survive should gladly toil on her behalf.

The praise of the city is the praise of these men, for they made her great. Good and bad, rich and poor alike, preferred death to dishonour.

'I have dwelt upon the greatness of Athens because 42
I want to show you that we are contending for a higher prize than those who enjoy none of these privileges, and to establish by manifest proof the merit of these men whom I am now commemorating. Their loftiest praise has been already spoken. For in magnifying the city I have magnified them, and men like them whose virtues made her glorious. And of how few Hellenes can it be said as of them, that their deeds when weighed in the balance have been found equal to their fame! Methinks that a death such as theirs has been gives the true measure of a man's worth; it may be the first revelation of his virtues, but is at any rate their final seal. For even those who come short in other ways may justly plead the valour with which they have fought for their country; they have blotted out the evil with the good, and have benefited the state more by their public services than they have injured her by their private actions. None of these men were enervated by wealth or hesitated to resign the pleasures of life; none of them put off the evil day in the hope, natural to poverty, that a man, though poor, may one day become rich. But, deeming that the punishment of their enemies was sweeter than any of these things, and that they could fall in no nobler cause, they determined at the hazard of their lives to be honourably avenged, and to leave the rest. They resigned to hope their unknown chance of happiness; but in the face of death they resolved to rely upon them-

selves alone. And when the moment came they were minded to resist and suffer, rather than to fly and save their lives; they ran away from the word of dishonour, but on the battle-field their feet stood fast, and [a] in an instant, at the height of their fortune, they passed away from the scene, not of their fear, but of their glory [a].

Contemplate and love Athens, and you will know how to value them. They were united in their deaths, but their glory is separate and single. Their sepulchre is the remembrance of them in the hearts of men. Follow their example without fear: it is the prosperous, not the unfortunate, who should be reckless.

43 'Such was the end of these men; they were worthy of Athens, and the living need not desire to have a more heroic spirit, although they may pray for a less fatal issue. The value of such a spirit is not to be expressed in words. Any one can discourse to you for ever about the advantages of a brave defence, which you know already. But instead of listening to him I would have you day by day fix your eyes upon the greatness of Athens, until you become filled with the love of her; and when you are impressed by the spectacle of her glory, reflect that this empire has been acquired by men who knew their duty and had the courage to do it, who in the hour of conflict had the fear of dishonour always present to them, and who, if ever they failed in an enterprise, would not allow their virtues to be lost to their country, but freely gave their lives to her as the fairest offering which they could present at her feast. The sacrifice which they collectively made was individually repaid to them; for they received again each one for himself a praise which grows not old, and the noblest of all sepulchres—I speak not of that in which their remains are laid, but of that in which their glory survives, and is proclaimed always and on every

---

[a] Or, taking τύχης with καιροῦ: 'while for a moment they were in the hands of fortune, at the height, not of terror but of glory, they passed away.'

fitting occasion both in word and deed. For the whole earth is the sepulchre of famous men; not only are they commemorated by columns and inscriptions in their own country, but in foreign lands there dwells also an unwritten memorial of them, graven not on stone but in the hearts of men. Make them your examples, and, esteeming courage to be freedom and freedom to be happiness, do not weigh too nicely the perils of war. The unfortunate who has no hope of a change for the better has less reason to throw away his life than the prosperous who, if he survive, is always liable to a change for the worse, and to whom any accidental fall makes the most serious difference. To a man of spirit, cowardice and disaster coming together are far more bitter than death striking him unperceived at a time when he is full of courage and animated by the general hope.

'Wherefore I do not now commiserate the parents of the 44
dead who stand here; I would rather comfort them. You know that your life has been passed amid manifold vicissitudes; and that they may be deemed fortunate who have gained most honour, whether an honourable death like theirs, or an honourable sorrow like yours, and whose days have been so ordered that the term of their happiness is likewise the term of their life. I know how hard it is to make you feel this, when the good fortune of others will too often remind you of the gladness which once lightened your hearts. And sorrow is felt at the want of those blessings, not which a man never knew, but which were a part of his life before they were taken from him. Some of you are of an age at which they may hope to have other children, and they ought to bear their sorrow better; not only will the children who may hereafter be born make them forget their own lost ones, but the city

The parents of the dead are to be comforted rather than pitied. Some of them may yet have children who will lighten their sorrow and serve the state; while others should remember how large their share of happiness has been, and be consoled by the glory of those who are gone.

will be doubly a gainer. She will not be left desolate, and she will be safer. For a man's counsel cannot have equal weight or worth, when he alone has no children to risk in the general danger. To those of you who have passed their prime, I say: "Congratulate yourselves that you have been happy during the greater part of your days; remember that your life of sorrow will not last long, and be comforted by the glory of those who are gone. For the love of honour alone is ever young, and not riches, as some say, but honour is the delight of men when they are old and useless."

Sons and brothers will find their example hard to imitate, for men are jealous of the living, but envy follows not the dead. Let the widows restrain their natural weakness, and avoid both praise and blame.

45 'To you who are the sons and brothers of the departed, I see that the struggle to emulate them will be an arduous one. For all men praise the dead, and, however preeminent your virtue may be, hardly will you be thought, I do not say to equal, but even to approach them. The living have their rivals and detractors, but when a man is out of the way, the honour and good-will which he receives is unalloyed. And, if I am to speak of womanly virtues to those of you who will henceforth be widows, let me sum them up in one short admonition: To a woman not to show more weakness than is natural to her sex is a great glory, and not to be talked about for good or for evil among men.

So have I paid a due tribute of words to the dead. The city will pay them in deeds, as by this funeral, so too by the maintenance of their children.

46 'I have paid the required tribute, in obedience to the law, making use of such fitting words as I had. The tribute of deeds has been paid in part; for the dead have been honourably interred, and it remains only that their children should be maintained at the public charge until they are grown up: this is the solid prize with which, as with a garland, Athens crowns her sons living and dead, after a struggle like theirs. For where the rewards of virtue are greatest, there the noblest citizens

are enlisted in the service of the state. And now, when you have duly lamented, every one his own dead, you may depart.'

47 Such was the order of the funeral celebrated in this winter, with the end of which ended the first year of the Peloponnesian War. As soon as summer returned, the Peloponnesian army, comprising as before two-thirds of the force of each confederate state, under the command of the Lacedaemonian king Archidamus, the son of Zeuxidamus, invaded Attica, where they established themselves and ravaged the country. They had not been there many days when the plague broke out at Athens for the first time. A similar disorder is said to have previously smitten many places, particularly Lemnos, but there is no record of such a pestilence occurring elsewhere, or of so great a destruction of human life. For a while physicians, in ignorance of the nature of the disease, sought to apply remedies; but it was in vain, and they themselves were among the first victims, because they oftenest came into contact with it. No human art was of any avail, and as to supplications in temples, enquiries of oracles, and the like, they were utterly useless, and at last men were overpowered by the calamity and gave them all up.

Second invasion of Attica; outbreak of the plague,

B.C. 430. Ol. 87, 3.

48 The disease is said to have begun south of Egypt in Aethiopia; thence it descended into Egypt and Libya, and after spreading over the greater part of the Persian empire, suddenly fell upon Athens. It first attacked the inhabitants of the Piraeus, and it was supposed that the Peloponnesians had poisoned the cisterns, no conduits having as yet been made there. It afterwards reached the upper city, and then the mortality became far greater. As to its probable origin or the causes which might or could have produced such a disturbance of nature, every man, whether a physician or not, will give his own opinion. But I shall

which commenced in Aethiopia. The origin and causes of it are unknown, but I shall confine myself to the facts. I was myself a sufferer.

describe its actual course, and the symptoms by which any one who knows them beforehand may recognise the disorder should it ever reappear. For I was myself attacked, and witnessed the sufferings of others.

The characteristics of the disease.

49 The season was admitted to have been remarkably free from ordinary sickness; and if anybody was already ill of any other disease, it was absorbed in this. Many who were in perfect health, all in a moment, and without any apparent reason, were seized with violent heats in the head and with redness and inflammation of the eyes. Internally the throat and the tongue were quickly suffused with blood, and the breath became unnatural and fetid. There followed sneezing and hoarseness; in a short time the disorder, accompanied by a violent cough, reached the chest; then fastening lower down, it would move the stomach and bring on all the vomits of bile to which physicians have ever given names; and they were very distressing. An ineffectual retching producing violent convulsions attacked most of the sufferers; [a] some as soon as the previous symptoms had abated, others not until long afterwards [a]. The body externally was not so very hot to the touch, nor yet pale; it was of a livid colour inclining to red, and breaking out in pustules and ulcers. But the internal fever was intense; the sufferers could not bear to have on them even the finest linen garment; they insisted on being naked, and there was nothing which they longed for more eagerly than to throw themselves into cold water. And many of those who had no one to look after them actually plunged into the cisterns, for they were tormented by unceasing thirst, which was not in the least assuaged whether they drank little or much. They could not sleep; a restlessness which was intolerable never left them. While the disease was at its height the body, instead of wasting away,

---

[a] Or, taking λωφήσαντα with σπασμόν: 'these convulsions in some cases soon abated, in others not until long afterwards.'

held out amid these sufferings in a marvellous manner, and either they died on the seventh or ninth day, not of weakness, for their strength was not exhausted, but of internal fever, which was the end of most; or, if they survived, then the disease descended into the bowels and there produced violent ulceration; severe diarrhoea at the same time set in, and at a later stage caused exhaustion, which finally with few exceptions carried them off. For the disorder which had originally settled in the head passed gradually through the whole body, and, if a person got over the worst, would often seize the extremities and leave its mark, attacking the privy parts and the fingers and the toes; and some escaped with the loss of these, some with the loss of their eyes. Some again had no sooner recovered than they were seized with a forgetfulness of all things and knew neither themselves nor their friends.

Even the animals and birds of prey refused to touch the corpses.

The general character of the malady no words can 50
describe, and the fury with which it fastened upon each sufferer was too much for human nature to endure. There was one circumstance in particular which distinguished it from ordinary diseases. The birds and animals which feed on human flesh, although so many bodies were lying unburied, either never came near them, or died if they touched them. This was proved by a remarkable disappearance of the birds of prey, which were not to be seen either about the bodies or anywhere else; while in the case of the dogs the result was even more obvious, because they live with man.

Nothing availed against the disease.

Such was the general nature of the disease: I omit 51
many strange peculiarities which characterised individual cases. None of the ordinary sicknesses attacked any one while it lasted, or, if they did, they ended in the plague. Some of the sufferers died from want of care, others equally who were receiving the greatest attention. No single remedy could

be deemed a specific; for that which did good to one did harm to another. No constitution was of itself strong enough to resist or weak enough to escape the attacks; the disease carried off all alike and defied every mode of treatment. Most appalling was the despondency which seized upon any one who felt himself sickening; for he instantly abandoned his mind to despair and, instead of holding out, absolutely threw away his chance of life.

Rapidity with which the infection spread. None could visit the sick with impunity except those who had already been attacked and had recovered.

Appalling too was the rapidity with which men caught the infection; dying like sheep if they attended on one another; and this was the principal cause of mortality. When they were afraid to visit one another, the sufferers died in their solitude, so that many houses were empty because there had been no one left to take care of the sick; or if they ventured they perished, especially those who aspired to heroism. For they went to see their friends without thought of themselves and were ashamed to leave them, at a time when the very relations of the dying were at last growing weary and ceased even to make lamentations, overwhelmed by the vastness of the calamity. But whatever instances there may have been of such devotion, more often the sick and the dying were tended by the pitying care of those who had recovered, because they knew the course of the disease and were themselves free from apprehension. For no one was ever attacked a second time, or not with a fatal result. All men congratulated them, and they themselves, in the excess of their joy at the moment, had an innocent fancy that they could not die of any other sickness.

52 The crowding of the people out of the country into the

The misery aggravated by the overcrowding of the city.

city aggravated the misery; and the newly-arrived suffered most. For, having no houses of their own, but inhabiting in the height of summer stifling huts, the mortality among them was dreadful, and they perished in wild disorder. [a]The dead lay as they had died, one upon another, while others hardly alive wallowed[a] in the streets and crawled about every fountain craving for water. The temples in which they lodged were full of the corpses of those who died in them; for the violence of the calamity was such that men, not knowing where to turn, grew reckless of all law, human and divine. The customs which had hitherto been observed at funerals were universally violated, and they buried their dead each one as best he could. Many, having no proper appliances, because the deaths in their household had been so numerous already, lost all shame in the burial of the dead[b]. When one man had raised a funeral pile, others would come, and throwing on their dead first, set fire to it; or when some other corpse was already burning, before they could be stopped, would throw their own dead upon it and depart.

General violation of ancient customs of burial.

All legal and religious restraint disappears in the terror of the plague.

There were other and worse forms of lawlessness 53
which the plague introduced at Athens. Men who had hitherto concealed what they took pleasure in, now grew bolder. For, seeing the sudden change,—how the rich died in a moment, and those who had nothing immediately inherited their property,—they reflected that life and riches were alike transitory, and they resolved to enjoy themselves while they could, and to think only of pleasure. Who would be willing to sacrifice himself to the law of honour when he knew not whether he would ever live to be held in honour? The pleasure of the moment and any sort of thing which conduced to it took the place both of honour and of expediency. No fear of Gods or law of man deterred a criminal. Those who saw all perishing alike, thought that the worship or neglect of the Gods

---

[a] More literally: 'They, dying, lay dead one upon another, or wallowed hardly alive' &c.

[b] See note *ad loc.*

made no difference. For offences against human law no punishment was to be feared; no one would live long enough to be called to account. Already a far heavier sentence had been passed and was hanging over a man's head; before that fell, why should he not take a little pleasure?

54 Such was the grievous calamity which now afflicted the Athenians; within the walls their people were dying, and without, their country was being ravaged. In their troubles they naturally called to mind a verse which the elder men among them declared to have been current long ago:—

'A Dorian war will come and a plague with it.'

Dispute about an ancient oracle: whether limos *or* loimos *was the word.*

There was a dispute about the precise expression; some saying that *limos*, a famine, and not *loimos*, a plague, was the original word. Nevertheless, as might have been expected, for men's memories reflected their sufferings, the argument in favour of *loimos* prevailed at the time. But if ever in future years another Dorian war arises which happens to be accompanied by a famine, they will probably repeat the verse in the other form. The answer of the oracle to the Lacedaemonians when the God was asked 'whether they should go to war or not,' and he replied 'that if they fought with all their might, they would conquer, and that he himself would take their part[a],' was not forgotten by those who had heard of it, and they quite imagined that they were witnessing the fulfilment of his words. The disease certainly did set in immediately after the invasion of the Peloponnesians, and did not spread into Peloponnesus in any degree worth speaking of, while Athens felt its ravages most severely, and next to Athens the places which were most populous. Such was the history of the plague[b].

---

[a] Cp. i. 118 fin. [b] Cp. iii. 87

After the Peloponnesians had wasted the plain they 55
entered what are called the coast lands (*Paralus*) and penetrated as far as Laurium, where are the silver mines belonging to the Athenians. First they ravaged that part of the coast which looks towards Peloponnesus, and afterwards that situated towards Euboea and Andros. But Pericles, who was still general, continued to insist, as in the former invasion, that the Athenians should remain within their walls.

The Peloponnesians at Laurium. Pericles still restrains the people from going out, but sends a hundred ships to ravage Peloponnesus.

Before, however, the Peloponnesians had left the plain 56
and moved forward into the coast lands he had begun to equip an expedition of a hundred ships against Peloponnesus. When all was ready he put to sea, having on board four thousand Athenian hoplites and three hundred cavalry conveyed in horse transports which the Athenians then constructed for the first time out of their old ships. The Chians and Lesbians joined them with fifty vessels. The expedition did not actually put to sea until the Peloponnesians had reached the coast lands. Arriving at Epidaurus in Peloponnesus the Athenians devastated most of the country and attacked the city, which at one time they were in hopes of taking, but did not quite succeed. Setting sail again they ravaged the territory of Troezen, Halieis, and Hermionè, which are all places on the coast of Peloponnesus. Again putting off they came to Prasiae, a small town on the coast of Laconia, ravaged the country, and took and plundered the place. They then returned home and found that the Peloponnesians had also returned and were no longer in Attica.

All the time during which the Peloponnesians remained 57
in the country and the armament of the Athenians continued at sea the plague was raging both among the troops and in the city. The fear which it inspired was said to have induced the enemy to leave Attica sooner than they intended; for they heard from deserters that the disease

The Peloponnesians leave Attica after a stay of forty days.

was in the city, and likewise saw the burning of the dead. Still in this invasion the whole country was ravaged by them, and they remained about forty days, which was the longest stay they ever made.

Expedition against Potidaea. The plague breaks out among the troops, and the reinforcements return to Athens.

58 In the same summer, Hagnon the son of Nicias, and Cleopompus the son of Cleinias, who were colleagues of Pericles in his military command, took the fleet which he had employed and sailed forthwith against the Thracian Chalcidians and against Potidaea, which still held out. On their arrival they brought engines up to the walls, and tried every means of taking the town. But they did not succeed; nor did the result by any means correspond to the magnitude of their armament; for thither too the plague came and made dreadful havoc among the Athenian troops. Even the soldiers who were previously there and had been in good health caught the infection from the forces under Hagnon. But the army of Phormio[a] escaped; for he and his sixteen hundred troops had left Chalcidicè. And so Hagnon returned with his fleet to Athens, having lost by the plague out of four thousand hoplites a thousand and fifty men in about forty days. But the original armament[b] remained and prosecuted the siege.

The Athenians sue for peace and are rejected. They turn upon Pericles. His defence.

59 After the second Peloponnesian invasion, now that Attica had been once more ravaged, and the war and the plague together lay heavy upon the Athenians, a change came over their spirit. They blamed Pericles because he had persuaded them to go to war, declaring that he was the author of their troubles; and they were anxious to come to terms with the Lacedaemonians. Accordingly envoys were despatched to Sparta, but they met with no success. And now, being completely at their wits' end, they turned upon Pericles. He saw

---

[a] Cp. i. 64 med. [b] Cp. i. 59, 61 init.

that they were exasperated by their misery and were behaving just as he had always anticipated that they would. And so, being still general, he called an assembly, wanting to encourage them and to convert their angry feelings into a gentler and more hopeful mood. At this assembly he came forward and spoke as follows:—

'I was expecting this outburst of indignation; the 60
causes of it are not unknown to me. And I have summoned an assembly that I may remind you of your resolutions and reprove you for your inconsiderate anger against me, and want of fortitude in misfortune. In my judgment it would be better for individuals themselves that the citizens should suffer and the state flourish than that the citizens should flourish and the state suffer. A private man, however successful in his own dealings, if his country perish is involved in her destruction; but if he be an unprosperous citizen of a prosperous city he is much more likely to recover. Seeing then that states can bear the misfortunes of individuals, but individuals cannot bear the misfortunes of the state, let us all stand by our country and not do what you are doing now, who because you are stunned by your private calamities are letting go the hope of saving the state, and condemning not only me who advised, but yourselves who consented to, the war. Yet I with whom you are so angry venture to say of myself, that I am as capable as any one of devising and explaining a sound policy; and that I am a lover of my country, and incorruptible. Now a man may have a policy which he cannot clearly expound, and then he might as well have none at all; or he may possess both ability and eloquence, but if he is disloyal to his country he cannot, like a true man, speak in her interest; or again he may be unable to resist a bribe, and then all his other good qualities will be sold for money. If, when you determined to go to war,

Your anger is inconsiderate and unmanly; you forget that the fortunes of the individual depend on those of the state. If you believed that I was wise, loyal, disinterested, when you consented to the war, why should you attack me now?

you believed me to have somewhat more of the statesman in me than others, it is not fair that I should now be charged with anything like crime.

I am not changed, but you are changed by misfortune. Such a change is unbecoming the citizens of Athens: you should forget your sorrows, and think only of the public good.

61 'I allow that for men who are in prosperity and free to choose it is great folly to make war. But when they must either submit and at once surrender independence, or strike and be free, then he who shuns and not he who meets the danger is deserving of blame. For my own part, I am the same man and stand where I did. But you are changed; for you have been driven by misfortune to recall the consent which you gave when you were yet unhurt, and to think that my advice was wrong because your own characters are weak. The pain is present and comes home to each of you, but the good is as yet unrealised by any one; and your minds have not the strength to persevere in your resolution, now that a great reverse has overtaken you unawares. Anything which is sudden and unexpected and utterly beyond calculation, such a disaster for instance as this plague coming upon other misfortunes, enthralls the spirit of a man. Nevertheless, being the citizens of a great city and educated in a temper of greatness, you should not succumb to calamities however overwhelming, or darken the lustre of your fame. For if men hate the presumption of those who claim a reputation to which they have no right, they equally condemn the faint-heartedness of those who fall below the glory which is their own. You should lose the sense of your private sorrows and cling to the deliverance of the state.

62 'As to your sufferings in the war, if you fear that they may be very great and after all fruitless, I have shown you already over and over again that such a fear is groundless. If you are still unsatisfied I will indicate [a] one element of

[a] Or, taking ὑπάρχον ὑμῖν absolutely: 'a consideration which, however obvious, appears to have escaped you.' Or, again, taking μεγέθους

your superiority which appears to have escaped you[a], although it nearly touches your imperial greatness. I too have never mentioned it before, nor would I now, because the claim may seem too arrogant, if I did not see that you are unreasonably depressed. You think that your empire is confined to your allies, but I say that of the two divisions of the world accessible to man, the land and the sea, there is one of which you are absolute masters, and have, or may have, the dominion to any extent which you please. Neither the great King nor any nation on earth can hinder a navy like yours from penetrating whithersoever you choose to sail. When we reflect on this great power, houses and lands, of which the loss seems so dreadful to you, are as nothing. We ought not to be troubled about them or to think much of them in comparison; they are only the garden of the house, the superfluous ornament of wealth; and you may be sure that if we cling to our freedom and preserve that, we shall soon enough recover all the rest. But, if we are the servants of others, we shall be sure to lose not only freedom, but all that freedom gives. And where your ancestors doubly succeeded, you will doubly fail. For their empire was not inherited by them from others but won by the labour of their hands, and by them preserved and bequeathed to us. And to be robbed of what you have is a greater disgrace than to attempt a conquest and fail. Meet your enemies therefore not only with spirit but with disdain. A coward or a fortunate fool may brag and vaunt, but he only is capable of disdain whose conviction that he is

Do you fear that your sufferings will be fruitless? I tell you that you are absolute masters of the sea, which is half the world. What are your possessions in comparison with freedom? Keep that, and you will soon regain the rest. Meet your enemies with disdain, as having a rational conviction of your superiority.

πέρι with ἐνθυμηθῆναι: 'one element of your superiority which nearly touches your empire, but of which you never seem to have considered the importance.'

stronger than his enemy rests, like our own, on grounds of reason. Courage fighting in a fair field is fortified by the intelligence which looks down upon an enemy; an intelligence relying, not on hope, which is the strength of helplessness, but on that surer foresight which is given by reason and observation of facts.

63 'Once more, you are bound to maintain the imperial dignity of your city in which you all take pride; for you should not covet the glory unless you will endure the toil. And do not imagine that you are fighting about a simple issue, freedom or slavery; you have an empire to lose, and there is the danger to which the hatred of your imperial rule has exposed you. Neither can you resign your power, if, at this crisis, any timorous or inactive spirit is for thus playing the honest man. For by this time your empire has become a tyranny which in the opinion of mankind may have been unjustly gained, but which cannot be safely surrendered. The men of whom I was speaking, if they could find followers, would soon ruin a city, and if they were to go and found a state of their own, would equally ruin that. For inaction is secure only when arrayed by the side of activity; nor is it expedient or safe for a sovereign, but only for a subject state, to be a servant.

Your empire is at stake, and it is too late to resign it; for you have already incurred the hatred of mankind.

64 'You must not be led away by the advice of such citizens as these, nor be angry with me; for the resolution in favour of war was your own as much as mine. What if the enemy has come and done what he was certain to do when you refused to yield? What too if the plague followed? That was an unexpected blow, but we might have foreseen all the rest. I am well aware that your hatred of me is aggravated by it. But how unjustly, unless to me you also ascribe the credit of any extraordinary

Nothing has happened, except the plague, but what we all anticipated when we agreed on war. Do not lose the spirit which has made Athens great and, even though she fall, will render her glorious for all time.

success which may befall you[a]! The visitations of heaven should be borne with resignation, the sufferings inflicted by an enemy with manliness. This has always been the spirit of Athens, and should not die out in you. Know that our city has the greatest name in all the world because she has never yielded to misfortunes, but has sacrificed more lives and endured severer hardships in war than any other; wherefore also she has the greatest power of any state up to this day; and the memory of her glory will always survive. Even if we should be compelled at last to abate somewhat of our greatness (for all things have their times of growth and decay), yet will the recollection live, that, of all Hellenes, we ruled over the greatest number of Hellenic subjects; that we withstood our enemies, whether single or united, in the most terrible wars, and that we were the inhabitants of a city endowed with every sort of wealth and greatness. The indolent may indeed find fault, but [b]the man of action[b] will seek to rival us, and he who is less fortunate will envy us. To be hateful and offensive has ever been at the time the fate of those who have aspired to empire. But he judges well who accepts unpopularity in a great cause. Hatred does not last long, and, besides the immediate splendour of great actions, the renown of them endures for ever in men's memories. Looking forward to such future glory and present avoidance of dishonour, make an effort now and secure both. Let no herald be sent to the Lacedaemonians, and do not let them know that you are depressed by your sufferings. For those are the greatest states and the greatest men, who, when misfortunes come, are the least depressed in spirit and the most resolute in action.'

By these and similar words Pericles endeavoured to 65
appease the anger of the Athenians against himself, and

---

[a] Cp. i. 140 init.

[b] Or, taking καὶ αὐτὸς with βουλόμενος: 'he who is ambitious like ourselves.'

to divert their minds from their terrible situation. In the conduct of public affairs they took his advice, and sent no more embassies to Sparta; they were again eager to prosecute the war. Yet in private they felt their sufferings keenly; the common people had been deprived even of the little which they possessed, while the upper class had lost fair estates in the country with all their houses and rich furniture. Worst of all, instead of enjoying peace, they were now at war. The popular indignation was not pacified until they had fined Pericles; but, soon afterwards, with the usual fickleness of a multitude, they elected him general and committed all their affairs to his charge. Their private sorrows were beginning to be less acutely felt, and for a time of public need they thought that there was no man like him. During the peace while he was at the head of affairs he ruled with prudence; under his guidance Athens was safe, and reached the height of her greatness in his time. When the war began he showed that here too he had formed a true estimate of the Athenian power. He survived the commencement of hostilities two years and six months; and, after his death, his foresight was even better appreciated than during his life. For he had told the Athenians that if they would be patient and would attend to their navy, and not seek to enlarge their dominion while the war was going on, nor imperil the existence of the city, they would be victorious; but they did all that he told them not to do, and in matters which seemingly had nothing to do with the war, from motives of private ambition and private interest they adopted a policy which had disastrous effects in respect both of themselves and of their allies; their measures,

The Athenians follow Pericles' advice, but are not appeased until they have fined him. He soon regains their esteem, and takes the lead of affairs. After his death his wisdom was even better appreciated than during his life. His advice about the war was sound if the Athenians would only have followed it. But they were continually embarking on rash enterprises, and the city was distracted by the struggles of rival demagogues, whereas Pericles had been their natural leader.

[a]had they been successful, would only have brought[a] honour and profit to individuals, and, when unsuccessful, crippled the city in the conduct of the war. The reason of the difference was that he, deriving authority from his capacity and acknowledged worth, being also a man of transparent integrity, was able to control the multitude in a free spirit; he led them rather than was led by them; for, not seeking power by dishonest arts, he had no need to say pleasant things, but, on the strength of his own high character, could venture to oppose and even to anger them. When he saw them unseasonably elated and arrogant, his words humbled and awed them; and, when they were depressed by groundless fears, he sought to reanimate their confidence. Thus Athens, though still in name a democracy, was in fact ruled by her greatest citizen. But his successors were more on an equality with one another, and, each one struggling to be first himself, they were ready to sacrifice the whole conduct of affairs to the whims of the people. Such weakness in a great and imperial city led to many errors, of which the greatest was the Sicilian expedition; not that the Athenians miscalculated their enemy's power, but they themselves, instead of consulting for the interests of the expedition which they had sent out, were occupied in intriguing against one another for the leadership of the democracy[b], and not only hampered the operations of the army, but became embroiled, for the first time, at home. And yet after they had lost in the Sicilian expedition the greater part of their fleet and army, and were now distracted by revolution, still they held out three years not only against their former enemies, but against the Sicilians who had combined with them, and against most of their own allies who had risen in revolt. Even when Cyrus the son of the King joined

Even after the Sicilian disaster they held out against their old enemies and many new ones, and were at last only ruined by themselves. So that Pericles was quite right after all.

[a] Or, 'while they continued to succeed, only brought.'

[b] Cp. vi. 28.

in the war and supplied the Peloponnesian fleet with money, they continued to resist, and were at last overthrown, not by their enemies, but by themselves and their own internal dissensions. So that at the time Pericles was more than justified in the conviction at which his foresight had arrived, that the Athenians would win an easy victory over the unaided forces of the Peloponnesians.

66 During the same summer the Lacedaemonians and their allies sent a fleet of a hundred ships against the island of Zacynthus, which lies opposite Elis. The Zacynthians are colonists of the Peloponnesian Achaeans, and were allies of the Athenians. There were on board the fleet a thousand Lacedaemonian hoplites, under the command of Cnemus the Spartan admiral. They disembarked and ravaged the greater part of the country; but as the inhabitants would not come to terms, they sailed away home.

The Lacedaemonians attack Zacynthus without result.

67 At the end of the same summer, Aristeus the Corinthian, the Lacedaemonian ambassadors Aneristus, Nicolaus, and Stratodemus, Timagoras of Tegea, and Pollis of Argos who had no public mission, were on their way to Asia in the hope of persuading the King to give them money and join in the war. They went first of all to Sitalces son of Teres, in Thrace, wishing if possible to detach him from the Athenians, and induce him to lead an army to the relief of Potidaea, which was still blockaded by Athenian forces; they also wanted him to convey them across the Hellespont on their intended journey to Pharnaces, the son of Pharnabazus, who was to send them on to the King. At the time of their arrival two Athenian envoys, Learchus the son of Callimachus, and Ameiniades the son of Philemon, chanced to be at the court of Sitalces; and they entreated his son Sadocus, who had been made

Envoys sent from the Peloponnesian cities to the King are detained by Sitalces and given up to the Athenians. They are carried to Athens and put to death.

an Athenian citizen [a], to deliver the envoys into their hands, that they might not find their way to the King and so injure a city which was in some degree his own. He consented, and, sending a body of men with Learchus and Ameiniades, before they embarked, as they were on their way through Thrace to the vessel in which they were going to cross the Hellespont, seized them; they were then, in accordance with the orders of Sadocus, handed over to the Athenian envoys, who conveyed them to Athens. On the very day of their arrival the Athenians, fearing that Aristeus, whom they considered to be the cause of all their troubles at Potidaea and in Chalcidicè, would do them still further mischief if he escaped, put them all to death without trial and without hearing what they wanted to say; they then threw their bodies down precipices. They considered that they had a right to retaliate on the Lacedaemonians, who had begun by treating in the same way the traders of the Athenians and their allies when they caught their vessels off the coast of Peloponnesus. For at the commencement of the war, all whom the Lacedaemonians captured at sea were treated by them as enemies and indiscriminately slaughtered, whether they were allies of the Athenians or neutrals.

The Ambraciots make war without success upon the Amphilochian Argives.

About the end of the same summer the Ambraciots, 68
with a large Barbarian force which they had called out, made war upon the Amphilochian Argos and upon Amphilochia. The original cause of their enmity against the Argives was as follows:—The Amphilochian territory had been occupied and the city founded by Amphilochus the son of Amphiaraus, who on returning home after the Trojan War was dissatisfied at the state of Argos. He fixed the site on the shore of the Ambracian Gulf, and called the new city by the name of his native place; it was the greatest city in that region, and its

[a] Cp. ii. 29 fin.

inhabitants were the most powerful community. Many generations afterwards, these Amphilochians in a time of distress invited their neighbours the Ambraciots to join in the settlement, and from them they first learned the Hellenic language which they now speak; the other Amphilochians are Barbarians. After a while the Ambraciots drove out the Amphilochian Argives and themselves took possession of the city. The expelled Amphilochians placed themselves under the protection of the Acarnanians, and both together called in the Athenians, who sent them a fleet of thirty ships under the command of Phormio. When Phormio arrived, they stormed Argos, and sold the Ambraciots into slavery; and the Amphilochians and Acarnanians dwelt together in the place. The alliance between the Acarnanians and Athenians then first began. The hatred of the Ambraciots towards the Amphilochian Argives commenced with the enslavement of their countrymen; and now when the war offered an opportunity they invaded their territory, accompanied by the Chaonians and some others of the neighbouring Barbarians. They came as far as Argos and made themselves masters of the country; but not being able to take the city by assault they returned, and the several tribes dispersed to their own homes. Such were the events of the summer.

Phormio at Naupactus. Melesander sent to collect tribute in Lycia and Caria is defeated and slain.

69 In the following winter the Athenians sent twenty ships on an expedition round Peloponnesus. These were placed under the command of Phormio, who, stationing himself at Naupactus, guarded the straits and prevented any one from sailing either out of or into Corinth and the Crisaean Gulf. Six other vessels were sent to collect tribute in Lycia and Caria; they were under the command of Melesander, who was to see that Peloponnesian privateers did not establish themselves in those parts, and damage merchant vessels coming from Phaselis and Phoenicia and all that region. But he, going up the country into Lycia with an army composed

of Athenians taken from the crews and of allied troops, was defeated, and himself and a part of his forces slain.

In the same winter the Potidaeans, who were still 70
blockaded, found themselves unable to hold out'; for the Peloponnesian invasions of Attica did not make the Athenians withdraw; and they had no more food. When they had been reduced to such straits as actually in some cases to feed on human flesh, they entered into communications with the Athenian generals, Xenophon the son of Euripides, Hestiodorus the son of Aristocleides, and Phanomachus the son of Callimachus, to whom the siege had been entrusted. They, seeing that the army was suffering from the exposed situation, and considering that the city had already spent two thousand talents[a] on the siege, accepted the terms proposed. The Potidaeans, with their wives and their children, and likewise the foreign troops[b], were to come out of the city, the men with one garment, the women with two, and they were allowed a certain fixed sum of money for their journey. So they came out under a safe-conduct, and went into Chalcidicè, or wherever they could find a home. But the Athenians blamed the generals for coming to terms without their authority, thinking that they could have made the city surrender at discretion. Soon afterwards they sent thither colonists of their own. Such were the events of the winter. And so ended the second year in the Peloponnesian War of which Thucydides wrote the history.

The Potidaeans are compelled by hunger to surrender. The Athenians blame their generals for giving easy terms.

In the following summer the Peloponnesians and their 71
allies under the command of Archidamus the son of Zeuxidamus, the Lacedaemonian king, instead of invading Attica, made an expedition against Plataea. There he encamped and was about to ravage the

B.C. 429. Ol. 87, 4.

Expedition of the Peloponnesians under Archidamus against Plataea.

[a] £400,000. [b] Cp. i. 60.

country, when the Plataeans sent envoys to him bearing the following message:—

Protest of the Plataeans.

You are violating the promise of independence which Pausanias made us after the battle of Plataea.

'Archidamus, and you Lacedaemonians, in making war upon Plataea you are acting unjustly, and in a manner unworthy of yourselves and of your ancestors. Pausanias the son of Cleombrotus, the Lacedaemonian, when he and such Hellenes as were willing to share the danger with him fought a battle in our land and liberated Hellas from the Persian, offered up sacrifice in the Agora of Plataea to Zeus the God of Freedom, and in the presence of all the confederates then and there restored to the Plataeans their country and city to be henceforth independent; no man was to make unjust war upon them at any time or to seek to enslave them; and if they were attacked, the allies who were present promised that they would defend them to the utmost of their power. These privileges your fathers granted to us as a reward for the courage and devotion which we displayed in that time of danger. But you are acting in an opposite spirit; for you have joined the Thebans, our worst enemies, and have come hither to enslave us. Wherefore, calling to witness the Gods to whom we all then swore, and also the Gods of your race and the Gods who dwell in our country, we bid you do no harm to the land of Plataea. Do not violate your oaths, but allow the Plataeans to be independent, and to enjoy the rights which Pausanias granted to them.'

72 To this appeal Archidamus rejoined:—

Archidamus offers peace if they will either join the Lacedaemonian confederacy or remain neutral.

'What you say, Plataeans, is just, but your acts should correspond to your words. Enjoy the independence which Pausanias granted to you, but also assist us in freeing the other Hellenes who were your sworn confederates in that time of danger and are now in subjection to the Athenians. With a view to the emancipation of them and of the other subject states, this great war has been undertaken and all these preparations made. It would be best for you to join with us, and observe the oaths yourselves which you would have us observe. But if you prefer to be neutral, a course which we have already once proposed to you, retain possession of your lands, and receive both sides in peace, but neither for the purposes of war; and we shall be satisfied.'

The Plataeans reply that they cannot act without the Athenians, and also that they distrust the Thebans.

The Plataean ambassadors then returned to the city and reported these words of Archidamus to the people, who made answer that they could not do what they were asked without the sanction of the Athenians, in whose power they had left their wives and children, and that they also feared for the very existence of their state. When the Lacedaemonians were gone the Athenians might come and not allow them to carry out the treaty; or the Thebans, who would be included in the clause requiring them 'to receive both sides,' might again attempt to seize their town. To this Archidamus, wanting to reassure them, made the following answer:—

Archidamus then asks them to surrender the city till the end of the war.

'Then deliver over your city and houses to the Lacedaemonians; mark the boundaries of your land, and number your fruit-trees and anything else which can be counted. Go yourselves whithersoever you please, while the war lasts, and on the return of peace we will give back to you all that we have received. Until then we will hold your property in trust, and will cultivate your ground, paying you such a rent as will content you.'

The Plataeans, obtaining permission to consult the Athenians, are encouraged by them to resist.

73 Upon hearing these words the envoys again returned into the city, and, after holding a consultation with the people, told Archidamus that they wished first to communicate his proposals to the Athenians, and if they could get their

consent they would do as he advised; in the meantime they desired him to make a truce with them, and not to ravage their land. So he made a truce which allowed sufficient time for their ambassadors to return from Athens; and meanwhile he spared their land. The Plataean envoys came to Athens, and after advising with the Athenians they brought back the following message to their fellow-citizens:—'Plataeans, the Athenians say that never at any time since you first became their allies[a] have they suffered any one to do you wrong, and that they will not forsake you now, but will assist you to the utmost of their power; and they adjure you, by the oaths which your fathers swore, not to forsake the Athenian alliance.'

They reply that they cannot accept the Lacedaemonian proposals.

74 When the answer came, the Plataeans resolved not to desert the Athenians, but patiently to look on, if they must, while the Lacedaemonians wasted their country, and to endure the worst. No one was henceforward to leave the town, but answer was to be made from the walls that they could not possibly consent to the Lacedaemonian proposal. King Archidamus, as soon as he received the reply, before proceeding to action, fell to calling upon the Gods and heroes of the country in the following words:—

Archidamus appeals to the Gods.

'O ye Gods and heroes who possess the land of Plataea, be our witnesses that our invasion of this land in which our fathers prayed to you when they conquered the Persians, and which you made a propitious battle-field to the Hellenes, has thus far been justified, for the Plataeans first deserted the alliance; and that if we go further we shall be guilty of no crime, for we have again and again made them fair proposals and they have not listened to us. Be gracious to us and grant that the real authors of the iniquity may be punished, and that they may obtain revenge who lawfully seek it.'

---

[a] Herod. vi. 108.

After this appeal to the Gods he began military operations. In the first place, the soldiers felled the fruit-trees and surrounded the city with a stockade, that henceforth no one might get out. They then began to raise a mound against it, thinking that with so large an army at work this would be the speediest way of taking the place. So they cut timber from Cithaeron and built on either side of the intended mound a frame of logs placed cross-wise in order that the material might not scatter. Thither they carried wood, stones, earth, and anything which would fill up the vacant space. They continued raising the mound seventy days and seventy nights without intermission; the army was divided into relays, and one party worked while the other slept and ate. The Lacedaemonian officers who commanded the contingents of the allies stood over them and kept them at work. The Plataeans, seeing the mound rising, constructed a wooden frame, which they set upon the top of their own wall opposite the mound; in this they inserted bricks, which they took from the neighbouring houses; the wood served to strengthen and bind the structure together as it increased in height; they also hung curtains of skins and hides in front; these were designed to protect the wood-work and the workers, and shield them against blazing arrows. The wooden wall rose high, but the mound rose quickly too. Then the Plataeans had a new device;—they made a hole in that part of the wall against which the mound pressed and drew in the earth. 75

The siege operations begin: the Peloponnesians raise a mound, which the Plataeans counteract by raising the height of a part of their wall and by drawing away earth from the mound.

The Peloponnesians discovered what they were doing, and threw into the gap clay packed in wattles of reed, which could not scatter and like the loose earth be carried away. Whereupon the Plataeans, baffled in one plan, resorted to another. Calcu- 76

This plan being defeated, the Plataeans build a second line of defence within their old wall in the form of a crescent.

lating the direction, they dug a mine from the city to the mound and again drew the earth inward. For a long time their assailants did not find them out, and so what the Peloponnesians threw on was of little use, since the mound was always being drawn off below and settling into the vacant space. But in spite of all their efforts, the Plataeans were afraid that their numbers would never hold out against so great an army; and they devised yet another expedient. They left off working at the great building opposite the mound, and beginning at both ends, where the city wall returned to its original lower height, they built an inner wall projecting inwards in the shape of a crescent, that if the first wall were taken the other might still be defensible. The enemy would be obliged to begin again and carry the mound right up to it, and as they advanced inwards would have their trouble all over again, and be exposed to missiles on both flanks. While the mound was rising the Peloponnesians brought battering engines up to the wall; one which was moved forward on the mound itself shook a great part of the raised building, to the terror of the Plataeans. They brought up others too at other points of the wall. But the Plataeans dropped nooses over the ends of these engines and drew them up; they also let down huge beams suspended at each end by long iron chains from two poles leaning on the wall and projecting over it. These beams they drew up at right angles to the advancing battering-ram, and whenever at any point it was about to attack them they slackened their hold of the chains and let go the beam, which fell with great force and snapped off the head of the ram.

By ingenious devices they disable the battering-rams of the enemy.

77 At length the Peloponnesians, finding that their engines were useless, and that the new wall was rising opposite to the mound, and perceiving that they could not without more formidable means of attack hope to take the city, made preparations for a blockade. But first of all they

The Peloponnesians nearly succeed in setting the city on fire.

resolved to try whether, the wind favouring, the place, which was but small, could not be set on fire; they were anxious not to incur the expense of a regular siege, and devised all sorts of plans in order to avoid it. So they brought faggots and threw them down from the mound along the space between it and the wall, which was soon filled up when so many hands were at work; then they threw more faggots one upon another into the city as far as they could reach from the top of the mound, and casting in lighted brands with brimstone and pitch, set them all on fire. A flame arose of which the like had never before been made by the hand of man; I am not speaking of fires in the mountains, when the forest has spontaneously blazed up from the action of the wind and mutual attrition. There was a great conflagration, and the Plataeans, who had thus far escaped, were all but destroyed; a considerable part of the town was unapproachable, and if a wind had come on and carried the flame that way, as the enemy hoped, they could not have been saved. It is said that there was also a violent storm of thunder and rain, which quenched the flames and put an end to the danger.

The Peloponnesians, having failed in this, as in their 78
former attempts, sent away a part of their army but retained the rest[a], and dividing the task among the contingents of the several cities, surrounded Plataea with a wall. Trenches, out of which they took clay for the bricks, were formed both on the inner and the outer side of the wall. About the rising of Arcturus[b] all was completed. They then drew off their army, leaving a guard on one half of the wall, while the other half was guarded by the Boeotians; the disbanded troops returned to their homes. The Plataeans had already conveyed to Athens[c] their wives, children, and old men,

Failing in their attempt, they draw a double wall round the city and retire, leaving a guard of themselves and the Boeotians.

[a] Retaining in the text τὸ δὲ λοιπὸν ἀφέντες.

[b] i. e. about the middle of September.

[c] ii. 6 fin.

with the rest of their unserviceable population. Those who remained during the siege were four hundred Plataeans, eighty Athenians, and a hundred and ten women to make bread. These were their exact numbers when the siege began. There was no one else, slave or freeman, within the walls. In such sort was the blockade of Plataea completed.

The Athenians attack Spartolus. An engagement takes place, in which they are at first victorious, but Chalcidian reinforcements arriving, the engagement is renewed and they are defeated with loss.

79 During the same summer, when the corn was in full ear, and about the time of the attack on Plataea, the Athenians sent an expedition against the Chalcidians of Thrace and against the Bottiaeans, consisting of two thousand heavy-armed troops of their own and two hundred horsemen under the command of Xenophon the son of Euripides, and two others. They came close up to the Bottian Spartolus and destroyed the crops. They expected that the place would be induced to yield to them by a party within the walls. But the opposite party sent to Olynthus and obtained from thence a garrison, partly composed of hoplites, which sallied out of Spartolus and engaged with the Athenians under the walls of the town. The Chalcidian hoplites and with them certain auxiliaries were defeated and retreated into Spartolus, but their cavalry and light-armed troops had the advantage over those of the Athenians. They were assisted by a few targeteers, who came from the district called Crusis. The engagement was scarcely over when another body of targeteers from Olynthus came up to their aid. Encouraged by the reinforcement and their previous success, and supported by the Chalcidian horse and the newly-arrived troops, the light-armed again attacked the Athenians, who began to fall back upon the two companies which they had left with their baggage: as often as the Athenians charged, the enemy retired; but when the Athenians continued their retreat, they pressed upon them and hurled darts at them. The Chalcidian

cavalry too rode up, and wherever they pleased charged the Athenians, who now fled utterly disconcerted and were pursued to a considerable distance. At length they escaped to Potidaea, and having recovered their dead under a flag of truce, returned to Athens with the survivors of their army, out of which they had lost four hundred and thirty men and all their generals. The Chalcidians and Bottiaeans, having set up a trophy and carried off their dead, disbanded and dispersed to their several cities.

In the same summer, not long afterwards, the Ambraciots and Chaonians, designing to subjugate the whole of Acarnania and detach it from the Athenian alliance, persuaded the Lacedaemonians to equip a fleet out of the confederate forces, and to send into that region a thousand hoplites. They said that if the Lacedaemonians would join with them and attack the enemy both by sea and land, the Acarnanians on the sea-coast would be unable to assist the inland tribes, and they might easily conquer Acarnania. Zacynthus and Cephallenia would then fall into their hands, and the Athenian fleet would not so easily sail round Peloponnesus. They might even hope to take Naupactus. The Lacedaemonians agreed, and at once despatched Cnemus, who was still admiral[a], with the thousand hoplites in a few ships; they ordered the rest of the allied navy to get ready and at once sail to Leucas. The interests of the Ambraciots were zealously supported by Corinth, their mother city. The fleet which was to come from Corinth, Sicyon, and the adjacent places was long in preparation; but the contingent from Leucas, Anactorium, and Ambracia was soon equipped, and waited at Leucas. Undiscovered by Phormio, the commander of the twenty Athenian ships which were keeping guard at 80

The Ambraciots persuade the Lacedaemonians to send a land and sea force under Cnemus against Acarnania. Disembarking his troops, he is joined by a number of barbarous tribes and marches towards Stratus.

[a] Cp. ii. 66.

Naupactus, Cnemus and his thousand hoplites crossed the sea and began to make preparations for the land expedition. Of Hellenes he had in his army Ambraciots, Leucadians, Anactorians, and the thousand Peloponnesians whom he brought with him,—of Barbarians a thousand Chaonians, who, having no king, were led by Photyus and Nicanor, both of the governing family and holding the presidency for a year. With the Chaonians came the Thesprotians, who, like them, have no king. A Molossian and Atintanian force was led by Sabylinthus, the guardian of Tharypas the king, who was still a minor; the Paravaeans were led by their king Oroedus, and were accompanied by a thousand Orestians placed at the disposal of Oroedus by their king Antiochus. Perdiccas also, unknown to the Athenians, sent a thousand Macedonians, who arrived too late. With this army Cnemus, not waiting for the ships from Corinth, began his march. They passed through the Argive territory and plundered Limnaea, an unwalled village. At length they approached Stratus, which is the largest city in Acarnania, thinking that, if they could take it, the other places would soon come over to them.

The Acarnanians, being refused aid by Phormio, confine themselves to the defence of their cities. Cnemus marches on Stratus in three divisions. While the Hellenes encamp, the Chaonians, rushing forward, attempt to storm the place, but fall into an ambush and are routed.

81 The Acarnanians, seeing that a great army had invaded their territory, and that the enemy was threatening them by sea as well as by land, did not attempt any united action, but guarded their several districts, and sent to Phormio for aid. He replied that a fleet of the enemy was about to sail from Corinth, and that he could not leave Naupactus unguarded. Meanwhile the Peloponnesians and their allies marched in three divisions towards Stratus, intending to encamp near and try negotiations; if these failed, they would take stronger measures and assault the wall. The Chaonians and the other Barbarians advanced in the centre; on the

right wing were the Leucadians, Anactorians, and their auxiliaries; on the left was Cnemus with the Peloponnesians and Ambraciots. The three divisions were a long way apart, and at times not even in sight of one another. The Hellenic troops maintained order on the march and kept a look out, until at length they found a suitable place in which to encamp; the Chaonians, confident in themselves, and having a great military reputation in that part of the country, would not stop to encamp, but they and the other Barbarians rushed on at full speed, hoping to take the place by storm and appropriate to themselves the glory of the action. The Stratians perceiving their approach in time, and thinking that, if they could overcome them before the others arrived, the Hellenic forces would not be so ready to attack them, set ambuscades near the city. When they were quite close, the troops came out of the city and from the ambuscades and fell upon them hand to hand. Whereupon the Chaonians were seized with a panic and many of them perished; the other Barbarians, seeing them give way, no longer stood their ground, but took to flight. Neither of the Hellenic divisions knew of the battle; the Chaonians were far in advance of them, and were thought to have hurried on because they wanted to choose a place for their camp. At length the Barbarians in their flight broke in upon their lines; they received them, and the two divisions uniting during that day remained where they were, the men of Stratus not coming to close quarters with them, because the other Acarnanians had not as yet arrived, but slinging at them from a distance and distressing them greatly. For they could not move a step without their armour. Now the Acarnanians are famous for their skill in slinging.

When night came on, Cnemus withdrew his army in 82
haste to the river Anapus, which is rather more than nine miles from Stratus, and on the following day carried off his dead under a flag of truce. The people of Oeniadae

were friendly and had joined him; to their city therefore he retreated before the Acarnanians had collected their forces. From Oeniadae all the Peloponnesian troops returned home. The Stratians erected a trophy of the battle in which they had defeated the Barbarians.

Cnemus withdraws his troops to Oeniadae, whence they are conveyed home.

83 The fleet from Corinth and the other allied cities on the Crisaean Gulf, which was intended to support Cnemus and to prevent the Acarnanians on the sea-coast from assisting their friends in the interior of the country, never arrived, but was compelled, almost on the day of the battle of Stratus, to fight with Phormio and the twenty Athenian ships which were stationed at Naupactus. As they sailed by into the open sea, Phormio was watching them, preferring to make his attack outside the gulf. Now the Corinthians and their allies were not equipped for a naval engagement, but for the conveyance of troops into Acarnania, and they never imagined that the Athenians with twenty ships would venture to engage their own forty-seven. But, as they were coasting along the southern shore, they saw the Athenian fleet following their movements on the northern; they then attempted to cross the sea from Patrae in Achaea to the opposite continent in the direction of Acarnania, when they again observed the enemy bearing down upon them from Chalcis and the mouth of the river Evenus. They had previously endeavoured to anchor under cover of night [a], but had been detected. So at last they were compelled to fight in the middle of the channel. The ships were commanded by generals of the cities which had furnished them; the Corinthian squadron by Machaon, Isocrates, and Agatharchidas. The Peloponnesians

The fleet of the Peloponnesians which was intended to support Cnemus is compelled to engage by Phormio.

---

[a] Or, reading ἀφορμισάμενοι, 'they had weighed anchor before it was light, but had been detected.'

arranged their ships in such a manner as to make the largest possible circle without leaving space to break through, turning their prows outwards and their sterns inwards; within the circle they placed the smaller craft which accompanied them, and five of their swiftest ships that they might be close at hand and row out at whatever point the enemy charged them.

Their ships form a circle.

The Athenians ranged their ships in a single line and 84
sailed round and round the Peloponnesian fleet, which they drove into a narrower and narrower space, almost touching as they passed, and leading the crews to suppose that they were on the point of charging. But they had been warned by Phormio not to begin until he gave the signal, for he was hoping that the enemy's ships, not having the steadiness of an army on land, would soon fall into disorder and run foul of one another; they would be embarrassed by the small craft, and if the usual morning breeze, for which he continued waiting as he sailed round them, came down from the gulf, they would not be able to keep still for a moment. He could attack whenever he pleased, because his ships were better sailers; and he knew that this would be the right time. When the breeze began to blow, the ships, which were by this time crowded into a narrow space and were distressed at once by the force of the wind and by the small craft which were knocking up against them, fell into confusion; ship dashed against ship, and they kept pushing one another away with long poles; there were cries of 'keep off' and noisy abuse, so that nothing could be heard either of the word of command or of the coxswains' giving the time; and the difficulty which unpractised rowers had in clearing the water in a heavy sea made the vessels disobedient to the helm. At that moment Phormio gave the signal; the Athenians, falling upon the

The Athenians sail round and round till the morning wind rises and throws the enemy's vessels into confusion, when they make their attack and win a complete victory.

enemy, began by sinking one of the admirals' vessels, and then wherever they went made havoc of them; at last such was the disorder that no one any longer thought of resisting, but the whole fleet fled away to Patrae and Dymè in Achaea. The Athenians pursued them, captured twelve ships, and taking on board most of their crews, sailed away to Molycrium. They set up a trophy on Rhium, and having there dedicated a ship to Poseidon, retired to Naupactus. The Peloponnesians likewise, with the remainder of their fleet, proceeded quickly along the coast from Dymè and Patrae to Cyllenè, where the Eleans have their docks. Cnemus with the ships from Leucas, which should have been joined by these, arrived after the battle of Stratus at Cyllenè.

The Lacedaemonians send Brasidas and two others to advise Cnemus.

85 The Lacedaemonians at home now sent to the fleet three commissioners, Timocrates, Brasidas, and Lycophron, to advise Cnemus. He was told that he must contrive to fight again and be more successful; he should not allow a few ships to keep him off the sea. The recent sea-fight had been the first attempt of the Lacedaemonians, and they were quite amazed and could not imagine that their own fleet was so inferior to that of the enemy. They suspected that there had been cowardice, not considering that the Athenians were old sailors and that they were only beginners[a]. So they despatched the commissioners in a rage. On their arrival they and Cnemus sent round to the allied cities for ships, and equipped for action those which were on the spot. Phormio likewise sent home messengers to announce the victory, and at the same time to inform the Athenians of the preparations which the enemy were making. He told them to send him immediately as large a reinforcement as possible, for he might have to fight any day. They sent

The Athenians send reinforcements to Phormio, but order them to go to Crete first.

---

[a] Cp. i. 142.

him twenty ships, but ordered the commander of them to go to Crete first; for Nicias of Gortys in Crete, who was the proxenus of the Athenians, had induced them to send a fleet against Cydonia, a hostile town which he promised to reduce. But he really invited them to please the Polichnitae, who are neighbours of the Cydoniatae. So the Athenian commander took the ships, went to Crete, and joined the Polichnitae in ravaging the lands of the Cydoniatae; there, owing to contrary winds and bad weather, a considerable time was wasted.

The Peloponnesians and Phormio take up a position opposite to each other, outside the Crisaean Gulf.

While the Athenians were detained in Crete the Pelo- 86
ponnesians at Cyllene, equipped for a naval engagement, coasted along to Panormus in Achaia, whither the Peloponnesian army had gone to co-operate with them. Phormio also coasted along to the Molycrian Rhium and anchored outside the gulf with the twenty ships which had fought in the previous engagement. This Rhium was friendly to the Athenians; there is another Rhium on the opposite coast in Peloponnesus; the space between them, which is rather less than a mile, forms the mouth of the Crisaean Gulf. When the Peloponnesians saw that the Athenians had come to anchor, they likewise anchored with seventy-seven ships at the Rhium which is in Achaia, not far from Panormus where their land forces were stationed. For six or seven days the two fleets lay opposite one another, and were busy in practising and getting ready for the engagement—the one resolved not to sail into the open sea, fearing a recurrence of their disaster, the other not to sail into the strait, because the confined space was favourable to their enemies. At length Cnemus, Brasidas, and the other Peloponnesian generals determined to bring on an engagement at once, and not wait until the Athenians too received their reinforcements. So they assembled their soldiers and, seeing that they were generally dispirited at their former defeat

and reluctant to fight, encouraged them in the following words:—

87 'The late sea-fight, Peloponnesians, may have made some of you anxious about the one which is impending, but it really affords no just ground for alarm. In that battle we were, as you know, ill-prepared, and our whole expedition had a military and not a naval object. Fortune was in many ways unpropitious to us, and this being our first sea-fight we may possibly have suffered a little from inexperience. The defeat which ensued was not the result of cowardice; nor should the unconquerable quality which is inherent in our minds, and refuses to acknowledge the victory of mere force, be depressed by the accident of the event. For though fortune may sometimes bring disaster, yet the spirit of a brave man is always the same, and while he retains his courage he will never allow inexperience to be an excuse for misbehaviour. And whatever be your own inexperience, it is more than compensated by your superiority in valour. The skill of your enemies which you so greatly dread, if united with courage, may be able in the moment of danger to remember and execute the lesson which it has learned, but without courage no skill can do anything at such a time. For fear makes men forget, and skill which cannot fight is useless. And therefore against their greater skill set your own greater valour, and against the defeat which so alarms you set the fact that you were unprepared. But now you have a larger fleet; this turns the balance in your favour; and you will fight close to a friendly shore under the protection of heavy-armed troops. Victory is generally on the side of those who are more numerous and better equipped. So that we have absolutely no reason for anticipating failure. Even our mistakes will be an additional advantage, because they will be a lesson to us. Be of good courage, then, and

You are terrified by our late mishap. But you were then unprepared. Your superior courage outweighs their superior skill, for without courage skill is useless. We for our part will arrange the attack better. But you must all do your duty.

let every one of you, pilot or sailor, do his own duty and maintain the post assigned to him. We will order the attack rather better than your old commanders, and so give nobody an excuse for cowardice. But, if any one should be inclined to waver, he shall be punished as he deserves, while the brave shall be honoured with the due rewards of their valour.'

Such were the words of encouragement addressed to 88
the Peloponnesians by their commanders. Phormio too, fearing that his sailors might be frightened, and observing that they were gathering in knots and were evidently apprehensive of the enemy's numbers, resolved to call them together and inspirit them by a suitable admonition. He had always been in the habit of telling them and training their minds to believe that no superiority of hostile forces could justify them in retreating. And it had long been a received opinion among the sailors that, as Athenians, they were bound to face any quantity of Peloponnesian ships. When, however, he found them dispirited by the sight which met their eyes, he determined to revive their drooping courage, and, having assembled them together, he spoke as follows:—

Phormio, seeing his sailors dispirited, assembles and addresses them.

'Soldiers, I have summoned you because I see that you 89
are alarmed at the numbers of the enemy, and I would not have you dismayed when there is nothing to fear. In the first place, the reason why they have provided a fleet so disproportionate is because we have defeated them already, and they can see themselves that they are no match for us; next, [a] as to the courage which they suppose to be native to them and which is the ground of their confidence when they attack us [a], that reliance is merely inspired by the success which their experience on land

[a] Or, taking the antecedent to ᾧ as supplied by the clause *οὐ δι' ἄλλο τι θαρσοῦσιν . . . κατορθοῦντες*: 'as to the ground of the confidence with which they attack us as if courage were native to them.'

usually gives them, and will, as they fancy, equally ensure them by sea. But the superiority which we allow to them on land we may justly claim for ourselves at sea; for in courage at least we are their equals, and the superior confidence of either of us is really based upon greater experience. The Lacedaemonians lead the allies for their own honour and glory; the majority of them are dragged into battle against their will; if they were not compelled they would never have ventured after so great a defeat to fight again at sea. So that you need not fear their valour; they are far more afraid of you and with better reason, not only because you have already defeated them, but because they cannot believe that you would oppose them at all if you did not mean to do something worthy of that great victory. [a]For most men when, like these Peloponnesians, they are a match for their enemies[a] rely more upon their strength than upon their courage; but those who go into battle against far superior numbers and under no constraint must be inspired by some extraordinary force of resolution. Our enemies are well aware of this, and are more afraid of our surprising boldness than they would be if our forces were less out of proportion to their own. Many an army before now has been overthrown by smaller numbers owing to want of experience; some too through cowardice; and from both these faults we are certainly free. If I can help I shall not give battle in the gulf, or even sail into it. For I know that where a few vessels which are skilfully handled and are better sailers engage with a larger number which are badly

I see that you fear the number of the enemy. Yet (1) their fleet is only so large because you defeated them before; (2) they boast of their courage, but it is only a courage on land; (3) they go unwillingly to battle, for (4) they believe that your very disproportion shows your superiority. I will not, if possible, sail into the gulf, where the confined space would baffle your skill. Do you keep your presence of mind, for the maritime supremacy of Athens is at stake.

[a] Or, 'For men who, like these Peloponnesians, are numerically superior to the enemy whom they face.'

managed the confined space is a disadvantage. Unless the captain of a ship see his enemy a good way off he cannot come on or strike properly; nor can he retreat when he is pressed hard. The manœuvres suited to fast-sailing vessels, such as breaking of the line or returning to the charge, cannot be practised in a narrow space. The sea-fight must of necessity be reduced to a land-fight [a] in which numbers tell. For all this I shall do my best to provide. Do you meanwhile keep order and remain close to your ships. Be prompt in taking your instructions, for the enemy is near at hand and watching us. In the moment of action remember the value of silence and order, which are always important in war, especially at sea. Repel the enemy in a spirit worthy of your former exploits. There is much at stake; for you will either destroy the rising hope of the Peloponnesian navy, or bring home to Athens the fear of losing the sea. Once more I remind you that you have beaten most of the enemy's fleet already; and, once defeated, men do not meet the same dangers with their old spirit.' Thus did Phormio encourage his sailors.

The Peloponnesians by a feigned attack on Naupactus draw the Athenians into the gulf, and, suddenly turning upon them, drive most of their vessels upon shore. Bravery of the Messenians.

The Peloponnesians, when they found that the Athenians 90
would not enter the straits or the gulf, determined to draw them in against their will. So they weighed anchor early in the morning, and, ranging their ships four deep, stood in towards the gulf [b] along their own coast [b], keeping the order in which they were anchored. The right wing, consisting of twenty of their fastest vessels, took the lead. These were intended to close upon the Athenians and prevent them from eluding their attack and getting beyond the wing in case Phormio, apprehending an attack upon Naupactus, should sail along

[a] Cp. vii. 62. [b] Reading παρά for ἐπί with the Laurentian and three other MSS. Or, adopting the conjecture ἐκείνων for ἑαυτῶν: 'making for the enemy's shore, and' &c.

shore to its aid. He, when he saw them weighing anchor, was alarmed, as they anticipated, for the safety of the town, which was undefended. Against his will and in great haste he embarked and sailed along the shore; the land forces of the Messenians followed. The Peloponnesians, seeing that the enemy were in single file and were already within the gulf and close to land, which was exactly what they wanted, at a given signal suddenly brought their ships round, and the whole line faced the Athenians and bore down upon them, every ship rowing at the utmost speed, for they hoped to cut off all the Athenian fleet. Eleven vessels which were in advance evaded the sudden turn of the Peloponnesians, and rowed past their right wing into the open water; but they caught the rest, forced them aground, and disabled them. All the sailors who did not swim out of them were slain. Some of the empty ships they fastened to their own and began to tow away; one they had already taken with the crew, but others were saved by the Messenians, who came to the rescue, dashed armed as they were into the sea, boarded them, and, fighting from their decks when they were being already towed away, finally recovered them.

The Lacedaemonians chase the eleven Athenian ships, which had escaped, to Naupactus. One of these by a sudden turn sinks her pursuer.

91 While in this part of the engagement the Lacedaemonians had the victory and routed the Athenian ships, their twenty vessels on the right wing were pursuing the eleven of the Athenians which had escaped from their attack into the open water of the gulf. These fled and, with the exception of one, arrived at Naupactus before their pursuers. They stopped off the temple of Apollo, and, turning their beaks outward, prepared to defend themselves in case the enemy followed them to the land. The Peloponnesians soon came up; they were singing a paean of victory as they rowed, and one Leucadian ship far in advance of the rest was chasing the single Athenian ship which had been left behind. There chanced to be anchored in the deep water a merchant

vessel, round which the Athenian ship rowed just in time, struck the Leucadian amidships, and sank her. At this sudden and unexpected feat the Peloponnesians were dismayed; they had been carrying on the pursuit in disorder because of their success. And some of them, dropping the blades of their oars, halted, intending to await the rest, which was a foolish thing to do when the enemy were so near and ready to attack them. Others, not knowing the coast, ran aground.

When the Athenians saw what was going on their hopes 92
revived, and at a given signal they charged their enemies with a shout. The Lacedaemonians did not long resist, for they had made mistakes and were all in confusion, but fled to Panormus, whence they had put to sea. The Athenians pursued them, took six of their ships which were nearest to them, and recovered their own ships which the Peloponnesians had originally disabled and taken in tow near the shore. The crews of the captured vessels were either slain or made prisoners. Timocrates the Lacedaemonian[a] was on board the Leucadian ship which went down near the merchant vessel; when he saw the ship sinking he killed himself; the body was carried into the harbour of Naupactus. The Athenians then retired and raised a trophy on the place from which they had just sailed out to their victory. They took up the bodies and wrecks which were floating near their own shore, and gave back to the enemy, under a flag of truce, those which belonged to them. The Lacedaemonians also set up a trophy of the victory which they had gained over the ships destroyed by them near the shore; the single ship which they took they dedicated on the Achaean Rhium, close to the trophy. Then, fearing the arrival of the Athenian reinforcements, they sailed away at nightfall to the Crisaean Gulf and to

The Athenians, taking advantage of the confusion, turn upon the enemy and gain a complete victory.

[a] Cp. ii. 85 init.

Corinth, all with the exception of the Leucadians. And not long after their retreat the twenty Athenian ships from Crete, which ought to have come to the assistance of Phormio before the battle, arrived at Naupactus. So the summer ended.

The Peloponnesians determine to make an attempt on the Piraeus, but losing heart, only sail to Salamis and ravage the island.

93 Before breaking up the fleet which had returned to Corinth and the Crisaean Gulf, Cnemus, Brasidas, and the other Peloponnesian commanders, it being now the beginning of winter, wished to make an attempt, suggested by some Megarians, on Piraeus, the harbour of Athens. The entrance was unclosed and unguarded; as was natural, since the Athenians were complete masters of the sea. Each sailor was to carry his cushion and his oar with its thong, and cross on foot with all haste from Corinth to the Athenian side of the Isthmus; they were to go to Megara and from Nisaea, the harbour of Megara, to launch forty ships which happened to be lying in the docks; thence they were to sail straight for the Piraeus. No guard ships were stationed there, for no one ever expected [a] that the enemy would attempt a surprise of this kind. As to an open and deliberate attack, how was he likely to venture on that? and if he even entertained such a design, would he not have been found out in time [a]? The plan was immediately carried out. Arriving at night, they launched the ships from Nisaea and sailed away, but not to the Piraeus; the danger seemed too great, and also the wind is said to have been unfavourable. So they gave up their original idea and made for the projecting point of Salamis which looks towards Megara; here there was a fort, and three ships were stationed in order to prevent anything being conveyed by sea into or out of Megara. This fort they

[a] Or, taking ἐπεί differently, and καθ' ἡσυχίαν in the sense of 'without interference:' 'that the enemy would make a sudden attack of this kind. An attempt so bold and open was not likely to be unopposed, or the very design, if entertained, to escape detection.'

assailed, towed away the ships without their crews, and ravaged the rest of Salamis which was unprepared for their attack.

By this time fire-signals had carried the alarm to Athens. 94
Nothing which happened in the war caused a greater panic. The inhabitants of the city thought that the enemy had already sailed into the Piraeus; the belief in the Piraeus was that Salamis had been taken and that the enemy were on the point of sailing into the harbour, which, if they had been bolder, they might easily have done, and no wind would have prevented them. But as soon as day dawned, the Athenians, coming down with the whole strength of the city to the Piraeus, launched their ships and, embarking in tumultuous haste, sailed to Salamis, while their land-forces remained and guarded the Piraeus. When the Peloponnesians saw the fleet coming they sailed quickly back to Nisaea, but not until they had ravaged the greater part of Salamis and taken many prisoners and much spoil, as well as the three ships which lay off the fort of Budorum. There was some apprehension about their own ships; for they had long been lain up and were not sea-worthy. Arriving at Megara they marched back again to Corinth, and the Athenians, having failed to overtake them in Salamis, sailed back likewise. Henceforth they kept more careful watch over the Piraeus, among other precautions closing the entrance to the harbour.

Temporary panic at Athens. Relief is immediately sent to Salamis, and the Peloponnesians retire.

About the same time, at the beginning of winter, Sitalces 95
the Odrysian, the son of Teres, king of Thrace, made war upon Perdiccas, the son of Alexander, king of Macedon, and upon the Thracian Chalcidians. There were two promises, of which he wished to perform one, and exact fulfilment of the other. The promise of which he claimed fulfilment had been made to him by Perdiccas, when, being hard pressed at the

Sitalces king of Thrace, in alliance with Athens, attacks Perdiccas and the Thracian Chalcidians.

beginning of the war, he wanted Sitalces to reconcile him to the Athenians[a], and not to restore and place on the throne his brother Philip, who was his enemy; but Perdiccas did not keep his word. The other was a promise which Sitalces had himself made to the Athenians when he entered into alliance with them, that he would put an end to their war with the Chalcidians. For these two reasons he invaded the country, taking with him Amyntas the son of Philip, whom he intended to make king of Macedon, and also certain Athenian envoys who had just come to remind him of his engagement, and an Athenian commander Hagnon. For the Athenians on their part were bound to assist him against the Chalcidians with ships and with as large an army as they could provide.

The forces of Sitalces.

96 Accordingly Sitalces, beginning with the Odrysae, made a levy of all his Thracian subjects dwelling between Mount Haemus and Mount Rhodope as far as the shores of the Euxine and of the Hellespont. Beyond the Haemus he made a levy of the Getae and of all the tribes lying more towards the Euxine on this side of the Ister. Now the Getae and their neighbours border on the Scythians, and are equipped like them, for they are all horse-archers. He also summoned to his standard many of the highland Thracians, who are independent and carry dirks; they are called Dii, and most of them inhabit Mount Rhodopè; of these some were attracted by pay, while others came as volunteers. He further called out the Agrianians, the Laeaeans, and the other Paeonian nations who were his subjects. These tribes were the last within his empire; they extended as far as the Graaean Paeonians and the river Strymon, which rises in Mount Scombrus and flows through the country of the Graaeans and Laeaeans; there his dominion ended and the independent Paeonians began. In the

[a] The reconciliation had been effected through the instrumentality of Nymphodorus; ii. 29.

direction of the Triballi, who are likewise independent, the Treres and the Tilataeans formed his boundary. These tribes dwell to the north of Mount Scombrus and reach westward as far as the Oscius. This river rises in the same mountains as the Nestus and the Hebrus, an uninhabited and extensive range which adjoins Rhodopè.

The empire of the Odrysae measured by the coast-line 97
reaches from the city of Abdera to the mouth of the Ister in the Euxine. The voyage round can be made by a merchant vessel, if the wind is favourable the whole way, at the quickest in four days and as many nights. Or an expeditious traveller going by land from Abdera to the mouth of the Ister, if he takes the shortest route, will accomplish the journey in eleven days. Such was the extent of the Odrysian empire towards the sea: up the country the land journey from Byzantium to the Laeaeans and to the Strymon, this being the longest line which can be drawn from the sea into the interior, may be accomplished by an expeditious traveller in thirteen days. The tribute which was collected from the Hellenic cities and from all the barbarous nations in the reign of Seuthes, the successor of Sitalces, under whom the amount was greatest, was valued at about four hundred talents of coined money [a], reckoning only gold and silver. Presents of gold and silver equal in value to the tribute, besides stuffs embroidered or plain and other articles, were also brought, not only to the king himself, but to the inferior chiefs and nobles of the Odrysae. For their custom was the opposite of that which prevailed in the Persian kingdom; they were more ready to receive than to give; and he who asked and was refused was not so much discredited as he who refused when he was asked. The same custom prevailed among the other Thracians in a less degree, but among the Odrysae, who were richer, more extensively; nothing could be done without presents. By these means

Extent and wealth of the Odrysian empire.

---

[a] £80,000.

the kingdom became very powerful, and in revenue and general prosperity exceeded all the nations of Europe which lie between the Ionian Sea and the Euxine; in the size and strength of their army being second only, though far inferior, to the Scythians. For if the Scythians were united, there is no nation which could compare with them, or would be capable of resisting them[a]; I do not say in Europe, but even in Asia—not that they are at all on a level with other nations in sense, or in that intelligence which uses to advantage the ordinary means of life.

98 Such was the great country over which Sitalces ruled.

Sitalces and his army enter Macedonia.

When he had collected his army and his preparations were complete he marched into Macedonia, passing first of all through his own territory, and then through Cercinè, a desert mountain which lies between the Sinti and the Paeonians. He went by the road which he had himself constructed when he made his expedition against the Paeonians and cut down the forest. As he left the Odrysian territory in going through the mountain he had on the right hand the Paeonians and on the left hand the Sinti and Maedi; on quitting the mountain he arrived at Doberus in Paeonia. He lost no part of his army on the march, except by sickness, but rather increased it; for many of the independent Thracian tribes followed him of their own accord in hopes of plunder. The whole number of his forces was estimated at a hundred and fifty thousand, of which about two-thirds were infantry and the rest cavalry. The largest part of the cavalry was furnished by the Odrysae themselves, and the next largest by the Getae. Of the infantry, those armed with dirks who came from the independent tribes of Mount Rhodopè were the most warlike. The remainder of the army was a mixed multitude, chiefly formidable from its numbers.

99 Having mustered at Doberus, they made ready to

---

[a] Cp. Herod. iv. 46.

descend over the heights into the plains of Macedonia, which were the territory of Perdiccas. *Early history of the Macedonian kingdom.* There is an upper Macedonia, which is inhabited by Lyncestians, Elimiots, and other tribes; these are the allies and tributaries of the lower Macedonians, but have kings of their own. The maritime country which we now call Macedonia was conquered and formed into a kingdom by Alexander the father of Perdiccas and his ancestors the Temenidae, who originally came from Argos [a]. They defeated and drove out of Pieria the Pierians, who afterwards settled in Phagres and other places at the foot of Mount Pangaeus, beyond the Strymon; the land which lies under Mount Pangaeus towards the sea is still called the Pierian vale. They also drove out of Bottia, as it is called, the Bottiaeans, who are now the neighbours of the Chalcidians, and they acquired a narrow strip of Paeonia by the river Axius, reaching down to Pella and the sea. Beyond the Axius they possess the country called Mygdonia reaching to the Strymon, out of which they have driven the Edonians. They expelled from the country still called Eordia the Eordians, of whom the greater part perished, but a small remnant of them settled in the neighbourhood of Physca; and from Almopia the Almopians. They and their subjects further subdued and still hold various places belonging to other tribes, Anthemus, Grestonia, Bisaltia, and a great part of the original Macedonia. But the whole of this country is now called Macedonia, and was under the rule of Perdiccas the son of Alexander at the time of the invasion of Sitalces.

The Macedonians were unable to defend themselves 100
against the onset of so vast a host; they therefore retired into their strongholds and forts, which at that time were few. For those which now exist were built by Archelaus the son of Perdiccas, who, when he became king, made straight roads and in various ways improved the country.

[a] Herod. viii. 137–139.

In his force of cavalry and infantry and in his military resources generally he surpassed all the eight kings who preceded him.

The Macedonians retire into their strongholds. Their cavalry oppose the invaders, but are compelled by their inferiority of numbers to desist.

The Thracian army, leaving Doberus, invaded first of all the country which had formerly been the principality of Philip, and took Eidomenè by storm. Gortynia, Atalantè, and some other towns came to terms out of regard for Amyntas the son of Philip, who accompanied the expedition. They also besieged but failed to take Europus; they next advanced into that part of Macedonia which lay on the left of Pella and Cyrrhus. Farther south into Bottiaea and Pieria they did not penetrate, but were content to ravage the territory of Mygdonia, Grestonia, and Anthemus. The Macedonians had no idea of facing them with infantry, but sent for additional cavalry from their allies in the upper part of the country, and, although a handful of men, dashed in amongst the great Thracian host wherever they pleased. No one withstood their onset; for they were excellent horsemen and well protected with coats of mail. But hemmed in as they continually were by a multitude many times their own number, they ran into great danger. At last, feeling that they were not strong enough to encounter such superiority of force, they desisted.

Sitalces holds a conference with Perdiccas, and after an unsuccessful campaign in Botticè and Chalcidicè, is persuaded by his nephew Seuthes (who had been gained over by Perdiccas) to return home. Alarm in Hellas.

101 Sitalces now held a conference with Perdiccas touching the matters which gave occasion to the war. The fleet which the Athenians had promised never arrived; for not believing that Sitalces would come, they only sent gifts and envoys to him. After waiting for them in vain he despatched a part of his army against the Chalcidians and Bottiaeans, and, driving them within their walls, devastated the country. While he was encamped in these parts, the Thessalians, who lie towards the south, the

Magnesians and other dependants of the Thessalians, and all the Hellenes as far as Thermopylae were afraid that his army would move on them, and took measures of precaution. Those independent Thracian tribes to the north beyond the Strymon who dwelt in the plains, namely the Panaeans, Odomantians, Droans, and Dersaeans, were also in great alarm. A belief arose, which spread far and wide among the enemies of Athens, that the Athenians meant to lead their Odrysian allies against the rest of Hellas. Meanwhile Sitalces overran and ravaged Chalcidicè, Botticè, and Macedonia, but could not effect his objects; and, his army being without food and suffering from the winter, he was persuaded by his nephew, who next to himself had the greatest authority, Seuthes the son of Spardacus [a], to return home at once. Now Perdiccas had secretly gained over Seuthes, promising to give him his sister in marriage, with a portion. And so Sitalces and his army, having remained thirty days in all, of which eight were passed among the Chalcidians, returned home in haste. Perdiccas in fulfilment of his promise gave his sister Stratonicè in marriage to Seuthes. Thus ended the expedition of Sitalces.

The Athenians, under Phormio, make an expedition into Acarnania.

During the same winter the Athenian forces at Naupactus, after the Peloponnesian fleet had dispersed, made an expedition under the command of Phormio into the centre of Acarnania with four hundred hoplites of their own taken from the fleet [b] and four hundred Messenian hoplites. They first coasted along towards Astacus [c] and disembarked. From Stratus, Coronta, and other places they expelled those of the inhabitants whom they distrusted, and restoring Cynes the son of Theolytus to Coronta, they returned to their ships. Oeniadae, of which the inhabitants, unlike the rest of 102

[a] Cp. iv. 101 fin.

[b] Cp. ii. 83 init.; 92 fin.

[c] Cp. ii. 30; 33.

the Acarnanians, were their persistent enemies, was unapproachable in winter. For the town is in the midst of a marsh formed by the river Achelous, which, rising in Mount Pindus and passing first through the territory of the Dolopians, Agraeans, and Amphilochians, and then through the Acarnanian plain, at some distance from its mouth flows by the city of Stratus and finds an exit into the sea near Oeniadae: an expedition in winter is thus rendered impossible by the water. Most of the islands called Echinades are situated opposite to Oeniadae and close to the mouth of the Achelous. The consequence is that the river, which is large, is always silting up: some of the islands have been already joined to the mainland, and very likely, at no distant period, they may all be joined to it. The stream is wide and strong and full of mud; and the islands are close together and serve to connect the deposits made by the river, not allowing them to dissolve in the water. For, lying irregularly and not one behind the other, they prevent the river from finding a straight channel into the sea. These islands are small and uninhabited. The story is that when Alcmaeon the son of Amphiaraus was wandering over the earth after the murder of his mother, he was told by Apollo that here he should find a home, the oracle intimating that he would never obtain deliverance from his terrors until he discovered some country which was not yet in existence and not seen by the sun at the time when he slew his mother; there he might settle, but the rest of the earth was accursed to him. He knew not what to do, until at last, according to the story, he spied the deposit of earth made by the Achelous, and he thought that a place sufficient to support life must have accumulated in the long time during which he had been wandering since his mother's death. There, near Oeniadae, he settled, and, becoming

Oeniadae was inaccessible, owing to the flooding of the Achelous. Opposite to the town lie the Echinades, islands formed by the deposits of the river. Here Alcmaeon, after the murder of his mother, is said to have found a home which was indicated to him by the oracle of Apollo.

ruler, left to the country the name of his son Acarnan. Such is the tradition which has come down to us concerning Alcmaeon.

The Athenians under Phormio sailed back from Acar- 103
nania to Naupactus, and later at the beginning of spring returned to Athens, bringing with them the ships which they had captured, besides the prisoners of free birth whom they had taken in the naval engagements. These were exchanged man for man. And so the winter ended, and with it the third year in the Peloponnesian War of which Thucydides wrote the history.

The Athenians return to Naupactus, and in the spring sail back to Athens.

BOOK III

1 IN the following summer, when the corn was in full ear, the Peloponnesians and their allies, under the command of Archidamus, the son of Zeuxidamus, the Lacedaemonian king, invaded Attica, and encamping wasted the country. The Athenian cavalry as usual attacked them whenever an opportunity offered, and prevented the great body of the light-armed troops from going beyond their lines and injuring the lands near the city. The invaders remained until their supplies were exhausted; they were then disbanded, and returned to their several homes.

B.C. 428. Ol. 88.

Third invasion of Attica by the Peloponnesians.

2 No sooner had the Peloponnesians quitted Attica than the whole people of Lesbos, with the exception of the Methymnaeans, revolted from Athens. They had entertained the design before the war began, but the Lacedaemonians gave them no encouragement. And now they were not ready, and were compelled to revolt sooner than they had intended. For they were waiting until they had completed the work of closing their harbours, raising walls, and building ships, and they had not as yet received from Pontus the force of archers, the corn and the other supplies for which they had sent. But the inhabitants of Tenedos, who were not on good terms with them, and the Methymnaeans, and individual citizens who were of the opposite faction and

The Lesbians, with the exception of the Methymnaeans, revolt, but sooner than they had intended, information of their plans having been sent to Athens from Tenedos, Methymna, and Mytilenè itself.

were proxeni of Athens, turned informers and told the Athenians that the Mytilenaeans were forcibly making Mytilenè the centre of government for the whole island; that the preparations which they were pressing forward had been throughout undertaken by them in concert with the Lacedaemonians and with their Boeotian kinsmen, and meant revolt; and that if something were not immediately done, Lesbos would be lost to Athens.

The Athenians determine to surprise Mytilenè at a festival, and send Cleïppides thither with forty ships. The inhabitants are forewarned.

The Athenians, who were suffering severely from the 3
plague and from the war, of which they had begun to feel the full effects, reflected that it was a serious matter to bring upon themselves a second war with a naval power like Lesbos, whose resources were unimpaired; and so, mainly because they wished that the charges might not be true, they at first refused to listen to them. But, when they had sent envoys to Mytilenè and found that the Mytilenaeans, in spite of remonstrances, continued their preparations and persisted in the attempt to concentrate the government in Mytilenè, they took alarm and determined to be beforehand with them. Without losing a moment, they sent to Lesbos, under the command of Cleïppides the son of Deinias, and two others, forty ships which had been intended to cruise about Peloponnesus. They had heard that there was a festival of Apollo Maloeis held outside the walls in which the whole population took part, and that if they made haste they might hope to surprise them. The attempt would very likely succeed; but, if not, they might bid the Mytilenaeans give up their fleet and dismantle their walls, and in case they refused they might go to war with them. So the ships sailed; and as there happened to be at Athens ten Mytilenaean triremes, serving in accordance with the terms of the alliance, the Athenians seized them and threw their crews into prison. But the Mytilenaeans were warned by a messenger from Athens, who crossed to Euboea and went on foot to Geraestus; there

he found a merchant vessel just about to sail; he took ship, and arriving at Mytilenè on the third day after he left Athens, announced the coming of the Athenian fleet. Whereupon the Mytilenaeans abstained from going out to the temple of Apollo Maloeis. They also kept good watch about their walls and harbours, and barricaded the unfinished works.

The Mytilenaeans, after a slight resistance at sea, negotiate an armistice. They send envoys openly to Athens, secretly to Sparta.

4 Soon afterwards the Athenians arrived. The commanders of the fleet, seeing that they were foiled, delivered the message entrusted to them; the city refused to yield and they commenced hostilities. Taken by surprise, and unprepared for the war which was forced upon them, the Mytilenaeans came out once and made a show of fighting a little in front of the harbour; but they were soon driven back by the Athenian ships, and then they began to parley with the generals, in the hope of obtaining tolerable terms of some kind, and getting rid of the fleet for the time. The Athenian generals accepted their proposals, they too fearing that they were not strong enough to make war against the whole island. Having got the armistice, the Mytilenaeans sent envoys to Athens; one of them was a person who had given information against his fellow-citizens, but was now repentant. They had a faint hope that the Athenians would be induced to withdraw their ships and believe in their good intentions. But as they did not really expect to succeed in their Athenian mission, they also sent an embassy to Lacedaemon, unperceived by the Athenian fleet, which was stationed at Malea[a] to the north of the city[a]. After a troublesome voyage through the open sea, the envoys arrived at Lacedaemon and solicited aid for their countrymen.

---

[a] Or, to avoid the geographical contradiction (see notes), we may take the words with ἀποστέλλουσιν: 'they also sent an embassy . . . northward from the city.'

The envoys return from Athens without success. A battle ensues, in which the Mytilenaeans have the advantage; but they remain inactive, awaiting aid from Peloponnesus.

The other envoys who had been sent to Athens met 5
with no success. When they returned, the Mytilenaeans and the rest of Lesbos, with the exception of Methymna, commenced hostilities; the Methymnaeans, with the Imbrians, Lemnians, and a few of the allies, had come to the support of the Athenians. The Mytilenaeans with their whole force sallied out against the Athenian camp, and a battle took place, in which they got the better; but they had no confidence in themselves, and, instead of encamping on the field, retired. They then remained quiet, being unwilling to risk an engagement without the additional help which they were expecting from Peloponnesus and elsewhere. For Meleas a Lacedaemonian, and Hermaeondas a Theban, had now arrived at Mytilenè; they had been sent before the revolt, but the Athenian fleet anticipated them, and they sailed in by stealth after the battle in a single trireme. The envoys recommended the Mytilenaeans to send an embassy of their own in another trireme to accompany them on their return to Sparta; which they accordingly did.

The Athenians blockade Mytilenè by sea.

The Athenians, greatly encouraged by the inactivity of 6
their adversaries, summoned their allies, who came all the more readily because they saw that the Lesbians displayed no energy. They then anchored the fleet round the south of the city, and having fortified two camps, one on either side of it, they established a blockade of both the harbours. Thus they excluded the Mytilenaeans from the sea. They likewise held the country in the immediate neighbourhood of their two camps; but the Mytilenaeans and the other Lesbians, who had now taken up arms, were masters of the rest of the island. At Malea the Athenians had, not a camp, but a station for their ships and for their market.

Such was the course of the war in Lesbos. In the same 7
summer, and about the same time, the Athenians sent

thirty ships to Peloponnesus; they were placed under the command of Asopius, the son of Phormio; for the Acarnanians had desired them to send out a son or relation of Phormio to be their leader. The ships in passing ravaged the coast of Laconia, and then Asopius sent most of them home, but kept twelve, with which he sailed to Naupactus. Next he made a general levy of the Acarnanians and led his forces against Oeniadae, his ships sailing up the river Achelous, while his army ravaged the country by land. As the inhabitants refused to yield, he disbanded his land-forces, but himself sailed to Leucas and made a descent upon Nericus, where he and part of his army in returning to their ships were slain by the inhabitants, assisted by a few Peloponnesian guards. The Athenians then put to sea, and received their dead from the Leucadians under a flag of truce.

Asopius with thirty Athenian ships ravages the Laconian coast, and, dismissing eighteen, sails to Oeniadae, which he is unable to capture.

He is killed in a descent upon Leucas.

8 The envoys whom the Mytilenaeans had sent out in their first vessel were told by the Lacedaemonians to come to the Olympic festival, in order that the allies, as well as themselves, might hear them and determine what should be done. So they went to Olympia, The Olympiad was that in which the Rhodian Dorieus won his second victory. When the festival was over, the allies met in council, and the ambassadors spoke as follows:—

The Mytilenaean envoys meet the allies in council at Olympia. Their speech.

9 'We know, Lacedaemonians and allies, that all Hellenes entertain a fixed sentiment against those who in time of war revolt and desert an old alliance. Their new allies are delighted with them in as far as they profit by their aid; but they do not respect them, for they deem them traitors to their former friends. And this opinion is reasonable enough; but only when the rebels, and those from whom they sever

There is a natural feeling against those who desert their friends, but the friendship must be real and equal.

themselves, are naturally united by the same interests and feelings and equally matched in power and resources, and when there is no reasonable excuse for a revolt. But our relation to the Athenians was of another sort, and no one should be severe upon us for deserting them in the hour of danger although we were honoured by them in time of peace.

'Since an alliance is our object, we will first address 10
ourselves to the question of justice and honour. We know that no friendship between man and man, no league between city and city, can ever be permanent unless the friends or allies have a good opinion of each other's honesty, and are similar in general character. For the diversity in men's minds makes the difference in their actions.

Before asking for your alliance, we must show that we deserve your respect.

'Now our alliance with the Athenians first began when you ceased to take part in the Persian War, and they remained to complete the work. But we were never the allies of the Athenians in their design of subjugating Hellas; we were really the allies of the Hellenes, whom we sought to liberate from the Persians. And while in the exercise of their command they claimed no supremacy, we were very ready to follow them. But our fears began to be aroused when we saw them relaxing their efforts against the Persians and imposing the yoke of their dominion upon the allies, who could not unite and defend themselves, for their interests were too various. And so they were all enslaved, except ourselves and the Chians. We forsooth were independent allies, free men—that was the word—who fought at their side. But, judging from previous examples, how could we any longer have confidence in our leaders? For they had subjugated others to whom, equally with ourselves, their faith was pledged; and how

We became allies of the Athenians because we wanted to complete the deliverance of Hellas from the Persians. But when we saw the allies, excepting the Chians and ourselves, successively enslaved by them, what wonder that we lost confidence in them!

could we who survived expect to be spared if ever they had the power to destroy us?

11 'Had all the allies retained their independence, we should have had better assurance that they would leave us as we were; but when the majority had been subjugated by them, they might naturally be expected to take offence at our footing of equality; they would contrast us who alone maintained this equality with the majority who had submitted to them; they would also observe that in proportion as their strength was increasing, our isolation was increasing too. Mutual fear is the only solid basis of alliance; for he who would break faith is deterred from aggression by the consciousness of inferiority. And why were we left independent? Only because they thought that to gain an empire they must use fair words and win their way by policy and not by violence. On the one hand, our position was a witness to their character. For, having an equal vote with them, we could not be supposed to have fought in their wars against our will, but those whom they attacked must have been in the wrong. On the other hand, they were thus enabled to use the powerful against the weak; they thought that they would leave us to the last; when the lesser states were removed, the stronger would fall an easier prey. But if they had begun with us while the power of the allies was still intact, and we might have afforded a rallying-point, they would not so easily have mastered them. Besides, our navy caused them some apprehension; they were afraid that we might join you, or some other great power, and that the union would be dangerous to them. For a time, too, we saved ourselves by paying court to the people and to the popular leaders of the day. But we were not likely to have survived long, judging by the conduct of the Athenians towards others, if this war had not arisen.

We were an offence to them, but they left us free because (1) our voluntary adherence was a testimony to their character, (2) they wanted to use the strong against the weak, and so isolate us, (3) they feared our navy, (4) we paid court to their demagogues.

'What trust then could we repose in such a friendship 12
or such a freedom as this? The civility which we showed to one another was at variance with our real feelings. They courted us in time of war because they were afraid of us, and we in time of peace paid a like attention to them. And the faith which is generally assured by mutual good-will had with us no other bond but mutual fear; from fear, and not from love, we were constrained to maintain the alliance, and which ever of us first thought that he could safely venture would assuredly have been the first to break it. And therefore if any one imagines that we do wrong in striking first, because they delay the blow which we dread, and thinks that we should wait and make quite sure of their intentions, he is mistaken. If we were really on an equality with them and in a position to counteract their designs and imitate their threatening attitude, how was it consistent with this equality that we had still to be at their mercy? The power of attack is always in their hands, and the power of anticipating attack should always be in ours.

It was not mutual love but mutual fear which united us. We struck first because we were not on an equality with them; we were always liable to be attacked, and were therefore at their mercy.

'These were the reasons, Lacedaemonians and allies, 13
and the grievances which led us to revolt. They were clear enough to prove to all hearers the justice of our cause, and strong enough to alarm us and drive us to seek some deliverance. We have acted from no sudden impulse; long ago, before the war began, we sent envoys to you, and proposed to revolt. But we could not, because you refused our request. Now, however, when the Boeotians have invited us, we have at once obeyed the call. We were intending to make a double severance of ourselves, from the

Our revolt, though premature, was not rash; it had a double motive: we feared the Athenians and sympathised with Hellas. But we look to you for help. Now is your opportunity for attacking Athens by sea. The battle must be fought in the countries on which Athens depends.

Hellenes and from the Athenians; from the guilt, that is, of oppressing the Hellenes, in concert with the Athenians, instead of aiding in their liberation, and from the ruin which the Athenians were sooner or later sure to bring upon us, unless we anticipated them. But the step has been taken hastily and without due preparation; hence you are the more bound to receive us into alliance and to send us speedy help, thereby showing that you are ready to protect those who have claims upon you and to strike a blow at your enemies. Never was there such an opportunity before. The Athenians are exhausted by pestilence and by a costly war; some of their ships are cruising about your shores; the remainder are threatening us; so that they are not likely to have many to spare if you, in the course of this summer, make a second attack upon them by land and by sea. They will not be able to meet you at sea; or, if they do, they will have to withdraw their forces both from Lesbos and from Peloponnesus. And let no one say to himself that he is going to incur a danger which will be his own on behalf of a country which is not his own. He may think that Lesbos is a long way off; but he will find that the help which we bring will be very near him. For the war will not be fought in Attica, as might be imagined; but in those countries by which Attica is supported. The revenues of the Athenians are derived from their allies, and, if they subdue us, will be greater than ever; no one will revolt again, and our resources will be added to theirs; and we shall suffer worse things than those who have been enslaved already. But, if you assist us heartily, you will gain the alliance of a great naval power, and a navy is your chief want; you will draw away the allies of the Athenians, who will fearlessly come over to you; thus you will more easily overthrow the power of Athens. And you will no longer incur, as in times past, the reproach of deserting those who revolt[a].

---

[a] Cp. i. 40 fin.; i. 69.

If you come forward as their liberators your final triumph will be assured.

14 'Do not then for very shame frustrate the hopes which the Hellenes rest on you, or dishonour the name of Olympian Zeus in whose temple we are in a manner suppliants, but be our allies and helpers. Do not betray us; we, the people of Mytilenè, risk our lives alone in the common cause of Hellas: universal will be the benefit which we confer if we succeed, and still more universal the ruin if you are inflexible and we fall. Wherefore prove yourselves worthy of your reputation in Hellas, and be such as we in our fear would have you.'

Do not then betray us, for our cause is the cause of Hellas.

These were the words of the Mytilenaeans.

15 The Lacedaemonians and the allies immediately accepted their proposals and took the Lesbians into alliance. The confederates, who were present at Olympia, were told to make ready quickly for another expedition into Attica, and to assemble at the isthmus, bringing the usual contingent of two-thirds. The Lacedaemonians arrived first, and at once set to work making machines for hauling ships over the isthmus, from Corinth to the Saronic Gulf. For they intended to attack the Athenians both by sea and land. But although they were energetic themselves, the other allies assembled slowly; they were gathering in their fruits and in no mood for war.

The Mytilenaeans are taken into alliance, and the confederates are directed to meet at the isthmus, but come in slowly.

16 The Athenians, perceiving that the activity of the Lacedaemonians was due to a conviction of their weakness, determined to show them their mistake, and to prove that, without moving the fleet from Lesbos, they were fully able to repel this new force which threatened them. They manned a hundred ships, in which they embarked, both metics and citizens[a],

The Lacedaemonians for the first time prepare to attack Attica by sea, but the Athenians man a hundred ships, and the attempt is given up.

[a] Cp. i. 143 init.

all but the highest class and the Knights; they then set sail, and, after displaying their strength along the shores of the isthmus, made descents upon the Peloponnesian coast wherever they pleased. The Lacedaemonians were astounded, and thought that the Lesbians had told them what was not true. Their allies too had not yet arrived, and they heard that the Athenians in the thirty ships [a] which had been sent to cruise around Peloponnesus were wasting their country districts; and so, not knowing what else to do, they returned home. However, they afterwards prepared a fleet to go to Lesbos, and ordered the allies to equip forty ships: these they placed under the command of Alcidas, who was to take them out. When the Athenians saw that the Peloponnesians had gone home, they and their fleet of a hundred ships did the same.

Perfection of the Athenian navy at this time. Great expenditure on the navy and the siege of Potidaea in the first year of the war.

17 At the time when the fleet was at sea, the Athenians had the largest number of ships which they ever had all together, effective and in good trim, although the mere number was as large or even larger at the commencement of the war. For then there were a hundred which guarded Attica, Euboea, and Salamis, and another hundred which were cruising off Peloponnesus [b], not including the ships employed in blockading Potidaea and at other places; so that in one and the same summer their fleet in all numbered two hundred and fifty. This and the money spent in the war against Potidaea was the chief call upon their treasury. Every one of the hoplites engaged in the siege received two drachmae [c] a-day, one for himself, and one for his servant; the original force amounted to three thousand [d], and this number was maintained as long as the siege lasted. Sixteen hundred more came with Phormio, but went away before

[a] Cp. iii. 7 init. [b] Cp. ii. 17 fin. [c] About 1*s.* 4*d.*
[d] Cp. i. 57 fin.; 61 init.

the end [a]. The sailors in the fleet all received the same pay as the soldiers. So great was the drain on the resources of the Athenians in the early part of the war, and such was the largest number of ships which they ever manned.

The Mytilenaeans make an unsuccessful attempt upon Methymna. The Methymnaeans attack Antissa, but are defeated. Reinforcements from Athens arrive under Paches, who blockades Mytilenè by land.

While the Lacedaemonians were at the isthmus, the 18
Mytilenaeans and their auxiliaries marched against Methymna, which they expected to be betrayed to them, but, making an assault, and finding that they were mistaken, they went off to Antissa, Pyrrha, and Eresus; and, having strengthened the walls of these places and established their interest in them, they hastily returned. As soon as they had retired, the Methymnaeans retaliated by making an expedition against Antissa; but the people of Antissa and their auxiliaries sallied out and defeated them with heavy loss; the survivors made a hasty retreat. The Athenians heard that the Mytilenaeans were masters of the country, and that their own troops in Lesbos were not sufficient to confine them within the walls. So about the beginning of autumn they sent to Mytilenè, under the command of Paches the son of Epicurus, a thousand Athenian hoplites who handled the oars themselves. On arriving, they surrounded the town with a single line of wall; and in some strong places forts were erected which formed part of the wall. Thus Mytilenè was effectually blockaded both by sea and by land. The winter now began to set in.

The Athenians raise a property-tax; and Lysicles is sent to collect tribute; he is killed in Caria.

The Athenians, being in want of money to carry on the 19
siege, raised among themselves for the first time a property-tax of two hundred talents [b], and sent out twelve ships to collect tribute among the allies, under the command of Lysicles and four others. He sailed to various places and exacted

[a] Cp. i. 64 med.; ii. 58 med.

[b] £40,000.

tribute; but as he was going up from Myus in Caria, through the plain of the Maeander, he was attacked at the hill of Sandius by the Carians and the Samians of Anaea[a], and, with a great part of his army, perished.

20 *The Plataeans resolve to break out of Plataea, but only two hundred and twenty persevere. They estimate the height of the enemy's wall by the layers of bricks.*

During the same winter the Plataeans, who were still besieged by the Peloponnesians and Boeotians, began to suffer from the failure of provisions. They had no hope of assistance from Athens and no other chance of deliverance. So they and the Athenians who were shut up with them contrived a plan of forcing their way over the enemy's walls. The idea was suggested by Theaenetus the son of Tolmides, a diviner, and Eupompidas, the son of Daïmachus, one of their generals. At first they were all desirous of joining, but afterwards half of them somehow lost heart, thinking the danger too great, and only two hundred and twenty agreed to persevere. They first made ladders equal in length to the height of the enemy's wall, which they calculated by the help of the layers of bricks on the side facing the town, at a place where the wall had accidentally not been plastered. A great many counted at once, and, although some might make mistakes, the calculation would be oftener right than wrong; for they repeated the process again and again, and, the distance not being great, they could see the wall distinctly enough for their purpose. In this manner they ascertained the proper length of the ladders, taking as a measure the thickness of the bricks.

21 *Plan of the Peloponnesian wall.*

The Peloponnesian wall was double, and consisted of an inner circle looking towards Plataea, and an outer intended to guard against an attack from Athens; they were at a distance of about sixteen feet from one another. This interval of sixteen feet was partitioned off into lodgings for the soldiers, by which the two walls were joined together, so that they appeared

[a] Cp. iii. 32 init.; iv. 75 med.

to form one thick wall with battlements on both sides. At every tenth battlement there were large towers, filling up the space between the walls, and extending both to the inner and outer face; there was no way at the side of the towers, but only through the middle of them. During the night, whenever there was storm and rain, the soldiers left the battlements and kept guard from the towers, which were not far from each other and were covered overhead. Such was the plan of the wall with which Plataea was invested.

When the Plataeans had completed their preparations 22
they took advantage of a night on which there was a storm of wind and rain and no moon, and sallied forth. They were led by the authors of the attempt. First of all they crossed the ditch which surrounded the town; then they came right up to the wall of the enemy. The guard did not discover them, for the night was so dark that they could not be seen, while the clatter of the storm drowned the noise of their approach. They marched a good way apart from each other, that the clashing of their arms might not betray them; and they were lightly equipped, having the right foot bare that they might be less liable to slip in the mud. They now set about scaling the battlements, which they knew to be deserted, choosing a space between two of the towers. Those who carried the ladders went first and placed them against the wall; they were followed by twelve others, armed only with sword and breastplate, under the command of Ammeas the son of Coroebus: he was the first to mount; after him came the twelve, ascending the wall and proceeding to the towers on the right and left, six to each[a]. To these succeeded more men lightly armed with short spears, others following who bore their shields, that they might have less difficulty in mounting the wall; the shields were

The Plataeans sally forth. They are discovered by an accident. Their friends in the city make an attack from the opposite side.

[a] See note on the passage.

to be handed to them as soon as they were near the enemy. A considerable number had ascended, when they were discovered by the guards in the towers. One of the Plataeans, taking hold of the battlements, threw down a tile which made a noise in falling: immediately a shout was raised and the army rushed out upon the wall; for in the dark and stormy night they did not know what the alarm meant. At the same time, in order to distract their attention, the Plataeans who were left in the city made a sally against the Peloponnesian wall on the side opposite to the place at which their friends were getting over. The besiegers were in great excitement, but every one remained at his own post, and dared not stir to give assistance, being at a loss to imagine what was happening. The three hundred who were appointed to act in any sudden emergency marched along outside the walls towards the spot from which the cry proceeded; and fire-signals indicating danger were raised towards Thebes. But the Plataeans in the city had numerous counter signals ready on the wall, which they now lighted and held up, thereby hoping to render the signals of the enemy unintelligible, that so the Thebans, misunderstanding the true state of affairs, might not arrive until the men had escaped and were in safety.

The Plataeans, protected by parties of men who hold the towers, first get over the wall; they then cross the ditch.

23 Meanwhile the Plataeans were scaling the walls. The first party had mounted, and, killing the sentinels, had gained possession of the towers on either side. Their followers now began to occupy the passages, lest the enemy should come through and fall upon them. Some of them placed ladders upon the wall against the towers, and got up more men. A shower of missiles proceeding both from the upper and lower parts of the towers kept off all assailants. Meanwhile the main body of the Plataeans, who were still below, applied to the wall many ladders at once, and, pushing down the battlements, made their way over

through the space between the towers. As each man got to the other side he halted upon the edge of the ditch, whence they shot darts and arrows at any one who came along under the wall and attempted to impede their passage. When they had all passed over, those who had occupied the towers came down, the last of them not without great difficulty, and proceeded towards the ditch. By this time the three hundred were upon them; they had lights, and the Plataeans, standing on the edge of the ditch, saw them all the better out of the darkness, and shot arrows and threw darts at them where their bodies were exposed; they themselves were concealed by the darkness, while the enemy were dazed by their own lights. And so the Plataeans, down to the last man of them all, got safely over the ditch, though with great exertion and only after a hard struggle; for the ice in it was not frozen hard enough to bear, but was half water, as is commonly the case when the wind is from the east and not from the north. And the snow which the east wind brought in the night had greatly swollen the water, so that they [a] could scarcely accomplish the passage [a]. It was the violence of the storm, however, which enabled them to escape at all.

From the ditch the Plataeans, leaving on the right hand 24
the shrine of Androcrates, ran all together along the road to Thebes. They made sure that no one would ever suspect them of having fled in the direction of their enemies. On their way they saw the Peloponnesians pursuing them with torches on the road which leads to Athens by Cithaeron and Dryoscephalae. For nearly a mile the Plataeans continued on the Theban road; they then turned off and went by the way up the mountain leading to Erythrae and Hysiae, and so, getting to the hills, they escaped to Athens. Their number was

They first go towards Thebes, and then strike over the mountains to Athens.

[a] Taking ὑπερέχειν in the sense of 'superare': or, 'could hardly keep above the surface in crossing.'

two hundred and twelve[a], though they had been originally more, for some of them went back to the city and never got over the wall; one who was an archer was taken at the outer ditch. The Peloponnesians at length gave up the pursuit and returned to their lines. But the Plataeans in the city, knowing nothing of what had happened, for those who had turned back had informed them that not one was left alive, sent out a herald at daybreak, wanting to make a truce for the burial of the dead; they then discovered the truth and returned. Thus the Plataeans scaled the wall and escaped.

25 At the end of the same winter Salaethus the Lacedaemonian was despatched in a trireme from Lacedaemon to Mytilenè. He sailed to Pyrrha, and thence, proceeding on foot, made his way, by the channel of a torrent at a place where the line of the Athenian wall could be crossed, undiscovered into Mytilenè. He told the government that there was to be an invasion of Attica, and that simultaneously the forty ships which were coming to their assistance would arrive at Lesbos; he himself had been sent in advance to bring the news and take charge of affairs. Whereupon the Mytilenaeans recovered their spirits, and were less disposed to make terms with the Athenians. So the winter ended, and with it the fourth year in the Peloponnesian War of which Thucydides wrote the history.

Salaethus is sent from Lacedaemon to Mytilenè, with the news that help is on the way.

26 With the return of summer the Peloponnesians despatched the two and forty ships which they intended for Mytilenè in charge of Alcidas, the Lacedaemonian admiral. They and their allies then invaded Attica, in order that the Athenians, embarrassed both by sea and land, might have their attention distracted from the ships sailing to Mytilenè. Cleomenes led the invasion. He was acting in the place

B.C. 427.
Ol. 88, 2.

After despatching a fleet under Alcidas to Lesbos, the Peloponnesians invade Attica, causing great distress.

---

[a] Cp. iii. 20 med.

of his nephew, the king Pausanias, son of Pleistoanax, who was still a minor. All the country which they had previously overrun, wherever anything had grown up again, they ravaged afresh, and devastated even those districts which they had hitherto spared. This invasion caused greater distress to the Athenians than any, except the second. For the Peloponnesians, who were daily expecting to hear from Lesbos of some action on the part of the fleet, which they supposed by this time to have crossed the sea, pursued their ravages far and wide. But when none of their expectations were realised, and their food was exhausted, they retired and dispersed to their several cities.

Meanwhile the Mytilenaeans, finding as time went on 27
that the ships from Peloponnesus never came, and that their provisions had run short, were obliged to make terms with the Athenians. The immediate cause was as follows:—Salaethus himself began to despair of the arrival of the ships, and therefore he put into the hands of the common people (who had hitherto been light-armed) shields and spears, intending to lead them out against the Athenians. But, having once received arms, they would no longer obey their leaders; they gathered into knots and insisted that the nobles should bring out the corn and let all share alike; if not, they would themselves negotiate with the Athenians and surrender the city.

Salaethus, despairing of help, arms the people, who turn upon the nobles.

The magistrates, knowing that they were helpless, and 28
that they would be in peril of their lives if they were left out of the convention, concluded a general agreement with Paches and his army, stipulating that the fate of the Mytilenaeans should be left in the hands of the Athenians at home. They were to receive him and his forces into the city; but might send an embassy

The government, feeling their helplessness, surrender the city to Paches, on condition that the Athenians at home should decide on the fate of the inhabitants.

to Athens on their own behalf. Until the envoys returned, Paches was not to bind, enslave, or put to death any Mytilenaean. These were the terms of the capitulation. Nevertheless, when the army entered, those Mytilenaeans who had been principally concerned with the Lacedaemonians were in an agony of fear, and could not be satisfied until they had taken refuge at the altars. Paches raised them up, and promising not to hurt them, deposited them at Tenedos until the Athenians should come to a decision. He also sent triremes to Antissa, of which he gained possession, and took such other military measures as he deemed best.

The Peloponnesian fleet intended for Mytilenè wastes time. Alcidas, hearing of its fall, sails to Embatum, and holds a council. Speech of Teutiaplus.

29 The forty ships of the Peloponnesians, which should have gone at once to Mytilenè, lost time about the Peloponnese, and proceeded very leisurely on their voyage. They arrived safely at Delos, before they were heard of at Athens; but on touching at Icarus and Myconus they found, too late, that Mytilenè was taken. Wanting to obtain certain information, they sailed to Embatum near Erythrae, which they reached, but not until seven days after the fall of Mytilenè. Having now made sure of the fact, they consulted as to what measures should next be taken, and Teutiaplus, an Elean, addressed them as follows:—

Let us hurry on to Mytilenè. We shall find the Athenians off their guard. The art of the general is to surprise others, never to be surprised.

30 'My opinion, Alcidas, and you, my fellow-commanders of the Peloponnesian forces, is that we should attack Mytilenè at once, just as we are, before our arrival is known. In all probability we shall find that men who have recently gained possession of a city will be much off their guard, and entirely so at sea, on which element they do not fear the attack of an enemy, and where at this moment we can strike with effect. Probably too their land forces, in the carelessness of victory, will be scattered up and

down among the houses of the city. If we were to fall upon them suddenly by night, with the help of our friends inside, should there be any left, I have no doubt that Mytilenè would be ours. The danger should not deter us; for we should consider that the execution of a military surprise is always dangerous, and that the general who is never taken off his guard himself, and never loses an opportunity of striking at an unguarded foe, will be most likely to succeed in war.'

It is also proposed to occupy some town, and raise a revolt in Ionia. But Alcidas rejects both propositions. He hurries home.

His words failed to convince Alcidas; whereupon some 31
Ionian exiles and the Lesbians who were on board the fleet[a] recommended that, if this enterprise appeared too hazardous, he should occupy one of the Ionian towns or the Aeolian Cymè: having thus established their head-quarters in a city, the Peloponnesians might raise the standard of revolt in Ionia. There was a good chance of success, for every one was glad of his arrival; they might cut off a main source of Athenian revenue; and although they themselves would incur expense, for the Athenians would blockade them[b], the attempt was worth making. Pissuthnes might very likely be persuaded to co-operate. But Alcidas objected to this proposal equally with the last; his only idea was, now that he had failed in saving Mytilenè, to get back as fast as he could to Peloponnesus.

The Samian exiles remonstrate with him for his impolicy in slaying the captives whom he had taken.

Accordingly he sailed from Embatum along the coast, 32
touching at Myonnesus in the territory of Teos; he there slew most of the captives whom he had taken on his voyage. He then put into harbour at Ephesus, where a deputation from the Samians of Anaea[c] came to him. They told him that it was an ill manner of liberating Hellas, to have put to death

[a] i.e. the envoys who had been sent to Sparta. Cp. iii. 4 fin., 5 fin.

[b] Adopting with Bekker the conjecture ἐφορμοῦσιν.

[c] Cp. iii. 19 fin.; iv. 75 med.

men who were not his enemies and were not lifting a hand against him, but were allies of Athens from necessity: if he went on in this way he would convert few of his enemies into friends, and many of his friends into enemies. He was convinced by them, and allowed such of the Chian prisoners as he had not yet put to death and some others to go free. They had been easily taken, because, when people saw the ships, instead of flying, they came close up to them under the idea that they were Athenian; the thought never entered into their minds that while the Athenians were masters of the sea, Peloponnesian ships would find their way across the Aegean to the coast of Ionia.

He sails from Ephesus direct for Peloponnesus, having been sighted by the Paralus and Salaminia, and is pursued as far as Patmos by Paches.

33 From Ephesus Alcidas sailed away in haste, or rather fled; for while he was at anchor near Clarus he had been sighted by the Athenian sacred vessels, Paralus and Salaminia, which happened to be on a voyage from Athens. In fear of pursuit he hurried through the open sea, determined to stop nowhere, if he could help it, until he reached Peloponnesus. News of him and his fleet was brought to Paches from the country of Erythrae, and indeed kept coming in from all sides. For Ionia not being fortified, there was great apprehension lest the Peloponnesians, as they sailed along the coast, might fall upon the cities and plunder them, even though they had no intention of remaining. And the Paralus and Salaminia reported that they had themselves seen him at Clarus. Paches eagerly gave chase and pursued him as far as the island of Patmos, but, seeing that he was no longer within reach, he returned. Not having come up with the fleet of the Peloponnesians upon the open sea, he congratulated himself that they had not been overtaken somewhere near land, where they would have been forced to put in and fortify themselves on shore, and the Athenians would have had the trouble of watching and blockading them.

As he was sailing along the coast on his return he 34
touched at Notium, the port of Colophon. Here some inhabitants of the upper town had taken up their abode; for it had been captured by Itamenes and the Barbarians, who had been invited into the city by a certain local faction. The capture took place about the time of the second invasion of Attica. The refugees who settled in Notium again quarrelled among themselves. The one party, having introduced Arcadian and Barbarian auxiliaries whom they had obtained from Pissuthnes, stationed them in a fortified quarter of the town; the Persian faction from the upper city of Colophon joined them and were living with them. The other party had retired from the city, and being now in exile, called in Paches. He proposed to Hippias, the commander of the Arcadians in the fortress, that they should hold a conference, undertaking, if they could not agree, to put him back in the fort, safe and sound. So he came out, and Paches kept him in custody without fetters. In the meantime he made an attack upon the unsuspecting garrison, took the fortress, and slaughtered all the Arcadians and Barbarians whom he found within. He then conducted Hippias into the fort, according to the agreement, and when he was inside seized him and shot him to death with arrows. He next handed over Notium to the Colophonians, excluding the Persian party. The Athenians afterwards gathered together all the Colophonians who could be found in the neighbouring cities and colonised the place, to which they gave laws like their own, under new founders whom they sent out from Athens.

Paches on his return puts in at Notium, the port of Colophon, on the invitation of an anti-Persian faction which had been driven out. He takes the citadel, and treacherously kills the commander Hippias. The Athenians re-establish the Colophonians in Notium.

On returning to Lesbos, Paches reduced Pyrrha and 35
Eresus, and finding Salaethus, the Lacedaemonian governor, concealed in Mytilenè, sent him to Athens. He

Salaethus is captured and sent to Athens with the Mytilenaean rebels.

also sent thither the Mytilenaeans whom he had deposited in Tenedos, and any others who seemed to have been implicated in the revolt. He then dismissed the greater part of his army, and, by the aid of the remainder, settled as seemed best to him the affairs of Mytilenè and Lesbos.

The Athenians put Salaethus to death, and order the slaughter of all the grown-up citizens of Mytilenè. On the next day they begin to repent, and the Mytilenaean envoys persuade the magistrates to call another assembly.

36 When the captives arrived at Athens the Athenians instantly put Salaethus to death, although he made various offers, and among other things promised to procure the withdrawal of the Peloponnesians from Plataea, which was still blockaded. Concerning the other captives a discussion was held, and in their indignation the Athenians determined to put to death not only the men then at Athens, but all the grown-up citizens of Mytilenè, and to enslave the women and children; the act of the Mytilenaeans appeared inexcusable, because they were not subjects like the other states which had revolted, but free. That Peloponnesian ships should have had the audacity to find their way to Ionia and assist the rebels contributed to increase their fury; and the action showed that the revolt[a] was a long premeditated affair[a]. So they sent a trireme to Paches announcing their determination, and bidding him put the Mytilenaeans to death at once. But on the following day a kind of remorse seized them; they began to reflect that a decree which doomed to destruction not only the guilty, but a whole city, was cruel and monstrous. The Mytilenaean envoys who were at Athens[b] perceived the change of feeling, and they and the Athenians who were in their interest prevailed on the magistrates to bring the question again before the people; this they were the more willing to do, because they saw themselves that the majority of the citizens were anxious to have an opportunity given them of reconsidering

[a] Or, 'was part of an extensive scheme.' [b] Cp. iii. 28 med.

their decision. An assembly was again summoned, and different opinions were expressed by different speakers. In the former assembly, Cleon the son of Cleaenetus had carried the decree condemning the Mytilenaeans to death. He was the most violent of the citizens, and at that time exercised by far the greatest influence over the people[a]. And now he came forward a second time and spoke as follows:—

Speech of Cleon.

'I have remarked again and again that a democracy 37
cannot manage an empire, but never more than now, when I see you regretting your condemnation of the Mytilenaeans. Having no fear or suspicion of one another in daily life[b], you deal with your allies upon the same principle, and you do not consider that whenever you yield to them out of pity or are misled by their specious tales, you are guilty of a weakness dangerous to yourselves, and receive no thanks from them. You should remember that your empire is a despotism[c] exercised over unwilling subjects, who are always conspiring against you; they do not obey in return for any kindness which you do them to your own injury, but in so far as you are their masters; they have no love of you, but they are held down by force. Besides, what can be more detestable than to be perpetually changing our minds? We forget that a state in which the laws, though imperfect, are inviolable, is better off than one in which the laws are good but ineffective[d]. Dullness and modesty are a more useful combination than cleverness and licence; and the more simple sort generally make better citizens than the more astute. For the latter desire to be thought wiser than the laws[e]; they want to be always getting their own way in public discussions; they think that they can

You do not know how to manage an empire; you are foolishly kind to your allies, who do not love you; and with your quick wits are always changing your minds.

---

[a] Cp. iv. 21 med. [b] Cp. i. 68 init. [c] Cp. ii. 63 med.
[d] Cp. vi. 18 fin. [e] Cp. i. 84 med.

nowhere have a finer opportunity of displaying their intelligence[a], and their folly generally ends in the ruin of their country; whereas the others, mistrusting their own capacity, admit that the laws are wiser than themselves: they do not pretend to criticise the arguments of a great speaker; and being impartial judges, not ambitious rivals, they hit the mark. That is the spirit in which we should act; not suffering ourselves to be so excited by our own cleverness in a war of wits as to advise the Athenian people contrary to our own better judgment.

Why is their punishment delayed? Will any one pretend that their crimes do us good? or would any one speak on their behalf if he was not well paid, and you were not blind to facts and at the mercy of every clever talker?

38 'I myself think as I did before, and I wonder at those who have brought forward the case of the Mytilenaeans again, thus interposing a delay which is in the interest of the evil-doer. For after a time the anger of the sufferer waxes dull, and he pursues the offender with less keenness; but the vengeance which follows closest upon the wrong is most adequate to it and exacts the fullest retribution. And again I wonder who will answer me, and whether he will attempt to show that the crimes of the Mytilenaeans are a benefit to us, or that when we suffer, our allies suffer with us. Clearly he must be some one who has such confidence in his powers of speech as to contend[b] that you never adopted what was most certainly your resolution[b]; or else he must be some one who, under the inspiration of a bribe, elaborates a sophistical speech in the hope of diverting you from the point. In such rhetorical contests the city gives away the prizes to others, while she takes the risk upon herself. And you are to blame, for you order these contests amiss. When speeches are to be heard, you are too fond of using your eyes, but, where actions are concerned, you trust your ears; you estimate

---

[a] Cp. iii. 40 init.

[b] Or, 'that what all men believe to be true is absolutely false.'

the possibility of future enterprises from the eloquence of an orator, but as to accomplished facts, instead of accepting ocular demonstration, you believe only what ingenious critics tell you [a]. No men are better dupes, sooner deceived by novel notions, or slower to follow approved advice. You despise what is familiar, while you are worshippers of every new extravagance. Not a man of you but would be an orator if he could; when he cannot, he will not yield the palm to a more successful rival: he would fain show that he does not let his wits come limping after, but that he can praise a sharp remark before it is well out of another's mouth; he would like to be as quick in anticipating what is said, as he is slow in foreseeing its consequences. You are always hankering after an ideal state, but you do not give your minds even to what is straight before you. In a word, you are at the mercy of your own ears, and sit like spectators attending a performance of sophists, but very unlike counsellors of a state.

'I want you to put aside this trifling, and therefore I say 39
to you that no single city has ever injured us so deeply as Mytilenè. I can excuse those who find our rule too heavy to bear, or who have revolted because the enemy has compelled them. But islanders who had walls, and were unassailable by our enemies, except at sea, and on that element were sufficiently protected by a fleet of their own, who were independent and treated by us with the highest regard, when they act thus, they have not revolted (that word would imply that they were oppressed), but they have rebelled, and entering the ranks of our bitterest enemies have conspired with them to seek our ruin. And

No city has done us so much harm as Mytilenè; none ever had so little reason. Our indulgence has made them insolent. Nobles and people should be punished alike, for they are equally guilty. If you pardon them your other subjects will be encouraged to revolt; and we must neglect our enemies to fight our own allies.

[a] Cp. vii. 48 med.

surely this is far more atrocious than if they had been led by motives of ambition to take up arms against us on their own account. They learned nothing from the misfortunes of their neighbours who had already revolted and been subdued by us, nor did the happiness of which they were in the enjoyment make them hesitate to court destruction. They trusted recklessly to the future, and cherishing hopes which, if less than their wishes, were greater than their powers, they went to war, preferring might to right. No sooner did they seem likely to win than they set upon us, although we were doing them no wrong. Too swift and sudden a rise is apt to make cities insolent and, in general, ordinary good-fortune is safer than extraordinary. Mankind apparently find it easier to drive away adversity than to retain prosperity. We should from the first have made no difference between the Mytilenaeans and the rest of our allies, and then their insolence would never have risen to such a height; for men naturally despise those who court them, but respect those who do not give way to them. Yet it is not too late to punish them as their crimes deserve. And do not absolve the people while you throw the blame upon the nobles. For they were all of one mind when we were to be attacked. Had the people deserted the nobles and come over to us, they might at this moment have been reinstated in their city; but they considered that their safety lay in sharing the dangers of the oligarchy, and therefore they joined in the revolt. Reflect: if you impose the same penalty upon those of your allies who wilfully rebel and upon those who are constrained by the enemy, which of them will not revolt upon any pretext however trivial, seeing that, if he succeed, he will be free, and, if he fail, no irreparable evil will follow? We in the meantime shall have to risk our lives and our fortunes against every one in turn. When conquerors we shall recover only a ruined city, and, for the future, the revenues which are our strength will be lost to us[a]. But if we fail, the

[a] Cp. iii. 46 med.

number of our adversaries will be increased. And when we ought to be employed in repelling the enemies with whom we have to do, we shall be wasting time in fighting against our own allies.

'Do not then hold out a hope, which eloquence can 40
secure or money buy, that they are to be excused and that their error is to be deemed human and venial. Their attack was not unpremeditated; that might have been an excuse for them; but they knew what they were doing. This was my original contention, and I still maintain that you should abide by your former decision, and not be misled either by pity, or by the charm of words, or by a too forgiving temper. There are no three things more prejudicial to your power. Mercy should be reserved for the merciful, and not thrown away upon those who will have no compassion on us, and who must by the force of circumstances always be our enemies. And our charming orators will still have an arena[a], but one in which the questions at stake will not be so grave, and the city will not pay so dearly for her brief pleasure in listening to them, while they for a good speech get a good fee. Lastly, forgiveness is naturally shown to those who, being reconciled, will continue friends, and not to those who will always remain what they were, and will abate nothing of their enmity. In one word, if you do as I say, you will do what is just to the Mytilenaeans, and also what is expedient for yourselves; but, if you take the opposite course, they will not be grateful to you, and you will be self-condemned. For, if they were right in revolting, you must be wrong in maintaining your empire. But if, right or wrong, you are resolved to rule, then rightly or wrongly they must be chastised for your good. Otherwise you must

Do not be misled by pity, fine words, or a forgiving temper. If you have no right to chastise rebels, you have no right to rule. Treat them as they, fearing your vengeance, would have treated you. You will have no trouble with your allies when they know that rebellion will be punished by death.

[a] Cp. iii. 37 fin.

give up your empire, and, when virtue is no longer dangerous, you may be as virtuous as you please. Punish them as they would have punished you; let not those who have escaped appear to have less feeling than those who conspired against them. Consider: what might not they have been expected to do if they had conquered?—especially since they were the aggressors. For those who wantonly attack others always rush into extremes, and sometimes, like these Mytilenaeans, to their own destruction. They know the fate which is reserved for them by an enemy who is spared: [a]when a man is injured wantonly he is more dangerous if he escape than the enemy who has only suffered what he has inflicted[a]. Be true then to yourselves, and recall as vividly as you can what you felt at the time; think how you would have given the world to crush your enemies, and now take your revenge. Do not be soft-hearted at the sight of their distress, but remember the danger which was once hanging over your heads. Chastise them as they deserve, and prove by an example to your other allies that rebellion will be punished with death. If this is made quite clear to them, your attention will no longer be diverted from your enemies by wars against your own allies.'

Speech of Diodotus.

41 Such were the words of Cleon; and after him Diodotus the son of Eucrates, who in the previous assembly had been the chief opponent of the decree which condemned the Mytilenaeans, came forward again and spoke as follows:—

42 'I am far from blaming those who invite us to reconsider our sentence upon the Mytilenaeans, nor do I approve of the censure which has been cast on the practice of deliberating more than once about matters so critical. In my opinion the two things most adverse to good counsel are haste and passion; the former is generally a mark

[a] Or, referring the words to the Mytilenaeans: 'He who has gone out of his way to bring a calamity upon himself is more dangerous if he be allowed to escape than the enemy who only retaliates.'

of folly, the latter of vulgarity and narrowness of mind. When a man insists that words ought not to be our guides in action[a], he is either wanting in sense or wanting in honesty: he is wanting in sense if he does not see that there is no other way in which we can throw light on the unknown future; and he is not honest if, seeking to carry a discreditable measure, and knowing that he cannot speak well in a bad cause, he reflects that he can slander well and terrify his opponents and his audience by the audacity of his calumnies. Worst of all are those who, besides other topics of abuse, declare that their opponent is hired to make an eloquent speech. If they accused him of stupidity only, when he failed in producing an impression he might go his way having lost his reputation for sense but not for honesty; whereas he who is accused of dishonesty, even if he succeed, is viewed with suspicion, and, if he fail, is thought to be both fool and rogue. And so the city suffers; for she is robbed of her counsellors by fear. Happy would she be if such citizens could not speak at all, for then the people would not be misled. The good citizen should prove his superiority as a speaker, not by trying to intimidate those who are to follow him in debate, but by fair argument; and the wise city ought not to give increased honour to her best counsellor, any more than she will deprive him of that which he has; while he whose proposal is rejected not only ought to receive no punishment, but should be free from all reproach. Then he who succeeds will not say pleasant things contrary to his better judgment in order to gain a still higher place in popular favour, and he who fails will not be striving to attract the multitude to himself by like compliances.

We are right in reconsidering the case of the Mytilenaeans. He is foolish, even if he be honest, who would have no deliberation: still worse is he who insinuates that his opponent is corrupt, instead of meeting him by fair arguments. The wise city makes room for all, and shows favour to none.

---

[a] Cp. ii. 40 med.

But you are too clever: you are always suspecting that a speaker has some interested motive. You punish the giver of bad advice, and not yourselves for following him.

43 'But we take an opposite course; and still worse. Even when we know a man to be giving the wisest counsel, a suspicion of corruption is set on foot; and from a jealousy which is perhaps groundless we allow the state to lose an undeniable advantage. It has come to this, that the best advice when offered in plain terms is as much distrusted as the worst; and not only he who wishes to lead the multitude into the most dangerous courses must deceive them, but he who speaks in the cause of right must make himself believed by lying. In this city, and in this city only, to do good openly and without deception is impossible, because you are too clever; and, when a man confers an unmistakeable benefit on you, he is rewarded by a suspicion that, in some underhand manner, he gets more than he gives. But, whatever you may suspect[a], when great interests are at stake, we who advise ought to look further and weigh our words more carefully than you whose vision is limited. And you should remember that we are accountable for our advice to you, but you who listen are accountable to nobody. If he who gave and he who followed evil counsel suffered equally, you would be more reasonable in your ideas; but now, whenever you meet with a reverse, led away by the passion of the moment you punish the individual who is your adviser for his error of judgment, and your own error you condone, if the judgments of many concurred in it.

The question is one of policy, not of law. Your anger ought not to make you prefer justice to expediency.

44 'I do not come forward either as an advocate of the Mytilenaeans or as their accuser; the question for us rightly considered is not, what are their crimes? but, what is for our interest? If I prove them ever so guilty, I will not on that account bid you put them to death, unless it is expedient. Neither,

[a] Reading ἀξιοῦντι.

if perchance there be some degree of excuse for them, would I have you spare them, unless it be clearly for the good of the state. For I conceive that we are now concerned, not with the present, but with the future. When Cleon insists that the infliction of death will be expedient and will secure you against revolt in time to come, I, like him taking the ground of future expediency, stoutly maintain the contrary position; and I would not have you be misled by the apparent fairness of his proposal, and reject the solid advantages of mine. You are angry with the Mytilenaeans, and the superior justice of his argument may for the moment attract you; but we are not at law with them, and do not want to be told what is just; we are considering a question of policy, and desire to know how we can turn them to account.

'To many offences less than theirs states have affixed 45
the punishment of death; nevertheless, excited by hope, men still risk their lives. No one when venturing on a perilous enterprise ever yet passed a sentence of failure on himself. And what city when entering on a revolt ever imagined that the power which she had, whether her own or obtained from her allies, did not justify the attempt? All are by nature prone to err both in public and in private life, and no law will prevent them. Men have gone through the whole catalogue of penalties in the hope that, by increasing their severity, they may suffer less at the hands of evil-doers. In early ages the punishments, even of the worst offences, would naturally be milder; but as time went on and mankind continued to transgress, they seldom stopped short of death. And still there are transgressors. Some greater terror then has yet to be discovered; certainly death is no deterrent. For poverty inspires necessity with daring; and wealth engenders avarice in pride and insolence; and the various conditions of human life, as they severally fall

Experience abundantly proves that the penalty of death is no deterrent. Men, and still more states, are carried away by their passions and by trust in fortune.

under the sway of some mighty and fatal power, lure men through their passions to destruction. Desire and hope are never wanting, the one leading, the other following the one devising the enterprise, the other suggesting that fortune will be kind; and they are the most ruinous, for, being unseen, they far outweigh the dangers which are seen. Fortune too assists the illusion, for she often presents herself unexpectedly, and induces states as well as individuals to run into peril, however inadequate their means; and states even more than individuals, because they are throwing for a higher stake, freedom or empire, and because when a man has a whole people acting with him, [a] he magnifies himself [a] out of all reason. In a word then, it is impossible and simply absurd to suppose that human nature when bent upon some favourite project can be restrained either by the strength of law or by any other terror.

46 'We ought not therefore to act hastily out of a mistaken reliance on the security which the penalty of death affords. Nor should we drive our rebellious subjects to despair; they must not think that there is no place for repentance, or that they may not at any moment give up their mistaken policy. Consider: at present, although a city may actually have revolted, when she becomes conscious of her weakness she will capitulate while still able to defray the cost of the war and to pay tribute for the future; but if we are too severe, will not the citizens make better preparations, and, when besieged, resist to the last, knowing that it is all the same whether they come to terms early or late? Shall not we ourselves suffer? For we shall waste our money by sitting down before a city which refuses to surrender; when the place is taken it will be a mere wreck, and we shall in

The threat of severe punishment will make rebels fight to the last, and, if we succeed, we shall only gain a ruined city. Our true policy is prevention, not punishment.

[a] Or, reading αὐτῶν, 'he exaggerates the importance of his aims.'

future lose the revenues derived from it[a]; and in these revenues lies our military strength. Do not then weigh offences with the severity of a judge, when you will only be injuring yourselves, but have an eye to the future; let the penalties which you impose on rebellious cities be moderate, and then their wealth will be undiminished and at your service. Do not hope to find a safeguard in the severity of your laws, but only in the vigilance of your administration. At present we do just the opposite; a free people under a strong government will always revolt in the hope of independence; and when we have put them down we think that they cannot be punished too severely. But instead of inflicting extreme penalties on free men who revolt, we should practise extreme vigilance before they revolt, and never allow such a thought to enter their minds. When however they have been once put down we ought to extenuate their crimes as much as possible.

'Think of another great error into which you would fall 47
if you listened to Cleon. At present the popular party are everywhere our friends; either they do not join with the oligarchs, or, if compelled to do so, they are always ready to turn against the authors of the revolt; and so in going to war with a rebellious state you have the multitude on your side. But, if you destroy the people of Mytilenè who took no part in the revolt, and who voluntarily surrendered the city as soon as they got arms into their hands; in the first place they were your benefactors, and to slay them would be a crime; in the second place you will play into the hands of the oligarchic parties, who henceforward, in fomenting a revolt, will at once have the people on their side; for you will have proclaimed to

If you destroy the Mytilenaeans who put their city into your hands, you will show ingratitude and alienate the popular party everywhere. Even if they were guilty, it would be more expedient to pardon them.

[a] Cp. iii. 39 fin.

all that the innocent and the guilty will share the same fate. Even if they were guilty you should wink at their conduct, and not allow the only friends whom you have left to be converted into enemies. Far more conducive to the maintenance of our empire would it be to suffer wrong willingly, than for the sake of justice to put to death those whom we had better spare. Cleon may speak of a punishment which is just and also expedient, but you will find that, in any proposal like his, the two cannot be combined.

48 'Assured then that what I advise is for the best, and yielding neither to pity nor to lenity, for I am as unwilling as Cleon can be that you should be influenced by any such motives, but simply weighing the arguments which I have urged, accede to my proposal: Pass sentence at your leisure on the Mytilenaeans whom Paches, deeming them guilty, has sent hither; but leave the rest of the inhabitants where they are. This will be good policy for the future, and will strike present terror into your enemies. For wise counsel is really more formidable to an enemy than the severity of unreasoning violence.'

Pass sentence at leisure on the prisoners sent hither by Paches, and spare the rest.

49 Thus spoke Diodotus, and such were the proposals on either side which most nearly represented the opposing parties. In spite of the reaction, there was a struggle between the two opinions; the show of hands was very near, but the motion of Diodotus prevailed. The Athenians instantly despatched another trireme, hoping that, if the second could overtake the first[a], which had a start of about twenty-four hours, it might be in time to save the city. The Mytilenaean envoys provided wine and barley for the crew, and promised them great rewards if they arrived first. And such was their energy that they continued rowing

The motion of Diodotus is just carried. A trireme is despatched, which by great exertions arrives in time to save Mytilenè.

---

[a] Reading δευτέρας.

whilst they ate their barley, kneaded with wine and oil, and slept and rowed by turns. Fortunately no adverse wind sprang up, and, the first of the two ships sailing in no great hurry on her untoward errand, and the second hastening as I have described, the one did indeed arrive sooner than the other, but not much sooner. Paches had read the decree and was about to put it into execution, when the second appeared and arrested the fate of the city.

So near was Mytilenè to destruction.

The captives whom Paches had sent to Athens as being 50
the most guilty numbered about a thousand, or rather more [a]; these the Athenians, upon the motion of Cleon, put to death. They razed the walls of the Mytilenaeans and took away their fleet. Then, instead of imposing tribute on them, they divided the whole island, exclusive of the territory of Methymna, into three thousand portions, of which they dedicated three hundred to the Gods; the remainder they let out to cleruchi [b] taken from their own citizens, whom they chose by lot and sent to Lesbos. The Lesbians undertook to pay them a yearly rent of two minae [c] for each portion and cultivated the land themselves. The Athenians also took possession of the towns on the continent which the Mytilenaeans held [d], and these henceforward were subject to Athens.

The captives at Athens are put to death. The lands of Lesbos are divided among Athenian citizens.

Thus ended the revolt of Lesbos.

During the same summer, after the recovery of Lesbos, 51
the Athenians, under the command of Nicias the son of Niceratus, made an expedition against the island of Minoa, which lies in front of Megara; the Megarians had built a fort there and used the island as a military station. But

The Athenians under Nicias capture and fortify the island of Minoa.

[a] See note. The number must be considered doubtful. [b] Cleruchi, literally 'portioners,' Athenians who received land in a conquered country, but remained citizens. [c] £6 13*s*. 4*d*. [d] Cp. iv. 52 med.

Nicias wanted the Athenians to keep a watch over Megara, not as hitherto from Budorum in Salamis, but from this spot, which was nearer, the Peloponnesians would then be no longer able to send out triremes, as they had already done on one occasion[a], or privateers from the harbour unobserved, and nothing could be brought in by sea to Megara. First of all he took[b] two projecting towers on the side of the island towards Nisaea[b] by the help of engines from the sea, and, having thus freed a way into the channel dividing Minoa from the coast of Megara, he fortified the point nearest the mainland, where, by a bridge through a lagoon, aid could be brought by the enemy to the island, lying as it did at that point close to the shore. The work was completed in a few days. Nicias then proceeded to build a fort on the island, and, leaving a garrison, returned with the rest of his army.

The Plataeans surrender to the Lacedaemonians, and a commission of five is sent from Sparta to decide their fate. They obtain leave to speak in their own defence.

52 In this summer and about the same time the Plataeans, who had exhausted their food and could no longer hold out, capitulated to the Peloponnesians. The enemy had assaulted their wall and they were unable to defend themselves. But the Lacedaemonian commander knew their weakness, and was desirous that the place should be surrendered and not stormed; he had instructions from home to this effect, the intention being that if some day a treaty of peace were concluded, and both parties agreed to give up all the places which they had taken by force of arms[c], Plataea might be excepted on the ground that the inhabitants had come to terms of their own accord. So he sent a herald to enquire whether they would surrender the place to the Lacedaemonians and submit to their decision; the guilty were to be punished, but no one without a just cause. The Plataeans,

[a] Cp. ii. 93, 94.
[b] Or, 'two towers projecting from Nisaea.'
[c] Cp. v. 17 med.

now in the last stage of weakness, surrendered the city; and for a few days, until the five men who were appointed judges came from Lacedaemon, the Peloponnesians supplied them with food. On the arrival of the judges no accusation was brought against them; they were simply asked one by one, Whether they had done any kind of service to the Lacedaemonians or to their allies in the present war. Before making their reply they requested leave to speak at length, and appointed two of their number, Astymachus the son of Asopolaus, and Lacon the son of Aeimnestus, who was the Lacedaemonian proxenus, to be their advocates. They came forward and spoke as follows:—

'Men of Lacedaemon, we surrendered our city because 53
we had confidence in you; we were under the impression that the trial to which we submitted would be legal, and of a very different kind from this; and when we accepted you and you alone to be our judges, which indeed you are, we thought that at your hands we had the best hope of obtaining justice. But we fear that we are doubly mistaken, having too much reason to suspect that in this trial our lives are at stake, and that you will turn out to be partial judges. So we must infer, because no accusation has been preferred against us calling for a defence, but we speak at our own request; and because your question is a short one, to which the answer, if true, condemns us, and, if false, is exposed at once. In the extremity of our helplessness, our only and our safest course is to sa something, whatever may be our fate; for men in ir condition are sure to reproach themselves with en, silence, and to fancy that the unuttered word, if would have saved them.

We hoped to have a legal trial and to receive justice at your hands, but we are disappointed. We now fear that we are to be sacrificed to the Thebans.

'But by what arguments can we ever co rht with you? If we were unacquainted with one another you were advantage adduce in evidence matters of ignorant, but now you know all that we can say; and we are afraid, not that we are criminals in your eyes because you have decided that we fall short of your own standard of virtue [a], but that we are being sacrificed to please others, and that the cause which we plead is already prejudged.

Treat us either as friends or as open enemies. Remember our conduct (1) *in the Persian War,* (2) *in the revolt of the Helots.*

54 'Still we may urge our claims of justice against our Theban enemies, and our claims of gratitude upon you and the other Hellenes; the recollection of our good deeds may perhaps move you. To your short question, "Whether in this war we have done any service to the Lacedaemonians and their allies," we reply that "if we are enemies you are not wronged, because you have received no good from us; and if you deem us friends, you who have made war upon us, and not we, are to blame." During the late peace and in the Persian War our conduct was irreproachable; we were not the first to violate the peace, and we were the only Boeotians who took part in repelling the Persian invader and in the liberation of Hellas. Although we are an inland city, we joined in the sea-fight off Artemisium; we were at your side when you fought in our land under Pausanias, and, whatever dangers the Hellenes underwent in those days, we took a share beyond our strength in all of them. And you, Lacedaemonians, more especially should remember how at the time when Sparta was panic-stricken by the rebellion of the Helots, who seized Ithomè after the earthquake [b], we sent a third part of our own citizens to your aid; these are things not to be forgotten.

'Such was the spirit which animated us in the great ...ys of old; not until later did we become your enemies, ... that was originally your own fault. For when we sought ... help against the violence of the Thebans, you had ...d us and had bade us turn to the Athenians, who were

[a] Cp. iii. 57 init. [b] Cp. i. 101.

now in the last stage of weakness, surrendered the city; and for a few days, until the five men who were appointed judges came from Lacedaemon, the Peloponnesians supplied them with food. On the arrival of the judges no accusation was brought against them; they were simply asked one by one, Whether they had done any kind of service to the Lacedaemonians or to their allies in the present war. Before making their reply they requested leave to speak at length, and appointed two of their number, Astymachus the son of Asopolaus, and Lacon the son of Aeimnestus, who was the Lacedaemonian proxenus, to be their advocates. They came forward and spoke as follows:—

We hoped to have a legal trial and to receive justice at your hands, but we are disappointed. We now fear that we are to be sacrificed to the Thebans.

'Men of Lacedaemon, we surrendered our city because 53
we had confidence in you; we were under the impression that the trial to which we submitted would be legal, and of a very different kind from this; and when we accepted you and you alone to be our judges, which indeed you are, we thought that at your hands we had the best hope of obtaining justice. But we fear that we are doubly mistaken, having too much reason to suspect that in this trial our lives are at stake, and that you will turn out to be partial judges. So we must infer, because no accusation has been preferred against us calling for a defence, but we speak at our own request; and because your question is a short one, to which the answer, if true, condemns us, and, if false, is exposed at once. In the extremity of our helplessness, our only and our safest course is to say something, whatever may be our fate; for men in our condition are sure to reproach themselves with their silence, and to fancy that the unuttered word, if spoken, would have saved them.

'But by what arguments can we ever convince you? If we were unacquainted with one another we might with advantage adduce in evidence matters of which you were ignorant, but now you know all that we can say; and we are afraid, not that we are criminals in your eyes because you have decided that we fall short of your own standard of virtue[a], but that we are being sacrificed to please others, and that the cause which we plead is already prejudged.

Treat us either as friends or as open enemies. Remember our conduct (1) in the Persian War, (2) in the revolt of the Helots.

54 'Still we may urge our claims of justice against our Theban enemies, and our claims of gratitude upon you and the other Hellenes; the recollection of our good deeds may perhaps move you. To your short question, "Whether in this war we have done any service to the Lacedaemonians and their allies," we reply that "if we are enemies you are not wronged, because you have received no good from us; and if you deem us friends, you who have made war upon us, and not we, are to blame." During the late peace and in the Persian War our conduct was irreproachable; we were not the first to violate the peace, and we were the only Boeotians who took part in repelling the Persian invader and in the liberation of Hellas. Although we are an inland city, we joined in the sea-fight off Artemisium; we were at your side when you fought in our land under Pausanias, and, whatever dangers the Hellenes underwent in those days, we took a share beyond our strength in all of them. And you, Lacedaemonians, more especially should remember how at the time when Sparta was panic-stricken by the rebellion of the Helots, who seized Ithomè after the earthquake[b], we sent a third part of our own citizens to your aid; these are things not to be forgotten.

55 'Such was the spirit which animated us in the great days of old; not until later did we become your enemies, and that was originally your own fault. For when we sought your help against the violence of the Thebans, you had rejected us and had bade us turn to the Athenians, who were

[a] Cp. iii. 57 init.

[b] Cp. i. 101.

near, whereas you were at a distance. Yet even in this war you have neither suffered nor were ever likely to suffer anything very atrocious at our hands. If we refused to revolt from the Athenians at your bidding, we were quite right; for they assisted us against the Thebans when you shrank from the task; and after this it would have been dishonourable to betray them. They had been our benefactors; we had been at our own request admitted to their alliance, and we shared the rights of citizenship with them. How could we refuse to respond loyally to their call? When you or they in the exercise of your supremacy have acted, it may be, wrongly and led your allies into evil courses, the leaders and not the followers are to be blamed.

B.C. 519. Ol. 65, 2.

We only left you at the bidding of the Athenians and you originally forced us to become their allies. They helped us then, and how could we abandon them?

'The Thebans have inflicted many injuries upon us, 56
and their latest crime, as you are well aware, is the cause of our present misfortunes. They came, not only in time of peace, but at a holy season, and attempted to seize our city; we righteously and in accordance with univeral law defended ourselves and punished the aggressor; and there is no reason why we should now suffer for their satisfaction. If you take your own present advantage and their present hatred to be the measure of justice, you will prove yourselves, not upright and impartial judges, but the slaves of expediency. The Thebans may appear serviceable now, but of far greater service to you were we and the other Hellenes when you were in far greater danger. For now you invade and menace others, but in those days the Barbarian was threatening to enslave us all, and they were on his side. May we not fairly set our former patriotism against our present offence, if indeed we have offended? You will find that the one more than

The Thebans attacked us in time of peace: were we wrong in resisting them? If we have erred at all, is not the error outweighed by our former patriotism? Yet the same principle on which we acted then made us refuse to leave the Athenians.

outweighs the other; for our service to you was performed at a time when very few Hellenes opposed their courage to the power of Xerxes; they were then held in honour, not[a] who, looking to their own advantage, made terms with the invader[a] and were safe, but who, in the face of danger, dared the better part. Of that number were we, and there was a time when we received the highest honour at your hands, but now we fear that these same principles, which have led us to prefer a just alliance with the Athenians to an interested alliance with you, will be our destruction. Yet when men have been consistent in their conduct, others should show themselves consistent in their judgment of it[b]. For true expediency is only this—to have an enduring sense of gratitude towards good allies for their services, while we[c] do not neglect our own immediate interest.

Remember your own reputation: do not outrage Hellenic sentiment by allowing Plataea, whose name your fathers inscribed on the Delphian tripod, to be blotted out in order to please the Thebans.

57 'Consider, before you act, that hitherto you have been generally esteemed among Hellenes to be a pattern of nobility; if you decide unjustly (and this judgment cannot be hidden, for you, the judges, are famous, and we, who are judged by you, are of good repute), mankind will be indignant at the strange and disgraceful sentence which will have been passed against good men by men still better[d]. They will not endure to see spoils taken from us, the benefactors of Hellas, dedicated by our enemies in the common temples. Will it not be deemed a monstrous thing that the Lacedaemonians should desolate Plataea; that they, whose fathers inscribed the name of the city on the tripod at Delphi in token of her valour[e], should for the sake of the Thebans blot out the

---

[a] Or, reading αὐτοῖς, and referring the word to the Persians: 'who, looking to advantage, forwarded the course of the invader.' [b] This may refer to the judgment of the Spartans on the Plataeans, or to the adhesion of the Plataeans to the Athenians; see note. [c] Reading ἡμῖν. [d] Cp. iii. 53 fin. [e] Cp. i. 132 init.

whole people from the Hellenic world? For to this we have come at last. When the Persians conquered our land, we were all but ruined; and now, when we plead before you, who were once our dearest friends, the Thebans have prevailed against us. We have had to meet two terrible trials, the danger first of starvation, if we had not given up the city; and secondly, of condemnation to death. The Plataeans, who were zealous in the cause of Hellas even beyond their strength, are now friendless, spurned and rejected by all. None of our old allies will help us, and we fear that you, O Lacedaemonians, our only hope, are not to be depended upon.

Do not bring infamy upon yourselves by slaying suppliants. Your ancestors are buried in our land, and we have honoured them by yearly gifts. Will you give them up to their murderers and enslave the country in which the freedom of Hellas was won?

'Yet once more for the sake of those Gods in whose 58
name we made a league of old, and for our services to the cause of Hellas, relent and change your minds, if the Thebans have at all influenced you: [a] in return for the wicked request which they make of you, ask of them the righteous boon that you should not slay us to your own dishonour [a]. Do not bring upon yourselves an evil name merely to gratify others. For, although you may quickly take our lives, you will not so easily obliterate the infamy of the deed. We are not enemies whom you might justly punish, but friends who were compelled to go to war with you; and therefore piety demands that you should spare our lives. Before you pass judgment, consider that we surrendered ourselves, and stretched out our hands to you; the custom of Hellas does not allow the suppliant to be put to death. Remember too that we have ever been your benefactors. Cast your eyes upon the sepulchres of your fathers slain by the Persians and buried in our land, whom we have honoured by a yearly public

[a] Or, 'ask of them the boon that you should not kill those whom you ought not, and receive an honest gratitude from us, instead of a disgraceful gratitude from them.'

offering of garments, and other customary gifts. We were their friends, and we gave them the firstfruits in their season of that friendly land in which they rest; we were their allies too, who in times past had fought at their side; and if you now pass an unjust sentence, will not your conduct strangely contrast with ours? Reflect: when Pausanias buried them here, he thought that he was laying them among friends and in friendly earth. But if you put us to death, and make Plataea one with Thebes, are you not robbing your fathers and kindred of the honour which they enjoy, and leaving them in a hostile land inhabited by their murderers? Nay more, you will enslave the land in which the Hellenes won their liberty; you bring desolation upon the temples in which they prayed when they conquered the Persians; and you will take away the sacrifices which our fathers instituted from the city which ordained and established them.

We entreat you by the common gods of Hellas, by your fathers' oaths, not to betray us. We did not surrender to the Thebans: we would rather have died of hunger: if you will not hear us, put us back in our city, and let us meet our fate.

59 'These things, O Lacedaemonians, would not be for your honour. They would be an offence against the common feeling of Hellas and against your ancestors. You should be ashamed to put us to death, who are your benefactors and have never done you any wrong, in order that you may gratify the enmity of another. Spare us, and let your heart be softened towards us; be wise, and have mercy upon us, considering not only how terrible will be our fate, but who the sufferers are; think too of the uncertainty of fortune, which may strike any one however innocent. We implore you, as is becoming and natural in our hour of need, by the Gods whom the Hellenes worship at common altars, to listen to our prayers. We appeal to the oaths which your fathers swore, and entreat you not to forget them. We kneel at your fathers' tombs, and we call upon the dead not to let us be betrayed into the hands of the Thebans, their dearest

friends to their bitterest enemies. We remind you of the day on which we shared in their glorious deeds—we who on this day are in danger of meeting a fearful doom. And now we say no more; to men in our case, though we must, there is nothing harder than to make an end; for with the end comes the decisive hour. Our last word is that we did not surrender Plataea to the Thebans,—far rather would we have perished from hunger, the most miserable of deaths,—but to you, in whom we trusted, and, if you will not listen to us, you ought at least to replace us in the same position, and allow us to choose our destiny, whatever it may be. We adjure you not to deliver us, the Plataeans, who were so loyal to the cause of Hellas, and who are now suppliants to you, O Lacedaemonians, out of your own hands and your own good faith, into the hands of the Thebans, our worst enemies. Be our saviours. You are liberating the other Hellenes; do not destroy us.'

The Thebans also obtain leave to speak.

Such were the words of the Plataeans; whereupon the 60
Thebans, fearing that the Lacedaemonians might give way, came forward and said that since, against their judgment, the Plataeans had been allowed, instead of answering the question, to make a long defence, they too wished to speak. Permission was granted, and they spoke as follows:—

We should not have spoken if the Plataeans had not. But you must hear our case as well as theirs. They separated themselves from their own nation and went over to the Athenians.

'We should never have asked to speak, if the Plataeans 61
had briefly answered the question which was put to them[a], and had not turned upon us and arraigned us while they made a long and irrelevant defence of their own doings, excusing themselves from charges which nobody brought against them, and praising what nobody blamed. We must answer their accusations of us, and look a little closely into their glorification of themselves,

[a] Cp. i. 37 init. 73; vi. 82.

that neither our baseness nor their superior reputation may benefit them, and that, before you judge, you may hear the truth both about us and them. Our quarrel with them arose thus:—Some time after our first occupation of Boeotia [a] we settled Plataea and other places, out of which we drove a mixed multitude. But the Plataeans refused to acknowledge our leadership according to the original agreement, and, separating themselves from the other Boeotians, deserted the traditions of their ancestors. When force was applied to them they went over to the Athenians, and, assisted by them, did us a great deal of mischief; and we retaliated.

They say that we sided with the Persian in the war of liberation. To which we reply that we were not our own masters, and that afterwards we fought at Coronea for the liberation of Hellas from Athens, and are now fighting for it.

62 'They say that when the Barbarian invaded Hellas they were the only Boeotians who did not join the Persian; and this is their great glory, and our great reproach. But we say that if they did not side with the Persians, it was only because the Athenians did not; and on the same principle, they alone of all the Boeotians afterwards sided with the Athenians when the liberties of Hellas were attacked by them. But, consider how different were the circumstances in which we and they acted. In those days our state was not governed by an oligarchy which granted equal justice to all, nor yet by a democracy; the power was in the hands of a small cabal, than which nothing is more opposed to law or to true political order, or more nearly resembles a tyranny. The rulers of the state, hoping to strengthen their private interest if the Persian won, kept the people down and brought him in. The city at large, when she acted thus, was not her own mistress; and she cannot be fairly blamed for an error which she committed when she had no constitution. After the Persian departed and she obtained a constitution, you may see how we fought against the Athenians when they became

[a] Cp. i. 12.

aggressive and endeavoured to subjugate us as well as the rest of Hellas. Owing to our divisions they actually conquered the greater part of the country; but we defeated them at Coronea, and liberated Boeotia[a]; and at this moment we are zealously co-operating in the liberation of Hellas, providing cavalry and munitions of war more largely than any of the allies. Thus much in answer to the charge respecting our Persian tendencies.

'And now we will proceed to show that you, and not 63
we, have done the greater wrong to Hellas, and are deserving of every sort of punishment. You say that you became allies and citizens of Athens in order that you might be protected against us. If so, you ought to have invited their aid only against us, and not to have assisted them in their attacks upon others; such a course was certainly open to you: even if you had been in some degree constrained against your will by the Athenians, you had previously made the alliance with the Lacedaemonians against the Persians, to which you are so fond of appealing. That alliance would at any rate have restrained our hands, and above all would have secured to you freedom of deliberation. But you acted willingly, and were no longer under compulsion when you made common cause with the Athenians. Your allegation is that they were your benefactors and that you could not honourably betray them; but how far more dishonourable and wicked to betray all the Hellenes with whom you had sworn alliance, than the Athenians only, the one the liberators, the other the enslavers of Hellas! The return which you made to them is unequal, nay, infamous; you say that you invited them to assist you because you were wronged, and then you became their accomplices in wronging others. Surely ingratitude is shown in refusing to return an honourable kindness, when it can be done honourably, not in refusing to return

But they of their own free-will abetted the Athenians in their aggressions upon Hellas. They plead obligation, but no obligation can justify a crime.

[a] Cp. iv. 92 fin.

a kindness which, however justly due, cannot be repaid without a crime.

64 'You have thus made it plain that, when you alone among the Boeotians refused to join the Persian cause, this was not out of any love for Hellas[a], but because the Athenians did not[a]; and that you wanted to act with them and not with us; and now you claim the benefit of the virtue which others inspired in you. But this is not reasonable; having once chosen the Athenians, fight on their side, and do not at the last moment be saying that the old alliance ought to save you. For you have abandoned it, and by the violation of it, instead of striving to

When they resisted the Persian it was only because the Athenians resisted him. They have now shown themselves in their true light, and have forfeited all their claims upon Hellas.

B.C. 456. Ol. 81. prevent, have aided in the enslavement of the Aeginetans and of other members of the alliance. And you were not, like us, under compulsion, but free, living under your ancient laws. Moreover, you persisted in refusing that last offer of peace and neutrality which we made to you before the siege began[b]. Who more thoroughly than you deserve the hatred of the Hellenes? than you who have only displayed your virtues to their injury? You have given proof that the merit which you claim for your former actions does not properly belong to you! Your true nature and constant desire are now revealed in the light of day; for you have followed the Athenians in the path of injustice. Thus much we have to say as to our involuntary dealings with the Persians, and your voluntary dealings with the Athenians.

65 'The last offence which you lay to our charge is that we unlawfully assailed your city in time of peace, and at a holy season; even in that affair we do not think ourselves more in fault than you. We do not deny that we were wrong if of

They say that we broke into their city. True, because we were invited by the most influential and patriotic of their citizens.

---

[a] Or reading ὅτι οὐδ' Ἀθηναῖοι, ἡμεῖς δέ, 'but because the Athenians did not and we did.'

[b] Cp. ii. 72, 73.

our own mere motion we went to your city, fought with you, and ravaged your land. But when certain of the noblest and richest of your citizens, who wished to withdraw you from a foreign alliance and to bring you back to the national institutions of Boeotia, came and invited us, wherein are we to blame? As you say yourselves, the leaders rather than the followers are the transgressors [a]. But in our opinion, neither we nor they were really guilty. Like yourselves they were citizens, and they had a greater stake in the country than you have; they opened their own gates and received us into their native city, not as her enemies but as her friends. They desired that the bad among you should not grow worse, and that the good should have their reward. They wanted to reform the principles of your citizens, and not to banish their persons; they would have brought them back into a natural union with their kindred, that Plataea might be at peace with all and the enemy of none.

'And the proof that we acted in no hostile spirit is that 66
we did no harm to any one, but made a proclamation that whoever wished to live under the national institutions of Boeotia should join us. You came to us gladly, and, entering into an agreement, for a time offered no opposition; but afterwards, when you discovered that we were few, you turned upon us. Even allowing that we did act somewhat inconsiderately in entering your town without the consent of your whole people, still how different was your conduct and ours! For if you had followed our example you would have used no violence, but thought only of getting us out by persuasion, whereas you broke the agreement and attacked us. Now we do not so much complain of the fate of those whom you slew in battle—for they indeed suffered by a kind of law—but there were others who

At first they were ready to join us, but after a while they set upon us, and slew our citizens whom they had sworn to spare.

[a] Cp. iii. 55 fin.

stretched out their hands to you; and although you gave them quarter, and then promised to us that you would spare them, in utter defiance of law you took their lives—was not that a cruel act? Here are three crimes which you committed within a few hours; the breach of the agreement, the slaughter of the prisoners which followed, and the lying promise which you made to us that you would not slay them if we did no injury to your property in the fields; and yet you insist that we are the criminals, and that you ought to be acquitted. Not so; if the Lacedaemonians give just judgment: but for all these offences you shall suffer.

You should know the truth about the Plataeans. If they had the virtues to which they pretend, they deserve a double punishment. Pity not them, but their victims. For their misfortunes they may thank themselves. Put the question to them again.

67 'We have entered into particulars, Lacedaemonians, both for your sakes and for our own, that you may know the sentence which you are going to pass on them to be just, and still more righteous the vengeance which we have taken. Do not let your hearts be softened by tales about their ancient virtues, if they ever had any; such virtues might plead for the injured, but should bring a double penalty[a] on the authors of a base deed, because they are false to their own character. Let them gain nothing by their pitiful lamentations, or by appealing to your fathers' tombs and their own desolate condition. We tell you that a far sadder fate was inflicted by them on our murdered youth, of whose fathers some fell at Coronea in the act of bringing Boeotia to join you, while others are left in their old age by their solitary hearths, and entreat you, with far better reason, to punish the Plataeans. Men who suffer an unworthy fate are indeed to be pitied, but there should be joy over those who suffer justly, as these do. For their present desolation they may thank themselves; they might have chosen the worthier alliance, but

[a] Cp. i. 86 init.

they wilfully renounced it. They sinned against us though we had never injured them; the spirit of hatred and not of justice possessed them, and even now they are not punished half enough. For they are going to suffer by a lawful sentence, not, as they pretend, stretching out their suppliant hands on the field of battle, but delivering themselves up to justice under the terms of a capitulation. Maintain then, Lacedaemonians, the common Hellenic law which they have outraged, and give to us, who have suffered contrary to law, the just recompense of our zeal in your cause. Do not be moved by their words to spurn and reject us[a], but show Hellas by example that, when a cause is tried at your tribunal, deeds and not words will prevail. If the deeds be good, a brief statement of them is enough; if they be evil, speeches full of fine sentiments do but veil them. If all persons in authority were like you, and would sum up a case in a short question, and pass sentence upon all the offenders at once, men would be less tempted to seek out fair words in order to excuse foul deeds.'

The Plataeans are put to death, and their city razed to the ground.

Thus spoke the Thebans. The Lacedaemonian judges 68
thought that no objection could be made to their question, whether the Plataeans had done them any service in the war. [b]For they pretended to have expected neutrality from them in the times before the war, on the strength of the original treaty concluded with Pausanias after the defeat of the Persians. And just before the siege they had made to them a proposal[b] of neutrality in accordance with the terms of the same treaty; but the Plataeans had refused. Considering that they had been wronged by them, after their own fair proposals

---

[a] Cp. iii. 57 fin. [b] Or, taking ἠξίουν in a different sense, and repeating it before καὶ ὅτε ὕστερον: 'For they had been constantly requesting them, as they said, to remain neutral in the times before the war, . . . and they had repeated the request when just before the siege they had made to them a proposal,' &c.

had released them from the obligations of the treaty, they again brought up the Plataeans one after another, and asked each of them separately, Whether he had done any service to the Lacedaemonians and their allies in the war? When he said No, they took him away and slew him; no one was spared. They put to death not less than two hundred Plataeans, as well as twenty-five Athenians who had shared with them in the siege; and made slaves of the women. For about a year the Thebans gave possession of the city to certain Megarians, who had been driven out by a revolution [a], and to any surviving Plataeans who were of their own party; but they afterwards razed the whole place to the very foundations, and built near the precinct of Herè an inn forming a square of two hundred feet; it had two stories, and chambers all round. They used the roofs and the doors of the Plataeans; and of the brass and iron articles of furniture found within the walls they made couches, which they dedicated to Herè; they also built in her honour a stone temple a hundred feet long. The Plataean territory they converted into public land, and let it out for terms of ten years; some of their own citizens occupied it. Throughout the whole affair the severity shown by the Lacedaemonians to the Plataeans was mainly promoted by a desire to gratify the Thebans, who seemed likely to be useful allies to them in the war
B.C. 519. Ol. 65, 2. then just beginning. Such was the fate of Plataea, which was overthrown in the ninety-third year after the Plataeans entered into alliance with Athens [b].

Return of Alcidas. He and Brasidas make ready an expedition to Corcyra.

69 The forty Peloponnesian ships which had been sent to the aid of Lesbos, as they fled through the open sea pursued by the Athenians [c], were caught in a storm near Crete, and, making their way in a straggling condition from Crete to the Peloponnesus, found at Cyllene thirteen Leucadian and Ambraciot

[a] Cp. iv. 66 init. [b] Cp. Herod. vi. 108. [c] Cp. iii. 33.

triremes, and Brasidas the son of Tellis, who had been sent out as a commissioner to advise Alcidas. The Lacedaemonians at home, after the failure of their attempt on Lesbos, had determined to increase their navy and sail to Corcyra, which was in a state of revolution. The Athenian squadron at Naupactus consisted of twelve ships only, and the Lacedaemonians wanted to reach the island before any more vessels could arrive from Athens. Brasidas and Alcidas made their preparations accordingly.

Unsettled state of Corcyra, originating in the intrigues of the prisoners who had returned from Corinth.

Now Corcyra had been in an unsettled state ever since 70
the return of the prisoners who were taken at sea in the Epidamnian war[a], and afterwards released by the Corinthians. They were nominally let out on bail for a sum of eight hundred talents[b] on the security of their proxeni, but in reality they had been induced to try and gain over Corcyra to the Corinthian interest. They went from one citizen to another, and did their best with them to bring about a revolt from Athens. On the arrival of an Athenian and also of a Corinthian vessel conveying ambassadors, there was a discussion in the assembly, and the Corcyraeans voted that they would continue allies of Athens according to their agreement[c], but would renew their former friendship with the Peloponnesians. A certain Peithias, who voluntarily acted as the proxenus of the Athenians and was the popular leader, was summoned by the partisans of the Peloponnesians to take his trial, they affirming that he wanted to bring Corcyra under the yoke of Athens. He was acquitted, and then he in turn summoned their five richest men, declaring that they were in the habit of cutting poles for vines in the sacred precinct of Zeus and Alcinous; now

Trial of Peithias, the popular leader. His acquittal. Trial of the oligarchs, and murder of Peithias and of sixty others.

[a] Cp. i. 55 med. [b] £160,000. [c] Cp. i. 44.

for each pole the penalty was fixed at a stater[a]. They were condemned; but the fine was so excessive that they went and sat as suppliants in the temple of Zeus and Alcinous, begging that they might pay the money by instalments. Peithias, who happened to be a member of the senate as well as the popular leader, persuaded the senators to put the law in execution. The culprits, knowing that the law was against them, and perceiving that Peithias[b] as long as he remained in the senate would try to induce the people[b] to make an alliance offensive and defensive with Athens, conspired together, and, rushing into the council chamber with daggers in their hands, slew him and others to the number of sixty, as well private persons as senators. A few who were of the same party with him took refuge in the Athenian trireme, which had not yet left.

71 The next step taken by the conspirators was to assemble the people and tell them that they had acted for the best, and in order to secure them against the tyranny of Athens. For the future they should receive neither Athenians nor Peloponnesians, unless they came peaceably with one ship; to bring more should be deemed the act of an enemy; and this proposal they compelled the people to ratify. They also sent envoys to Athens, who were to put the most favourable colour on the affair, and to dissuade the refugees who had fled thither from taking any inconvenient step which might lead to a counter-revolution.

Temporary triumph of the oligarchs.

72 When the envoys arrived, the Athenians arrested them as disturbers of the peace, and deposited them in Aegina, together with any of the refugees whom they had gained over. In the meantime, the

Envoys from Corcyra are arrested at Athens. Defeat of the popular party.

[a] If the gold stater, about 16*s.*; if the silver Athenian stater, about 2*s.* 8*d.*; if the silver Corinthian stater (didrachmon) (tetradrachmon), about 1*s.* 4*d.*

[b] Or, 'before he ceased to be a senator would persuade the people.'

Corcyraean oligarchs who were now in power, on the arrival of a Corinthian trireme and Lacedaemonian envoys, attacked and defeated the people, who at nightfall took refuge in the Acropolis and the higher parts of the city, and there concentrated their forces. They also held the Hyllaic harbour; the other party seized the Agora, where most of them lived, and the adjacent harbour which looked towards the continent.

On the following day they skirmished a little, and both 73
parties sent messengers round the country inviting the slaves to join them, and promising them liberty; the greater number came to the aid of the people, while the other faction was reinforced by eight hundred auxiliaries from the mainland.

Reinforcements arrive.

After resting a day they fought again, and the people, 74
who had the advantage in numbers and in the strength of their positions, gained the victory. Their women joined vigorously in the fray, hurling tiles from the housetops, and showing amid the uproar a fortitude beyond their sex. The conflict was decided towards evening; the oligarchy, fearing lest the people should take the arsenal with a sudden rush and so make an end of them, set fire to the private houses which surrounded the Agora, as well as to the larger blocks of buildings, sparing neither their own property nor that of any one else in their determination to stop them. Much merchandise was burnt, and the whole city would have been destroyed if the wind had carried the flame in that direction. Both parties now left off fighting, and kept watch in their own positions during the night. When the popular cause triumphed, the Corinthian vessel stole away and most of the auxiliaries crossed over unobserved to the continent.

In a second conflict the people are victorious.

On the following day, Nicostratus the son of Diitrephes, 75
an Athenian general, arrived from Naupactus with twelve ships and five hundred Messenian hoplites. He tried to

effect a reconciliation between the two parties, and on his suggestion they agreed to bring to trial ten of the most guilty persons, who immediately fled. The rest were to live together, and to make peace with one another, and with Athens an alliance offensive and defensive. Having accomplished his purpose he was about to sail away, when the leaders of the people induced him to leave five of his own vessels, that the enemy might be less inclined to stir, promising to man five ships of their own and send them with him. He agreed, and they selected the crews of the ships out of the opposite faction. But the men were afraid of being sent to Athens, and sat as suppliants in the temple of the Dioscuri. Nicostratus sought to raise them up and reassure them, but they would not trust him; whereupon the people armed themselves, arguing that their mistrust and unwillingness to sail was a proof of their evil designs. They took their enemies' arms out of their houses, and some of them whom they chanced to meet would have been slain if Nicostratus had not interfered. The rest, to the number of about four hundred, when they saw what was going on, took refuge afresh in the temple of Herè. But the people, fearing that they would resort to violence, persuaded them to rise and conveyed them at once to the island that lies in front of the temple of Herè, whither provisions were regularly sent to them.

Arrival of twelve Athenian ships under Nicostratus, who vainly tries to reconcile the contending parties.

76 At this stage of the revolution, on the fourth or fifth day after the suppliants had been conveyed to the island, the Peloponnesian ships from Cyllene, which since the expedition to Ionia had been in harbour there[a], arrived on the scene, fifty-three in number, still under the command of Alcidas. Brasidas his adviser was on board. They anchored for the night at Sybota, a harbour on the mainland, and when the morning broke they sailed upon Corcyra.

Appearance of the Peloponnesian fleet.

[a] Cp. iv. 69.

The whole place was in an uproar; the people dreaded 77
their enemies within the city no less than the Peloponnesian fleet. They hastened to equip sixty ships, and as fast as they were manned sent them out against the Peloponnesians, although the Athenians entreated to be allowed to sail out first, leaving them to follow as soon as they had got their fleet together. But when in this straggling fashion their ships approached the enemy, two of them at once deserted; in others the crews were fighting with one another, and everything was in disorder. The Peloponnesians, seeing the confusion, employed twenty ships only against the Corcyraeans, and opposed the remainder of their fleet to the twelve Athenian ships, of which two were the Salaminia and Paralus.

Confused battle of the Corcyraeans and Athenians against the Peloponnesians.

The Corcyraeans, coming up few at a time and in this 78
disorderly fashion, had trouble enough among themselves. The Athenians, afraid of being surrounded by superior numbers, did not attack the main body nor the centre of those opposed to them, but fell upon the wings and sank a single ship; then, the enemy forming in a circle, they sailed round them and endeavoured to throw them into confusion. But those who were opposed to the Corcyraeans, seeing this movement and fearing a repetition of what happened at Naupactus[a], came to the rescue, and the united fleet charged the Athenians. Thereupon they rowed astern, hoping that by retreating very leisurely they might give the Corcyraeans time to escape, especially as the attack of the enemy was now directed against themselves. The naval engagement ended at sunset.

Diversion effected by the Athenians, who slowly retreat.

The Corcyraeans, who were afraid that the victorious 79
enemy would sail to the city and have recourse to some decisive measure, such as taking on board the prisoners

[a] Cp. ii. 84.

in the island, conveyed them back to the temple of Herè and guarded the city. But the Peloponnesians, although they had won the battle, did not venture to attack the city, but returned to their station on the mainland with thirteen Corcyraean ships which they had taken. On the next day they still hesitated, although there was great panic and confusion among the inhabitants. It is said that Brasidas advised Alcidas to make the attempt, but he had not an equal vote with him. So they only disembarked at the promontory of Leucimnè and ravaged the country.

The Peloponnesian fleet, instead of attacking the city, retire;

80 Meanwhile the people of Corcyra, dreading that the fleet of the Peloponnesians would attack them, held a parley with the other faction, especially with the suppliants, in the hope of saving the city; they even persuaded some of them to go on board the fleet; for the Corcyraeans still contrived to man thirty ships. But the Peloponnesians, after devastating the land till about midday, retired. And at nightfall the approach of sixty Athenian vessels was signalled to them from Leucas. These had been sent by the Athenians under the command of Eurymedon the son of Thucles, when they heard of the revolution and of the intended expedition of Alcidas to Corcyra.

and soon afterwards, hearing that sixty Athenian vessels are approaching, return home.

81 The Peloponnesians set out that very night on their way home, keeping close to the land, and transporting the ships over the Leucadian isthmus, that they might not be seen sailing round[a]. When the Corcyraeans perceived that the Athenian fleet was appoaching, while that of the enemy had disappeared, they took the Messenian troops, who had hitherto been outside the walls, into the city, and ordered the ships which they had manned to sail round into the Hyllaic harbour. These proceeded on their way. Meanwhile

Massacre of the oligarchs.

---

[a] Cp. iv. 8 init.

they killed any of their enemies whom they caught in the city. On the arrival of the ships they disembarked those whom they had induced to go on board, and despatched them[a]; they also went to the temple of Herè, and persuading about fifty of the suppliants to stand their trial condemned them all to death. The majority would not come out, and, when they saw what was going on, destroyed one another in the enclosure of the temple where they were, except a few who hung themselves on trees, or put an end to their own lives in any other way which they could. And, during the seven days which Eurymedon after his arrival remained with his sixty ships, the Corcyraeans continued slaughtering those of their fellow-citizens whom they deemed their enemies; they professed to punish them for their designs against the democracy, but in fact some were killed from motives of personal enmity, and some because money was owing to them, by the hands of their debtors. Every form of death was to be seen; and everything, and more than everything, that commonly happens in revolutions, happened then. The father slew the son, and the suppliants were torn from the temples and slain near them; some of them were even walled up in the temple of Dionysus, and there perished. To such extremes of cruelty did revolution go; and this seemed to be the worst of revolutions, because it was the first.

For not long afterwards nearly the whole Hellenic world 82
was in commotion; in every city the chiefs of the democracy and of the oligarchy were struggling, the one to bring in the Athenians, the other the Lacedaemonians. Now in time of peace, men would have had no excuse for introducing either, and no desire to do so; but, when they were

The conflict of democracy and oligarchy, encouraged as it is by the hope of Athenian or Lacedaemonian help, ruins states and disorganises society.

[a] Reading with a few MSS. *ἀπεχρῶντο*, (which is quoted from Thucydides by the Lexicographers,) instead of *ἀνεχώρησαν*, which gives no sense.

at war[a], the introduction of a foreign alliance on one side or the other to the hurt of their enemies and the advantage of themselves was easily effected by the dissatisfied party[a]. And revolution brought upon the cities of Hellas many terrible calamities, such as have been and always will be while human nature remains the same, but which are more or less aggravated and differ in character with every new combination of circumstances. In peace and prosperity both states and individuals are actuated by higher motives, because they do not fall under the dominion of imperious necessities; but war, which takes away the comfortable provision of daily life, is a hard master and tends to assimilate men's characters to their conditions.

Changes in men's moral principles and in their use of language.

When troubles had once begun in the cities, those who followed carried the revolutionary spirit further and further, and determined to outdo the report of all who had preceded them by the ingenuity of their enterprises and the atrocity of their revenges. The meaning of words had no longer the same relation to things, but was changed by them as they thought proper. Reckless daring was held to be loyal courage; prudent delay was the excuse of a coward; moderation was the disguise of unmanly weakness; to know everything was to do nothing. Frantic energy was the true quality of a man. A conspirator who wanted to be safe was a recreant in disguise. The lover of violence was always trusted, and his opponent suspected. He who succeeded in a plot was deemed knowing, but a still greater master in craft was he who detected one. On the other hand, he who plotted from the first to have nothing to do with plots was a breaker up of parties and a poltroon who was afraid of the enemy. In a word, he who could outstrip another in a bad action was

[a] Omitting the comma inserted in Bekker's text after προσποιήσει, or retaining it 'and both sides could easily obtain allies to the hurt of their enemies and the advantage of themselves, the dissatisfied party were only too ready to invoke foreign aid'; see note on the passage.

applauded, and so was he who encouraged to evil one who had no idea of it. The tie of party was stronger than the tie of blood, because a partisan was more ready to dare without asking why. (For party associations are not based upon any established law, nor do they seek the public good; they are formed in defiance of the laws and from self-interest.) The seal of good faith was not divine law, but fellowship in crime. If an enemy when he was in the ascendant offered fair words, the opposite party received them not in a generous spirit,[a] but by a jealous watchfulness of his actions[a]. Revenge was dearer than self-preservation. Any agreements sworn to by either party, when they could do nothing else, were binding as long as both were powerless. But he who on a favourable opportunity first took courage, and struck at his enemy when he saw him off his guard, had greater pleasure in a perfidious than he would have had in an open act of revenge; he congratulated himself that he had taken the safer course, and also that he had overreached his enemy and gained the prize of superior ability. In general the dishonest more easily gain credit for cleverness than the simple for goodness; men take a pride in the one, but are ashamed of the other.

Causes and effects of the revolutionary spirit. Disregard of all laws, human and divine.

The cause of all these evils was the love of power, originating in avarice and ambition, and the party-spirit which is engendered by them when men are fairly embarked in a contest. For the leaders on either side used specious names, the one party professing to uphold the constitutional equality of the many, the other the wisdom of an aristocracy, while they made the public interests, to which in name they were devoted, in reality their prize. Striving in every way to overcome each other, they committed the most monstrous crimes; yet even these were surpassed by the magnitude of their revenges

[a] Or, 'but by active precautions.'

which they pursued to the very utmost[a], neither party observing any definite limits either of justice or public expediency, but both alike making the caprice of the moment their law. Either by the help of an unrighteous sentence, or grasping power with the strong hand, they were eager to satiate the impatience of party-spirit. Neither faction cared for religion; but any fair pretence which succeeded in effecting some odious purpose was greatly lauded. And the citizens who were of neither party fell a prey to both; either they were disliked because they held aloof, or men were jealous of their surviving.

Universal distrust. Force of character, not intellect, prevailed.

83 Thus revolution gave birth to every form of wickedness in Hellas. The simplicity which is so large an element in a noble nature was laughed to scorn and disappeared. An attitude of perfidious antagonism everywhere prevailed; for there was no word binding enough, nor oath terrible enough to reconcile enemies. Each man was strong only in the conviction that nothing was secure; he must look to his own safety, and could not afford to trust others. Inferior intellects generally succeeded best. For, aware of their own deficiencies, and fearing the capacity of their opponents, for whom they were no match in powers of speech, and whose subtle wits were likely to anticipate them in contriving evil, they struck boldly and at once. But the cleverer sort, presuming in their arrogance that they would be aware in time, and disdaining to act when they could think, were taken off their guard and easily destroyed.

84 Now in Corcyra most of these deeds were perpetrated, and for the first time. There was every crime which men could commit in revenge who had been governed not wisely, but tyrannically, and now had the oppressor at their mercy. There were the dishonest designs of others

---

[a] Placing the comma after μείζους instead of after ἐπεξῄεσάν τε.

who were longing to be relieved from their habitual poverty, and were naturally animated by a passionate desire for their neighbour's goods; and there were crimes of another class which men commit, not from covetousness, but from the enmity which equals foster towards one another until they are carried away by their blind rage into the extremes of pitiless cruelty. At such a time the life of the city was all in disorder, and human nature, which is always ready to transgress the laws, having now trampled them under foot, delighted to show that her passions were ungovernable, that she was stronger than justice, and the enemy of everything above her. If malignity had not exercised a fatal power, how could any one have preferred revenge to piety, and gain to innocence? But, when men are retaliating upon others, they are reckless of the future, and do not hesitate to annul those common laws of humanity to which every individual trusts for his own hope of deliverance should he ever be overtaken by calamity; they forget that in their own hour of need they will look for them in vain.

(1) *Fury of the oppressed,* (2) *discontent of the poor,* (3) *party hatred among equals, were the great incentives to crime. Human nature when inspired by revenge is too much for justice, conscience, or prudence.*

Such were the passions which the citizens of Corcyra 85
first of all Hellenes displayed towards one another. After the departure of Eurymedon and the Athenian fleet the surviving oligarchs, who to the number of five hundred had escaped, seized certain forts on the mainland, and thus became masters of the territory on the opposite coast which belonged to Corcyra. Thence issuing forth, they plundered the Corcyraeans in the island, and did much harm, so that there was a great famine in the city. They also sent ambassadors to Lacedaemon and Corinth, begging that they might be restored, but, failing of their object, they procured boats and auxiliaries, and passed over to Corcyra about six

The surviving oligarchs seize some forts on the opposite coast, but soon return to the island and occupy Mount Istonè.

hundred in all; then, burning their boats, that they might have no hope but in the conquest of the island, they went into Mount Istonè, and building a fort there, became masters of the country to the ruin of the inhabitants of the city.

86 At the end of the same summer the Athenians sent twenty ships to Sicily under the command of Laches the son of Melanopus, and Charoeades the son of Euphiletus. Syracuse and Leontini were now at war with one another. All the Dorian cities, except Camarina, were in alliance with Syracuse; they were the same which at the beginning of the war were reckoned in the Lacedaemonian confederacy, but they had taken no active part[a]. The allies of the Leontines were the Chalcidian cities and Camarina. In Italy the Locrians sided with the Syracusans, and the Rhegians with the Leontines, who were their kinsmen[b]. The Leontines and their allies sent to Athens, and on the ground, partly of an old alliance, partly of their Ionian descent, begged the Athenians to send them ships, for they were driven off both sea and land by their Syracusan enemies. The Athenians sent the ships, professedly on the ground of relationship, but in reality because they did not wish the Peloponnesians to obtain corn from Sicily. Moreover they meant to try what prospect they had of getting the affairs of Sicily into their hands. So the commanders of the fleet came to Rhegium in Italy, where they established themselves, and carried on the war in concert with their allies. Thus the summer ended.

War in Sicily between the Syracusans and Leontines; the latter obtain assistance from Athens.

87 In the following winter the plague, which had never entirely disappeared, although abating for a time, again attacked the Athenians. It continued on this second occasion not less than a year, having previously lasted for two years. To the power of Athens certainly nothing was more ruinous; not less than

Reappearance of the plague after it had abated. At the same time numerous earthquakes occur.

[a] Cp. ii. 7 med. [b] Cp. vi. 44 fin.

four thousand four hundred Athenian hoplites who were on the roll died, and also three hundred horsemen; how many of the common people could never be ascertained. This too was the time when the frequent earthquakes occurred at Athens, in Euboea, and in Boeotia, especially at Orchomenos[a].

During the same winter the Athenians in Sicily and the 88
Rhegians made an expedition with thirty ships against the islands of Aeolus, as they are called, which in summer time cannot be attacked owing to the want of water. These islands belong to the Liparaeans, who are colonists of the Cnidians: they inhabit one of them, which is not large, and is called Lipara; from this they go and cultivate the rest, Didymè, Strongylè, and Hiera. The inhabitants believe that the forge of Hephaestus is in Hiera, because the island sends up a blaze of fire in the night-time and clouds of smoke by day. The Aeolian islands lie off the territory of the Sicels and Messenians; they were in alliance with Syracuse. The Athenians wasted the country, but finding that the inhabitants would not yield, sailed back to Rhegium. And so ended the winter, and with it the fifth year in the Peloponnesian War of which Thucydides wrote the history.

Fruitless expedition against the Aeolian islands.

In the ensuing summer the Peloponnesians and their 89
allies, under the command of Agis the son of Archidamus, the Lacedaemonian king, came as far as the isthmus. They intended to invade Attica, but were deterred from proceeding by numerous earthquakes[b], and no invasion took place in this year. About the time when these earthquakes prevailed, the sea at Orobiae in Euboea, retiring from what was then the line of coast and rising in a great wave, overflowed a part of the city; and although

The earthquakes conceived by Thucydides to have been the cause of the great ebb and flow of the sea at Orobiae in Euboea, and at Atalantè.

B.C. 426. Ol. 88, 3.

[a] Cp. ch. 89, and i. 23 med.

[b] Cp. ch. 87.

it subsided in some places, yet in others the inundation was permanent, and that which was formerly land is now sea. All the people who could not escape to the high ground perished. A similar inundation occurred in the neighbourhood of Atalantè, an island on the coast of the Opuntian Locri, which carried away a part of the Athenian fort [a], and dashed in pieces one of two ships which were drawn up on the beach. At Peparethus also the sea retired, but no inundation followed; an earthquake, however, overthrew a part of the wall, the Prytaneum, and a few houses. I conceive that, where the force of the earthquake was greatest, the sea was driven back, and the suddenness of the recoil made the inundation more violent; and I am of opinion that this was the cause of the phenomenon, which would never have taken place if there had been no earthquake.

90 During the same summer war was going on in various parts of Sicily, the Hellenes in Sicily fighting against one another, the Athenians helping their own allies. I will mention the chief actions in which the Athenians took part, whether by the help of their allies attacking, or attacked by their enemies. Charoeades, the Athenian general, had been killed in battle by the Syracusans, and, Laches having taken the entire command of the fleet, he and the allies made an expedition against Mylae, a town belonging to Messenè. Two tribes of the Messenians were keeping guard there, and they had set an ambuscade for the force which they were expecting to land; but the Athenians and their allies put to flight with heavy loss the troops which came out of the ambush. Then, attacking the fortress, they compelled its defenders to come to terms, surrender the citadel, and march with them against Messenè. Finally, upon the approach of the Athenians and their allies, the Messenians themselves came to terms,

Capture by Laches of Mylae in Sicily, and submission of Messenè.

[a] Cp. ii. 32.

giving hostages and the other pledges which were required of them.

In the same summer the Athenians sent thirty ships 91
round the Peloponnese under the command of Demosthenes the son of Alcisthenes, and Procles the son of Theodorus. They also sent sixty ships and two thousand hoplites to Melos, under the command of Nicias the son of Niceratus, wishing to subdue the Melians, who, although they were islanders, resisted them and would not join their alliance [a]. So they ravaged their country, but finding that the Melians would not yield, they sailed away to Oropus, opposite Euboea. There they put in at nightfall, and the hoplites disembarking went at once by land to Tanagra in Boeotia. Meanwhile the entire Athenian force, under the command of Hipponicus the son of Callias, and Eurymedon the son of Thucles, upon a signal given marched to meet them at the same spot. There they encamped, and all together devastated the country, remaining at Tanagra during that day and the following night. On the morrow they defeated the Tanagraeans who sallied out upon them, and also some Thebans who had come to their aid; they then took up the arms of the slain, raised a trophy, and returned, the one part of the forces back again to the city, the other to their ships. Nicias with his sixty ships then sailed to the coast of Locris; after ravaging the country he returned home.

Thirty Athenian ships under Demosthenes sail round the Peloponnese. Sixty more under Nicias go to Melos, and after ravaging the island sail to Oropus. At Tanagra his troops, in concert with the Athenian land-forces, defeat the inhabitants.

About the same time the Lacedaemonians founded 92
Heraclea, their colony in Trachinia. The intention was as follows:—The Trachinians are one of the three Melian tribes; the other two being the Paralians and the Hiereans. These Trachinians, having suffered greatly in war from their neigh-

To help the Trachinians and their own mother state Doris, the Lacedaemonians found the colony of Heraclea.

---

[a] Cp. v. 84.

bours the Oetaeans, at first thought of attaching themselves to the Athenians, but, fearing that they could not trust them[a], sent Tisamenus, whom they appointed their envoy, to Lacedaemon. The Dorians, who were the mother state of Lacedaemon, joined in the embassy and also requested help, for they too were suffering from the Oetaeans. The Lacedaemonians heard their appeal, and, being desirous of assisting both the Trachinians and Dorians, made up their minds to send out a colony. They also thought that the situation of the new city would be convenient for carrying on the war against the Athenians. There a navy could be equipped if they wanted to attack Euboea, which was quite near, and the station would be handy for the conveyance of troops to Chalcidicè. For every reason they were eager to colonise the place. First they enquired of the God at Delphi; he bade them go, and they sent out settlers taken from their own citizens and the Perioeci, announcing that any Hellenes who desired, not being of the Ionian, Achaean, or certain other races, might accompany them. The leaders of the colony were three Lacedaemonians, Leon, Alcidas, and Damagon. They set to work and built afresh the walls of the city, which received the name of Heraclea, and is situated about four miles and a half from Thermopylae and a little more than two from the sea. They also constructed docks[b], beginning the works near Thermopylae, at the pass, that the city might be perfectly defended.

The new colony is gradually worn out by the persistent opposition of the Thessalians, and by the brutality of the Lacedaemonian governors.

93 While the new colonists were collecting at Heraclea, the Athenians grew alarmed; the scheme appeared to be aimed at Euboea, for Cape Cenaeum on the opposite coast is within a short sail. But their fears were not realised; no harm whatever ensued. The reasons were these:—In the first place the Thessalians are strong in

[a] Cp. iii. 113 fin.

[b] Or, reading εἶρξαν τὸ——, 'and blockaded the defile at Thermopylae.'

that part of the country, and fearing that Heraclea, which was built to control them, would be a powerful and dangerous neighbour, they carried on uninterrupted war against the young colony until they completely wore the settlers out, although originally they had been very numerous. For every one joined without hesitation, encouraged by the promise of security which a Lacedaemonian colony seemed to offer. But another great cause of the ruin and depopulation of the place was the conduct of the governors sent out from Lacedaemon, who frightened the people away by their severe and often unjust administration [a]. Thus the Heracleans fell an easy prey to their neighbours.

During the same summer, and just about the same time 94
when the Athenians were engaged at Melos, the troops which were cruising in the thirty Athenian ships [b] about Peloponnesus set an ambuscade at Ellomenus in Leucadia and killed a few of the guards of the country. They next attacked Leucas itself with a larger armament, consisting of the Acarnanians, who followed them with their whole forces, all but the inhabitants of Oeniadae [c], and some Zacynthians and Cephallenians, together with fifteen ships from Corcyra. The Leucadians saw their territory both on the mainland and within the isthmus, where the town of Leucas and the temple of Apollo are situated, ravaged by the enemy; but being powerless against a superior force, they remained inactive. The Acarnanians begged Demosthenes, the Athenian general, to cut Leucas off by a wall, thinking that they could easily take the city and so rid themselves of an old enemy. But just then he was persuaded by the Messenians that, having such an army in the field, it would be a great thing to attack the Aetolians: they were the enemies of Naupactus, and if he defeated them he would

Attack upon Leucas. Demosthenes, instead of completing the blockade, is persuaded by the Messenians to invade Aetolia.

[a] Cp. v. 52 init. [b] Cp. iii. 91 init. [c] Cp. ii. 102 init.

easily subjugate the adjoining part of the mainland to the Athenians. The Aetolians, they said, though a large and warlike people, dwelt in unwalled villages, which were widely scattered, and as they had only light-armed soldiers, they would be subdued without difficulty before they could combine. They told him that he should first attack the Apodotians, then the Ophioneans, and after them the Eurytanians. The last are the largest tribe of the Aetolians; they speak a dialect more unintelligible than any of their neighbours, and are believed to eat raw flesh. They said that, if he conquered these, the rest would readily come over to him.

95 He was influenced by his regard for the Messenians, and still more by the consideration that without reinforcements from Athens, and with no other help than that of the allies on the mainland, to whom he hoped to add the Aetolians, he could make his way by land to attack Boeotia. He might proceed through the Ozolian Locri to the Dorian Cytinium, keeping Mount Parnassus on the right, until he came down upon the Phocians. They would probably be eager to join in the expedition because they had always been friendly to Athens, or, if unwilling, they might be coerced; and once in Phocis he would be on the borders of Boeotia. So he left Leucas with all his army, much against the will of the Acarnanians, and sailed to Sollium. He there communicated his design to them, but they would not accompany him because he had refused to blockade Leucas; so with the remainder of his army, which consisted of Cephallenians, Messenians, Zacynthians, and three hundred marines belonging to the Athenian fleet[a], the fifteen Corcyraean vessels having left, he marched against the Aetolians, starting from Oeneon in Locris. The Ozolian Locrians were allies of the Athenians, and

He determines to make his way through Aetolia and Phocis into Boeotia, which he hopes to attack with an allied force.

[a] Cp. ch. 94 init.

they were to meet him with their whole force in the interior of the country. They dwelt on the border of the Aetolians, and as they were armed in a similar manner and knew their country and ways of fighting, their help in the expedition seemed likely to be very valuable.

He encamped the first night at the temple of Nemean 96
Zeus, where the poet Hesiod is said to have been killed by the inhabitants in fulfilment of an oracle which foretold that he should die at Nemea. Early the next morning he proceeded on his march into Aetolia. On the first day he took Potidania, on the second Crocyleium, on the third Teichium. There he stayed and sent back the spoils to Eupalium in Locris. For he did not intend to attack the Ophioneans yet; when he had subjugated the rest of the country he would return to Naupactus and make a second expedition against them if they continued to resist. The Aetolians were aware of his designs from the very first; and no sooner did he enter their territory than they all collected in great force; even the most distant of the Ophioneans, the Bomieans and Callieans who reach down towards the Malian Gulf, came to the aid of their countrymen.

The Aetolians collect their forces.

The Messenians repeated the advice which they had 97
originally given to Demosthenes. They assured him that there would be no difficulty in conquering the Aetolians, and told him to march as quickly as he could against the villages. He should not wait until they could combine and meet him with an army, but should endeavour to take any place which was nearest. He, trusting to their advice, and confident in his good fortune since everything was going favourably, did not wait for the Locrians, who should have supplied his deficiency in javelin-men, but at once marched towards Aegitium, which he attacked, and forced his way in. The inhabitants had stolen away and taken up a position on the top of the hills overhanging the town, which was itself built upon

Demosthenes hurries on against the Aetolian villages, but receives a check at Aegitium.

heights at a distance of about nine miles from the sea. The other Aetolians, who had by this time come to the rescue of Aegitium, attacked the Athenians and their allies. Some ran down from one hill and some from another and hurled darts at them; when the Athenian army advanced they retired, and when the Athenians retreated they pressed upon them. The battle, which lasted long, was nothing but a series of pursuits and retreats, and in both the Athenians were at a disadvantage.

The Aetolians press upon the Athenians, who at length fly. The survivors with difficulty return to Naupactus, and thence to Athens. Demosthenes remains behind.

98 While their archers had arrows and were able to use them, the Athenians maintained their ground, for the Aetolians, being light-armed, were driven back by the arrows. But at length the captain of the archers was slain, and the forces under his command no longer kept together. The Athenians themselves grew weary of the long and tedious struggle. The Aetolians came closer and closer, and never ceased hurling darts at them. At last they turned and fled, and falling into ravines, out of which there was no way, or losing themselves in a strange country, they perished. Their guide, Chromon the Messenian, had been killed. The Aetolians, who were light-armed and swift of foot, followed at their heels, hurling darts, and caught and slew many of them in the actual rout. The greater number missed their way and got into the woods, out of which no path led; and their enemies brought fire and burnt the wood about them. So the Athenian army tried every means of escape and perished in all manner of ways. The survivors with difficulty made their way to the sea at Oeneon in Locris, whence they had set out. Many of the allies fell, and of the Athenian heavy-armed about a hundred and twenty, all in the flower of their youth; they were the very finest men whom the city of Athens lost during the war. Procles, one of the two generals, was also killed. When they had received the bodies of their dead under a flag of truce from the Aetol-

ians, they retreated to Naupactus, and returned in their ships to Athens. Demosthenes remained behind in Naupactus and the neighbourhood; for, after what had happened, he feared the anger of the Athenians.

About the same time the Athenian forces engaged in 99
Sicily, sailing to the territory of Locri and there disembarking, defeated the Locrians who came out to meet them, and took a small garrison fort, which was situated upon the river Halex.

The Italian Locrians defeated.

During the same summer the Aetolians, who had some 100
time before despatched Tolophus the Ophionean, Boriades the Eurytanian, and Tisander the Apodotian on an embassy to Corinth and Lacedaemon, induced the Lacedaemonians to aid them by sending an army against Naupactus, in order to punish the inhabitants for inviting the Athenian invasion [a]. So in the autumn they sent out three thousand hoplites of their allies, including five hundred from Heraclea, the newly-founded city in Trachis. Eurylochus, a Spartan, was general, and with him were associated in the command Macarius and Menedaeus, also Spartans.

The Aetolians persuade the Lacedaemonians to send an expedition against Naupactus.

When the army was collected at Delphi, Eurylochus 101
sent a herald to the Ozolian Locrians, for he had to pass through their country on the way to Naupactus; and he also wished to detach them from the Athenian alliance. Of the Locrians, the inhabitants of Amphissa were most willing to co-operate with him, being anxious for protection against their enemies the Phocians; they were the first who gave hostages, and by them the other Locrians, who were alarmed at the impending invasion, were persuaded to do the like:—first their neighbours the Myoneans, who commanded the most difficult pass into Locris; then the Ipneans, Messapians, Tritaeeans,

Eurylochus the Lacedaemonian commander starts from Delphi and marches through Locris.

[a] Cp. iii. 94 med.

Chalaeans, Tolophonians, Hessians, and Oeantheans; all these tribes also joined the expedition. The Olpaeans gave hostages but did not join; the Hyaeans would not give hostages until the Lacedaemonians had taken one of their villages, called Polis.

102 When everything was ready, and Eurylochus had deposited the hostages at Cytinium of the Dorians, he marched with his army against Naupactus, through the territory of the Locrians. On his march he took Oeneon[a] and Eupalium[b], two Locrian towns which refused to come to terms. When they had arrived in the territory of Naupactus and the Aetolians had at length joined them, they devastated the country, and after taking the unwalled suburbs of the town marched against Molycrium, a colony of the Corinthians subject to Athens, which they captured. But Demosthenes the Athenian, who after his misfortune in Aetolia was still in the neighbourhood of Naupactus, having previous intelligence, and fearing for the town, went and persuaded the Acarnanians, much against their will—for they had not forgotten his withdrawal from Leucas—to assist Naupactus. So they sent with him on board the Athenian ships[c] a thousand hoplites; these got in and saved the place, which was in danger of having to capitulate, owing to the extent of the wall and the paucity of its defenders. Eurylochus and his soldiers, when they saw that the garrison had been reinforced, and that there was no possibility of taking the city by storm, instead of going back to Peloponnesus, retired into the country of Aeolis, which is now called by the names of the towns Calydon and Pleuron, and to other places in the neighbourhood; also to Proschium in Aetolia. For the Ambraciots sent and persuaded them to take part in an attack on the Amphilochian Argos and the rest of Amphi-

Demosthenes with the help of the Acarnanians saves Naupactus. The Lacedaemonians retire, and in concert with the Ambraciots project an attack on the Amphilochian Argos.

[a] Cp. iii. 95 fin. [b] Cp. iii. 96 med. [c] Cp. iii. 105 fin

lochia and Acarnania, declaring that, if they gained possession of these places, all the tribes of the mainland would at once come over to the Lacedaemonians. Eurylochus assented and, dismissing the Aetolians, waited with his army in that region until the time for the Ambraciots to make their expedition and for him to join them in the neighbourhood of Argos. Thus the summer ended.

In the following winter the Athenians in Sicily and their 103
Hellenic allies made an attack upon the Sicel fort of Inessa, a Sicel town of which the citadel was held by the Syracusans. They were joined by many of the Sicels, who had formerly been allies to the Syracusans, and, having been held down by them, had now revolted to the Athenians. The attempt failed, and they retreated. But during their retreat the Syracusans sallied out and fell upon the allies who were in the rear of the Athenians, routed them, and put to flight a part of their forces with great loss. Soon afterwards, Laches and the Athenians in the fleet made several descents upon Locris. At the river Caecinus they defeated about three hundred Locrians who came out to meet them under Proxenus the son of Capaton, took arms from the slain, and returned.

The Athenians are defeated at Inessa, but are victorious in Locris.

In the same winter the Athenians, by command of an 104
oracle, purified the island of Delos. Pisistratus the tyrant had already purified it, but imperfectly, for the purification only extended to that part which was within sight of the temple. The whole island was now purified in the following manner:—The Athenians took away all the coffins of the dead which were in Delos[a], and passed a decree that henceforward no one should die or give birth to a child there, but that the inhabitants when they were near the time of either should be carried across to Rhenea. Now Rhenea is near to Delos, so near

The Athenians renew the purification of Delos and restore the Delian games.

---

[a] Cp. i. 8 init.; v. 1.

indeed that Polycrates the tyrant of Samos, who for a time had a powerful navy, attached this island, which he conquered with the rest of the islands and dedicated to the Delian Apollo, by a chain to Delos. After the purification, the Athenians for the first time celebrated the Delian games, which were held every four years. There had been in ancient days a great gathering of the Ionians and the neighbouring islanders at Delos; whither they brought their wives and children to be present at the Delian games, as the Ionians now frequent the games at Ephesus. Musical and gymnastic contests were held there, and the cities celebrated choral dances. The character of the festival is attested by Homer in the following verses, which are taken from the hymn to Apollo:—

The old festival of Delos is celebrated by Homer.

'At other times, Phoebus, Delos is dearest to thy heart,
Where are gathered together the Ionians in flowing robes,
With their wives and children in thy street:
There do they delight thee with boxing and dancing and song,
Making mention of thy name when they gather at the assembly.'

And that there were musical contests which attracted competitors is implied in the following words of the same hymn. After commemorating the Delian dance of women, Homer ends their praises with these lines, in which he alludes to himself:—

'And now may Apollo and Artemis be gracious,
And to all of you, maidens, I say farewell.
Yet remember me when I am gone;
And if some other toiling pilgrim among the sons of men
Comes and asks: O maidens,
Who is the sweetest minstrel of all who wander hither,
And in whom do you delight most?
Make answer with one voice, in gentle words,
The blind old man of Chios' rocky isle.'

Thus far Homer, who clearly indicates that even in days of old there was a great gathering and festival at Delos. In after ages the islanders and the Athenians led choruses in procession, and sacrificed. But the games and the greater part of the ceremonies naturally fell into disuse, owing to the misfortunes of Ionia. The Athenians now restored the games and for the first time introduced horse-races.

During the same winter the Ambraciots, in fulfilment of the promise by which they had induced Eurylochus and his army to remain[a], made an expedition against the Amphilochian Argos with three thousand hoplites. They invaded the Argive territory and seized Olpae, a strong fort on a hill by the sea-side, which in former days the Acarnanians had fortified and used as a common hall of justice. The place is about three miles from Argos, which is also on the sea-shore. One division of the Acarnanians came to the aid of Argos, while another encamped at a spot called the Wells, where they could lie in wait for Eurylochus and the Peloponnesians, and prevent them from joining the Ambraciots unobserved. They also despatched a messenger to Demosthenes, who had led the Athenian expedition into Aetolia, asking him to be their commander, and sent for twenty Athenian ships which were just then cruising about the Peloponnese under the command of Aristoteles the son of Timocrates, and Hierophon the son of Antimnestus. The Ambraciots sent a messenger from Olpae to their own citizens, bidding them come and help them with their entire force; for they were afraid that Eurylochus and his followers might not be able to make their way through the Acarnanians, and then they would have either to fight alone, or to attempt a hazardous retreat. 105

Eurylochus and the Ambraciots combine their forces against the Amphilochian Argos, which the Amphilochians, Acarnanians, and Athenians unite to protect. The Ambraciots seize Olpae, and send for reinforcements.

Eurylochus and the Peloponnesians, when they heard that the Ambraciots had arrived at Olpae, left Proschium and went with all speed to help them. Passing over the river Achelous they marched through 106

March of the Peloponnesians, who effect a junction with the Ambraciots at Olpae.

[a] Cp. iii. 102 fin.

Acarnania, leaving the city and garrison of Stratus on the right hand, and the rest of Acarnania on their left. The land was deserted, for the inhabitants had gone to the assistance of Argos. Crossing the territory of Stratus they proceeded through Phytia and by the extreme border of Medeon, and so through Limnaea; at last they left Acarnania, and reached the friendly territory of the Agraeans. Then taking to Mount Thyamus, which is open country, they marched on and descended into the plain of Argos after dark. Making their way unobserved between the city of Argos and the Acarnanian force stationed at the Wells, they at length reached the Ambraciots at Olpae.

Athenian reinforcements arrive. Demosthenes takes the command. He encamps near Olpae, where preparing for action he places troops in an ambuscade.

107 The two armies having effected this junction moved at break of day to a place called Metropolis, and there encamped. Soon afterwards the Argives received the expected reinforcement of twenty Athenian ships, which arrived in the Ambracian Gulf. With them came Demosthenes, who brought two hundred Messenian hoplites and sixty Athenian archers. The ships anchored about the hill of Olpae, while the Acarnanians and a few of the Amphilochians (the greater part of them were prevented from stirring by the Ambraciots[a]), having mustered at Argos, were now preparing to give battle. They associated Demosthenes with their own generals in the command of the allied forces. He led them to the neighbourhood of Olpae, and there encamped at a place where they were divided from the enemy by a great ravine. During five days they remained inactive; on the sixth day both armies drew up in battle array. Demosthenes, fearing that he would be surrounded by the Peloponnesians who were more numerous and extended beyond his own line, placed hoplites and light-armed troops,

[a] Cp. iii. 114 fin.

numbering altogether four hundred, in a deep lane overgrown with brushwood, intending them to lie in wait until the moment of conflict, when they were to rush out from the rear on the line of the enemy where it overlapped. The preparations of both armies were now complete and they engaged. Demosthenes led his own right wing, on which were the Messenians and a few Athenians, while the other was held by the Acarnanians, who were disposed according to their cities, and by the Amphilochian javelin-men who were in the battle. The Peloponnesians and Ambraciots were intermingled, with the exception of the Mantineans, who were all collected on the left wing; but the extremity of the wing was occupied by Eurylochus and his division, who were opposed to the Messenians under Demosthenes.

When the two armies were at close quarters, the left 108
wing of the Peloponnesians out-flanked the right wing of their opponents and threatened to surround them; whereupon the Acarnanians, coming upon them from behind out of the ambuscade, charged and turned them. They fled without striking a blow, and their panic caused the greater part of the army to run with them. For, when they saw Eurylochus and their best troops routed, they lost whatever courage they had. The Messenians, who were in this part of the field under the command of Demosthenes, were foremost in the action. The right wing of the enemy, however, and the Ambraciots, who are the most warlike nation in those parts, vanquished their opponents and drove them back to Argos. But, returning, they saw the greater part of the army defeated, and were hard pressed by the victorious division of the Acarnanians, whereupon, escaping with difficulty, they made their way to Olpae. Numbers of the defeated were killed, for they dashed into the fort wildly and in confusion, except the Mantineans, who kept together and retreated

The Peloponnesian left wing is panic-stricken by the troops coming out of the ambush, and flies. The right wing is victorious at first, but finally driven back to Olpae.

in better order than any other part of the army. The battle, which had lasted until evening, now ended.

109 On the next day Menedaeus took the command, for Eurylochus and Macarius, the two other generals, had been slain [a]. He knew not what to do after so serious a defeat. He could not hope, if he remained, to stand a siege, hemmed in as he was by land, and at sea blockaded by the Athenian ships; neither could he safely retire; so entering into a parley with Demosthenes and the Acarnanian generals about the burial of the dead, he tried to negotiate with them at the same time for a retreat. The Athenians gave back to the enemy their dead, erected a trophy, and took up their own dead, in number about three hundred. They would not openly agree to the proposal for a general retreat, but Demosthenes and his Acarnanian colleagues made a secret treaty with the Mantineans, and Menedaeus, and the other Peloponnesian generals and chief persons, allowing their army to depart. He wanted partly to isolate the Ambraciots and their foreign mercenary troops, but much more to take away the character of the Lacedaemonians and Peloponnesians among the Hellenes in those parts and convict them of selfishness and treachery. Accordingly the Peloponnesians took up their dead, and burying them quickly as well as they could, consulted secretly how those who had permission could best depart.

Difficulties of the Lacedaemonian commander, who negotiates with Demosthenes a secret treaty for the Peloponnesians only.

110 Meanwhile news was brought to Demosthenes and the Acarnanians that the whole remaining force of the Ambraciots, who some time previously had been summoned from the city [b] to join the troops in Olpae, were now on their way through the territory of the Amphilochians and were in entire ignorance of what had occurred. Whereupon he at once sent forward a part of

Approach of the main army of the Ambraciots. Demosthenes prepares to cut them off.

[a] Cp. iv. 38 init.

[b] Cp. iii. 105 fin.

his army to lie in ambush in the roads and to occupy the strong places, himself at the same time preparing to support them with the rest of his forces.

In the meantime the Mantineans and the others who 111
were included in the truce went out on pretence of gathering herbs and sticks, and stole away one by one, picking up as they went along what they pretended to be looking for. But, as they got farther away from Olpae, they quickened their steps, and then the Ambraciots and others who happened to collect on the instant, when they saw that they were leaving, ran after them at full speed, wanting to get up with them. The Acarnanians at first thought that none of those who were going away were protected by a truce, and pursued the Peloponnesians. Some of the generals tried to keep them back and explained how matters stood; whereupon a soldier, suspecting that there was treachery, hurled a javelin at them. At length the soldiers understood, and let the Mantineans and other Peloponnesians go, but began to kill the Ambraciots. There was great dispute and uncertainty as to who was an Ambraciot and who a Peloponnesian. Of the former they killed about two hundred; the Peloponnesians escaped into the neighbouring country of Agraea, and were received by king Salynthius who was their friend.

The Peloponnesians steal away from Olpae, and escape to Agraea. The Ambraciots who try to follow them are slain.

Meanwhile the reinforcement from the city of Ambracia 112
had reached Idomenè, which is the name of two lofty peaks. The higher of the two had been already occupied unobserved at nightfall by the troops which Demosthenes had sent forward; of the lower the Ambraciots first obtained possession and encamped there. As soon as it was dark, after supper, Demosthenes advanced with the rest of his army, himself leading half of them towards the pass between the mountains, while the rest made their way

Demosthenes, having sent on forces which occupy the hill opposite to that whereon the Ambraciots are encamped at Idomenè, surprises and routs them.

through the Amphilochian hills. At the first dawn of day he fell upon the Ambraciots, who were still half-asleep, and so far from knowing anything of what had happened that they imagined his troops to be their own comrades. For Demosthenes had taken care to place the Messenians in the first rank and desired them to speak to the enemy in their own Doric dialect, thereby putting the sentinels off their guard; and as it was still dark, their appearance could not be distinguished. So they fell upon the Ambraciots and routed them. Most of them were slain on the spot; the remainder fled over the mountains. But the paths were beset; the Amphilochians were lightly-armed, and in their own country which they knew, while their enemies were heavy-armed and the country was strange to them. And so, not knowing which way to turn, they fell into ravines and into ambuscades which had been set for them, and perished. Every means of escape was tried. Some even fled to the sea which was not far distant, and seeing the Athenian ships which were sailing by while the action was taking place, swam out to them, thinking in the terror of the moment that they had better be killed, if die they must, by the Athenians in the ships than by their barbarous and detested enemies the Amphilochians. So the Ambraciots were cut to pieces, and but few out of many returned home to their city. The Acarnanians, having despoiled the dead and raised trophies, returned to Argos.

113 On the following day there arrived a herald from the Ambraciots who had escaped out of Olpae to the Agraeans. He came to recover the bodies of the dead who had been slain subsequently to the first engagement, when, unprotected by the treaty, they tried to get out of Olpae in company with the Mantineans and others protected by it. The herald saw the arms of the Ambraciot troops from the city and wondered at the number of them; he knew nothing of the

Despair of the herald who came from the fugitive Ambraciots when he heard of the second and greater defeat.

later disaster, and he imagined that they belonged to his own division of the army. Some one present thought that the herald had come from the army defeated at Idomenè, and asked why he looked so astonished, and how many of their men had fallen; he replied, 'about two hundred [a]'; whereupon the other rejoined, 'These which you see are not the arms of two hundred men, but of more than a thousand.' The herald replied, 'Then they cannot be the arms of our men.' The other answered, 'They must be, if you were fighting yesterday at Idomenè.' 'But yesterday we did not fight at all; it was the day before, in the retreat.' 'All I know is that we fought yesterday with these men, who were marching to your aid from Ambracia.' When the herald heard these words, and knew that the army coming from the city had perished, he uttered a cry of anguish, and, overwhelmed by the greatness of the blow, went away at once without doing his errand, no longer caring to demand the dead. And indeed in the whole war no such calamity happened within so few days to any Hellenic state [b]. I have not ventured to set down the number of those who fell, for the loss would appear incredible when compared with the size of the city. Of this I am certain, that if the Acarnanians had been willing to destroy Ambracia as Demosthenes and the Athenians desired, they might have taken it at the first onset. But they were afraid that the Athenians, if they once got possession of the place, would be more troublesome neighbours than the Ambraciots [c].

Division of the spoils.

After assigning a third part of the spoils to the Athenians, the Acarnanians divided the remainder among their cities. The spoils of the Athenians were captured on the voyage. But three hundred panoplies which were allotted to Demosthenes he brought home with him, and they are still preserved in the Athenian temples. This good service 114

[a] Cp. iii. 111 fin. [b] Cp. vii. 30 fin. [c] Cp. iii. 92 init.

of his enabled him to return to Athens with less apprehension after his misfortune in Aetolia. The twenty Athenian ships sailed away to Naupactus. The Acarnanians and Amphilochians, after the Athenians and Demosthenes had left them, granted a truce to the Ambraciots and Peloponnesians who had fled to Salynthius and the Agraeans; they were thus enabled to return home from Oeniadae, whither they had removed from the country of Salynthius. The Acarnanians and Amphilochians now made a treaty of alliance for one hundred years with the Ambraciots, of which the terms were as follows:—'The Ambraciots shall not be required to join the Acarnanians in making war on the Peloponnesians, nor the Acarnanians to join the Ambraciots in making war on the Athenians. But they shall aid in the defence of one another's territory. The Ambraciots shall give up such places or hostages of the Amphilochians as they possess[a], and they shall not assist Anactorium' (which was hostile to the Acarnanians)[b]. Upon these terms they put an end to the war. Soon afterwards the Corinthians sent a force of their own, consisting of three hundred hoplites under the command of Xenocleidas the son of Euthycles, to guard Ambracia, whither they made their way with some difficulty by land. Such was the end of the Ambracian war.

Return of Demosthenes and the Athenian fleet. Treaty of the Acarnanians and Amphilochians with the Ambraciots.

115 During the same winter the Athenian fleet in Sicily, sailing to Himera, made a descent upon the country in concert with the Sicels, who had invaded the extreme border of the Himeraeans from the interior; they also attacked the Aeolian Isles. Returning to Rhegium, they found that Pythodorus son of Isolochus, one of the Athenian generals, had superseded Laches in the command of the fleet. The allies of

The Athenians resolve to take a more active part in the affairs of Sicily. They send out Pythodorus.

---

[a] Cp. iii. 107 init. [b] Cp. i. 55 init.

the Athenians in Sicily had sailed to Athens, and persuaded the Athenians to send a larger fleet to their aid; for their territory was in the power of the Syracusans, and they were kept off the sea by a few ships only; so they were preparing to resist, and had begun to collect a navy. The Athenians manned forty ships for their relief, partly hoping to finish the war in Sicily the sooner, partly because they wanted to exercise their fleet. They despatched one of the commanders, Pythodorus, with a few ships, intending to send Sophocles the son of Sostratides, and Eurymedon the son of Thucles, with the larger division of the fleet afterwards. Pythodorus, having now succeeded Laches in the command, sailed at the end of the winter against the Locrian fort which Laches had previously taken[a], but he was defeated by the Locrians and retired.

In the early spring the burning lava, not for the first time, 116
issued from Mount Aetna, which is the highest mountain in Sicily, and devastated a portion of the territory of the Catanaeans who dwell on the skirts of Aetna. The last eruption is said to have taken place fifty years before; and altogether three eruptions are recorded since the Hellenes first settled in Sicily. Such were the events of the winter; and so ended the sixth year in the Peloponnesian War of which Thucydides wrote the history.

Eruption of Aetna.

---

[a] Cp. iii. 99.